THE **NEW** TERROR

HOOVER NATIONAL SECURITY FORUM SERIES

THE **NEW** TERROR

Facing the Threat of Biological and Chemical Weapons

Edited by
Sidney D. Drell
Abraham D. Sofaer
George D. Wilson

HOOVER INSTITUTION PRESS
Stanford University Stanford, California

www-hoover.stanford.edu

Hoover Institution Press Publication No. 462
Copyright © 1999 by the Board of Trustees of the
    Leland Stanford Junior University

First printing, 1999
05   04   03   02   9   8   7   6   5   4   3   2

Manufactured in the United States of America
The paper used in this publication meets the minimum requirements
of American National Standard for Information Sciences—Permanence
of Paper for Printed Library Materials, ANSI Z39.48–1984. ♾

Cover photo: Riot police don their gas masks and antichemical gloves prior to their
inspection at a commune of the Aum Shinrikyo cult in Kamikuishiki (100 km west
of Tokyo), March 24, 1995. AFP PHOTO, Yoshikazu Tsuno.

Library of Congress Cataloging-in-Publication Data
The new terror : facing the threat of biological and chemical weapons / edited by
Sidney D. Drell, Abraham D. Sofaer, and George D. Wilson.
        p.   cm.
    Based on papers presented at a conference held Nov. 16–18, 1998 at the Hoover
Institution.
    Includes bibliographical references and index.
    ISBN 0-8179-9701-6 (alk. paper) — ISBN 0-8179-9702-4 (pbk. : alk. paper)
    1. Biological weapons—Congresses.   2. Biological arms control—Congresses.
3. Chemical weapons—Congresses.   4. Chemical arms control—Congresses.
I. Drell, Sidney D. (Sidney Drell), 1926–   II. Sofaer, Abraham D.
III. Wilson, George D., 1961–   IV. Hoover Institution on War, Revolution, and
Peace.
UG447.8.N48   1999
327.1'745—dc21
                                                            99-041989
                                                                CIP

Contents

Foreword

In 1998, the Hoover Institution inaugurated the National Security Forum. The forum, as part of the Hoover Institution program on International Rivalries and Global Cooperation, is an annual effort that involves scholars, practitioners, and government officials who examine and discuss challenges to international security. The principal goal of the forum is to produce a book that summarizes and synthesizes the dialogue of the experts for a general audience.

An important goal of the Hoover Institution is to heighten awareness of public policy issues and to disseminate pertinent information, data, and analysis that contribute to a meaningful dialogue. The first National Security Forum, which was launched with an event that took place November 16–18, 1998, is consistent with this goal, calling our attention to the serious threat of biological and chemical weapons. Rogue states and devoted terrorists pose serious security problems to civilized governments and policing agencies. Of these threats and challenges, none is more ominous than the threat of unleashing biological and chemical weapons.

Hoover fellows Sidney D. Drell, Abraham D. Sofaer, and George D. Wilson, the editors of this book and the coordinators of the related conference, have compiled the presentations of more than twenty experts made at the 1998 Hoover conference. Discussed and dissected are the full range of technical, legal, military, social, and medical issues associated with the threat of biological and chemical weapons, including their serious and malevolent threat and portents for the future. Some writers believe that this threat can be controlled; others are not so sure. However, the book does offer some optimism and constructive recommendations. In making suggestions in the areas of intelligence, scientific research, treaties and inspection, crisis control, and defense, the contributors leave us with the message that we must remain ever vigilant in our efforts to deter aggression, without compromise to our individual freedoms. We must not be held hostage by this significant threat.

An undertaking this size can only be completed through the combined efforts of many. I first want to thank Abe Sofaer, the George P. Shultz Senior Fellow at the Hoover Institution, for proposing to me the concept of a national security forum and for agreeing to lead this important institutional effort. Sid Drell had a vision for a conference and book that would address biological and chemical weapons as the first installment of this new forum. George Wilson joined Abe and Sid to define the issues, to identify the key participants, and to convene them at the Hoover conference. As joint editors, they have performed remarkably in assembling an impressive and important volume on biological and chemical weapons, thanks ultimately to the participants at the conference and the contributors to the book.

Associate Director Richard Sousa deserves significant credit in keeping the project in focus and on schedule. In addition, Richard, together with Jonathan B. Tucker, the 1999–2000 Robert Wesson Fellow in Scientific and Public Policy at the Hoover Institution, worked closely with the editors on all aspects of the book and provided advice and guidance on all facets of the conference.

Hoover conferences also require the effort of many dedicated staff; I am delighted to thank Kristan Austin, Kelly Hauge, Teresa Judd, Bonnie Rose, and Craig Snarr for their efforts in this regard. As always, Patricia Baker and the staff of the Hoover Institution Press contributed mightily and tirelessly to produce this volume.

Finally, and most important, we are deeply grateful to Ellis J. Alden and Mary Mochary, who provided financial support for the production of this book. Ellis also afforded us the hospitality of his Monterey Plaza Hotel for a sequestered meeting of the editors for the book's final review, revision, and editing.

John Raisian
Director
Hoover Institution

George P. Shultz

Preface

My role at the November 16–18, 1998, conference on biological and chemical weapons (BCW) at the Hoover Institution was to welcome the participants, just as it is to welcome the readers in this volume based on the conference. But somehow the word "welcome" does not seem quite right, since the subject is certainly not a welcome one, but it is necessary to address. And I want to address some of the reasons in these brief remarks.

First, we see the emergence of all sorts of weapons—lethal weapons—that are readily available. You can read, and even receive instruction, about them on the internet. Undoubtedly the most important of these are BCW.

Second, we see—at least as I fathom it, and I wish it were otherwise—the virtual disappearance of any sort of world security system that is rooted in accountability. It seems clear that we continue to face the existence of BW, and probably CW; certainly, in Iraq, Saddam Hussein is getting away with it.

So we have the existence of BCW and we have people in the world, people with power—and not only Saddam Hussein—who are willing to use these weapons and capable of doing so. No one likes to think that they are going to be used, and so we try to resist that thought. But realistically we must face up to the likelihood that it is not a question of "if" but of "when." At the present time, we lack a system with which to manage the problems raised by this reality. The United Nations Security Council is too divided to take any reasonably decisive action. So the real question is: How are we going to deal with the consequences?

This question reminds me of a small book entitled *Plagues and Peoples*[1] that I read quite a number of years ago. It was written by a great historian, William McNeill. Bill was a collegue of mine when I was at the University of Chicago. The thesis of the book was that plagues have played an enormous role in human history and have influenced events in very serious ways. But historians, by and large, have not paid enough attention to the impact of plagues. The book is full of examples taken from all parts of the world.

The example I remember particularly concerned Mexico. When the Spaniards—only 600 or so of them—first arrived in Mexico they encountered a very large population of natives. How in the world could that small band of Spaniards have conquered the much larger group of local people? The author ticks off various possible explanations, but the one he finds most compelling is that the Spaniards brought the contagious smallpox virus with them, although they themselves had developed an immunity to the virus. The people they encountered had no previous exposure to the disease and about a third of them were wiped out by it. The survivors were amazed;

1. William H. McNeill, *Plagues and Peoples* (Garden City, NY: Anchor Press, 1976).

they could not understand why so many of their people had gotten ill and died, but the Spaniards did not succumb to the disease. In awe of the Spaniards' "special powers," they adopted the Spaniards' religion and many aspects of Spanish culture. The smallpox plague had a huge impact on history.

In times past, plagues must have seemed mysterious; people simply did not understand what was happening or why, so all sorts of drastic measures were taken to deal with them. Today, we face a different problem: People are now considering creating plagues deliberately, creating something over which they have no control. No doubt some of the people who will develop BCW in a given country will be highly professional, and will know what they are doing. But there are also going to be amateurs, who may not fully understand what they are doing. And there will be madmen who do not care. So you can easily imagine a situation that goes out of control—a man-made plague.

In addressing the difficult problems created by the existence of BCW, we must build upon the sound foundation already laid by US policy. I believe that the participants in the conference contributed to the building process, but more needs to be done to raise people's awareness not only of the existence of the problem but also of the urgency of putting in place an international security system—rooted in accountability—capable of managing the dangers such weapons pose. Otherwise, I am afraid, we will see the devastation of man-made plagues caused by BCW.

Sidney D. Drell, Abraham D. Sofaer, George D. Wilson

Overview

The threat of biological and chemical weapons (BCW) presents a troubling and difficult challenge to society. A conference, held November 16–18, 1998, at the Hoover Institution, Stanford University, addressed the BCW challenge in all its aspects.

Participants with a broad variety of training and experience in science, medicine, intelligence, international and constitutional law, diplomacy, public health, and administration contributed to the conference discussions. But in a fundamental sense all the participants were amateurs on the topic; and that is our good fortune. No recent, major BCW terrorist incidents have occurred at home or on the battlefield with US troops. We hope this record is maintained, but it would be unrealistic and irresponsible to plan on that basis.

Most of the conference discussion addressed concerns about the use of BCW directly against US society, whether initiated by other governments or by terrorists, foreign or domestic. One cannot, of course, dismiss their battlefield use. The brutally frank admission by Tariq Aziz, reported at the conference by Ambassador Rolf Ekéus, that CW saved Iraq from overwhelming Iranian forces during the Iran–Iraq War of 1980–88, must be taken into account by strategic planners. However, the tactical military value of BCW is limited due to their delayed lethal action and uncertain dispersal patterns.

The existence of a direct threat from abroad to the US homeland is not new. Nuclear weapons (NW) have posed one for more than fifty years, and caused US civil defense exercises in the early years of the Cold War. But the present threat is not posed by just one or two nuclear-armed nations. It is much more pervasive. With modern advances in biotechnology and pharmaceutical manufacturing, there is a threat of attack against US society from a growing number of nations and terrorist units.

John C. Gannon, Chairman of the National Intelligence Council, expressed his hope that the conference would "develop a set of concrete action items to get us moving in harness against the BCW threat." That was, and is, precisely our aim. Although the BCW threat cannot be eliminated, the conference identified constructive steps—set forth in five essential areas: (1) intelligence, (2) research, (3) inspection, (4) consequence management, and (5) defense—that can reduce the dangers or mitigate the consequences of BCW attacks and perhaps even lead toward establishing a norm for the nonuse of BCW, such as has existed, de facto, for NW for more than fifty years. That a "nonuse norm" for NW exists is strongly indicated by the fact that the US, the former Soviet Union, France, and China have all been denied victories in military conflicts in which they nevertheless refrained from using their nuclear arsenals against nonnuclear-armed adversaries. Steps that would raise the cost-to-benefit ratio for the use of BCW would also reduce their attractiveness and thereby move the world along a path toward establishing another nonuse norm.

An agenda to deal with the BCW threat is essential, and feasible. Here are the five areas where actions can be effective in reducing the dangers and potential damage from the use of BCW:

1. *Intelligence:* A primary goal of an effective program against BCW is to obtain early and reliable intelligence and, best of all, clues as to the intentions of would-be perpetrators. Clues as to intentions are critically important for discovering emerging BCW threats. The relevant facilities, equipment, and material can have dual purposes. They may be used in legitimate civilian activities, such as manufacturing commercial drugs, pesticides, antibiotics, and vaccines, as well as in manufacturing and stockpiling BCW. Discerning intentions requires a strengthened, robust capability for human intelligence (HUMINT) and clandestine means of acquiring this information. On the domestic front, information gathering and surveillance by Department of Justice (DoJ), Federal Bureau of Investigation (FBI), and local law-enforcement personnel will be critical, but it must remain within legal restraints as mandated by the Constitution, consistent with the core values of our society. Care will be required to avoid the excesses that were practiced during, for example, the years of the "red scare" in the 1950s.

Comprehensive and timely databases maintained by health officials on disease and illness patterns can provide early evidence of hostile actions. Similar efforts by US agriculture officials monitoring crops and livestock conditions and contamination can provide vital intelligence warnings.

An overall information system and technical tools for detecting and identifying developing threats (or actual attacks) can be upgraded in significant ways. Possibilities exist for detecting small quantities of agents with compact, covert, autonomous, as well as remote, sensors—using technologies such as DNA swipes and chemical chromatographs. DARPA (Defense Advanced Research

Projects Agency), in the Department of Defense (DoD), is developing new sensors of great sensitivity for warning and detection. The
Department of Energy's (DoE) weapons laboratories are also important assets, and are applying their experience with nuclear sensors to the advancement of sensor technology for use against BCW,
a task currently supported by the federal Nunn-Lugar-Domenici
legislation. Better intelligence of traditional types will be important
against delivery systems and, in particular, against theater or short-
and intermediate-range ballistic missiles, such as the SCUDs and
their derivatives that (together with their launchers) the US failed
to locate during the Gulf War.

2. *Research:* On both the scientific and medical frontiers, a
strong research base is vital to stay ahead of naturally occurring
bacteria and viruses as they mutate into forms that evade current
antibiotics and vaccines. A strong public health system supporting
good health practice will help provide a database and a system on
which to build for recovery. Improved techniques are needed for
simply and reliably detecting infections during the early incubation
period, for example, by using sputum tests, nose swipes, or sophisticated sensors. Above all, the biomedical community should get
more heavily involved in these efforts.

The community of physicists was shocked by the atomic bombs
detonated over Hiroshima and Nagasaki, and by concerns of fallout
from atmospheric testing. Physicists quickly became intensely involved in efforts to control and reduce the dangers of NW through
contributions both to technical issues and to public understanding.
They are still "working the problem" in an effort to extend the over-
half-century of nonuse and to reduce the danger of such weapons.

The biomedical and chemical communities have, most fortunately, escaped a similar shock introduction to the BCW danger
involving the US, if not the rest of the world. It is now increasingly
important, however, for doctors and scientists with relevant expertise to become more deeply involved in helping address what can

and cannot be done technically, in developing ethical standards for their own activities, and in educating the public. An "extended" Hippocratic oath by the scientific and medical community, taking a moral stand against any actions violating the international BCW conventions, could be a powerful influence.

3. *Inspection:* The involvement of industry will be key to any success in efforts to develop protocols for inspections to implement the Biological Weapons Convention (BWC). This is the way a consensus was achieved in the US to support the signing and Senate ratification (April, 1997) of the Chemical Weapons Convention (CWC), a treaty banning all CW. Regrettably, the US implementing legislation adds unilateral waivers and exemptions that could weaken the regime and undercut its effectiveness. Implementing the BWC is a more difficult challenge because constraints based on the quantity of a biological agent are not effective, given the rapid rate at which such agents multiply. In addition, the pharmaceutical industry is extremely sensitive to the potential for loss of proprietary information. Experience with NW has demonstrated a need for effective challenge inspections. The International Atomic Energy Agency (IAEA) has recently developed a strengthened safeguard regime and is currently negotiating bilateral agreements with member states for its implementation. This is a difficult, but not impossible, problem to address for BCW. The value of routine inspections has been called into question, however, and should be determined on the basis of sound and objective criteria, to avoid unwarranted burdens. Emphasis should also be placed on the high costs to would-be proliferators if these efforts fail and they feel, somehow, that they must build up and maintain sophisticated BCW stockpiles and capabilities.

In both the NW and CW debates in the US, serious opposition to ratification of treaty limits or to accepting verification protocols has been based, in part, on the fear that success in negotiating a set of provisions and treaties will lull us into false confidence that we are safe or have accomplished more than, in reality, has been achieved. This points up the importance of not making excessive claims, of insisting upon effective verification as a necessary part of any control regime, and of diligent enforcement of compliance measures. Violations of treaties must not go unpunished. Furthermore, as former Secretary of State George P. Shultz noted during the conference, although the US should support the treaties and abide by them, it should at the same time proceed in its national-security planning with contingency preparations for appropriate responses to potential treaty violations and noncompliance.

We are currently facing similar concerns about whether the US can and will maintain an effective nuclear deterrent under a Comprehensive Test Ban Treaty (CTBT). These concerns lie at the heart of much of the current debate about ratification of the CTBT. So far, the US is doing what needs to be done to maintain its nuclear deterrent responsibly. The Stockpile Stewardship Program is receiving strong support, and the DoE weapons laboratories are addressing the technical challenge with seriousness of purpose. Success in this program can serve to increase faith in our nation's ability to avoid being lulled into a false sense of security by the BWC and CWC, as a result of advancing their prospects. At present, US concerns over protecting national security and proprietary information are still hampering progress in establishing acceptable "rules of the road" for the BW and CW treaty regimes.

4. *Consequence management:* A great deal remains to be done to enhance national, state, and local programs for managing the consequences of BCW attacks. The US must build a bottom-up system from the local level, making effective use of national resources, such as databases, information banks, and communication systems. We have to develop an effective process for making crisis decisions, both in periods of true catastrophe and in situations where panic is the greatest danger. A public affairs policy must also be crafted that applies available resources and benefits fairly in accord with US law

and codes of social justice, and that also establishes a proper balance between transparency and secrecy in making information available to ensure proper public awareness of dangers and actions without causing panic. We must honor our values as a society in any restriction on citizens' freedoms, including the right to travel, while at the same time preventing victims of contamination from contributing to the further spread of disease. This is a complex problem of information management and deserves serious and timely attention. Preparations for consequence management should also highlight the risks that will be faced by would-be perpetrators should they initiate BCW attacks.

5. *Defense:* Defense encompasses both passive and active efforts. Passive defenses, including equipment, preparations, and training of medical response and clean-up teams, can play an important role. Ongoing efforts for active defenses are also essential, but need continued, careful evaluation of their realistic potential and the prospect of operational countermeasures. Sanctions, and in particular trade as well as military sanctions, can be important, although their effectiveness against indigenous terrorist groups as opposed to state actors is highly doubtful. Export controls over critical substances and equipment are essential; the multilateral efforts of the Australia Group are far preferable to unilateral, and hence ineffective, measures.

Preemptive or preventive strikes have been, and will likely continue to be, taken regarding BCW. Accepted rules concerning such actions are elusive, however, and unilateral measures would be subject to satisfying stringent criteria under the United Nations (UN) Charter. Nations that act preemptively will have to be prepared to balance their unilateral aims against their international policy goals, as well as to defend their conduct by revealing intelligence as a basis for action—in addition to meeting the conventional requirements of proportionality and necessity for acting against a BCW threat. Such issues have to be addressed on a case-by-case basis. The economic and scientific strength of a nation, and even more its credibility, are important factors in its ability to dissuade, discourage, or even prevent a BCW attack. For this and other reasons, the US must maintain credibility by forgoing unwarranted threats, and by following through on such threats it does make—while insisting on, and subjecting itself to, strict accountability. As to what specific means, nuclear or otherwise, will or will not be employed in undertaking reprisal actions, little can be gained by explicitly "tipping one's hand." The prospect, however, that the fifty-year norm against use of NW would come to an end in response to the use of BCW is patently unappealing. Our policy should clearly show that we will seek to rely on other credible options, but it should stop short of ruling out any single action absolutely and totally.

Finally, examining the full range of issues relating to BCW conveys one overriding lesson. In every major respect, apart from battlefield use in open military conflict, the dangers posed by BCW—and the measures needed to manage and thereby reduce those dangers—are similar in principle to the dangers posed by—and the measures needed to manage—peacefully generated biological and chemical hazards.

The dangers created by chemicals to which humans are exposed include carcinogens, acids, poisonous gases, abrasives, and imbalances in the atmosphere. These may be generated by natural forces or caused by commercial or other nonaggressive, human activities. Animals, insects, and other living creatures—and even plants—also can injure or kill people with chemicals they expel or inject, including chemicals that attack the digestive, nervous, or other essential systems.

Similarly, the dangers created by natural and nonmilitary developments in the biological field are formidable. Malaria, for example, kills millions of people worldwide every year. Viruses and other disease-creating organisms mutate naturally and become resistant to methods of control. Standard vaccines and antibiotics are rapidly becoming incapable of neutralizing certain organisms, creating the risk—some would say the inevitability—of major outbreaks of particular diseases.

The public health infrastructure and methods needed to respond to naturally occurring and nonmilitary biological and chemical hazards overlap significantly with those required to deal with deliberately used BCW. The medical data needed to evaluate the incidence of injury or disease are the same for both peaceful and defensive purposes. The detection and evaluation technologies that are being developed in both the chemical and biological fields will serve equally critical roles, regardless of the source or motives behind the substances endangering the population. The infrastructure needed to deal with chemical and biological hazards is also the same: (a) properly equipped response teams able to circumscribe, neutralize, and decontaminate areas; (b) a system for informing the affected public, and for isolating and treating injured or contagious individuals; (c) the production, distribution, and administration of necessary medications; (d) securing public cooperation without causing panic; and (e) the development of long-term protection in the form of protective devices and treatments. The dilemmas and difficulties identified in several of the presentations at the conference, concerning such issues as the distribution of limited human and material resources to cope with chemical and biological emergencies, present the same difficult questions, irrespective of the cause of the emergency posed.

Important differences do exist between nondeliberate and deliberate chemical and biological hazards with respect to the measures that may be possible to regulate, deter, and defend against them. States that are threatened by identifiable regimes or terrorists may be able to slow or diminish the effectiveness of BCW programs by limiting the availability of necessary prerequisites, such as equipment, chemical precursors, biological media, or delivery systems. The dangerous Libyan CW program of Colonel Muammar Qaddafi, for instance, has been significantly slowed and limited through such efforts. Preemptive actions, such as the US attack on the Shifa pharmaceutical plant in Khartoum, Sudan, in August 1998, may also be possible.

Although potentially valuable, these measures are only feasible in the case of known enemies whose intentions are discernible and pose a substantial threat. The growing threat posed by BCW is largely composed of situations that fall outside this narrow category. In many, if not most, situations, it will be impossible to determine whether and where potential users are developing BCW, and it may often be impossible to know who is responsible for such attacks, or even whether a particular incident or outbreak of disease was deliberately caused.

The relative ease of access to BCW—even by nonstate actors— and the difficulties of using such weapons as a deterrent, strongly support the policies adopted in the CWC and BWC, prohibiting not only use but also possession and development. For the same reasons, however, it is essential to assume that no practical means exist to prevent all violations. Consequently, effective deterrence can only be assured through the imposition of severe sanctions for proven violations of the conventions. Significantly, no sanction has yet been imposed for such violations or use by states, groups, or individuals, and no prospect exists for including any in the conventions. Therefore, an effort to adopt an international convention to criminalize serious violations of the CWC and BWC is worthy of serious consideration—as has been suggested by the Harvard-Sussex Program on Chemical and Biological Warfare Armament and Arms Limitation in their proposal for a "Convention on the Prevention and Punishment of the Crime of Developing, Producing, Acquiring, Stockpiling, Retaining, Transferring or Using Biological or Chemical Weapons" (Harvard Draft Convention). In addition, it appears equally important to promote an initiative to persuade the UN Security Council to adopt a resolution for the mandatory imposition of appropriate, punitive measures by member states for BCW violations—as a threat to international peace and security under Chapter VII of the UN Charter—even with respect to those states that refuse to ratify the CWC and BWC.

The materials in this volume are arranged in six parts to reflect the major subject-matter areas covered at the conference. Part One describes the dimensions of the BCW problem, with chapters on biological and chemical agents and a description of likely BCW attack scenarios. Part Two covers the role of intelligence. Part Three deals with the current status of efforts to build BCW control regimes—including chapters providing background on the history and use of BCW, international treaties, and UN experience with inspections in Iraq. Part Four presents discussion of the legal constraints that exist on the regulation of BCW, especially US constitutional limitations and the tradition of not permitting the military to play a significant role on US territory. Part Five covers the subject of preparing for BCW attacks, with descriptions of existing initiatives at both the federal and local levels, as well as potential difficulties. Finally, Part Six deals with efforts to prevent such attacks, including coverage of strategic and legal options. Each part of the book opens with brief introductory remarks and concludes with a commentary that attempts to summarize the principal points made by participants at the conference sessions.

Abbreviations

AG   Australia Group

BCW   biological and chemical weapons

BW   biological weapons

BWC   Biological Weapons Convention (Convention on the Prohibition of the Development, Production and Stockpiling of Bacteriological [Biological] and Toxin Weapons and on Their Destruction)

CDC   Centers for Disease Control and Prevention

CIA   US Central Intelligence Agency

CM   consequence management

CTBT   Comprehensive Test-Ban Treaty

CW   chemical weapons

CWC	Chemical Weapons Convention (Convention on the Prohibition of the Development, Production, Stockpiling and Use of Chemical Weapons and on Their Destruction)
DCI	Director of Central Intelligence
DoD	US Department of Defense
DoE	US Department of Energy
DoJ	US Department of Justice
FBI	US Federal Bureau of Investigation
HHS	US Department of Health and Human Services
HUMINT	human intelligence
IC	US Intelligence Community
NATO	North Atlantic Treaty Organization
NPC	Nonproliferation Center of the DCI, CIA
NPT	Non-Proliferation Treaty
NW	nuclear weapons
OPCW	Organization for the Prohibition of Chemical Weapons
PHS	US Public Health Service
UK	United Kingdom of Great Britain and Northern Ireland
UN	United Nations
UNSCOM	United Nations Special Commission
US	United States
USG	United States Government
USSR	Union of Soviet Socialist Republics
WMD	weapons of mass destruction

Part One

Dimensions of the
BCW Problem

Sidney D. Drell

 **Introductory Remarks**

The growing, and already imminent, threat of biological and chemical weapons (BCW) prompted the organization of the Hoover Institution's November 16–18, 1998, conference. BCW are capable of indiscriminate destruction. Beyond their hideous potential on the battlefield, they create the frightening prospect of terrorist attacks by superempowered, angry individuals loose in our midst. What can we do? What should we be doing to prepare for this threat as we enter the twenty-first century? To address these questions, we brought together on the conference podium and in the audience knowledgeable leaders and thinkers on all of the broadly diverse aspects of this challenge: scientists, medical personnel, legal scholars—both domestic and international—law enforcement, intelligence, and crisis management personnel.

This book distills much of what we learned from one another

during our two and a half days together. The hope is that as a community we will understand much better the most pressing issues, as well as what are realistic options for preventing, or defending against and mitigating the consequences of, the use of BCW.

The BCW threat has been receiving greater attention and increased resources in Washington and elsewhere over the past few years. The challenge we face is to transform this newly enhanced activity into effective action.

This opening part of the conference proceedings focuses on practical scientific and operational issues—the evolving scientific and technical developments in BCW, and the scenarios and technical issues for utilizing such weapons. What is the nature and urgency of the threat today and what are prospects for the future? How are advances in biomedical science, in manufacturing processes, and in weapons technology enhancing the threat?

Michael L. Moodie

The Chemical Weapons Threat

Chemical weapons (CW) pose a challenge that is both old and new. The challenge is old in two senses. First, the use of gas as a weapon of war dates far back in time. "Toxic fumes" appeared in conflicts in India as far back as 2000 BC. In 400 BC, Sparta reportedly used wood saturated with pitch and sulfur under besieged city walls to choke defenders. In 1591, Germans used combinations of shredded hooves and horns with a fetid gum resin to produce noxious clouds to disrupt enemy forces.[1] Second, even "modern" CW have been around for some time; the science involved is not cutting edge. Sir Humphrey Davy prepared phosgene in 1811. Another English chemist, John Stenhouse, prepared

---

1. Javed Ali, Leslie Rodrigues, and Michael Moodie, *Jane's US Chemical-Biological Defense Guidebook* (Alexandria: Jane's Information Group, 1998), pp. 21–22.

chloropicrin in 1848, and the chemical today known as mustard gas was synthesized in 1854. The most lethal chemical agents, the nerve gases, were initially developed from German research into organophosphorus pesticides in the 1930s.

Despite their long history, however, CW also pose a new challenge. In particular, the context surrounding CW—both politically and technically—has changed, and those changes may influence calculations about their potential utility. The number of possible CW possessors has grown, and some of their arsenals are increasingly sophisticated. CW represent an option of increasing interest to nonstate actors, particularly terrorists. Scenarios in which CW could have a significant impact—on the outcome of military conflict, or on the well-being of civilians—have expanded.

CW remain the least glamorous of the weapons of mass destruction; but they have been the most used. CW must be dealt with on their own terms. They cannot be addressed as lesser-included cases of nuclear or even biological weapons. If we are complacent about our ability to respond effectively to the challenges posed by CW, we are likely only to increase the risks to our military forces and civilian populations alike.

This chapter summarizes the challenges posed by CW. It first examines the technical issues associated with their development, production, and dissemination. It then addresses the proliferation of CW both by states and by nonstate actors. Finally, it discusses some of the novel ways in which CW may be used.

CW: The Technical Dimension

CW capabilities can vary greatly in their sophistication, but each chemical agent uniquely combines a set of characteristics and properties that makes it appropriate for use as a weapon. These include:

- *Lethality:* the extent to which the agent will cause fatalities
- *Mode of action:* the route by which the agent causes its effects (inhalation, dermal exposure, mucous membrane, or oral ingestion)
- *Speed of action:* the time between exposure and effect
- *Stability:* the resistance of the agent to degradation, which is important during storage and dissemination
- *Persistence:* the length of time an agent remains a hazard once it is released into the environment
- *Toxicity:* the quantity of a substance required to achieve a given effect[2]

These characteristics for various categories of CW agents are summarized in table 1-1. Combinations of these different characteristics, of course, means that different agents have more or less utility for specific situations, depending on the objectives. An advanced CW capability would entail production of several agents with a mix of these different characteristics mated to a variety of delivery systems. In contrast, a crude program would be able to produce only one or two agents and few delivery systems.

Categories of Chemical Agents

CW agents are usually classified on the basis of their impact on the human body. People are the only target of a CW attack. These are perhaps the only weapons in which this is the case. They are usually categorized into choking, blister, blood, incapacitating, and nerve agents.

2. Toxicity can be measured by various factors such as LD_{50} (the dose that kills 50 percent of the exposed population) or ID_{50} (the dose that incapacitates 50 percent of the exposed population).

TABLE I-I

Chemical Agents and Their Characteristics

	Physical state	Persistency	Delivery	Route	Target
Blister agents	Liquid, solid	High	Vapor, aerosol, liquid	Lungs, eyes, skin	Man, animals
Blood agents	Liquid, vapors	Low	Vapor	Lungs	Man, animals
Choking agents	Liquid	Low	Vapor	Lungs, eyes, skin	Man, animals
Incapacitants	Liquid, solid	Low	Aerosol, liquid	Lungs, skin	Man, animals
Nerve agents	Liquid	Low to high	Vapor, aerosol, liquid	Lungs, eyes, skin	Man, animals

SOURCE: Gordon M. Burck, "Biological, Chemical, and Toxin Warfare Agents," in Susan Wright, ed., *Preventing a Biological Arms Race* (Cambridge, MA: MIT Press, 1990), Appendix A.

Choking agents, including chlorine and phosgene, are also called pulmonary agents because they attack lung tissue and cause pulmonary edema (excess fluid in the lungs). They were the first CW used during World War I and are estimated to have accounted for 80 percent of the chemical casualties during that conflict.[3] This CW category also highlights the problems confronting efforts to control CW proliferation in that the simple agents, such as chlorine, also have widespread commercial uses and are produced in the thousands, if not millions, of tons per year all around the world.

Blister agents, also known as vesicants, include mustard gas (both sulfur mustard and nitrogen mustard), and Lewisite. These chemicals burn the skin or other parts of the body; they can act on

3. *Jane's Defense Guidebook*, p. 50.

eyes, mucous membranes, and lungs. Mustard gas was used widely in World War I and in the Iran-Iraq War, and Japan may have used Lewisite against China in the 1930s. Blister agents, particularly mustard gas, were also a major component of both the US and Soviet CW arsenals.

Blood agents, in which cyanide is a critical component, are called such because their impact is carried through the body in the blood. Hydrogen cyanide and cyanogen chloride are the two most important agents in this category; they produce their effect by interfering with oxygen utilization at the cellular level. Although cyanide-based agents were used in World War I, they were largely unsuccessful because of the large amounts needed to saturate a given space and the fact that in vapor form it is difficult to maintain a lethal concentration. Cyanogen chloride was introduced to overcome this problem. As with chlorine, cyanide compounds are produced in vast quantities for commercial purposes, including mineral extraction, printing, photography, and paper, textile, and plastic production.

Incapacitating agents, such as BZ or LSD, produce either stimulant or depressive effects on the central nervous system. The results are disabling conditions that may persist for hours or days. Such agents are not usually lethal, and do not produce permanent injuries. Incapacitating agents have been more the subject of exploration than of systematic weaponization as agents. Iraq, however, was believed to be working before the Gulf War on a new incapacitant, known as "Agent 15," which is thought to be similar to BZ.[4]

Nerve agents, divided into G- and V-agents, are the most feared CW. Essentially, these agents affect the transmission of nerve impulses by inhibiting the functioning of the vital enzyme acetylcholinesterase, which hydrolizes acetylcholine wherever it is released.

---

4. "Iraq CW Capability During the Gulf War/Agent 15," UK Ministry of Defence Press Release (Feb. 10, 1998).

TABLE 1-2

Toxicity of Nerve Agents on Skin

Agent	LD_{50} *amount* (mg)
Tabun	1,000
Sarin	1,700
Soman	50
VX	10

SOURCE: *Medical Management of Chemical Casualties Handbook*, US Army Medical Research Institute of Chemical Defense (Sep. 1995).

They are the most toxic of CW (see tables 1-2 and 1-3). Some nerve agents, particularly VX, also tend to be highly persistent.

G-series nerve agents were discovered in 1936 by Gerhard Schrader of the German firm IG Farben while he was doing research on new organophosphorous pesticides, although G-agents can be 100 to 1,000 times more poisonous than those pesticides.[5] They are rapid-acting, and generally penetrate the body through inhalation, although they can also be absorbed through the skin. The V-series agents were originally discovered in 1948 by British scientists also involved in new pesticide research. Both the US and USSR conducted military development in the 1960s.[6] The major penetration route for an agent such as VX is through skin absorption rather than inhalation.

Today, nerve agents constitute 80 percent of the CW stockpile declared by Russia as part of its obligations under the Chemical Weapons Convention (CWC). The nerve agent sarin was also the agent used by the Aum Shinrikyo in its March 1995 attack on the

5. The differences in toxicity derive from the nature of the chemical groups surrounding the phosphorous atom. There are four such groups, one of which is a double-bonded oxygen.

6. Office of Technology Assessment, *Technologies Underlying Weapons of Mass Destruction* (Washington: Government Printing Office, 1993), p. 24.

TABLE 1-3
Lethal Toxicity Figures for Selected Chemical Agents

Agent	Ct_{50} $(mg\text{-}min/m^3)$*
Selected nerve agents	
Tabun	200–400
Sarin	100–200
Soman	50-70
VX	1–50
Selected blister agents	
Pure mustard	1,500 inhalation; 10,000 skin
Lewisite	Greater than 1,500
Selected blood agents	
Phosgene	3,200
Hydrogen cyanide	2,500–5,000
Cyanogen chloride	11,000

*Refers to the lethal concentration time that will kill 50 percent of the exposed population (milligram-minutes/cubic meter).

SOURCE: *US Army Handbook on the Field Aspects of NBC Defensive Operations*, Field Manual (FM) 8-9, Part III.

Tokyo subway. Prior to the Gulf War, Iraq produced 210 tons of tabun and 790 tons of sarin, some of which was weaponized. It also acknowledges having produced VX but denics loading it in munitions, a claim that is disputed by the US and other members of the international community.

Pathways to Proliferation

Securing a CW capability is not necessarily an easy task. An advanced program pursued by a state must include several dimensions, each of which involves several steps. These steps are summarized in figure 1-1.

Three important points must be made. First, producing the agent is not the same as developing a weapon. Depending on the

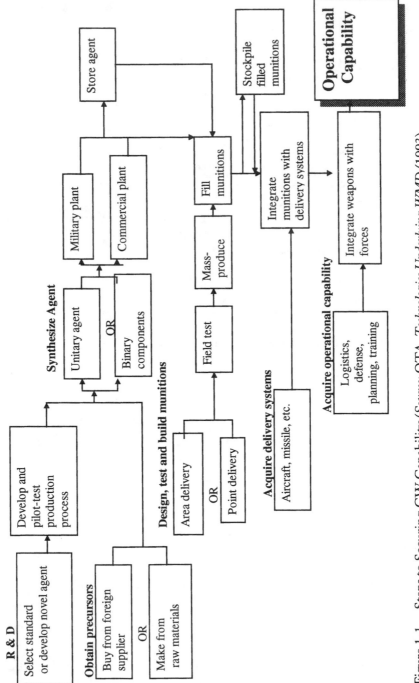

Figure 1-1. Steps to Securing CW Capability (*Source:* OTA, *Technologies Underlying WMD* (1993)

purpose of the weapon, many additional steps must be successfully taken before a weapons capability is achieved. Obviously, lesser performance requirements, such as those that terrorists might seek, create less demanding weapons-development processes.

Second, when comments are made—as the US government does—that a state is pursuing a CW program of concern, intelligence on which such comments are based is not always sufficient to locate the program's status precisely in this process. A country may be conducting research on various agents, for example, without necessarily having made the decision to go to full-scale production, let alone weaponization. In some cases, however, we just will not know the difference between a dabbler and a committed proliferator.

Third, while there are similarities in various programs, they are not necessarily identical, and it is wrong to assume that the current or future pathways for CW proliferation are the same as those that led to the development of CW capabilities in the past. Nine different production processes for sulfur mustard, for example, have been documented.[7] The US and Soviet Union produced VX through different processes, and methods used by Iraq and the US to develop G-category agents were also quite different.[8]

As the Office of Technology Assessment (OTA) has pointed out, each pathway "involves tradeoffs among simplicity, speed, agent shelf-life, and visibility. The choice of pathway would therefore be affected by the urgency of a country's military requirement for a CW stockpile, its desire to keep the program secret, its level of concern over worker safety and environmental protection, and the existence of embargoes on precursor materials and production equipment."[9]

7. Ibid., p. 21.
8. Ibid., p. 17
9. Ibid., p. 18

Weaponizing Chemical Agents

The critical requirements for turning an agent into an effective weapon is that it be toxic enough to produce the desired level of casualties and stable enough to survive dissemination either through explosion of the delivery mechanism or passage through a spray device. Meeting these requirements usually takes three steps:

1. Selecting and using chemical additives, including stabilizers, freezing-point depressants, thickeners, carriers, or antiagglomerants, to stabilize or augment the effects of the agent

2. Designing and producing munitions for dispersal of the agent

3. Filling, storage, and transport of the munitions

Filling operations, in particular, are extremely hazardous. The major technical hurdle is sealing the deadly agent inside the munition or delivery vehicle without leakage or contamination. Not all parties seeking a CW capability, however—whether states or terrorists— are concerned about the safety of either their personnel or the environment. Several members of the Aum Shinrikyo, for example, were injured and perhaps died in the process of the cult's developing its biological and chemical weapons.[10]

Chemical munitions are designed to convert a bulk payload of liquid or powdered agent into an aerosol of microscopic droplets that can be readily absorbed through the skin or inhaled. The optimal size for dermal absorption is about 70 microns and for inhalation 1 to 5 microns. Achieving the correct particle size or putting the particles into aerosol form can both pose problems for the pro-

10. Testimony of Kyle Olson, Hearings before the Permanent Subcommittee on Investigations of the Committee on Governmental Affairs, US Senate (Oct. 31, 1995), pp. 107–8.

liferator. The importance of aerosolizing the chemical agent was demonstrated by the Aum Shinrikyo subway attack. The fact that the sarin was allowed to evaporate rather than be delivered as an aerosol was one of the key factors in limiting casualties. Had Aum been able to develop an effective aerosolization mechanism—which they tried to do—the number of casualties would likely have been much higher.

The Iraqi CW program demonstrated that a wide variety of delivery platforms can be used to disseminate chemical agents. They can range from the unsophisticated plastic bags used by the Aum Shinrikyo to ballistic missiles, on which Iraq had loaded chemical warheads. Iraq also had chemical munitions for its rockets, aerial bombs, and artillery, as well as aerial spray tanks.[11] Delivery systems need not be high-tech, however, and can also include such "unconventional" systems as insect foggers, paint sprayers, and crop dusters.

Even if a proliferator can successfully engineer a CW delivery vehicle, the success of a CW attack is not necessarily guaranteed. Meteorological conditions will also play a role in determining the outcome. A number of atmospheric or ground conditions can influence the action of a chemical agent, including the following.

- *Air temperature:* The higher the temperature, the greater the rate of evaporation of particles, thereby decreasing their size; colder weather prevents evaporation, reducing concentrations in the air but lengthening the period of ground contamination.

- *Ground temperature:* This also influences the evaporation rate, thereby increasing or decreasing the duration of contamination.

11. "Iraq Weapons of Mass Destruction Program," US Government White Paper, United States Information Agency (Feb. 13, 1998), p. 11.

- *Exposure to sun:* This has a similar effect.

- *Humidity:* High relative humidity leads to enlargement of aerosol particles.

- *Precipitation:* Light rain disperses the agent, while heavy rain dilutes and displaces it; snow increases persistence of contamination by slowing down evaporation.

- *Wind speed and direction:* High winds disseminate the agent farther, but may dilute lethal concentrations sooner. Chemical clouds are most effective when winds are steady and at less than 4 knots.

- *Soil conditions:* Agent penetration of soil reduces the risk of contamination by contact but increases persistence because factors that could cause evaporation are prevented from acting.

Finally, CW attackers must take terrain into account. Open, flat terrain maximizes the lethal dispersion of the agent, while hilly or urban terrain can create atmospheric turbulence, which impedes even distribution of the agent and increases its vertical dilution, thereby reducing casualties.

Clearly, the use of chemical agents as effective weapons is not necessarily an easy task. The severity of the technical challenge depends on a number of factors, including the nature of the target (e.g., whether combat troops—protected or not—or civilians), the desired level of casualties, meteorological and topographical conditions, and choice of delivery system. This is not to argue that even the most demanding technical challenge is beyond the reach of many or most CW proliferators. Indeed, Iraq demonstrated what a committed proliferator can do. Nor is it to suggest that simpler technical challenges, such as use by terrorists, will not have significant effects. The case of Aum Shinrikyo was one in which luck played a big part in limiting the number of casualties. Rather, it is to argue that those who respond to the CW challenge must be as aware as the proliferators themselves of the full range of factors that influence the use of CW. Without such a comprehensive understanding, responses—at both policy and operational levels—could be off target.

Ongoing Challenges

An argument can be made that few military technologies have evolved as little as CW over the past fifty years.[12] This does not mean, however, that the problems posed by CW remain unchanged. Three developments in particular present ongoing challenges to those responsible for confronting the CW threat. They are the dual-use nature of much chemical material and equipment, the diffusion of chemical production capabilities, and the possibility of the development of new chemical agents.

First, dual use. The fact that many agents and much equipment involved in making CW also have legitimate commercial uses makes it a more difficult problem to control. A sulfur mustard plant using sulfur monochloride and ethylene (as the US and USSR did during World War II), for example, could be hidden at an oil refinery, which is an excellent source of ethylene and could also extract the necessary sulfur from petroleum or natural gas.[13] At the level of chemical agent, an excellent example of the dual-use problem is thiodiglycol, a key precursor for large-scale production of mustard gas, which also happens to be a key component of ballpoint-pen ink. More generally, many of the precursors that could be used in CW production are commercially used in quantities surpassing millions of tons per year.

---

12. See, e.g., *Technologies Underlying Weapons of Mass Destruction*, p. 18.
13. Ibid., p. 21.

The problem of dual use also creates alternatives for would-be proliferators. In the case of Iraq, for example, when confronted by a prospective embargo of thiodiglycol that it was importing from foreign sources, Baghdad developed an indigenous capability for mustard production based on reacting ethylene with hydrogen sulfide, both of which are widely available.[14] As an alternative to producing familiar chemical agents with different precursors, a proliferator might also look to develop more obscure CW using readily available precursors.

The international community has recognized the problem inherent in the dual-use nature of chemical material and equipment. It has attempted to regulate critical precursors through the activities of both the Australia Group (AG) and the CWC. The AG is an informal mechanism for the coordination of export controls related to chemical (and biological) materials and equipment. The 31-member AG is currently under attack from radical nonaligned countries, frequently led by Iran, for being discriminatory and as a violation of the spirit of the CWC. In response, members of the AG, frequently led by the US, argue that the AG not only is consistent with the CWC but also provides a mechanism for implementing the commitment of CWC parties not to transfer equipment or material that could facilitate development of another country's CW program. They also argue that the AG remains an important tool in the fight against BCW proliferation based on a continuing role for export controls (even if their focus shifts from denial to other functions),[15] the group's focus on material and equipment of greatest proliferation concern, and its enhancement of individual national efforts through coordination.

14. Ibid., p. 23.
15. For a discussion of this shift, see Brad Roberts, "Article III: Non-Transfer," in Graham S. Pearson and Malcolm Dando, eds., *Strengthening the Biological Weapons Convention: Key Points for the Fourth Review Conference*, Department of Peace Studies, University of Bradford (Sep. 1996), p. 37.

The CWC places limits on access to and flow of certain chemicals that are divided into three categories (defined by a combination of their utility in making CW and their commercial use and availability) and imposes on parties different sets of declaration and on-site obligations regarding these categories. The authors of the CWC recognized, however, that for precursors that were widely available and had widespread commercial utility, the ability to verify their nonuse in CW programs would be extremely difficult.

Second, diffusion. CW proliferation has been described as an "unfortunate side effect of a process that is otherwise beneficial and anyway impossible to stop: the diffusion of competence in chemistry and chemical technology from the rich to the poor parts of the world."[16] Trade and investment figures related to the chemical industry underline the extent of diffusion:

- Exports from the developed world to developing nations increased from $ 33 billion in 1980 to $ 57 billion in 1991.

- Annual direct investment in developing countries by US chemical manufacturers more than doubled from $4.05 billion in 1983 to $9.98 billion in 1993.

- The developing countries' share of US investment in overseas chemical industries remained a steady 21 percent in the decade from 1983 to 1993.[17]

The result of this diffusion of chemical production capability is that today more than 100 countries have the capability—if not the in-

16. Julian Perry Robinson, "Chemical Weapons Proliferation: The Problem in Perspective," in Trevor Findlay, ed., *Chemical Weapons and Missile Proliferation* (Boulder, CO: Lynne Rienner, 1991), p. 26.

17. Brad Roberts, "Rethinking Export Controls on Dual-Use Materials and Technologies: From Trade Restraints to Trade Enablers," *The Arena*, no. 2, Chemical and Biological Arms Control Institute (Jun. 1995), pp. 2–3.

tent—to produce at least simple CW, such as phosgene, hydrogen cyanide, or sulfur mustard. Obviously, a smaller number of countries can produce nerve agents, whose production involves more complex and difficult reaction steps. This diffusion of capability increasingly creates a world of "virtual CW programs" in which the critical factors shaping the proliferation landscape are not technical but political.

The diffusion of chemical production capabilities also increases the sources from which potential proliferators can purchase the necessary precursors. The Australia Group is limited in membership, and will remain so. Many countries do not belong to the AG and will not, and these nonmembers may not maintain export controls with the same tenacity as member countries. Moreover, despite the commitment of CWC parties to put effective export controls into place, global chemical trade is likely only to expand in the years ahead.

Another dimension of the diffusion problem is expertise. This aspect takes two forms. One is the leakage of experts from places (particularly the former Soviet Union) that had major CW programs. The second is the training of foreign nationals in the US and elsewhere in the West in disciplines, such as chemistry and chemical engineering, that might be exploited for CW purposes. This is not to say that all foreign students in the hard sciences or engineering are proliferation risks, but experience—such as that with Iraq—has demonstrated that foreign-trained nationals often take lead roles in a proliferator's WMD programs.

The third ongoing challenge is the prospect that, despite the fact that the number of CW agents has remained virtually static for many years, new chemical agents could be developed. This problem was highlighted by reports of Russia's development of a novel chemical agent called Novichok ("newcomer").

A September 20, 1992 *Moscow News* article coauthored by Vil Mirzayanov and Lev Fedorov alleged that the Russian CW complex was developing a new generation of CW.[18] The program, which began in 1982 and was code-named Foliant, had the apparent goal of developing new binary weapons in response to the Reagan Administration's CW initiatives. According to Mirzayanov, an employee for twenty-six years at the All-Union State Scientific Research Institute for Organic Chemistry and Technology where the program was conducted, by 1987 Soviet scientists had created the new nerve gas, Novichok, which has been alleged to be ten times more lethal than VX.[19] According to Mirzayanov, Novichok was based on chemical compounds developed between 1985 and 1991, dubbed Substance A-230 and A-232, with a toxicity that surpasses any known chemical agent by a factor of five to eight. Mirzayanov also claims that the Soviets developed in 1990 a binary CW code-named Substance 33, of which 15,000 tons were produced in the city of Novocheboksarsk while documentation was altered to give the impression that VX was being produced.[20] Responding to an investigation into Mirzayanov's claims by Russian authorities, the Institute's director wrote a letter to the Russian Security Ministry stating the institute had, "synthesized, studied, and tested a number of new chemical combinations of different classes that significantly surpass VX . . . ."[21]

If Mirzayanov's allegations are true, then Russia has covertly developed a new class of CW that it has not declared under the CWC. Moreover, it did so in a way consciously designed to circumvent the treaty by ensuring that the precursors for such an agent do not appear on the CWC schedules. Beyond the development of new agents, technological advances for more effective CW programs

18. Lev Fedorov and Vil Mirzayanov, "A Poisoned Policy," *Moscow News*, no. 39 (1992).
19. Will Englund, "Ex-Soviet Scientist Says Gorbachev's Regime Created New Nerve Gas in '91," *Baltimore Sun* (Sep. 16, 1992).
20. Vil Mirzayanov, *Wall Street Journal* (May 25, 1994).
21. 263 *Science* (Feb. 25,1994), p. 1083.

may result from current laboratory research on chemical defenses. Researchers are examining the impact of various agents at the molecular level. Although the purpose of such research is development of more effective antidotes, it could also assist in the development of novel compounds. An additional concern has been expressed about countries that are seeking to circumvent the CWC by modifying existing agents to avoid detection or by weaponizing "second string" agents of known but less effective poisons. A further worry is development of penetrant chemicals to defeat chemical defenses, particularly "mask breakers" capable of saturating gas-mask filters.[22] This is an example of the continuing risk that a novel technology will be developed to reverse the current ascendancy of defense over offense in the chemical field.

CW Proliferation

CW proliferation is a problem at both the state and nonstate actor levels. On the state level, US government spokesmen generally charge that as many as two dozen nations are pursuing CW programs of concern. Unfortunately, most public government discussions of this issue do not specify all of the countries on the list, but make the broad claim and then focus on the same limited number of countries of particular concern.

Table 1-4 summarizes nonofficial assessments of the CW proliferation problem at the state level. The countries identified as being suspected of pursuing CW programs were listed in a 1993 study by the OTA because they appeared on lists of suspected CW proliferators in more than two-thirds of the nongovernmental studies OTA assessed. Since that study, the CWC has entered into force (in 1997), requiring that all parties declare both existing or former CW production facilities and CW stockpiles. Prior to the CWC's entry

22. *Technologies Underlying Weapons of Mass Destruction*, p. 28.

TABLE 1-4
Chemical Weapons Programs: Declared or Suspected

Declared CW production facilities or stockpiles	Suspected CW production facilities or stockpiles
China	Egypt
France	Iran
Japan	Israel
India	Libya
Iraq	Myanmar
Russia	North Korea
South Korea	Syria
UK	Taiwan
US	Vietnam

SOURCES: Gordon Burck and Charles Flowerree, *International Handbook on Chemical Weapons Proliferation* (Westport, CT: Greenwood Press, 1991); Office of Technology Assessment, *Proliferation of Weapons of Mass Destruction: Assessing the Risks* (Washington: Government Printing Office, 1993).

into force only the US and the Soviet Union/Russia had declared CW stockpiles, and Iraq was forced to admit its program following the Gulf War. Following entry into force of the CWC, however, five other countries declared existing or former CW production facilities—China, France, the United Kingdom, Japan, and India.[23] The latter two, in particular, were surprising. Furthermore, in addition to the US and Russia, India and South Korea declared possession of a CW stockpile, and again the latter two surprised the international community.

Those declarations, while welcome, leave many questions unanswered about the existence or status of CW programs in other countries. Among suspected proliferators, most of the attention has focused on Iraq, Iran, Syria, Libya, and North Korea. A brief survey

23. "Declarations of Chemical Weapons Activities," Chemical and Biological Nonproliferation Project, Henry L. Stimson Center, http://www.stimson.org/cwc/declar.htm.

of these "rogue" states highlights some of the problems posed by CW proliferation at the state level.

Iraq

Iraq's CW program provides a disturbing example of the capabilities a committed proliferator can achieve. Iraq produced thousands of tons of CW beginning in the early 1980s, and weaponized them on a range of delivery systems, including artillery shells, rockets, gravity bombs, aerial spray tanks, and Scud-type missile warheads. It began to use some of these weapons early in the war with Iran, and by 1987 Iraq had developed the skills to use CW in direct support of ground operations.[24]

At the time of the Gulf War, Iraq had an inventory of about 1,000 metric tons of CW, split evenly between blister agents such as mustard and nerve agents. It was also beginning to weaponize VX. Iraq had made preparations for a CW offensive with chemical defense equipment and extensive written instructions in the Kuwaiti theater of operations.[25] The reason Iraq did not use CW against coalition forces is the subject of considerable debate. Explanations range from the mundane and technical (e.g., that the weather conditions were not appropriate) to the operational (e.g., that coalition forces moved too quickly to be found and present themselves as good CW targets), to the strategic (e.g., that Saddam Hussein was deterred from using CW by US threats of overwhelming retaliation[26]).

---

24. Anthony Cordesman, *Case Study 3: Iraq*, Deterrence Series (Alexandria: Chemical and Biological Arms Control Institute, 1998), p. 33.

25. Ibid., p. 34.

26. Iraqi Deputy Prime Minister Tariq Aziz indicated to Ambassador Rolf Ekéus, then Executive Chairman of the UN Special Commission on Iraq (UNSCOM), that Iraq interpreted the US threat to be one of nuclear retaliation. Ambassador Ekéus is reluctant to fully accept this explanation at face value, however, given the Iraqi propensity to tell their listeners what they think they want to hear.

Following the Gulf War, UNSCOM destroyed more than 40,000 CW munitions (28,000 filled and 12,000 empty), 480,000 liters of CW agent, 1,800,000 liters of chemical precursors, and eight different types of delivery systems.[27] Following the defection of Hussein Kamal, Iraq also admitted that it had:

- Produced larger amounts of VX than it had previously disclosed

- Researched in-flight mixing of binary CW

- Perfected techniques for the large-scale production of a VX precursor that is well suited to long-term storage

The ongoing dispute over Iraqi VX weaponization reflects continuing concerns over Baghdad's ability to reconstitute its CW program. According to one US estimate, Iraq could restart limited mustard agent production within a few weeks, full-scale production of sarin within a few months, and pre-Gulf War levels of production, including VX, within two to three years. Since the Gulf War, Iraq has also rebuilt two facilities it once used for CW production.[28]

Iran

During the Iran–Iraq War, Iran used CW to retaliate for Iraqi CW use. According to one study, at present, "chemical and biological weapons are seen as potentially important tactical force-multipliers and the core component of Iran's strategic forces."[29] For this reason, Iran has put a high priority on its CW program. According to the US Department of Defense, Iran now manufactures weapons for blister, blood, and choking agents, and is believed to be conduct-

---

27. "Iraqi Weapons of Mass Destruction Programs," p. 5.
28. Ibid., p. 6.
29. Michael Eisenstadt, *Case Study 4: Iran*, Deterrence Series (Alexandria: Chemical and Biological Arms Control Institute, 1998), p. 25.

ing research on nerve agents.[30] Its delivery systems include artillery shells and bombs. Despite its priority, the US government does not believe that Iran has in place yet a totally indigenous program, but remains dependent on foreign sources of supply, particularly China, for technology and equipment.[31]

Iran, however, has signed and ratified the CWC. As a consequence, it assumed an obligation to declare its current and past CW production activities as well as any existing stockpiles. That initial declaration was due in January 1998, thirty days after Iran became a party to the treaty; the submission was a year late. Unfortunately, the contents of Iran's declaration are not widely available. Its distribution even in the OPCW is highly restricted. What Iran has declared, therefore, is not possible to determine, although preparations are under way for the conduct of inspections there.

Syria

Syria is alleged to have a long-standing CW program, first begun in the 1970s. By the late 1980s, Syria was reported to have at least two CW facilities in operation, one near Damascus and the second near Homs.[32] The Syrian CW inventory is believed to contain both blister and nerve agents, although one report suggests that the Israelis at least believe that the bulk of the arsenal is made up of sarin.[33] Syrian delivery systems are said to include thousands of aerial bombs as well as some Scud-type warheads.[34]

As with Iran, Syria has relied on extensive external assistance in

---

30. US Department of Defense, *Proliferation: Threat and Response* (Dec. 1997), p. 5.

31. Ibid.

32. Ahmed Hashim, *Case Study 1: Syria*, Deterrence Series (Alexandria: Chemical and Biological Arms Control Institute, 1998), p. 7.

33. Ibid., p. 8.

34. M. Zuhair Diab, "Syria's Chemical and Biological Weapons: Assessing Capabilities and Motivations," *The Nonproliferation Review* (Fall 1997), p. 105.

its CW program. Former CIA Director William Webster stated in testimony that "West European firms were instrumental in supplying the required precursor chemicals and equipment."[35] Other sources of support are alleged to include China, India, North Korea, and Russia.[36]

Syria's primary security concern is its military balance with Israel, and its CW capabilities must be seen in that context. Their operational utility is likely to be considered most seriously in the context of a conflict that involves Syrian efforts to retake the Golan Heights. In this case, CW may be seen as a force-multiplier for Syrian forces on the offensive that would demoralize and disorganize Israeli forces defending the territory and disrupt Israeli plans to mobilize reserves and bring to bear the power of its air force.

Libya

Libya has both produced and used CW. Its program began in earnest in the 1980s with the completion of the CW plant at Rabta, which is alleged to have produced up to 100 tons of blister and nerve agent.[37] The plant was closed down after strong diplomatic efforts were made and media attention gave foreign involvement in its construction high visibility.[38] Analysts generally agree that Libya used some of its limited CW inventory in Chad.

35. Ahmed Hashim, p. 8.

36. M. Zuhair Diab, p. 106. The extent of Soviet/Russian support is the subject of some debate. Hashim, for example, suggests that far from supporting Syrian efforts, the Soviet Union sent a military delegation to warn Damascus that it would not support Syrian CW in combat. (Hashim, p. 8.) In contrast, Diab quotes Israeli Defense Minister Yitzhak Mordechai as saying in 1996 that Russian scientists were helping Syria to manufacture VX, an allegation the Russians denied. (Diab, p. 106.)

37. DoD, *Proliferation: Threat and Response*, p. 15.

38. German companies, in particular, took a lead role in the construction of the plant. The German firm Imhausen-Chemie, for example, was the prime contractor. Japanese companies were also involved, particularly in providing a metal-working plant with Japanese-made machine tools. French companies were alleged to have provided chemical reaction cauldrons, and Dutch and Hong Kong firms were used

Despite its efforts, however, the Libyan threat remains only marginally credible. Its stocks are low, making it impossible to sustain use. Moreover, its delivery capabilities are poor. In fact, the efforts to use CW in Chad were not all that effective. On one occasion, for example, artillery-delivered gas reportedly blew back across Libyan troops. The Libyan armed forces would also have enormous difficulties bringing its CW-armed artillery into play against any but the most unsophisticated opponent, given their vulnerability to modern counter-battery tactics and the dominance of the air that any Libyan opponent would likely secure.[39]

North Korea

One country whose CW program is far beyond marginally capable is North Korea. North Korea can produce significant quantities of a wide variety of CW—blister, choking, and nerve agents, including VX. According to defectors, North Korea produces twenty different chemical agents for use in weapons at more than a dozen sites.[40] Estimates suggest an annual production potential of 4,500 tons in peacetime and 12,000 tons in wartime with between 1,000 and 5,000 tons already stockpiled.[41]

The North Korean CW program began in the 1950s in the belief that they could provide a deterrent against aggression by South Korea and the US. By the 1990s, however, CW have come to be viewed primarily as "operational-level weapons," and the North Korean military is said to have studied both the Iran–Iraq War and Operation Desert Storm to determine how it can use its CW to best

---

for shipping and distribution. See OTA, *Technologies Underlying Weapons of Mass Destruction*, pp. 42–43.

39. Robert Waller, *Case Study 2: Libya*, Deterrence Series (Alexandria: Chemical and Biological Arms Control Institute, 1998), p. 7.

40. Joseph Bermudez, *Case Study 5: North Korea*, Deterrence Series (Alexandria: Chemical and Biological Arms Control Institute, 1998), p. 5.

41. Ibid., p. 9.

effect. North Korea could use its CW to attack US or allied forces deployed along the demilitarized zone as well as to isolate the peninsula from US strategic reinforcement by closing ports and airfields in the south. Some scenarios even suggest a threat of CW (and possibly BW) use against Japan as a further means of shutting down US military operations. Several US military planners suggest that any conflict on the Korean peninsula is likely to witness North Korean use of CW (and possibly BW) from the outset.

Although the proliferators summarized briefly here are remarkably diverse in their strategic cultures, doctrines, and decision-making processes, a common element is their continued willingness to resort to violence to settle disputes or secure national interests.[42] It may be they believe that it is good to be seen as a bit dangerous. Another common element that surfaces in looking at these countries is their emphasis on self-reliance. This emphasis is most pronounced in the case of North Korea with its philosophy of *juche*, but other countries such as Iran and Libya also stress the importance of not being dependent on others for their security. With peace treaties concluded between Israel and Egypt and Jordan, Syria sees itself as the last remaining Arab state with the will and the requirement to balance Israeli military capabilities—both conventional and unconventional—and appears to define its CW program in that context.

Enhancing freedom of action vis-à-vis developed countries does not appear to be a major motivation in the pursuit of CW thus far. This situation may be changing, however, as open discussion has occurred in some developing countries about the need for a capabil-

42. The brief discussion that follows is taken from Michael Moodie, *Chemical and Biological Weapons: Will Deterrence Work?* Deterrence Series (Alexandria: Chemical and Biological Arms Control Institute, 1998), pp. 29–31.

ity to deter intervention by developed states.[43] Only one example is the oft-quoted statement by an Indian general to the effect that a major lesson of the Gulf War is that a developing country should not go to war with the US without nuclear weapons (NW). For states that do not consider NW an option for political, technical, or financial reasons, BCW could become increasingly attractive alternatives as they search for leverage to exploit the weaknesses of stronger states. The use of BCW in such "asymmetric strategies" has become a key issue for US military planners.

Although the CW programs of the five countries briefly described here are usually considered the most serious proliferation problems, CW capabilities are not limited to these few states. Egypt is generally believed to have used CW in Yemen in the early 1960s, and there is no evidence that it has eliminated that now-aging capability. Egypt is not a party to the CWC, arguing that it will not join the treaty until Israel moves toward the Non-Proliferation Treaty. Israel, too, is generally considered to have a significant CW capability.[44] It has signed but not ratified the CWC, and a debate is now under way as to whether it should do so. Israeli military officials are questioning why they should relinquish this option that may have some value as a deterrent in kind in the region. In contrast, Israel's chemical industry worries that the limitations on trade with nonparties that will be introduced three years after the CWC's entry into force could injure their competitive position in the global chemical market. Taiwan is not allowed to sign the CWC, although it has

---

43. Former Indian Army Chief of Staff, General K. Sundarji, for example, has endorsed the notion of a "minimum deterrent" to discourage "US bullying" and possible "racist aggression from the West." Cited in Brad Roberts, "Between Panic and Complacency: Calibrating the Chemical and Biological Warfare Threat," in Stuart E. Johnson, *The Niche Threat: Deterring the Use of Chemical and Biological Weapons* (Washington: National Defense University Press, 1997), p. 27.

44. Gordon Burck and Charles Flowerree, *International Handbook on Chemical Weapons Proliferation* (Westport, CT: Greenwood Press, 1991).

indicated it would like to do so. In the meantime, concerns remain about its possible CW program, which lies well within the country's technical capacity. A number of other countries—Vietnam, Myanmar, and Pakistan—are also considered potential CW proliferators, although the extent of their programs does not seem to produce levels of anxiety comparable to those of the "rogues" described earlier.

The Nonstate Actor Challenge

The Aum Shinrikyo's sarin attack in the Tokyo subway in 1995, which killed 12 people and produced more than 5,000 casualties, stunned the world. The attack in Japan has sparked a global debate about whether the taboo against terrorist use of BCW has been broken, the extent to which nations should expect similar attacks in the future, and the steps countries should take to prepare for and respond to this new challenge. For some people, terrorist use of BCW presents the major threat from such weapons in the future.

Is such a concern justified in light of the historical record, which shows limited terrorist interest in BCW? Canadian intelligence analyst Ron Purver, who conducted an extensive survey of the unclassified literature dealing with terrorism,[45] has identified three categories of meaningful explanation for the nonuse of BCW by terrorists. The first category includes factors that relate to the nature and goals of terrorist groups, including fear of alienating public opinion, the perceived lack of control over the weapon itself, and the lack of suitable or commensurate demands that would make the threat of use of such weapons credible. A second category identifies factors that represent continuing constraints on terrorist BCW use, including the difficulty of ensuring group cohesion in the face of a

45. Ron Purver, *Chemical and Biological Terrorism: The Threat According to the Open Literature* (Jun. 1995).

possible controversial action, fear of government retaliation, and technical constraints which, although not insurmountable, add to the complexity and risks of an operation and could increase the prospect of failure. The third category of explanation highlights factors that are not always apposite, and could be losing their cogency. These factors include an alleged disinclination toward mass or indiscriminate killing, the absence of a need to resort to such weapons, alleged satisfaction with existing methods, and the perceived lack of precedent for BCW use.[46]

Have the factors that restrained terrorist use of BCW in the past so lost their cogency that we should expect widespread use of them in the future? Not necessarily. It is the case that technical factors have become less restrictive as a result of proliferation, technology diffusion, and the internet. But technical barriers were never all that high in the past; nor have they completely disappeared.[47] It is also true that trends in terrorist activity show that while the number of terrorist incidents in recent years has declined, the number of persons killed in such incidents has increased.[48] But terrorists always possessed the capacity to kill more people than they actually killed, even using traditional instruments such as guns and bombs. The ultimate impact of the changes in constraints on terrorist use of BCW remains ambiguous.

Has the taboo, then, been broken? Answering the question begins with the appreciation that change in the motivations propelling

46. These categories are presented in Ron Purver, "Understanding Past Non-Use of CBW by Terrorists," in Brad Roberts, ed., *Terrorism with Chemical and Biological Weapons: Calibrating Risks and Responses* (Alexandria: Chemical and Biological Arms Control Institute, 1997), pp. 71–72.

47. See Karl Lowe, "Analyzing Technical Constraints on Bio-Terrorism: Are They Still Important?" ibid., pp. 53–64.

48. Bruce Hoffman, "Viewpoint—Terrorism and WMD: Some Preliminary Hypotheses," *The Nonproliferation Review* (Spring-Summer 1997), p. 47.

terrorist groups has fostered a more complex array of groups, some of whom may indeed be attracted to the use of such weapons.

Brad Roberts identifies three types of traditional terrorist actors: those who use terror to demand a seat at the political table and compel respect for a cause, those who resort to violence in the hope of spurring such an overreaction by the state that the people rise up to overthrow it, and state-sponsored terrorists who are used by foreign powers to gain political leverage.[49] For a variety of reasons, none of these groups has been attracted to BCW use in the past, and there is little evidence to indicate that they are likely to find such weapons attractive for their purposes in the future.

The terrorism landscape has become more complicated, however, with the emergence of other groups. Terrorism expert Bruce Hoffman describes these new entrants as

> rather different terrorist "entities" with arguably less comprehensible nationalist or ideological motivations [which] frequently embrace not only far more amorphous religious and millenarian aims but are themselves less cohesive organizational entities, with a more diffuse structure and membership. Even more disturbing is that . . . their goals embrace mystical, almost transcendental, and divinely-inspired imperatives or a violently anti-government form of "populism reflecting far-fetched conspiracy notions based on a volatile mixture of seditious, racial, and religious dicta."[50]

Such groups hold different conceptions of political power and define their relationship with society in terms far different from those of the traditional terrorist. As a consequence, they also hold distinct views on the place of violence in their cause and the acceptability of inflicting mass casualties on innocent populations.

It is these groups that are likely to feel unrestrained in the use of

49. Brad Roberts, "Has the Taboo Been Broken?" in Roberts, *Terrorism with CBW*, pp. 129–30.
50. Bruce Hoffman, "Viewpoint—Terrorism and WMD," p. 47.

chemical or biological weapons. Aum Shinrikyo, for example, was a unique combination of millenarian cult, terrorist organization, and criminal enterprise that sought to hasten the collapse of the government of Japan and the conflict between Japan and the US that had been predicted by its charismatic leader, Shoko Asahara.[51] Closer to home, concern exists about the interest being demonstrated in BCW by elements of the so-called "Christian militia," particularly through their exchanges on the internet. One might ask, for example, why such groups are trying to recruit crop dusters from west Texas who used to fly for the former Nicaraguan dictator, Anastasio Somoza.

The more complex pattern of terrorism at the end of the twentieth century does not imply that terrorists will necessarily find it easy to acquire, develop, or effectively utilize CW on a regular basis. Nor does it suggest that such weapons will never be used. Trying to predict how and when CW will appear is a perilous undertaking. Terrorism expert Brian Jenkins, however, has offered the following propositions:

- Terrorists are more likely to threaten BCW use than actually to use them in attacks.

- CW will prove more prevalent than biological weapons because they are seen to be "easier" to produce and control.

- Small-scale attacks are more likely than large ones.

- Readily available chemicals, such as cyanide, are more likely to be used than more exotic agents (although the Aum attack with sarin suggests an interest in some of the more sophisticated substances).

---

51. For an excellent examination of the Aum Shinrikyo, see the testimony of John Sopko and the attached report, "Global Proliferation of Weapons of Mass Destruction: A Case Study of the Aum Shinrikyo," in *Global Proliferation of Weapons of Mass Destruction*, Hearings before the Permanent Subcommittee on Investigations, Committee on Governmental Affairs, US Senate, Part I (Oct. 31 and Nov. 1, 1995), pp. 15–102.

- Crude dispersal in enclosed areas is the most likely form of attack.

- While more instances of BCW attack will occur, they are not likely to become commonplace.[52]

If Jenkins's last point is correct, then policymakers confront one of their most vexing dilemmas: a potential contingency with low probability but high consequences. Such issues are the most difficult for defining appropriate policy responses. The threat must neither be hyped nor ignored. Shaping effective responses must be given some priority, but not always the highest. Financial resources directed to meeting that threat must be neither excessive nor inadequate. Drawing those lines is extremely difficult.

CW Use: A Range of Troubling Options

Current thinking about the threat posed by CW has been shaped in large part by the legacy of the Cold War. In the context of the East–West standoff, CW were a concern to NATO because the Warsaw Pact was viewed as capable of delivering chemical agents in huge quantities and of the proper type with precision delivery systems and to do so for prolonged periods of time so as to sustain lethal concentrations. The view was also that Soviet forces had the mobility and skill to exploit the tactical opportunities created by such action, thereby creating the prospect of dominating the battlefield. This focus on the impact of CW on battlefield outcomes was reinforced by the way CW were used in the Iran–Iraq War, the most significant use of CW since World War I.

---

52. Brian M. Jenkins, "Understanding the Link Between Motives and Methods," in Roberts, *Terrorism with CBW*, p. 51.

Thinking in such terms today is too narrow.[53] Even in major wars, CW have a broader range of uses than has generally been appreciated. Their use may be threatened, for example, to dissuade military action or deter intervention by an outside state or coalition before actual military conflict begins. CW may also be used to cripple the intervention in its early stages to prevent the conflict from progressing to a decisive encounter. Regimes defeated on the battlefield may also resort to CW to prevent the elaboration of a postconflict outcome that represents a strategic defeat and threatens the existence of the regime or severely limits its freedom of action.

Increasing US dependence on force projection and the accompanying military strategy premised on quick deployment of forces makes the US particularly vulnerable to these broader CW attacks. One government study, for example, highlighted this problem, noting on the basis of war games and other analyses that an

> enemy using relatively small quantities of chemical and biological weapons could exploit vulnerabilities . . . [and] that military operations conducted according to the tenets of power projection were executable only on delayed and disrupted schedules when CONUS deployment facilities, prepositioned materiel, or key reception sites in the area of responsibility were attacked with chemical and biological weapons.[54]

Major theater wars, however, are not likely to be the most frequent conflict situations in which US forces find themselves in the future. Rather, lower scale conflicts, such as peace enforcement operations, humanitarian assistance missions, or noncombatant evacuations are more likely scenarios. Confronting CW use in such sce-

---

53. This discussion is based in part on the work of Brad Roberts, who has done extensive analyses of unexpected uses of weapons of mass destruction.

54. "Assessment of the Impact of Chemical and Biological Weapons on Joint Operations in 2010 (The CB 2010 Study)," US Department of Defense, http// www.nbc-med.org/publications/cb2010.htm.

narios has been given almost no attention by defense planners or policymakers. Threatening use or even using CW to compel the departure of US forces in such situations is one possible contingency. So, too, is CW use to target congregating civilians preparing for evacuation. State-sponsored terrorism in the US in the context of such prewar or nonwar conflicts is perhaps a more likely contingency than an isolated attack by terrorists.

Policymakers and defense planners must pay greater attention to such potential uses of CW. In the context of the drive to eliminate CW as weapons of war, their use in these nonwar but intense conflicts could become the prevalent mode in which CW continue to be exploited by those seeking political and military advantage.

Conclusion

The changing context of post-Cold War security dynamics is creating a new environment that may change the calculations of the costs and benefits associated with developing, acquiring, and exploiting CW. The growing attraction of "asymmetrical strategies" and the emergence of new terrorist entities are only two aspects of this changing environment. Diminished technical barriers deriving from the diffusion of chemical-related materials, equipment, and expertise is another. The growing number of possible contingencies in which CW might be useful resulting from the more diverse forms of conflict the world is witnessing since the end of the Cold War creates additional opportunities.

The context may be new, but the challenge confronting those responsible for dealing with the CW threat remains much the same. In short, they must drive up the costs of pursuing and exploiting a CW capability as high as possible while minimizing the potential benefits that might be derived from doing so. The costs that must be imposed clearly go well beyond the financial to political and security losses as well. Minimizing benefits, particularly through exploiting defense capabilities—both active and passive—represents another means of deterring not just the use of the capability, but the political decisions to go down the CW road in the first place. The critical challenge is to shape the calculations of decisionmakers who might be contemplating the acquisition of CW capabilities in such a way that the only attractive option is one away from CW proliferation. Meeting that challenge will require a multifaceted strategy that relies on a panoply of policy tools. No one-policy element—intelligence, arms control, export controls, diplomacy, or military capabilities—will provide a complete answer. They must all be made to work together in a genuinely strategic approach. Only such an approach will maximize efforts to respond effectively to the threats posed by CW.

Steven M. Block

Living Nightmares: Biological Threats Enabled by Molecular Biology

This chapter draws on a 1997 summer study by JASON[1] that I led on the threat posed by the development and use of biological agents. Rather than address the myriad prob-

Thanks to the JASON Group, and especially to the participants in the 1997 Summer Study described in footnote 1 below, for their contributions to this chapter. Thanks also to Princeton University's Lynn Enquist (also editor, *Journal of Virology*) for his insight, encyclopedic knowledge, and patient tutorials in virology. Finally, thanks to Sidney Drell for inspiring me to think hard, for reawakening my latent activism, and for giving me the opportunity to do something about it.

1. This study was held during June and July of 1997. The JASONs are a collection of primarily academic scientists who dedicate a portion of their time to addressing problems of national interest, consulting for various US government agencies. According to their charter (JASON Charter, as amended November 13, 1991, Mitre Corp., McLean, VA):

> JASON exists to enable scientists to contribute to the enhancement of national security and to the public benefit by working as individuals or in groups on problems of impor-

lems posed by biological agents in general—a daunting and hopeless task—the JASON study focused instead, and from the outset, on one issue. Specifically, we took a hard look at what the near-term future of biological warfare held, based on how recent advances in the life sciences have changed the nature and scope of that threat. In brief, we concluded that progress in biomedical science inevitably has a dark side, and potentiates the development of an entirely new class of weapons of mass destruction (WMD): genetically engineered pathogens. The danger of such next-generation biological weapons (BW) in the twenty-first century is quite real, and they pose

tance supported by government organizations....

Formed during the Cold War era, the JASON group has been particularly active in confronting the nuclear threat. From the outset, its membership has included prominent scientists with backgrounds mainly in physics and mathematics. With the wind-down of the Cold War, however, the composition of the group shifted in keeping with the changing focus, and has grown today to include experts in computer science, electrical engineering, molecular biology, and other fields. In addition to the diversity of science represented by the group, individual JASON members have always been distinguished by their broad, cross-disciplinary interests. The 1997 Summer Study was carried out by me and the following fourteen individuals: Curtis Callan (Princeton University), J. Mike Cornwall (University of California, Los Angeles), William Dally (Stanford University), Freeman Dyson (Institute for Advanced Study), Norval Fortson (University of Washington), Gerald Joyce (Scripps Research Institute), H. Jeff Kimble (California Institute of Technology), Steven Koonin (California Institute of Technology), Claire Max (Lawrence Livermore National Labs), Thomas Prince (California Institute of Technology), Oscar Rothaus (Cornell University), Roy Schwitters (University of Texas), Peter Weinberger (Renaissance Technology), and W. Hugh Woodin (University of California, Berkeley). The study group included an MD/PhD as well as a biologist, in addition to one or more physicists, astronomers, mathematicians, computer scientists, and engineers. Many of the same individuals participated that summer in a study of the Human Genome Project (S. E. Koonin, "An Independent Perspective on the Human Genome Project," 279 Science (1998), pp. 36–37), undertaken on behalf of the Department of Energy. While assessing work at the forefront of life science, it seemed natural to contemplate at the same time the dangers of what has been termed "black biology." In this chapter, I write strictly as an individual, and not in any capacity on behalf of JASON, but it would be inappropriate not to acknowledge their vital role in shaping this presentation.

extraordinary challenges for detection, mitigation, and remediation.[2]

Prescience?

The JASON study proved to be rather timely. Shortly after our report was briefed, a popular account of bioterrorism with a genetically engineered pathogen was published, eventually making it onto the bestseller list: Richard Preston's *The Cobra Event*.[3] Although its plot was fictional—right down to the impossible supervirus it described—many of the supporting details in the novel were well researched and scientifically accurate. No question about it, this was scary stuff, a real eye-opener. Preston's book was reportedly read by President Clinton,[4] who was motivated to confer directly with a number of prominent biologists and biotechnologists about the credibility of Preston's scenario. Two Presidential Decision Directives have since emerged that address aspects of chemical, biological, and cyber threats, along with other security issues (PDDs 62 and 63). During 1997–98, prospects for some form of BW attack, involving either conventional or genetically engineered agents, were reported extensively by the news media.[5] Even the *Journal of the American Medical Association* devoted an entire issue to biological warfare concerns.[6]

2. The color figures that accompanied my presentation at the November 16–18, 1998, Hoover Institution conference on biological and chemical weapons have been rendered in black and white for this chapter.

3. Richard Preston, *The Cobra Event* (New York: Random House, 1997).

4. Judith Miller and William J. Broad, "Exercise Finds US Unable to Handle Germ War Threat," *New York Times* (Apr. 26, 1998), p. 1.

5. Coverage included television network specials on ABC (*PrimeTime Live*, Feb. and Jul. 1998), TBS (*The Coming Plague*, Apr. 98), and PBS (*Frontline*, Oct. 1998), plus a series of articles in the *New York Times*.

6. 278 *Journal of the American Medical Association* (no. 5) (Aug. 6, 1997), pp. 347–446.

This level of media attention undoubtedly aroused public interest in biological warfare—but was it alarmist hype, or largely warranted? On balance, I am inclined toward the latter view, for the following reason. Modern bioscience has led to the development of many powerful tools for manipulating genes. Such tools hold the key to revolutionary medical advances, among them gene therapy and the eventual abolition of fatal diseases such as cancer. But they make equally possible the creation of entirely new WMD, endowed with unprecedented power to destroy. It seems likely that such weapons will eventually come to exist, simply because of the lamentable ease with which they may be constructed. In contrast to nuclear weapons, BW do not require rare materials, such as enriched uranium or plutonium. They do not require rare finances: development and production are comparatively inexpensive. They do not require rare knowledge: most of the techniques involved are straightforward, well-documented, and in the public domain. Today, thousands of biologists worldwide possess the requisite skills, and more are trained every day (most often at US universities). Finally, they do not require rare infrastructure; some BW can be produced by small terrorist groups almost as easily as through national biological warfare programs. Inevitably, someone, somewhere, sometime seems bound to try something. So, for better or worse, genomics will change our world (see figure 2-1). It would be tragic if it took the biological equivalent of Hiroshima to muster our response. Like it or not, we need to begin certain preparations now.

Dimensions of the Threat

What can we anticipate? It seems reasonable to draw an analogy with the way that today's nuclear threat developed. In the pre-World War II era, the largest conventional bombs carried up to ~20 tons of TNT explosive. With the advent of the atomic bomb in 1945, explosions unleashed a 1,000-fold more power. The fission

> **Living nightmares: Next-generation BW threats**
>
> - Biotechnology is *very* powerful. It is also relatively inexpensive, and does not require special infrastructure. It is based on public knowledge. It is becoming ubiquitous.
> - Rapid advances in molecular biology make it necessary to contemplate new BW threats.
> - Genomics will change the world.

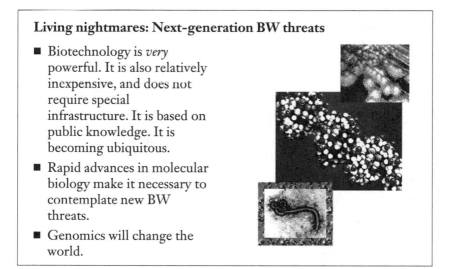

Figure 2-1

bombs dropped on Hiroshima ("Little Boy," August 6, 1945) and Nagasaki ("Fat Man," Aug. 9, 1945) released the equivalent of ~12 and ~23 kilotons of TNT, respectively. Within a decade, fusion-based devices were developed that made fission weapons seem puny by comparison. By 1954, H-bomb detonations in Operation Castle on the Bikini atoll released the equivalent of ~15 megatons of TNT—1,000-fold more than A-bombs, and 1,000,000-fold more than conventional weapons. By the height of the Cold War, the former USSR was testing thermonuclear weapons equivalent to 50 megatons of TNT. Each major breakthrough in weapons development produced roughly three orders of magnitude greater destructiveness. The type of biological weaponry made possible by genetic engineering may conceivably produce an analogous increase in virulence over conventional biological agents, which in turn have greater destructive potential than natural outbreaks of disease. If the analogy holds, this is bad news indeed.

In truth, there is little that is "conventional" about conventional

---

Conventional BW agents

- Bacterial agents: anthrax, plague, tularemia, brucellosis, typhoid fever

- Rickettsial agents: typhus, Rocky Mtn. spotted fever, Q fever

- Viral agents: smallpox, influenza, yellow fever, encephalitis (various), dengue fever, chikungunga, Rift Valley fever, hemorrhagic fevers (Ebola, Marburg, Lassa)

- Toxins: botulinum toxin, staphylococcus enterotoxin, shigella toxin, aflatoxin

- Fungal agents: coccidiodomyocosis

- Other: antiplant, antianimal, etc.

Figure 2-2

biological agents, which are already bad enough! These weapons comprise some of the worst scourges of mankind, such as smallpox, typhoid, typhus, anthrax, and plague. They include viral hemorrhagic fevers, such as Ebola, Lassa, and Marburg. They include potent toxins produced by microorganisms, such as botulinum toxin, aflatoxin, and shigella toxin. And the list goes on—see figure 2-2 for some examples.

In certain respects, a case can be made that anthrax is *already* a nearly perfect biological weapon in its natural form—indeed, it has long been the weapon of choice for many of the identified biological warfare programs. The anthrax bacterium, *Bacillus anthracis*, is ubiquitous and easily cultured from soil in areas that support livestock. It is readily propagated on inexpensive media. When grown appropriately, anthrax forms highly stable spores that retain their potency for decades as a dessicated powder,[7] ideal for weaponization. A mere

---

7. C. Redmond, M. J. Pearce, R. J. Manchee, and B. P. Berdal, "Deadly Relic of the Great War," 393 *Nature* (1998), pp. 747–8.

gram of spores contains thousands of lethal doses. Although deadly once contracted, anthrax is only weakly communicable, making it less prone to spread to friendly forces. Bacteria must enter directly into the lungs (*inhalation anthrax*, historically called woolsorter's disease) or into the bloodstream through a wound (*cutaneous anthrax*) to produce serious illness, although ingestion of badly contaminated meat may also produce disease (*intestinal anthrax*). When used as a biological weapon, inhalation anthrax is induced by exposure to large numbers of airborne spores. Enough spores in the lungs can produce death within a few days (the incubation period is one to six days, with a mortality rate of ~80 percent). However, the initial symptoms of pulmonary anthrax infection are fairly unremarkable (low fever, hacking cough, and weakness) and may make early diagnosis more difficult.

Anthrax is by no means the perfect bioweapon, however, for several excellent but unrelated reasons. First and foremost, it is nontrivial to target a ground population with any airborne agent, due to the many difficulties of dissemination, that is, producing just the right aerosol, adjusting for the vagaries of wind and weather, and so forth.[8] Second, prolonged exposure to sunlight kills most anthrax spores after release. Third, the minimal lethal dose for inhalation (reported to be 5,000 to 10,000 spores) is high compared with some other biological agents. Fourth, if diagnosed and treated early, anthrax may be cured with sufficient doses of penicillin-type antibiotics. Fifth, specific vaccines can be prepared that prevent infection by known strains of anthrax.

8. The Japanese terrorist cult Aum Shinrikyo (Aum Supreme Truth) is reported to have released quantities of anthrax in repeated biological attacks during the summer of 1993—all of which failed, and partly for this reason. In 1995, after apparently abandoning their biological warfare efforts, they released sarin gas in an attack on a Tokyo subway, killing 12 people and injuring 5,000. William J. Broad, "Sowing Death: A Special Report. How Japan Germ Terror Alerted the World," *New York Times* (May 26, 1998).

Novel BW threats

- Genetically engineered pathogens are qualitatively different from conventional BW agents.

- Attributes may include one or more of the following:
  - Safer handling and deployment
  - Easier propagation and/or distribution
  - Improved ability to target the host
  - Greater transmissivity, infectivity
  - More difficulty in detection
  - Greater toxicity, more difficulty in combating
  - More (self-limiting, self-enhancing ...)

Figure 2-3

Biological Warfare Desiderata

A scientist bent on producing a biological weapon more effective than airborne anthrax might consider ways to imbue the pathogen of his/her choice with any of a variety of desirable properties. These might include one or more of the following (see figure 2-3):

1. *Safer handling and deployment.* Biological warfare agents pose direct threats to those who use them, and many deaths appear to have resulted from accidental releases of agents, not from their use as weapons. What if this "boomerang problem" could be alleviated?

2. *Easier propagation and/or distribution.* Dried bacterial spores must have the right size and surface charge to disperse properly. Conversely, normally hydrated bioagents make poor aerosols. What if one could produce a better aerosol? Better

yet, what if one didn't need an aerosol at all, but relied on a different mechanism for distribution?

3. *Improved ability to target the host.* What if an agent could be developed that specifically targeted one or another population group? Or, what if some group could be protected against infection in advance?

4. *Greater transmissivity, infectivity.* What if one could engineer a viral disease with the lethality of (say) Ebola, but with the communicability of measles?

5. *More difficulty in detection.* What if the disease was hard to diagnose? Or had never even been encountered before? Or had a long latency? Or behaved in any other cryptic way?

6. *Greater toxicity, more difficulty in combating.* What if the disease had unusually high morbidity or mortality? What if it was resistant to all known antibacterial or antiviral agents? Or defeated all existing vaccines?

7. *More (self-limiting, self-enhancing . . .).* What if some pathogen could produce a localized outbreak but then render itself harmless? Conversely, what if a pathogen could continually alter itself in such a way as to evade treatment?

Clearly, some elements of this "wish list" seem rather far away from the current state of the art. But some may be closer to hand than one imagines. Recently, it was speculated in the *Times* of London that at least one country with a biological warfare program (Israel) was working on a bioweapon to target victims on the basis of ethnic origin.[9] Although this report seems scarcely credible (par-

9. U. Mahnaimi and M. Colvin, "Israel Planning Ethnic Bomb as Saddam Caves In" (London) *Sunday Times* (Nov. 15, 1999). The article contained the following text: "Israel is working on a biological weapon that would harm Arabs but not Jews, according to Israeli military and western intelligence sources. The weapon, targeting

ticularly in light of the history of the Holocaust and anti-Semitism in general) and was not picked up by other major media, what seems noteworthy is that the *theoretical possibility* of such a development is now taken seriously. As for some of the other attributes listed, there are plenty of existing pathogens with properties fitting the bill—and which might therefore be adapted by genetic engineering. For example, it is hard to imagine a disease more communicable, or much more virulent, than smallpox.[10] In terms of being hard to combat, the AIDS virus continually mutates and develops resistance to existing antiviral agents, such as AZT. Worse, it is a retrovirus, with a unique capacity to exist stably inside our cells and elude the immune system, making it nearly impossible to destroy. Exposure to minute levels of the agent aflatoxin produces fatal liver cancer, but only after a latency of years, making it hard to pin down the causative agent. And hospitals and health organizations must now come to grips with the worldwide emergence of virulent strains of multi-drug resistant bacteria (*streptococcus*, *staphylococcus*, *gonorrhea*, etc.) that have

---

victims by ethnic origin, is seen as Israel's response to Iraq's threat of chemical and biological attacks. . . . Porton Down, Britain's biological defence establishment, said last week that such weapons were theoretically possible. 'We have reached a point now where there is an obvious need for an international convention to control biological weapons,' said a spokesman."

10. Smallpox was declared eradicated by the World Health Organization (WHO) in May, 1980, and numerous frozen isolates of the virus (*Variola major*) are today maintained for the WHO by the US Centers for Disease Control (CDC) in Atlanta and by the Russian State Research Center of Virology and Biotechnology in Koltsovo. There are reports of unauthorized stocks elsewhere in the Soviet Union. The DNA sequence of *Variola* is known, and there is a controversial proposal to destroy all remaining stocks worldwide on June 30, 1999, under WHO supervision. A highly effective vaccine for smallpox has long existed, but it confers immunity for only about a decade. Therefore, adults who were vaccinated in their youth are no longer protected, and most civilian vaccination programs ceased worldwide in the 1960s and 70s. Some soldiers are still vaccinated.

emerged in response to the widespread overuse of antibiotics, both by humans and in the agricultural sector.[11]

There have been documented efforts to alter the properties of existing pathogens in such a way as to improve their effectiveness in biological warfare. Notable here is the work of Dr. Ken Alibek (formerly Dr. Kanatjan Alibekov, the Deputy Director of Biopreparat, the USSR's bioweapons program), who defected to the US in 1992. Alibek holds a doctorate in "industrial biotechnology," awarded in 1990 for his own contribution to the development of an anthrax strain designed specifically for weaponization purposes.[12] Alibek reports that he supervised, at one point, as many as 32,000 people in some forty separate facilities (there were reportedly some 60,000 people involved in the program overall). The size and scope of the former Soviet biological warfare program seem staggering; it represented an enterprise of a scale dwarfing worldwide efforts to sequence the human genome. The Soviet bioweapons program was carried out in violation of the 1972 Biological and Toxic Weapons Convention, to which the USSR was a signatory, and was reportedly dismantled in 1992 by order of Boris Yeltsin. However, Alibek and other experts have expressed reservations about whether biological warfare work in the former Soviet Union has actually ceased.[13]

It is not known to us, for example, whether Soviet strains of anthrax were engineered to carry a form of antibiotic resistance, nor

11. Arguably, the emergence of multidrug-resistant bacteria may pose more of an immediate threat to world health than any biological warfare agents, real or potential.

12. Richard Preston, "The Bioweaponeers," *New Yorker* (Mar. 9, 1998), pp. 52–65.

13. Ken Alibek, "Terrorist and Intelligence Operations: Potential Impact on the US Economy," Statement before the Joint Economic Committee, US Congress (May 20, 1998). Available online at: http://www.house.gov/jec/hearings/intell/alibek.htm.

whether conventional anthrax vaccine is effective against all the Soviet variants. However, Alibek has testified before the US Congress:

> It is important to note that, in the Soviet's view, the best biological
> agents were those for which there was no prevention and no cure.
> For those agents for which vaccines or treatment existed—such as
> plague, which can be treated with antibiotics—antibiotic-resistant
> or immunosuppressive variants were to be developed.[14]

Moreover, there is corroborative evidence that at least some level of
engineering of anthrax weapons had been attempted under the former Soviet Union. An outbreak of human anthrax in Sverdlosk (now
Yekaterinberg, Russia) in April 1979 has been attributed to the accidental release of spores from a secret military microbiological facility, after a shift-worker removed a crucial filter there for several
hours. Credible estimates placed the death toll in the range of 50 to
100 people, but patient hospital records were removed by the authorities. The incident was dismissed by Soviet authorities at the
time as being due to the consumption of anthrax-contaminated meat
from a local plant. In 1998, a study of DNA sequences extracted and
amplified from preserved samples taken from eleven of the Sverdlosk victims revealed the simultaneous presence of up to four distinct
genetic variants of B. anthracis, a finding that seems inconsistent with
any kind of natural outbreak (the latter would be expected to corre-
spond to just a single genetic variant).[15] However, this interpretation
has been challenged by Soviet experts. In any case, active spores
were not recovered, and it is not known whether the peculiar admix-
ture of strains that infected some of the Sverdlosk victims would

---

14. Ibid.
15. P. J. Jackson, M. E. Hugh-Jones, D. Adair, G. Green, K. K. Hill, C. R.
Kuske, L. M. Grinberg, F. A. Abramova, and P. Keim, "PCR Analysis of tissue
samples from the 1979 Sverdlosk anthrax victims: The presence of multiple Bacillus
anthracis strains in different victims," 95 Proc. Natl. Acad. Sci. USA (1998), pp. 1224–
9.

produce either a more virulent or more resistant form of the disease than a single "natural" strain.

The JASON List

Against this backdrop, the 1997 JASON summer study sought to identify avenues of future development for biological warfare agents. This exercise had several purposes: First, it provided an opportunity to assess the strengths and weaknesses of bioweaponry currently thought to exist.[16] Second, it provided a useful framework for projecting what might someday come into existence, both through traditional approaches and through recent advances in biotechnology. Third, it helped us to consider what countermeasures might usefully be brought to bear to defend populations—or at least to minimize the damage.

In the end, we arrived somewhat arbitrarily at six broad classes of unconventional pathogens that might, or might not, come to pose a threat during the twenty-first century. This list was never meant to be all-inclusive, but only to convey a sense of the spectrum of possibilities. These cover the full range, from trivial modifications of existing pathogens to full-up synthetic diseases and life forms. At one extreme, some of the more exotic constructs may appear to be rather fanciful, and at a minimum might take considerable develop-

---

16. The US abandoned its offensive biological warfare program in 1969 under President Nixon, while the former Soviet Union continued biological warfare work at least through the early 1990s. Offensive biological weapons programs reportedly exist today in perhaps a dozen countries worldwide, particularly in the Middle East and Asia. Countries currently listed as "proliferation concerns" by the Henry L. Stimson Center (Washington, DC) include China, Egypt, Iran, Iraq, Israel, Libya, North Korea, Syria, and Taiwan. Today, most developed nations maintain some form of defensive-only biological warfare capability, generally integrated with their public health systems, or with military medical services.

ment effort.[17] At the other extreme, some of the more straightforward modifications appear to be so obvious that they may even be
under development somewhere at this moment. All would pose formidable challenges for biodefense if ever successfully weaponized
and released. Finally, having gone through this exercise in imagination, I can only say that it hammers home the realization of just how
redoubtable conventional pathogens are, even before they are
adapted to other purposes.

Binary BW

One of the impediments to the deployment of BW is the danger
they pose to those who would handle or deploy them. A binary
biological weapon, by analogy with a binary chemical weapon, addresses this problem. It is fundamentally a two-component system
(see figure 2-4); neither of its major parts is toxic on its own, and
either one is therefore safe to handle. However, when suitably combined just prior to use, they generate a lethal mixture. How might a
binary biological weapon actually work?

As it turns out, nature has already done most of the hard work
of separating and compartmentalizing the needed components. Two
well-characterized instances of this phenomenon are worth review-

17. In some cases, certain next-generation possibilities don't fulfill traditional
criteria for being a "useful" biological warfare agent, but this fact can be misleading.
A propos of this issue, there are plenty of existing cases of unorthodox weapons
development. For example, in addition to formulating anthrax weapons, Iraq under
Saddam Hussein had reportedly been developing bioweapons based on *Clostridium
perfringens*, and also on aflatoxin (Source: US State Department White Paper,
"Iraq Weapons of Mass Destruction Programs" [Feb. 13, 1998], available online
at http://www.state.gov/www/regions/nea/iraq_white_paper.html). *C. perfringens*
causes gas gangrene and presumably would tend to infect only individuals already
wounded by traditional means. As for aflatoxin, a potent carcinogen, its effects can
take years to develop. The tactical effectiveness of weapons based on this seemingly
bizarre choice of agent has therefore been questioned. (No doubt, Saddam had
something rather different in mind.)

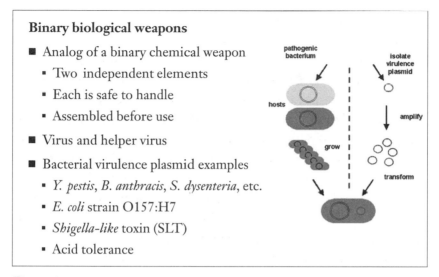

Binary biological weapons

- Analog of a binary chemical weapon
  - Two independent elements
  - Each is safe to handle
  - Assembled before use
- Virus and helper virus
- Bacterial virulence plasmid examples
  - *Y. pestis*, *B. anthracis*, *S. dysenteria*, etc.
  - *E. coli* strain O157:H7
  - *Shigella-like* toxin (SLT)
  - Acid tolerance

Figure 2-4

ing. The first is the case of the "satellite virus," which is an animal virus that cannot replicate inside a host cell on its own. Instead, it needs to coinfect the host together with another virus, which codes for key proteins that the helper requires for its own propagation. The classic example is hepatitis D (also called hepatitis delta), which has the smallest known virion of any animal virus, consisting of a small circle of just ~1,636 base pairs.[18] Hepatitis D needs to infect cells simultaneously with the unrelated virus hepatitis B; both are primarily transmitted through sexual contact or by contaminated blood or needles. The D virus takes advantage of the proteins expressed by the larger B virus, and greatly increases the severity of

18. Hepatitis delta is a remarkably compact RNA-based virus with special features. First, its highly abbreviated RNA message gets edited inside the cell, so that it winds up coding for two different proteins. Second, another portion of its RNA folds up to act as a *ribozyme*, or RNA-based catalyst, which is used to help with its replication. Then, like a sheep in wolf's clothing, it covers its replicated genetic material with a coat made from hepatitis B proteins.

the disease caused by hepatitis B. Infection by hepatitis D alone is not possible.

A second and more illustrative example, for our purposes, is the virulence plasmid. Most pathogenic bacteria carry small circular DNA elements that coexist with their main chromosomes. These are called "plasmids" (or episomes). Plasmids carry an autonomous origin of DNA replication and therefore can copy themselves independently of the chromosome itself. Bacterial cells sometimes contain multiple plasmids, each coding for its own particular cassette of genes. Plasmid gene cassettes endow bacteria with specialized functions: these are not often required for bacteria to grow and reproduce in the laboratory, but they aid survival in the wild. For example, genes used by *E. coli* bacteria to conjugate (i.e., for bacterial sex) are coded by a plasmid called the F' element. As it happens, the genes that cause virulence in bacteria are most often found on plasmids; this happens to be the case for the plague (*Yersinia pestis*), anthrax (*Bacillus anthracis*), dysentery (*Shigella dysenteria*), and other diseases. Both in the wild (by mechanisms unknown) and in the laboratory (through simple biotechnology), plasmids can be transferred among different kinds of bacteria across species barriers. Bacterial cells can also be "cured" of their plasmids, i.e., caused to lose them altogether.

One infamous example of a virulence happens in *E. coli* bacteria. Everyday strains of *E. coli*—such as the ones we have in our gut— don't produce toxins, but at least half of the known strains do. These toxins include various colicins, special molecules that target competing bacteria. Certain *E. coli* toxins cause forms of gastroenteritis in humans, but most of these are not life-threatening. However, there is a notable exception. In the case of *E. coli* strain O157:H7, the organism somehow picked up a rogue plasmid coding for a *Shigella*-like toxin (SLT) that produces a potentially deadly form of *hemorrhagic* enteritis when these bacteria multiply in the intestines. It is not yet known exactly where this plasmid came from, nor how it came to reside in this formerly benign strain. Not only does *E. coli*

O157:H7 code for a lethal toxin, but it has also developed the unusual ability to live in rather acid environments (down to pH 5.0),
such as those found in apple cider or cured sausage. These food
products normally have long shelf-lives and do not require sterili-
zation. The result is that a commonplace bacterium emerged as a
killer disease—and unpasteurized cider has become a thing of the
past.

Taking our cue from nature, a binary biological weapon could
be produced roughly as follows. First, a virulence plasmid is isolated
from a pathogenic parent strain and an antibiotic resistance gene is
introduced into it using standard molecular biology techniques. The
plasmid is then amplified directly, using biosynthetic-based methods,[19] such as the polymerase chain reaction (PCR). Independently,
the original parent strain is cured of its plasmid, and the resulting
nonvirulent isolate is cloned and grown up. Both components are
individually harmless, and can therefore be handled in significant
quantities without risk. The final step comes just before the weapon
is deployed, and consists of transforming the host strain back into a
pathogen. In practice, there are many ways to accomplish such a
transformation. Perhaps the simplest is to treat the bacteria briefly
with a solution of calcium chloride, which makes their cell walls
leaky. With small probability (roughly 1 in 100,000), the plasmid
DNA is taken up by the cell. If treated cells are then grown up in a
medium containing the right antibiotic, only those organisms that
have been successfully transformed will propagate, since the virulence plasmid also confers antibiotic resistance.

In actual practice, the final transformation (i.e., the combination
of cells and plasmids) and subsequent regrowth phase would pre-

19. Alternatively, the plasmid could be reintroduced into a different host where
it is rendered nontoxic but can nevertheless replicate successfully. The host is then
grown up in large quantities, broken apart, and its plasmid DNA isolated. The
choice of method depends, in part, on the size of the plasmid(s) involved.

sumably take place inside a small bioreactor that constituted the weapon itself, perhaps the size of a beer can. Because of their non-toxicity, all bioreactor ingredients may be handled with safety. The deployer of the weapon need not even be present to initiate the final transformation/regrowth phase, which would be accomplished automatically upon triggering the device.

There are many variations on this basic theme, including the use of multiple plasmids to reconstitute the pathogenic strain (the plasmid may be so small as to carry only a single critical gene, for example), or the use of a host strain that is genetically distinct from the parent originally used to isolate the virulence plasmid. The key point is that a binary weapon makes it feasible to grow up kilogram quantities of reagents without posing an undue risk to its manufacturer.

Designer Genes and Life Forms

The success of genome projects worldwide has led to knowledge of the complete genetic codes for literally hundreds of viruses, including most of the significant viral pathogens infecting humans. Today, we also know the DNA sequences of several dozen microorganisms, including *E. coli* and yeast. These microorganisms include many of the major bacterial pathogens (and potential biowarfare agents) such as *Yersinia, Salmonella, Streptococcus, Listeria, Leishmania, Legionella, Clostridium,* and others.[20] Recently, the first sequence of an entire multicellular organism was completed, the nematode worm *C. elegans.*[21] In a short time, the sequences for the fruit fly (*D. melanogaster*), mouse, and the human will be finished.

20. An updated listing of known bacterial sequences is maintained by the Institute for Genome Research (TIGR, Inc.) and available online at http://www.tigr.org/tdb/mdb/mdb.html

21. December 11, 1998 special issue; multiple articles. 282 *Science*, pp. 2011–46.

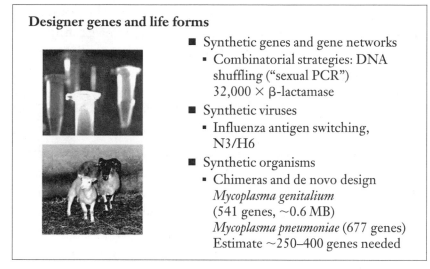

Designer genes and life forms

- Synthetic genes and gene networks
  - Combinatorial strategies: DNA shuffling ("sexual PCR") 32,000 × β-lactamase
- Synthetic viruses
  - Influenza antigen switching, N3/H6
- Synthetic organisms
  - Chimeras and de novo design *Mycoplasma genitalium* (541 genes, ~0.6 MB) *Mycoplasma pneumoniae* (677 genes) Estimate ~250–400 genes needed

Figure 2-5

All this new information raises the very real possibility of developing (in increasing complexity) synthetic genes, synthetic viruses, and even entire synthetic organisms. All three possibilities represent potential points of departure for would-be biological warfare developers (see figure 2-5). Perhaps the most straightforward—and arguably the most effective—way to increase the effectiveness of any bacterial warfare agent is to simply render it resistant to known antibiotics. A number of antibiotic-resistance genes already exist in nature: these include a gene that codes for the protein β-lactamase, which can break down penicillin. But the administration of large doses of antibiotic (or structural variants of that antibiotic) can overwhelm the activity of many natural resistance genes, and can therefore serve as an effective treatment. Using newly developed combinatorial strategies, however, it has become possible to carry out "evolution" in a test tube, and generate supergenes coding for antibiotic-destroying proteins with preternatural activity. The technique of DNA shuffling (also called "sexual PCR") developed by W.

P. Stemmer and colleagues is one such strategy.[22,23] The method is based on random recombination and reassembly of existing fragments of genes amplified by PCR. With appropriate selection, it is possible to evolve in just a few iterations a modified β-lactamase that works ~32,000-fold faster than the natural version, and is therefore capable of coping with correspondingly higher levels of antibiotics. This finding has serious implications for biological warfare: Organisms equipped with a whole bank of antibiotic-resistant supergenes might be impossible to stop. But DNA shuffling—like so many other powerful biotechniques—is a two-edged sword. It also holds the promise of developing organisms with genes that could detoxify poisonous wastes, such as arsenic[24] or oil spills. It might equally well be used to develop improved, recombinant vaccines that could play a major role in defense against biological warfare.

Synthetic viruses have now become possible, and once again nature points the way. Consider influenza, which despite its nuisance reputation in the workplace can be a deadly killer, as the pandemic of 1918 amply demonstrated, producing more deaths than all the battles of World War I. The flu is an extremely mutable and virulent virus. The variability of influenza is the reason for annual flu shots. The virus is able to mutate sufficiently rapidly during the course of a year that antibodies raised against the previous year's strain become largely ineffective. Influenza does this, in part, by periodically swapping out entire genes and replacing them with var-

22. W. P. Stemmer, "Rapid Evolution of a Protein in Vitro by DNA Shuffling," 370 *Nature* (1994), pp. 389–91. See also http://www.maxygen.com.

23. A. Crameri, S. A. Raillard, E. Bermudez, and W. P. Stemmer, "DNA Shuffling of a Family of Genes from Diverse Species Accelerates Directed Evolution," 391 *Nature* (1998), pp. 288–91.

24. A. Crameri, G. Dawes, E. Rodriguez, S. Silver, and W. P. Stemmer, "Molecular Evolution of an Arsenate Detoxification Pathway by DNA Shuffling," 15 *Nature Biotechnology* (1997), pp. 436–8.

iant forms. For the flu, the two main surface antigens are neuraminidase (N) and hemagglutinin (H). Gene swapping is thought to come about in a natural way. There are many forms of the flu in animals, including an avian form affecting birds such as geese and ducks, a swine form affecting pigs, and a human form affecting ourselves. Pigs can harbor *both* the avian and human forms, in addition to their own. In situations where ducks, pigs, and humans live in close proximity and under poor sanitary conditions (for example, on small farms in China), a pig can sometimes become infected simultaneously with two or more influenza strains, including one from ducks and one from humans. With some probability, the genes occasionally get mixed up inside pig cells and the result is the emergence of a novel, recombinant virus with a subset of components derived from each strain.

A bioweapons developer inspired by this state of affairs might attempt the *ab initio* construction of a synthetic virus using a kind of "erector set" strategy, building it up by literally mixing and matching known components of existing viruses. Alternatively, it may be sufficient to subtly alter the surface properties of the major antigens (the H and N proteins in flu, for example, for which many variants are known) in such a way that the virus retains virulence but loses an ability to be recognized by the immune system. In either case, the result could be a new human disease. Some animal viruses are so small that their entire genome can be stitched together, at least in principle, from machine-synthesized fragments using current technology. This raises the intriguing possibility that a virus could be created entirely from scratch, so to speak, rather than made by a cell.

The smallest known organisms are the mycoplasmas, tiny gram positive-like bacteria whose genomes are a scant ~0.6 megabase pairs (compare with *E. coli*, which is almost eight times larger, at 4.6 megabase pairs). The first mycoplasma to be sequenced, *Mycoplasma genitalium*, has just 541 genes.[25] The second mycoplasma, *Mycoplasma pneumoniae*, carried 677 genes,[26] and homologues of every one of the 541 genes from its relative were contained within that number (the rest are presumably nonessential). This fact has led to the speculation that as few as 250 to 400 genes may be required to create a complete organism. If the actual number turns out to be that small, we may not be so far from the day when creating an entirely synthetic organism becomes feasible. This, of course, has obvious implications for biological warfare.

Gene Therapy as a Weapon

The goal of gene therapy is to effect a change in the genetic makeup of an individual by introducing new information designed to replace or repair a faulty gene (see figure 2-6). In principle, gene therapy could be used to treat an enormous number of human diseases and conditions known to be associated with specific genetic defects, including diabetes, heart disease, cystic fibrosis, muscular dystrophy, immune disorders, hereditary anemias, cancer, and even mental illness. In view of its nearly unlimited and untapped potential to alleviate human suffering, it represents the Holy Grail of modern medicine. Small wonder that so many clinical and biotechnical programs now focus on gene therapy research. Gene therapy promises unimaginable benefits for mankind!

Broadly speaking, there are two classes of gene therapy: germline and somatic cell. Replacing or augmenting the DNA of a germline cell would, in principle, lead to a heritable change that could repair problems for all future generations. Somatic cell therapy, in

25. C. M. Fraser, et al., "The Minimal Gene Complement of *Mycoplasma genitalium*." 270 *Science* (1995), pp. 397–403.
26. R. Himmelreich, H. Hilbert, H. Plagens, E. Pirkl, B. C. Li, and R. Herrmann, "Complete Sequence Analysis of the Genome of the Bacterium *Mycoplasma pneumoniae*." 24 *Nucleic Acids Res.* (1996), pp. 4420–49.

Gene therapy as a weapon

- Goal: effect a permanent change in genetic makeup

- Approach: use transforming viruses or similar DNA vectors carrying "Trojan horse" genes: e.g., retrovirus, adenovirus, poxvirus, HSV-1, etc.

- Potential for misuse

  - Intentional

  - Unintentional

Figure 2-6

contrast, affects only the cells of the individual receiving it. For technical as well as ethical reasons, most current research has concentrated on the development of somatic cell gene therapy.

Gene therapy has additional prospects: It may be used as a kind of drug delivery system, to supply cytokines, blood clotting compounds, hormones, or other factors. It may equally well be used as a form of "vaccine," to confer immunity to certain diseases, such as AIDS. Finally, it could be used to delete (knock out) genes as well as to introduce them, or to change the expression patterns (or levels) of any genes.

Unfortunately, although there have been isolated and largely anecdotal successes, no one has any kind of reliable gene therapy working just yet. But it wouldn't be unreasonable to assume that some forms of gene therapy will become available early in the next century. Although complicated in practice, the idea behind gene therapy is simple: First you have to get the gene of choice into cells, and then you have to arrange for the gene to be stably expressed at the right levels. (This second bit is where most attempts fail, incidentally.) There are quite of few ways to go about doing this, in principle—including just adding "naked" DNA to cells and waiting for them to take it up. More often, though, a crippled virus is modified to serve as a kind of Trojan horse, or genetic vector. The virus is designed to retain its capacity to attach to and infect cells, and in certain cases to replicate or perhaps even to spread from cell to cell. But, importantly, the vector lacks critical genes that lead to viral disease. The gene of choice is then introduced into the virus vector along with special gene control elements designed to function once the vector reaches its cellular target. A great number of vectors are presently being constructed and tried. Some are based on transforming viruses, such as adenovirus (which causes disease in monkeys) and defective pox or herpes viruses. These animal viruses can exist for long periods inside our cells, but their DNA usually remains separate from the cell's own chromosomes. This separate identity can lead to eventual gene loss or instability. For this reason, some labs have chosen to work with an adeno-associated virus (AAV), which can integrate itself into chromosomes with some probability, to establish a latent state. Other labs are working to manufacture vectors based on retroviruses (such as the HIV virus that causes AIDS), which can permanently integrate single copies of themselves into the chromosomes, with a view to affording a more permanent and regulated transformation. It would be a singular irony if the great remedies of the twenty-first century were based on the last untreatable disease of the twentieth century.

Regardless of the vector technology that eventually will be developed, it seems clear that successful gene therapy is yet another example of a two-edged sword, with equal potential for misuse. Genes can be introduced for good or for evil, and they can induce disease as well as cure it. It has been speculated that some gene therapy vectors may be so easy to introduce that they will come in the form of a simple nasal spray. One quick whiff in a nostril trans-

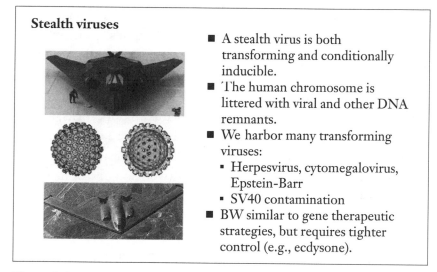

Stealth viruses

- A stealth virus is both transforming and conditionally inducible.
- The human chromosome is littered with viral and other DNA remnants.
- We harbor many transforming viruses:
  - Herpesvirus, cytomegalovirus, Epstein-Barr
  - SV40 contamination
- BW similar to gene therapeutic strategies, but requires tighter control (e.g., ecdysone).

Figure 2-7

fers the virus in aerosol form, and the vector takes care of the rest. If this sort of thing comes to pass, gene therapy vectors might be subverted to become potent BW of destruction.

Stealth Viruses

A "stealth virus" is another menacing possibility afforded by genetic engineering (see figure 2-7). The basic idea behind a stealth virus is to produce a tightly regulated, cryptic viral infection, using a vector that can enter and spread in human cells, remaining resident for lengthy periods without causing detectable harm. However, once triggered by an appropriate external (or internal) signal, the cryptic virus is activated and causes disease. Stealth viruses could be designed to be contagious, and therefore distribute themselves silently throughout a given population. They might even be designed against specific target groups. A population could be slowly preinfected with a stealth virus over an extended period, possibly years in advance, and then synchronously triggered. Stealth viruses therefore have utility beyond that of traditional bioweapons. For example, they could be disseminated and used to blackmail a population based merely on the threat of their activation.

At its core, a stealth virus is not so very different from any of the gene therapy vectors discussed in the previous section. It is based on the realization that most humans already carry a substantial and silent viral load.[27] For example, a significant fraction of the human population already carries herpes simplex (which in one of its forms causes cold sores), Epstein-Barr virus (which causes mononucleosis, or glandular fever), or human cytomegalovirus (found in up to 90 percent of urban populations). Some resident viruses, for example *herpes simplex I*, infect permanently but only produce symptoms periodically. Most of the time, the virus lies dormant inside cells (often in the trigeminal facial nerve, in the case of oral herpes), waiting to be triggered by some kind environmental assault. Examples of such assaults include cuts, chafing, exposure to ultraviolet rays (sunburn), infection by an unrelated disease, and physical or mental stress. The mechanism for triggering an active herpes infection is currently a subject of study.

Another example of a cryptic human infection, which remains a topic of controversy, dates to the widespread administration of Sabin type polio vaccines between 1955 and 1961.[28] These vaccines were prepared using live African green monkey kidney cells, and batches of polio vaccine became contaminated by low levels of a

27. In addition to silent (and complete) viruses, it has been estimated that the human genome is littered with various remnants of viruses from our past, amounting to 3 percent or more of the total DNA. This is probably true of all organisms, in fact. When the DNA sequence of *E. coli* was determined, it was found to harbor dozens of cryptic prophages, inactive remnants of bacterial viruses. F. R. Blattner, et al., "The Complete Genome Sequence of *Escherichia coli K-12*," 277 *Science* (1997), pp. 1453–62.

28. K. Shah and N. Nathanson, "Human Exposure to SV40: Review and Comment," 103 *Amer. J. Epidemiol.* (1976), pp. 1–12.

monkey virus, simian virus 40 (SV40), which eluded the quality control procedures of the day. As a result, large numbers of people—probably millions, in fact—were inadvertently exposed to SV40. The virus has since been shown to produce cancer in hamsters, although it does not do so in monkeys. It can also recombine with other monkey viruses, such as adenovirus. Evidently, however, the virus did not produce widespread problems for humans, and so my own generation may have dodged a bullet. Nevertheless, there is evidence that SV40 virus still exists in certain individuals exposed to the contaminated polio vaccine, and a great deal of speculation occurs about whether it may be responsible for some disease.

Taking a cue from this history, a stealth vector design could be based on one or more existing examples of dormant virus. In key respects, a stealth virus resembles a gene therapeutic vector. Just as in gene therapy, the vector must be able to enter the host and effect a stable transformation of cells. And just as in gene therapy, certain critical genes of the vector (in this case, those that lead to disease) must be regulated, so that their expression levels can be controlled. In contrast with gene therapeutic vectors, however, the genetic control must be extraordinarily tight, so that a potentially lethal disease is not released prematurely, but only in response to the desired trigger. This kind of exquisite control has not been easily achieved with genetically engineered systems, which tend to be "leaky." Recently, all that has changed with the advent of new, tighter control systems, such as those based on the insect hormone ecdysone.[29]

Host-Swapping Diseases

Viruses are basically parasites. They are symbiotic, and coevolve with their living hosts, depending upon them to furnish most of

29. D. No, T. P. You, and R. M. Evans, "Ecdysone-inducible gene expression in mammalians cells and transgenic mice," 93 *Proc. Natl. Acad. Sci. USA* (1996), pp. 3346–51.

Host-swapping diseases
- Parasites develop in evolutionary "equilibrium" with their hosts.
- Pathogens have narrow host ranges:
  - Equine encephalitis
  - Influenza, smallpox
  - CJD, BSE
- Example: *Canine parvovirus*
  - *Feline panleukopenia virus* +
    2 capsid protein mutations
    (appeared 1~974)
- Disruption of equilibrium tends to
  produce nothing, *or* high virulence!
  - AIDS
  - Hantavirus
  - Marburg, Ebola

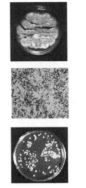

Figure 2-8

what is required to grow and propagate. Any virus that produces a disease so deadly that it kills off its host is committing suicide, because it rapidly comes to an evolutionary dead end. Indeed, any virus that even *distresses* its host to any significant degree will cause that same host to lose critical natural fitness, leading to another evolutionary dead end—albeit a slower one. Why, then, do viruses even cause disease? Perhaps surprisingly to some, the vast majority of viruses do not cause disease; they are utterly silent, in the sense discussed earlier. It is only the rare virus that disrupts the fragile evolutionary "equilibrium" between parasite and host. This can happen, in particular, when a virus skips out of its host range and accidentally targets a different species (see figure 2-8). It can also happen when a new virus is inadvertently created from the components of other viruses, or mutates, or picks up some genes by mistake. Viral diseases typically have short lifetimes on an evolutionary time scale. Smallpox, for example, is thought to have emerged in the modern human population only between three and ten thousand years ago.

Animal viruses tend to have narrow, well-defined host ranges—often just one to a few species. One example discussed earlier is human influenza. Another is SV40, which causes disease in hamsters but not in humans. Animal viruses tend to have a natural animal reservoir where they reside and cause little or no damage. The virus responsible for Eastern equine encephalitis (EEE), for example, grows mainly in water fowl, but it can be transmitted by mosquitoes that bite birds and then transfer it to horses or humans, where it can cause a fatal (but not contagious) disease. The animal reservoir for the deadly (to humans) hantavirus is the rodent, especially deer mice. The animal reservoir for Ebola virus is currently thought to be the bat,[30] where it can grow to high blood levels (titers) but does not apparently produce symptoms. Quite recently, it was established that the original source of the AIDS virus is likely to be the chimpanzee.[31] However, that virus has now mutated in humans to a form that causes AIDS even in chimps.[32]

The lesson, so to speak, is that when viruses are transferred out of their natural host reservoir, they tend to do one of two things. With high probability, they remain inactive and unable to propagate in a different host species. With lower probability, they can gain a toehold. Frequently, in such situations, they cause disease. Viruses can also jump out of their host range by acquiring one or more mutations that allow them access to cell surface receptors of a new host. An example of this is canine parvovirus, against which most pet dogs are now routinely vaccinated by veterinarians. Parvovirus is a deadly disease of dogs, but it was utterly unknown before about 1974. Around that time, a feline panleukopenia virus (cat distemper)

30. R. Swanepoel, et al., "Experimental Inoculation of Plants and Animals with Ebola Virus," 2 *Emerging Infectious Diseases* (no. 4) (1996), pp. 321–5.

31. F. Gao, et al., "Origin of HIV-1 in the chimpanzee *Pan troglodytes*," 397 *Nature* (1999), pp. 436–41.

32. F. J. Novembre, et al., "Development of AIDS in a Chimpanzee Infected with Human Immunodeficiency Virus Type 1," 71 *J. Virol.* (1997), pp. 4086–91.

somehow acquired just two capsid protein mutations, thereby turning it into a lethal dog disease. Since then, parvovirus has continued to evolve slightly, picking up a couple of additional mutations. There are many kinds of parvovirus in nature, including several variants that infect humans.

A determined developer seeking to create a new biological weapon might take inspiration from all this. If the proper mutations were introduced into a relatively benign animal virus, permitting it to escape from its normal host range and infect humans instead, it would have the potential to become a virulent human disease. Several highly lethal viral diseases, such as AIDS, Ebola and Marburg fevers, and hantavirus are now classified by the CDC as *emerging diseases*: They all qualify (more or less) as examples of this very phenomenon—only the "experiment" was performed by nature in this case, and not by the hand of man! However, with stringent genetic selection and appropriate biotechnology, it does not seem so far-fetched to suggest that the same type of experiment might be accomplished in the laboratory. The result, of course, would be a man-made emergent disease.

Designer Diseases

Our understanding of cellular and molecular biology is nearly to the point where it may be possible to contemplate a disease first, then construct the pathogen necessary to produce it second (for example, using one of the vectors discussed earlier). Such a "designer disease" might work through any of a variety of molecular signaling pathways that are critical to the health of humans. Like the HIV virus that causes AIDS, a disease might target the immune response, escaping our natural ability to fight it; or it might activate normally dormant genes and wreak havoc in our cells; or it might simply instruct the cells in our body to commit suicide, as follows.

Programmed cell death, or "apoptosis," is a facet of nature (see

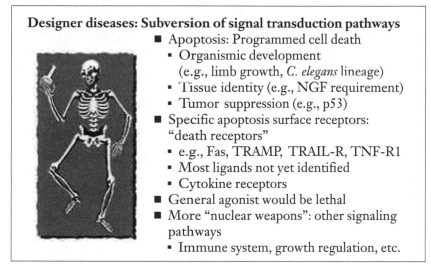

Designer diseases: Subversion of signal transduction pathways
- Apoptosis: Programmed cell death
  - Organismic development
    (e.g., limb growth, *C. elegans* lineage)
  - Tissue identity (e.g., NGF requirement)
  - Tumor suppression (e.g., p53)
- Specific apoptosis surface receptors:
  "death receptors"
  - e.g., Fas, TRAMP, TRAIL-R, TNF-R1
  - Most ligands not yet identified
  - Cytokine receptors
- General agonist would be lethal
- More "nuclear weapons": other signaling
  pathways
  - Immune system, growth regulation, etc.

Figure 2-9

figure 2-9). Human cells, it would seem, all contain one or more built-in signaling pathways which, when suitably activated, cause them to die. Apoptosis serves many useful purposes in organisms, from development to fighting cancer. For example, embryonically, human babies start out with webbed hands and feet. At a later stage, cells in the webbed areas are programmed to die off, leaving us with five distinct digits on each appendage. This kind of cellular die-off is critical to our forming human shapes, of course.

Apoptosis is also used in an entirely different way. When cells develop certain types of chromosomal instability or mutation, as is frequently the case in cancer or during viral infection, a *tumor suppressor* pathway is activated that causes the cells to chop up their own DNA into small bits and commit a very characteristic form of suicide. This pathway is mediated by a set of supervisory genes called *tumor suppressor genes*, the best known example of which is p53. Normally, once cancer begins to take over a cell, a tumor suppressor like p53 directs it to die altruistically—halting the transformation. But a loss of p53 function means that organisms lose their innate ability to stop the spread of cancer. That is why the p53 gene is found to be missing or mutated in so many forms of human cancer (up to 65 percent for colorectal cancer, 70 percent for lung cancer, and 60 percent for skin cancer).[33]

Tumor suppressors represent one set of genes involved in apoptosis, but there are others. Nerve cells grown in culture, for example, commit apoptosis unless a special small molecule, nerve growth factor (NGF), is supplied to the medium. Put differently, nerve cells are prepared to die the very moment they are deprived of NGF. They sense the presence of NGF levels via specific receptors in their membranes that bind to external NGF and signal to the rest of the apoptotic pathway. In other types of cells, death can be induced by the *addition*, rather than the deprivation, of other small signaling molecules, such as cytokines or necrosis factors.

Because of its intimate relation to cancer, apoptosis has been the subject of an enormous amount of recent work, and quite a few cell receptors have already been identified, with strange names (which keep changing) like Fas, TRAMP, TRAIL-R, and TNF-R1. These all hook up to a variety of "death pathways" that use a common mechanism to kill the cell.[34] Many of their natural ligands remain to be identified, however.

A designer disease might be created, for example, by subverting one or more of these apoptosis pathways. If a *general agonist* for apoptosis receptors were identified, i.e., a small compound that activated death pathways in all cells, it would potentially be more toxic than any known poison! A biological warfare viral vector designed

33. A database of human mutations is maintained at: http://www.umd.necker.fr/disease.html. A p53 database with frequency information can be found at: http://perso.curie.fr/Thierry.Soussi/p53_database.html.

34. C. M. Rudin and C. B. Thompson, "Apoptosis and Disease: Regulation and Clinical Relevance of Programmed Cell Death, " 48 *Annual Rev. Med.* (1997), pp. 267–81.

to direct the synthesis of such an agonist would lead to the mass suicide of otherwise healthy cells—and ultimately to the death of the organism.[35] This is only one kind of designer disease: quite a few others can by conjured up based on similar principles.

Concluding Remarks

This, then, is the *real* Y2K problem, or "millenium bug!" How do we protect ourselves from ourselves as we enter the next millenium? Like the nuclear threat, the specter of biological warfare presents a multifactorial problem, and it will call for multifactorial solutions. No one single remedy seems likely to make this thing go away. And, like the nuclear genie released from the bottle, the newfound power unleashed by advances in biotechnology will not be tamed by merely wishing it—or legislating it—away. Once knowledge is attained, there is no going back.

A large number of government and government-affiliated agencies are now investigating aspects of the biological warfare threat and developing specific recommendations. The JASON group, for example, developed its own set during the 1997 Summer Study. Rather than repeat these here, I will conclude by touching briefly on just some of the challenges faced in coping with the next generation of pathogens (see figure 2-10).

Anticipation and Detection

Identification and classification. We urgently require newer, faster, and more reliable ways to identify viruses and bacteria—both traditional and next-generation pathogens. We must also develop im-

35. Of course, no such general agonist may actually exist, for any of a variety of excellent reasons. Even so, the widespread—and therefore inappropriate—expression of the specific ligand for *any* of the many apoptosis pathways may be more than sufficient to cause disease.

The true Y2K problem!
- Anticipation and detection
  - Identification and classification: both old and new threats
  - Screening: develop and test indicators of threats
  - Vigilance: use of indicators to detect threats
- Mitigation and remediation
  - New vaccines, antibacterials, antivirals, anti-?
  - Medical infrastructure and response
- Political and military response
  - The nuclear threat redux—but worse!
- Education: *A Call from Arms*
  - Current lack of awareness and responsibility in the professional community
  - Bioethics training beyond Dolly

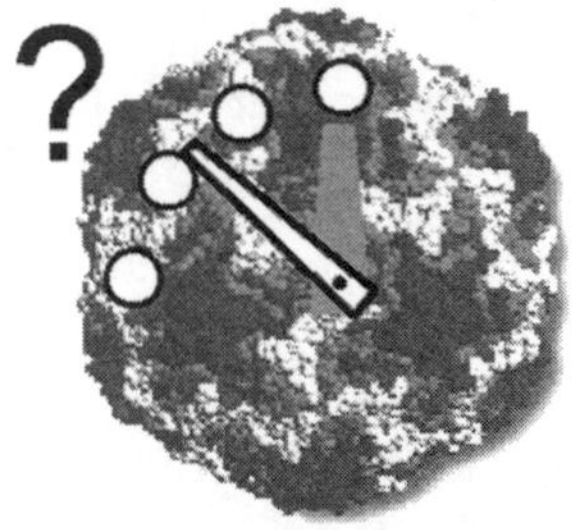

The Doomsday Clock:
Ticking since June 1947.
Reset on June 11, 1998,
to midnight minus
9 minutes.

Figure 2-10

proved ways of collecting, saving, and preparing biological samples. One sensitive method that holds great promise is based on PCR amplification of target DNA (or RNA, using RT-PCR). We need to develop ways to miniaturize and automate bio-detectors, and make these ready for use in the field, as well as in the laboratory. We also need to explore other promising technologies, including various forms of hybridization array, immunological detection methods, light- or mass-spectrometry, and so forth. Perhaps most important of all, we need to be able to anticipate the detailed nature and scope of next-generation biological warfare threats. Anticipation holds the key to detection: One can't readily develop a test for something one's not expecting to find! We need to try to stay one or more steps ahead of an adversary.

Screening. We need to be thorough in screening for presumptive pathogens throughout the whole of the environment. This implies not only developing and deploying appropriate sensors and detectors, but also becoming systematic about testing these and understanding their intrinsic limits. Moreover, "detectors" need not be limited to technology alone. There is a real and growing need for human intelligence as it relates to biological warfare, and this seems likely to remain a prime source of information.

Vigilance. Having produced detectors, we need to use these consistently and wisely. Perhaps more importantly, we need to update regularly our detectors,[36] to take advantage of the latest intelligence and technical developments. This is nontrivial.

Mitigation and Remediation

We must develop new vaccines, new antibacterials, and new antivirals. We must also develop entirely new ways to make such things. We must improve upon existing remedies. Much of this work will fall to the pharmaceutical and biotechnology sectors, which are already active in this area. The one saving grace of this whole gloomy scenario may be that the very same technologies that make possible BW may make it possible to defeat them.

The public health response to BW threats needs to be addressed and coordinated at federal, state, and local levels *as never before*. Biomedical, military, and legal authorities will all need to become involved. We need to produce and stockpile whatever materials will be needed for rapid deployment of health resources. We may also need to stockpile certain vaccines, or to develop a rapid pipeline for manufacture and delivery of them. We may even consider large-scale vaccination programs, but this remains to be seen. Finally, we need to give careful thought to implementing health measures that are consistent with our traditional constitutional protections and personal freedoms.

---

36. For the case of PCR-based biosensors, these devices are no better than the *primers* supplied (primers are short DNA fragments specific to the target, used to initiate the amplification of sequences). Particular care must be given to the design and selection of primers, and this will require an ongoing effort in the face of a changing biological landscape.

Political and Military Response

In many respects, the BW threat is just like the nuclear threat—
only worse! It poses significantly greater risks for the proliferation
and control of arms. Our nation will need continually to revise its
guidelines for political and military responses to BW use. The US
should take a leadership position in helping to strengthen the provisions of the international Biological and Toxin Weapons Convention (BWC) to include meaningful, multilateral inspections. The
worldwide ban on biological weaponry must be enforceable.

Education: A Call from Arms

I should like to close with a personal observation. There is a
regrettable lack of involvement by members of the professional biomedical community in issues related to BW, particularly among molecular biologists working in industry and academia. Some of this is
understandable, because it is an exceedingly unpleasant topic to contemplate. But I believe the issue goes much deeper than that. Some
folks simply do not take the threat seriously, but they should. Others
worry about provoking a widespread public backlash against biotechnology in general that might have a chilling effect on their own
legitimate biological research. Still others worry that by calling "unnecessary" attention to the problem, they will paradoxically hasten
its development. None of these excuses stands up to close scrutiny.

When the National Institutes of Health began work on the Human Genome Project, it set aside 5 percent of all funding to the
National Human Genome Research Institute (NHGRI) for a program in the Ethical, Legal, and Social Implications of the work
(ELSI, established in 1990).[37] Partly in response, most major univer-

---

37. The US Department of Energy, which also funds work on the Human
Genome Project, also sets aside funding for the same purpose.

sities receiving federal funds now offer biomedical ethics courses for graduate students and postdocs receiving training in molecular biology. These courses cover many timely and important topics, such as scientific misconduct, privacy issues related to DNA and human health, and the ethics of animal cloning. Rarely, however, do they attempt to educate young professionals on ethical issues related to BW. It is high time to offer biomedical ethics training "beyond Dolly." Biological scientists at all levels need to get involved. To quote Preston:

> The community of biologists in the United States has maintained a kind of hand-wringing silence on the ethics of creating bioweapons—a reluctance to talk about it with the public, even a disbelief that it's happening. Biological weapons are a disgrace to biology. The time has come for top biologists to assert their leadership and speak out, to take responsibility on behalf of their profession for the existence of these weapons and the means of protecting the population against them, just as leading physicists did a generation ago when nuclear weapons came along. Moral pressure costs nothing and can help; silence is unacceptable now.[38]

Amen! As George Orwell put it, "Life is a race between education and catastrophe."

---

38. Richard Preston, "Taming the Biological Beast" Op-Ed, *New York Times* (Apr. 21, 1998).

Dean A. Wilkening

BCW Attack Scenarios

This chapter provides a taxonomy of historical BCW attacks according to the method of transmission (injection, food or pharmaceutical contamination, water contamination, animal vectors, or airborne release); examines the logic and evidence behind the claim that the BCW threat is growing; and provides a glimpse of possible future attack scenarios, albeit at the high end of the threat spectrum—which probably are not the most likely scenarios. The argument that BCW threats are growing rests on three propositions: (1) the capability to make BCW is increasingly available to states, if not terrorist groups; (2) the intention to use these weapons is growing; and (3) civilian populations, and to a lesser extent military forces, are quite vulnerable to BCW attacks. Although the logic is clear, assessing the degree to which these propositions are valid is more difficult. With respect to future BCW scenarios, this chapter examines what would have happened in two historical cases had events turned out differently; specifically, if Saddam Hussein had used BCW-armed Al Hussayn missiles during the 1991 Gulf War and if the Aum Shinrikyo cult in Japan had been able to master BW. Finally, the chapter concludes with some observations about the severity of future BCW attack scenarios and implications for future options to deal with this emerging threat.

Taxonomy of BCW Attacks

The target of BCW attacks could be crops, livestock, or humans. The mode of transmission could be by injection or direct contact, food or pharmaceutical contamination, water contamination, animal vectors (e.g., fleas) for biological agents, or airborne release. Airborne scenarios produce the largest number of casualties and the largest contaminated areas. They come in two types: release within an enclosed space (e.g., a subway or a building), and open air release.

While the interest in chemical and biological weapons among states has been modest during the twentieth century, interest among terrorist groups has been relatively rare, accounting for only 52 cases out of more than 8,000 in the RAND Chronology of International Terrorism since 1968.[1] According to one estimate, terrorist incidents involving chemical or biological contamination have been historically distributed in the following manner: 13 percent involve injection/direct contact; 15 percent, food or drink contamination; 16 percent, pharmaceutical contamination; 11 percent, water contamination; and 17 percent, airborne dissemination; in 29 percent of the cases the dissemination method is unknown. This ignores hoaxes and false cases, which account for nearly half of all incidents.[2]

1. Bruce Hoffman, "Responding to Terrorism across the Technology Spectrum," 6 *Terrorism and Political Violence* (Autumn 1994), p. 368.
2. See Jessica E. Stern, "Would Terrorists Turn to Poison?," Orbis (Summer 1993), p. 404.

The prevalence of hoaxes following widespread media attention to a particular event (e.g., product tampering, BCW terrorism, and the like) is demonstrated by the recent rash of anthrax threats in the US. Since October 1998, there have been over 120 anthrax hoaxes reported in the media nationwide, with 45 incidents in February 1999 alone.[3] This rapid increase is presumably due to the widespread attention being paid to this particular biological agent (e.g., the announcement that US military personnel would be vaccinated against anthrax and frequent public discussions about anthrax as the classic BW agent).

Injection/Direct Contact

Injection or direct contact with chemical or biological agents most frequently is used for assassination. For example, in August 1974 the "Alphabet Bomber" threatened to kill the US President with nerve gas and, according to one account, he nearly succeeded in accumulating the necessary precursor chemicals. In 1976, Michael Townley was arrested for smuggling sarin into the US in a perfume bottle allegedly to be used to assassinate the Chilean Foreign Minister Orlando Letelier.[4] The classic example of biological assassination is the tactic developed by the Bulgarian secret police where ricin (a highly lethal toxin) contained within a pellet is shot from the tip of an umbrella into the victim's skin. In August 1978, the Bulgarian secret police attempted to assassinate Vladimir Kostov using this method. The attack apparently failed due to an insufficient dose of ricin. However, in September 1978 they assassinated

3. Private communication, Jason Pate, Center for Nonproliferation Studies, Monterey Institute of International Studies, Monterey, CA, based on statistics from the "Chemical and Biological Weapons Nonproliferation Project" database (Apr. 26, 1999).

4. See Ron Purver, "Chemical and Biological Terrorism: New Threat to Public Safety?," *Conflict Studies* 295, Research Institute for the Study of Conflict and Terrorism, London (Jan. 1997), p. 14.

the dissident Georgi Markov in London by this method. More recently, in 1992 the Minnesota Patriots Council threatened to assassinate several federal agents and IRS officials with ricin by coating door knobs with the toxin (they were convicted in 1995 under the Biological Weapons Anti-Terrorism Act of 1989 after 0.7 gram of ricin was seized);[5] and in April 1993 Thomas Lavy, a member of a neo-nazi survivalist group, was caught trying to smuggle 130 grams of relatively impure ricin across the Alaskan-Canadian border presumably to be used for assassinations (he later committed suicide in prison).[6] In April 1997, Thomas Leahy was arrested for possession of ricin as a weapon. He allegedly attempted to develop other biological agents also for the purpose of assassination, reportedly by delivering toxic packages in the mail.[7] Finally, the Aum Shinrikyo cult in Japan attempted to assassinate several critics, perceived adversaries, and several cult members by injecting or spraying them with small doses of chemical agents.[8]

A little known example of biological warfare against animals was the German use of glanders and other microbial agents to infect draft animals herded into ports within the US and Argentina enroute to the western front during World War I.[9] The method of

5. Ibid., p. 12.
6. See W. Seth Carus, "Bio-terrorism and Bio-crimes: The Illicit Use of Biological Agents in the 20th Century" (Washington: Center for Counter Proliferation Research Working Paper, National Defense University) (Aug., Nov. 1998), pp. 155–6.
7. Ibid., pp. 116–20.
8. Aum Shinrikyo reportedly assassinated a lawyer and his family (who were prosecuting the cult) with potassium chloride, newspaper critics with phosgene gas and sarin, and several cult member with VX. See Ron Purver, "Chemical and Biological Terrorism: New Threat to Public Safety?," p. 15; David E. Kaplan and Andrew Marshall, *The Cult at the End of the World* (New York: Crown Publishers, 1996), pp. 41–3.
9. Mark Wheelis, "Biological Sabotage in the First World War," in E. Geissler and J.E.V.C. Moon, eds., *Biological Warfare from the Middle Ages to 1945* (New York: Oxford University Press, 1999).

transmission was by injection as well as contamination of animal food. Evidence for the effectiveness of these attacks is equivocal, although there were reports that shiploads of animals did become sick while at sea and had to be thrown overboard. Nevertheless, these attacks appear to have had little impact on the war effort.

Food and Pharmaceutical Contamination

Foodborne contamination is the most frequent BCW terrorist threat, with chemical contamination more prevalent than biological contamination—the salmonella contamination by the Rajneeshee cult in Oregon to influence the outcome of a local election by making people too sick to vote being one of the few successful cases of food contamination with a biological agent. In terms of objectives, BCW contamination of food or agricultural products has been used to assassinate individuals, coerce individuals or companies, and for economic terrorism directed against a specific company or state.

Small-scale examples of this kind of terrorism are the Animal Liberation Front (ALF), who claimed in 1984 to have contaminated Mars candy bars in the United Kingdom with rat poison to protest tooth decay experiments on monkeys. Eight candy bars were found with ALF notes protesting such experiments; however, no poison was ever found. Later in 1984, four ALF members were charged with poisoning turkeys with mercury during the Christmas season. In 1989, the ALF again was suspected of poisoning eggs in British supermarkets.[10] A similar incident occurred in Japan when soft drinks and food sold in vending machines were contaminated in a series of incidents that led to ten deaths and thirty-five serious injuries.[11]

More troubling are possible scenarios involving BCW contamination of agricultural producs; for example, infecting livestock with

---

10. See Jessica E. Stern, "Would Terrorists Turn to Poison?," p. 396.
11. Ibid.

foot and mouth disease (a highly contagious virus), pigs with African Swine Fever, chickens with the Newcastle disease virus, or various crops (e.g., wheat, rice, corn, soy beans, etc.) with Karnal Bunt, stem rusts, or leaf rusts. Agricultural products are relatively attractive targets for BCW terrorism for several reasons. First, agriculture may constitute an important part of a state's or region's economy, e.g., US agricultural exports constitute a $140 billion-a-year industry. Second, the psychological impact of a threat or attack may greatly outweigh the physical effects of contamination. Recall Europe's reaction when bovine spongiform encephalopathy or "mad cow" disease was discovered in Great Britain in 1988 (British beef prices dropped considerably) and the subsequent reaction in 1996 when a possible link was discovered between eating contaminated meat and a variant of Creutzfeldt-Jakob disease in humans (the price temporarily dropped to zero), or the June 1999 ban in Europe and Asia on all Belgian chicken, pork, and beef products after dioxin was discovered in chicken and animal feed—a ban that according to one estimate cost the Belgian economy nearly $1 billion.[12] So sensitive is the public to food contamination that hoaxes alone may cause a substantial economic impact (e.g., hoaxes that affect agricultural futures markets may become a new form of market manipulation for financial gain). Third, agricultural products frequently present easy, concentrated targets (e.g., large herds, feedlots, or warehouses). For example, the United States imports approximately 30 billion tons of food each year and the US Food and Drug Administration samples less than 1 percent for possible contamination. Fourth, there are few effective deterrents against such acts, in part, because there is less public outrage if animals or crops are infected as opposed to people. Finally, low-level food contamination may be difficult to detect unless it is localized in space and time, due to the background level of

---

12. Steve Goldstein, "US Could Face New Terror Tactic: Agricultural Warfare," *Philadelphia Enquirer* (Jun. 22, 1999), p. 1.

approximately 9,000 deaths each year in the US due to food-borne diseases.[13]

There have been several historical examples of large-scale economic terrorism involving food or agricultural contamination. In 1979, a Palestinian extremist group injected liquid mercury into Israeli oranges destined for European markets. Contaminated oranges were found in the Netherlands, Belgium, Germany, Sweden, and the UK, with over a dozen people reportedly poisoned (none fatally). Israel was forced to curtail its orange exports by approximately 40 percent.[14] Another example is the 1986 threat by Tamil guerrillas operating in Sri Lanka to poison tea with potassium cyanide with the intent of crippling the Sri Lankan tea export industry.[15] As a final example, in 1989 an anonymous caller to the US Embassy in Santiago, Chile, claimed that Chilean grapes destined for US and Japanese markets had been contaminated with cyanide. The US placed a quarantine on all Chilean grapes and forced the growers to recall those that had already been shipped, causing approximately $333 million in damage to the Chilean grape industry. After a thorough investigation by the US Food and Drug Administration, traces of cyanide too small to cause harm were found on two grapes. This apparent hoax caused substantial damage to the Chilean fruit industry. To protest what the Chilean government and the grape growers and exporters believe was overreaction on the US side, they sued for $466 million in damages in US courts.[16]

Pharmaceutical contamination in many ways is similar to food poisoning, although it is more difficult to carry out today because of

13. See Christopher F. Chyba, *Biological Terrorism, Emerging Infectious Diseases, and National Security*, Project on World Security, Rockefeller Brothers Fund, New York (1998), p. 15.

14. See Ron Purver, "Chemical and Biological Terrorism: New Threat to Public Safety?," p. 13.

15. See Jessica E. Stern, "Would Terrorists Turn to Poison?," p. 396.

16. Ibid., pp. 395–6.

limited access to the product; most bottles and packages containing pharmaceuticals are sealed and access to the place of manufacture is carefully controlled. The classic example of pharmaceutical contamination is the 1982 Tylenol poisoning, where seven people died from potassium cyanide that had been placed in Tylenol capsules. In the wake of this event similar threats were directed at other pharmaceutical products, some of which resulted in deaths, demonstrating the copycat effect so well known in the study of terrorism. The perpetrator and the motive for the Tylenol tampering have never been discovered.[17]

Water Contamination

Waterborne contamination of large public reservoirs is relatively unattractive as a terrorist threat because large amounts of chemical or biological agents are required due to dilution, although this is not true for small, private reservoirs. In addition, most public water supplies are filtered and chlorinated to kill naturally occurring microorganisms, thus removing biological agents at the same time. Therefore, these threats tend to lack credibility unless they are directed against small, private water supplies. However, the psychological impact of water contamination will be difficult for public officials to ignore, even if the physical effects are limited.

Approximately 11 percent of past terrorist contamination cases involve waterborne contamination threats. For example, in 1972 the Order of the Rising Sun (RISE), a neo-nazi group, threatened to contaminate the water supplies of Chicago and several other Midwestern cities with typhoid.[18] In 1980, an individual threatened to poison the water supply of two Lake Tahoe casinos unless they paid $10 million in ransom. The herbicide Agent Orange was included

17. Private communication, Jason Pate, Center for Nonproliferation Studies, Monterey, CA.
18. Carus, "Bio-terrorism and Bio-crimes," pp. 124–5.

with the extortion note, although the attack never occurred. In 1987, fourteen white supremacists were indicted on charges of plotting to assassinate federal and elected officials, as well as to poison the water supplies of both Chicago and Washington with cyanide, 30 gallons of which was found on their rural compound in Arkansas.[19] In March 1992, the Kurdish Workers Party poisoned water tanks at a Turkish Air Force base with lethal concentrations of potassium cyanide, although the plot was discovered before any casualties occurred.[20] Finally, reports have surfaced that Iran plotted to contaminate US and European water supplies with an unspecified biological agent in February 1993, and that Israeli Arabs plotted to poison the water in Galilee with an "unidentified powder."[21]

Animal Vectors

Animal vectors—e.g., fleas, ticks, rats, and mice—have been the natural carriers of diseases for millennia. Some early attempts used vectors—most notably the Japanese program during World War II, which used plague-infected fleas—but most recent attempts have avoided animal vectors because they are difficult to keep alive in storage, during weapon delivery, and after dispersal.[22] Moreover, humans can protect themselves from animal vectors in numerous ways, thus reducing the likelihood of vector to human transmission. Hence, this method is unattractive compared to direct exposure to

19. See Bruce Hoffman, "Holy Terror: The Implications of Terrorism Motivated by Religious Imperative," RAND Corporation Paper P-7834 (1993), pp. 6, 8.

20. Ron Purver, "Chemical and Biological Terrorism: New Threat to Public Safety?," p. 14.

21. Ibid., pp. 12–13.

22. On the history of the Japanese program, see Peter Williams and David Wallace, *Unit 731: Japan's Secret Biological Warfare in World War II* (New York: Free Press, 1989); Sheldon H. Harris, *Factories of Death: Japanese Biological Warfare 1932–45 and the American Cover-up* (London: Routledge, 1994); and Ralph Blumenthal, "Japanese Germ-War Atrocities: A Half-Century of Stonewalling the World," *New York Times* (Mar. 4, 1999), p. A10.

biological agents. Therefore, most modern BW programs have not focused on delivery via vectors. The same is likely to be true in the future for both states and terrorist groups. Animal vectors are noted here simply for completeness.

Airborne BCW Releases

The scenarios with the greatest number of potential casualties involve airborne BCW releases. Releases within enclosed spaces (such as subways, buildings, domed sports arenas, airports, or train stations) require less BCW agent and are likely to be quite lethal because the agent remains concentrated in a confined space. However, open-air releases can potentially contaminate a much larger area and, hence, are associated with the most lethal BCW attacks.

The lethality of airborne attacks depends on the amount of BCW agent used and, for biological agents, the efficiency with which a respirable aerosol—i.e., particles in the 1 to 5 micron size range—can be generated, although particles above this size range can produce infections less efficiently in the upper respiratory tract.[23] For releases within enclosed spaces, relatively little agent is required—less than on the order of 1 kilogram for chemical agents and 1 gram for biological agents. Open-air attacks typically require on the order of 500 kilograms of chemical agent or 1 to 5 kilograms of biological agent.

Effective aerosol dissemination has been one of the more challenging hurdles to making biological weapons, although this may change in the future due to advances in commercial aerosol technologies. Biological agents may be aerosolized either by explosion or

23. Particles in the 1 to 5 micron diameter size range deposit efficiently in the lungs. Submicron particles tend to be exhaled and, hence, deposit less efficiently in the lungs. Particles with sizes above 5 microns tend to become trapped in the upper respiratory tract, where higher doses are required to start an infection. Particles above 20 microns in diameter tend to settle to the ground quickly and consequently do not travel far downwind.

by use of a spray nozzle. Explosive release tends to be inefficient (according to one estimate approximately 0.1 to 1 percent ends up in the 1 to 5 micron size range) because explosions create fine aerosols very inefficiently and because the heat and shock of the explosion can kill a lot of the agent. Spray release is more efficient (approximately 0.1 to 25 percent efficient for liquid slurries and up to 40 percent efficient for dry biological agents that are ground to the proper size prior to dispersal).[24] Obviously, spray release is more attractive for covert delivery. Of the two forms for the BW agents, wet and dry, wet slurries are relatively safe to manufacture and handle, but they tend to be difficult to spray into the 1 to 5 micron size range. Dry agents, on the other hand, are more difficult to manufacture and handle in a safe manner, but they are easier to spray into the proper size range. For example, the Iraqis manufactured relatively large quantities of anthrax and botulinum toxin; however, they apparently had difficulty developing efficient spray nozzles and, consequently, had to rely on explosive release for their BCW-armed Scud missiles. Similarly, the Aum Shinrikyo cult was able to grow modest quantities of anthrax and botulinum toxin (although they may not have had the correct strain), but they too had difficulty developing effective spray nozzles.

Examples of attempts to release BCW agents within enclosed spaces include a reported plot to introduce hydrogen cyanide gas into the United Nations building in New York City; and a similar plot in 1987 by the Confederate Hammer Skins, a white supremacist group, to put cyanide crystals in the air conditioning units of a Dallas Jewish community center.[25] More recently, Aum Shinrikyo placed three briefcases designed to spray botulinum toxin in the

24. William C. Patrick III, "Biological Terrorism and Aerosol Dissemination," 15 *Politics and the Life Sciences* (Sep. 1996), pp. 208–10.

25. Ron Purver, "Chemical and Biological Terrorism: New Threat to Public Safety?," p. 11.

Tokyo subway on March 15, 1995. The attack failed because the individual responsible for loading the briefcases apparently had qualms about carrying out the attack and substituted a nontoxic substance instead.[26] This failure prompted the cult leader, Shoko Asahara, to launch the notorious sarin attack in the Tokyo subway five days later on March 20, 1995. This attack was timed during the morning rush hour and the sarin was released on several different subway cars converging on the Kasumigaseki station beneath the federal police station and neighboring government office buildings. Twelve people died in the attack and nearly 3,800 people were injured, including approximately 1,000 that required hospitalization.[27] Over one month later, on May 5, 1995, Aum Shinrikyo struck again, this time attempting to release hydrogen cyanide with a crude device left in the restroom of a Tokyo subway station. However, the device accidentally caught fire, alerting subway workers who extinguished the fire before the chemicals mixed appreciably.[28]

Open-air BCW releases have the potential to affect the broadest area and create the highest number of casualties. Hence, they are the scenarios associated with battlefield BCW use. However, they also have become associated with terrorist attacks. The area contaminated in an open-air release is determined by the amount of BCW agent, or payload of the delivery vehicle, and the aerosol dissemination efficiency, just as for releases within enclosed spaces. In addition, open-air attacks are dependent on local meteorological conditions, environmental factors that degrade BCW agents, and any

26. David E. Kaplan and Andrew Marshall, *The Cult at the End of the World*, pp. 235–6.

27. Although the number of casualties associated with this attack is usually cited as 5,500, Kyle Olson claims the actual number is 3,796. See Kyle Olson, Talk on Aum Shinrikyo delivered at the National Symposium on Medical and Public Health Responses to Bioterrorism, sponsored by the Johns Hopkins Center for Civilian Biodefense Studies, held in Arlington, VA (Feb. 16–17, 1999).

28. David E. Kaplan and Andrew Marshall, *The Cult at the End of the World*, pp. 279–80.

protection afforded by being indoors when the BCW cloud drifts by outdoors.

The problem of aerosol dissemination is the same as discussed above. Once aerosolized, the wind speed determines the rate at which the agent is transported downwind and atmospheric stability determines the rate at which the agent diffuses in the vertical and horizontal directions. The presence of temperature inversions, in particular, may trap BCW agents close to the ground, increasing surface doses substantially. Rain washes most BCW agents out of the air. Some BCW agents may remain harmful in groundwater; however, most become harmless. BCW agents decay in the air due to humidity, thermal stress, the presence of oxygen, the "open-air factor" (associated with air pollution), and ultraviolet light—and the rate of decay differs widely for different BCW agents. Finally, if one is inside a closed building at the time a BCW plume passes outside, the integrated dose one receives is reduced by a factor of 2 or more for typical American homes, assuming the windows and doors are closed, and up to a factor of 10 or more for hermetically sealed office buildings, depending on the quality of the air filters in the heating, ventilation, and air conditioning system.[29] Taking these factors into account, a wide range of BCW attack outcomes is possible for open-air releases.

As for delivery means, ballistic missiles, aircraft, cruise missiles, unmanned aerial vehicles (especially for BW agents because of the small payloads required), artillery shells, and a variety of covert delivery means are possible. Ballistic missiles are not necessarily the preferred delivery option because BCW warheads, at least on long-range ballistic missiles, must be well insulated to protect the agent from reentry heating, and atmospheric dispersal is difficult at high reentry speeds. Covert delivery is the most worrisome scenario be-

---

29. See Lester L. Yuan, "Sheltering Effects of Buildings from Biological Weapons" (to be published; copy on file with author).

cause of the ease with which small amounts of BW agent can be concealed, the inability to detect BW agents in real time (BW agents are colorless, odorless, tasteless, and difficult for automated sensors to distinguish from naturally occurring airborne biological particles such as pollen—although this may change in the future), and the incubation period associated with most BW agents that gives the perpetrators time to escape.

Historically, states have released chemical agents in the air more often than biological agents. Obviously, the use of chemical agents on the battlefield in World War I is the most egregious example. In addition, Italy used chemical agents against Ethiopia in 1935–36 and Libya reportedly used chemical agents against Chad in 1986 and 1987.[30] A more well-documented example is Iraq's use of chemical agents in the Iran–Iraq War (1980–88). Iraq first used nonlethal riot control agents in 1982, but turned to the use of mustard gas and nerve agents to defend Basra against Iranian "human wave" attacks in 1984. Since Iranian soldiers lacked effective protective gear at that time, the Iraqi chemical attacks inflicted heavy casualties. In total, Iraq used chemical agents approximately 195 times during the war with the frequency of such attacks increasing in 1987–88. While it is difficult to make reliable estimates of Iranian casualties, Iran reported that prior to April 8, 1987, there had been 262 fatalities due to chemical attacks and over 27,000 casualties.[31] In the mid-1980s, Iran began to produce its own CW agents. It used them against Iraq late in the war. The Iranian attacks were not very effective, in part, because Iraqi troops used chemical protective gear. Both World War I and the Iran–Iraq War support the common claim that chem-

30. For a review of alleged BCW use prior to 1970, see Julian Perry Robinson, *The Problem of Chemical and Biological Warfare, Volume 1: The Rise of CB Weapons*, (New York: Stockholm International Peace Research Institute/Humanities Press, 1971), pp. 125–228.

31. See Thomas L. McNaugher, "Ballistic Missiles and Chemical Weapons: The Legacy of the Iran-Iraq War," 15 *International Security* (Fall 1990), pp. 5–34.

ical warfare is less lethal (by a factor of two to four) than high explosives used in similar circumstances, although chemical agents produce more casualties, thereby creating medical and logistics problems for the state attacked. Finally, Iraq also used chemical agents against its own people. In April 1988, Iraqi (and possibly Iranian) CW killed scores of Kurdish civilians in the city of Halabja, although it is not clear whether this was intentional or simply collateral damage from nearby battles, and in September 1988 Iraq used chemical agents to drive the Kurds from villages located on the Turkish border.[32]

Biological agents have been released by states much less frequently, the most notorious example being the Japanese biological program, i.e., Unit 731 located in the Manchuria, from 1932 to 1945. During this period the Japanese experimented with plague-infected fleas, anthrax, cholera, and several other diseases as biological warfare agents. Moreover, Japan conducted field trials against Chinese cities in the late 1930s. The biological agents were sprayed from aircraft and placed in water or food supplies, with mixed results. There were several plague outbreaks in Chinese cities; however, definitive evidence that these were caused by Japanese biological attacks instead of natural causes is difficult to obtain. In addition, Japan reportedly killed 1,700 of its own troops through BW mishaps.[33]

The only other open-air release of a biological agent by a state occurred by accident at a biological warfare facility in Sverdlovsk, Russia, on April 2, 1979, when a plume of anthrax was released that killed 66 of the 77 reported cases of pulmonary anthrax downwind from the release point. Livestock also died 10 to 100 kilometers

32. Ibid., pp. 21–4.
33. Nicholas D. Kristof, "Japan Confronting Gruesome War Atrocity," *New York Times* (Mar. 17, 1995), p. A1. See also Peter Williams and David Wallace, *Unit 731: Japan's Secret Biological Warfare in World War II*; and Sheldon H. Harris, *Factories of Death: Japanese Biological Warfare 1932–45 and the American Cover-up*.

downwind from the release point. Initially the Soviet government denied that the accident had occurred, claiming that the victims had eaten contaminated meat (which would not have caused pulmonary anthrax). However, in 1992 President Yeltsin finally admitted that the event had been due to an accident at a former Soviet BW facility, an admission corroborated by western researchers who were allowed to conduct an epidemiological investigation of the incident in 1993.[34]

Although some terrorist groups have been interested in open-air BCW releases, Aum Shinrikyo is the only group that has attempted such a feat.[35] Between 1990 and 1993, the cult reportedly attempted to release biological agents in the air on eight different occasions. The first four attempts used botulinum toxin, including three attempts in April 1990 when the cult reportedly attempted to spray botulinum toxin from trucks that drove around Japan's parliament building in Tokyo, the Yokosuka naval base near Tokyo, and Narita International Airport on the outskirts of Tokyo, and an attempt in early June 1993 to disrupt Prince Naruhito's wedding by spraying botulinum toxin from specially equipped automobiles.[36] None of these four attacks produced noticeable results. The cult then turned to anthrax. In late June 1993, they attempted to spray anthrax from the roof of the Aum Shinrikyo building in Tokyo. After nothing happened, they tried again in July 1993. Neither attempt produced any noticeable fatalities, although on the second

34. Matthew Meselson, Jeanne Guillemin, Martin Hugh-Jones, Alexander Langmuir, Ilona Popova, Alex Alexis, Shelokov, and Olga Yampolskaya, "The Sverdlovsk Anthrax Outbreak of 1979," 266 *Science* (Nov. 18, 1994), pp. 1202–8.

35. The Baader-Meinhof Gang, for example, threatened to use mustard gas against Stuttgart and possibly other cities after a large quantity of the agent was stolen from a US Army ammunition depot in West Germany. See Ron Purver, "Chemical and Biological Terrorism: New Threat to Public Safety?," p. 11.

36. See Sheryl WuDunn, Judith Miller, and William J. Broad, "How Japan Germ Terror Alerted World," *New York Times* (May 26, 1998), p. A10; David E. Kaplan and Andrew Marshall, *The Cult at the End of the World*, pp. 58–9, 93–6, and 234–6.

occasion neighbors complained of a foul smell in the air and later several pets were found dead. The police arrived at the scene but did not investigate further. Again in July 1993, the cult reportedly attempted to spray anthrax around the Japanese Diet building in central Tokyo, and in late July 1993 they apparently attempted to spray anthrax around the Imperial Palace using a spray device mounted on a truck. All four anthrax attempts also appear to have failed.

There is considerable debate about the causes of Aum Shinrikyo's failures. In the case of botulinum toxin, the cult grew the botulinum bacillus from a seed stock obtained in the wild on Hokkaido Island.[37] Hence, the strain may not have been one of the more virulent strains of botulinum (i.e., not type A). With respect to the anthrax seed stock, it may have been obtained from a laboratory at Tsukuba University and, hence, may have been a vaccine strain and not the virulent Volum B strain. In addition, the cult apparently had problems developing effective spray nozzles for aerosolizing the agent in the 1 to 5 micron size range. To the extent clouds were produced, they may have been too dilute for toxic effects due to the low flow rate of their nozzles. Finally, one cannot be positive that no fatalities occurred in any of these attacks because if only a few fatalities occurred, this may have gone unnoticed at local hospitals, given the number of deaths in any major city due to unknown infectious origins in the US.[38] At least there were no fatalities among the high-profile targets of these attacks (i.e., the Diet, the Imperial Palace, Narita Airport, and Yokosuka naval base, and Prince Naruhito's wedding party).

Due to these failures with biological agents, Shoko Asahara turned increasingly to chemical agents. Between 1993 and 1994, the

37. See Sheryl WuDunn, Judith Miller, and William J. Broad, "How Japan Germ Terror Alerted World."
38. See Christopher F. Chyba, *Biological Terrorism, Emerging Infectious Diseases, and National Security*, pp. 15–16.

cult was able to manufacture approximately 30 kilograms of sarin and experimented with the manufacture of several other chemical agents, including VX.[39] On June 27, 1994 the cult attempted to kill three judges that were presiding over different trials involving the cult by spraying sarin at night upwind from the apartment building where they slept. The attack affected approximately 160 people, killing 7 and permanently wounding 68. All three judges were sufficiently incapacitated so their trials had to be postponed. This, after all, was the purpose of the attack. The next time the cult struck with sarin was in the Tokyo subway on March 20, 1995.

Is Aum Shinrikyo's attempt to use BCW agents for mass murder a harbinger of things to come, or simply a freak event? Obviously, with only one data point, it is difficult to extrapolate with any reliability. However, Aum Shinrikyo does provide proof that groups with these motives do exist. In the past, scenarios like those attempted by Aum Shinrikyo would have been dismissed as exaggerations. One can no longer be so dismissive. On the other hand, one should not jump to the conclusion that events like those attempted by Aum Shinrikyo are likely to occur in the future; they require a motive to carry out such attacks, the necessary technical expertise in CW or BW, sufficient funds, and the opportunity to operate with relative impunity from local police—the Japanese police had very limited powers to investigate religious groups, of which Aum Shinrikyo was one.

How Serious Is the Threat?

The logic behind the belief that chemical and biological threats to the US are growing rests on three propositions: (1) that access to dual-use chemical and biological warfare technologies is increasing

39. See David E. Kaplan and Andrew Marshall, *The Cult at the End of the World*, pp. 85–6, 119–25, 132, 150, 185–6, 211–12.

both for states and terrorist groups, (2) that the motive to acquire, threaten, and use BCW is growing, and (3) that the US, as well as most other states, is vulnerable to chemical or biological attacks, especially against urban areas. The extent to which these propositions are valid is discussed below.

BCW Proliferation

The technologies, materials, and knowledge required to build BCW are inherently dual-use because they are used in a wide range of legitimate chemical industries, pharmaceutical companies, medical laboratories, and biotechnology companies. Therefore, the perennial problem for arms control—allowing activities and technologies with commercial benefit to proliferate while constraining those that lead to weapon programs—is particularly difficult in the area of BCW. The chemical precursors and facilities used to produce pesticides can also make nerve agents. The fermenters and growth medium used to produce microbial cells and viruses for a wide range of medical and commercial applications can also be used to produce anthrax and other biological agents. Vaccine production, biopesticide production, and medical research all have significant overlap with BW activities. In fact, biological toxins (e.g., ricin), have even been used to treat some forms of cancer. In summary, almost all BCW technologies can be found in a wide range of legitimate civilian applications. Moreover, the globalization of the chemical and biotechnology industries implies that the knowledge, materials, and technology have spread worldwide.

Rapid advances in bioengineering have made the BW proliferation problem worse, not because advances in recombinant DNA allow one to manufacture new agents with tailored effects, although this may be possible in the future, but rather because the genetic revolution has spurred tremendous advances in bioprocessing—for example, techniques for the large-scale culture of bacteria and viruses, techniques for separating and purifying bacteria, viruses, and toxins, and advanced diagnostic techniques to determine the nature of the biological material with which one is working.[40] These advances in bioprocessing have made it easier to produce the classic biological agents such as anthrax, botulinum toxin, and others. Finally, there has been a proliferation of manuals, especially on the internet, with explicit directions for making several common poisons and CW agents, along with instructions on how to use these weapons.

The collapse of the former Soviet Union has added a new dimension to the proliferation problem—namely, the potential for material, technology, knowledge, and possibly weapons to leak from the former Soviet BCW programs. Similar concerns, though of a smaller magnitude, exist with other former BCW programs (e.g., in South Africa). This source of proliferation has been recognized as a serious problem with respect to nuclear weapons; however, the problem is more daunting for the vast former Soviet BCW complex because most of these scientists and technicians are now unemployed and the level of safety and security associated with biological and chemical facilities is lower than at their nuclear counterparts. Finally, as political relations between Russia and the West continue to appear to deteriorate, the prospects for cooperating to prevent the leakage of BCW material, technology, and weapons expertise becomes less likely, including attempts to enhance the transparency of former Soviet BW activities.

Therefore, the supply of BCW material, technology, and expertise probably has already spread beyond any state's ability to control it. Consequently, attention should focus on the intention to use BCW because any state or terrorist group that wants to acquire these weapons probably can do so without much trouble (or money).

---

40. Malcolm Dando, "Biological Warfare in the 21st Century," *Brassey's* (UK), 1994, chap. 7.

This brings us to the second premise, namely, that the motives to acquire, threaten, or use BCW are growing.

State Motives for Acquiring, Threatening, or Using BCW

States may have a greater incentive to acquire BCW today for their security because the international system is less stable now than in the bipolar Cold War era. In particular, some states traditionally hostile to the US must now provide for their own security rather than rely on an alliance with the former Soviet Union. North Korea and Iraq provide examples that spring readily to mind. Given the global role the US has assumed in the post-Cold War era, some states may conclude that they need BCW, if not nuclear weapons, to deter regional intervention by the US or, if deterrence fails, to complicate US conventional military operations in a local theater. Not possessing economies that can sustain large modern conventional military forces, these states will likely turn to the least expensive weapons that offer impressive deterrence benefits vis-à-vis the US. Leaders may quickly conclude that BCW are the weapons of choice.

The objectives for threatening BCW attacks may differ from the objectives for actually carrying them out. At the strategic level, states may threaten BCW attacks to deter regional intervention by a larger power; to deter, coerce, or intimidate neighboring states, especially allies of a large power; or to deter larger powers from pressing wars to the point of total defeat for the regime. For example, although Iraq never used CW to attack Iranian cities during the Iran–Iraq War, the fear that such attacks might occur, either with aircraft or ballistic missiles, during the last six months of the war was manipulated by Iraq to intimidate an already war-weary Iranian leadership and population.[41] Threatening BCW attacks to deter the defeat of a state or regime is reminiscent of the role played by nuclear weapons during the Cold War—they were weapons of last resort. This may have been the role Saddam Hussein had in mind for his BCW in the Gulf War, namely, if coalition forces had attacked Baghdad and the collapse of Hussein's regime appeared imminent, he might have authorized the use of BCW against Israel, Saudi Arabia, and/or co- alition forces deployed in the region.[42]

The above objectives are particularly important vis-à-vis the US because many regional states will find it difficult to challenge US conventional military superiority directly and, hence, may seek "asymmetric" means to deter or defeat the US. Moreover, states may come to the conclusion that weapons of mass destruction (WMD) are the best means for deterring the US given America's supposed sensitivity to casualties.[43] By intimidating US allies, regional states may be able to fragment US-led coalitions or deny basing rights or overflight rights to US forces. At the very least, WMD raise the risks associated with regional intervention. This probably is what General Sundarji meant when he concluded that one of the lessons of the 1991 Gulf War is that states should acquire NW before they engage the US.[44] The argument applies with equal force to BW and perhaps with less force to CW.

41. See Thomas L. McNaugher, "Ballistic Missiles and Chemical Weapons: The Legacy of the Iran-Iraq War," pp. 21–4.

42. See Timothy V. McCarthy and Jonathan Tucker, "Saddam's Toxic Arsenal: Chemical and Biological Weapons and Missiles in the Gulf Wars," chap. 2, in *Planning the Unthinkable*, Peter Lavoy, Scott D. Sagan, and James Wirth, eds., forthcoming.

43. See Eric V. Larsen, "Casualties and Consensus: The Historical Role of Casualties in Domestic Support for US Military Operations," RAND Corporation Paper MR-726-RC (1996).

44. See George Quester and Victor Utgoff, "No-First-Use and Non-prolifera- tion: Redefining Extended Deterrence," 17(2) *Washington Quarterly* (Spring 1994), p. 107.

States may actually use CW or BW to carry out the strategic threats mentioned above, especially against unprotected civilian populations. Assuming no protection, chemical attacks against cities with several hundred kilograms of nerve agent may cause between 100 and 10,000 fatalities, with scenarios above 10,000 fatalities being possible if aircraft spray tanks are used against densely populated cities (e.g., Seoul, Tokyo, or New York). However, biological attacks can be much more devastating. Attacks using several tens of kilograms of anthrax, for example, could result in 1,000 to 100,000 fatalities, with fatalities reaching the millions if efficient spray devices are used under the right circumstances in densely populated urban areas. This is comparable to the fatalities that would result from a large nuclear bomb. Hence, biological, as opposed to chemical, weapons are a "poor man's nuclear bomb" for strategic attacks.

At the tactical level, BCW are not particularly attractive to modern militaries because their effects are weather-dependent and, hence, difficult to control; they can be difficult to handle in the field, especially for CW because chemical agents can be corrosive; CW, though not necessarily BW, are less lethal than high explosives, as discussed above; BCW agents may affect one's own troops if they overrun contaminated areas or if the wind changes direction; and the use of BW, in particular, may contaminate such large areas that the resulting collateral damage to neighboring civilian populations increases the chance of devastating reprisals. Finally, passive defenses can be quite effective (greater than 95 percent) for protecting military personnel against BCW threats, assuming the necessary equipment and training are provided to operate in a contaminated environment for days on end (such training currently is uncommon, however, even in western militaries).[45] Therefore, it should come as

45. The 5 percent failure rate for chemical suits is mostly due to poor mask fit. Suits that utilize positive overpressure within the mask and suit provide much greater protection, although they tend to be more cumbersome.

no surprise that most modern militaries prefer high explosives to BCW for tactical operations, especially with the advent of precision-guided conventional munitions.

Nevertheless, some states may still threaten or use CW or BW to harm, slow down, or demoralize opposing troops.[46] The incentive is greatest if the opposing troops do not have protective gear or if tactical surprise can catch the opponent in an unprotected state. Historically, BCW rarely have been used against protected troops, suggesting that passive defenses may dissuade their use. In both World War I and the Iran–Iraq War, the initial CW use was against unprotected troops, although chemical use continued after protective gear was provided. However, even with protective gear, troops cannot fight as efficiently due to the thermal and physical burden associated with chemical suits and masks, especially in hot, humid weather—suggesting that decreasing the operational tempo of a superior conventional force may be another reason for threatening, if not using, BCW.[47] While this has been a concern in the past, it will become less so in the future due to the advent of modern protective gear with relatively low thermal and physical burdens.

46. In terms of the weapons used, attacks with persistent chemical agents make it difficult to operate at military facilities such as airfields, ports, or logistics nodes without full protective gear. Covert attacks with biological agents also may be effective against these facilities if they occur without warning (e.g., prior to the outbreak of hostilities). Attacks against forces in the field are better conducted with nonpersistent chemical agents because of the possibility that one's own forces may overrun the same area a few hours or days after the attack. If BW are used against engaged forces, toxins are preferred because their effects are immediate, although the attacking force would have to take precautions in case it overran a contaminated area because the agent, if it survives in the soil, may be re-aerosolized by heavy troop or vehicular traffic. Again, the fact that biological attacks against military facilities may result in high civilian collateral casualties is problematic for an attacker because it increases the risk that the opponent may retaliate in devastating ways, including a possible nuclear response if the opponent is a nuclear power.

47. This is less true for biological attacks because only masks covering the mouth and nose are required, since biological agents are not absorbed efficiently through the skin.

The one area where BCW attacks may have a tactical or operational impact is against high-priority military facilities such as ports, airfields, logistics nodes, and command centers that are heavily dependent on civilian support personnel because civilians typically are not trained or equipped with BCW protective gear. If civilian stevedores at ports or truck drivers carrying munitions and logistic supplies are not protected, then BCW attacks may bring military operations to a halt. Therefore, despite the fact that BCW are not preferred by modern militaries, they can have substantial impact on modern military operations if the vulnerability of support personnel at critical military facilities is not addressed (for example, by providing adequate equipment and training for such personnel or by having adequate military manpower to take over civilian functions in the event of a BCW threat or attack).

North Korea provides an interesting illustration of these strategic and tactical objectives for threatening or using BCW. If North Korea were to attack South Korea in a replay of events of June 1950, the opening salvo of the attack might well involve the use of BCW against South Korean and US forces in the region. Chemical attacks against frontline troops might be used to defeat forces caught in an unprotected posture. The US strategy for the defense of South Korea hinges on the prompt infusion of additional forces and supplies, because the peacetime US presence in South Korea is relatively small. Hence, persistent chemical or biological agents might be used against ports and airfields to slow down the buildup and resupply of US forces. Such attacks could have a substantial effect if the civilian support personnel at these bases were vulnerable to BCW attacks. Next, North Korea might consider threatening biological attacks against Japan in an attempt to coerce it into staying out of the conflict, or at least to coerce the Japanese government into denying the use of Japanese airfields and ports for US offensive military operations against North Korea. If this coercive threat were successful, it could greatly complicate US efforts to conduct military operations on the Korean peninsula. Finally, if the war eventually turned against North Korea, as most people believe it would, and US and South Korean forces moved north of the 38th parallel in an attempt to unify the peninsula using military force, then the North Korean regime might threaten to attack Seoul or other major South Korean cities with BW, as well as Japanese and US cities if long-range delivery means were available, to deter the defeat of their regime.

Motives for Terrorist Organizations

BCW acquisition might be appealing to terrorist groups to end the state's monopoly on large-scale violence, to confer prestige on the group because it demonstrates a mastery of WMD, to copy others who have attempted to acquire these weapons before, or to threaten or use these weapons for specific objectives such as assassination, economic terrorism, or inflicting mass casualties. Moreover, the acquisition, threat, or use of BCW by a state to intimidate or defeat an opponent could encourage terrorist groups to emulate them. Although Iraq did not make overt BCW threats, US concern with possible Iraqi BCW use during the 1991 Gulf War apparently gave Shoko Asahara the idea of starting his own BCW program. After Aum Shinrikyo, the copycat phenomena may encourage others to do the same—although it is noteworthy that no copycat events have followed Aum Shinrikyo in the past four years, as have occurred with airline hijackings, the Tylenol poisoning, and other novel terrorist events.

Assassination is a frequent objective for the threat or actual use of BCW agents, whether by governments, terrorist organizations, or individuals. In the US, several right-wing militia groups and estranged individuals have shown interest in ricin for assassinations, as the examples of the Minnesota Patriots Council, Thomas Leahy, and Thomas Levy demonstrate. Aum Shinrikyo also reportedly murdered several people with chemical and biological agents. Although some of these examples are only threats, some involve possession with the intent to use BCW agents for assassination and others involve actual use.

Economic terrorism conducted by contaminating food, agricultural, or pharmaceutical products or infecting livestock may simply require threats, or the use of only trace amounts of hazardous chemical or biological substances, to have their effect. According to the estimate cited earlier, nearly 31 percent of the terrorist events involving contamination involve threats against food, agricultural, or pharmaceutical products. The objective of such threats could be financial gain (as in the extortion threats following the 1982 Tylenol poisoning); or it might have a larger political purpose, namely, destroying public confidence in a certain company, disrupting the export or import of specific goods and thereby damaging a specific economic sector (as was the case with the mercury poisoning of Israeli oranges and the cyanide threat that crippled Chilean grape exports to the US), or the threat might simply be directed at the overall economic well-being of a state. Moreover, as the Chilean grape case and the ALF's threat to poison Mars candy bars demonstrate, hoaxes can have tremendous economic impact because it is difficult to verify that chemical or biological poisons are *not* present and because such threats evoke a disproportionate sense of dread. Hoaxes may also be easier to perpetuate because less moral opprobrium is attached to hoaxes than actually poisoning innocent people. Hence, terrorists might expect less severe reactions from the state. Finally, if the threats are anonymous, a terrorist organization may not even shoulder the blame.

Inflicting mass casualties or mass killing (defined here to be more than 1,000 casualties or deaths) is a third objective for terrorist use of BCW. Some call this "catastrophic terrorism." Here the motive would simply be to create as many casualties as possible, to disrupt or possibly to hasten the collapse of what the terrorists believe is a corrupt national or international order, or as a sacramental act to a divine being that believes in retribution against a corrupt or degenerate world order. Threats to create mass casualties, as opposed to the actual use of BCW, are less likely because they are apt to be counterproductive. Few political objectives warrant threatening such BCW attacks because the means are disproportionate to most political ends. Hence, such threats make poor bargaining tools. Moreover, making such threats may trigger reprisals by the state or may lead to heightened security measures which would decrease the chance that subsequent attacks are successful. Therefore, if mass killing is the objective, terrorists are not likely to issue threats in advance.

Fear that mass killing is a growing motive among terrorists arises because some evidence suggests that indiscriminate violence is becoming more common; that religious, nihilist, and millenarian terrorist organizations are becoming more numerous; and that the means for carrying out such threats are becoming widely available. However, considerable debate exists regarding the evidence for, and the interpretation of, these trends—leaving this author with the impression that the evidence for the future use of BCW for mass killing by terrorists is equivocal.

Historical trends do not suggest that indiscriminate violence is very common. In the twentieth century fewer than a dozen terrorist attacks have caused more than 100 fatalities.[48] However, most of them are concentrated in the past two decades. The midair airline bombings in the 1980s; the February 1993 bombing of the World Trade Center in New York City along with the June 1993 plot to

---

48. For example, the 1979 arson attack on a cinema in Teheran that killed more than 400 people; the 1983 bombing of the US Marine barracks in Beirut that killed 241 people; the midair bombing of an Air India airplane in 1985 that killed 328 people; the midair bombing of Pan Am flight 103 over Lockerbie, Scotland, in 1988, killing 278 people; the 1989 midair bombing of a French UTA flight that killed 171 people; and the in-flight bombing of a Colombian Avianca aircraft in 1989 that killed 107 people. See Bruce Hoffman, "Responding to Terrorism across the Technological Spectrum," 6 *Terrorism and Political Violence* (Autumn 1994), n. 13.

free those terrorists;[49] and the April 1995 bombing of the Oklahoma City Federal Building suggest that large-scale, indiscriminate violence is becoming more common.[50] Nevertheless, it still is a leap from these events to the indiscriminate use of BCW against civilians—Aum Shinrikyo being the only example of this type.

Not only is the historical evidence for mass killing by terrorists scant, but there are also reasons to believe such scenarios will remain unlikely. Threats to retaliate against states that sponsor BCW terrorism should diminish the likelihood that states will assist terrorist groups in the use of such agents. Even if the assistance is covert, there is always the chance that it will be discovered. Presumably, strong domestic legislation of the sort recently passed in the US to punish nefarious BCW activities should deter individuals or groups from developing, producing, trafficking in, or storing BCW agents in quantities that have no justification for peaceful or prophylactic purposes, not to mention deterring individuals or groups from using BCW agents.

The traditional argument has been that organized secular terrorist groups will not resort to mass killing because these means are disproportionate to their ends. Mass killing would alienate public support, which frequently such organizations rely upon for new members as well as for financial and logistic support. In addition, inflicting mass casualties almost guarantees a strong response from the state in which the attack occurs—a response that may threaten the very survival of the group. Therefore, as Brian Jenkins once said,

49. The plot included the destruction of two commuter tunnels and a bridge linking New Jersey and Manhattan, blowing up the United Nations building, attacking the New York City FBI field office, and assassinating several public officials.

50. See Bruce Hoffman, "Responding to Terrorism across the Technological Spectrum," pp. 373–6.

secular terrorist organizations want "lots of people watching, not lots of people dead."[51]

However, the rise of religious, millenarian, and nihilist groups may weaken this traditional argument for doubting the likelihood of BCW terrorist attacks.[52] The secular terrorist attempts to change a political system that has ignored the aspirations of some disenfranchised group, but religious, millenarian, and nihilist groups may be more interested in destroying or overthrowing the existing political order. Many of these groups view themselves as a persecuted minority and the outside world as infidels, subhuman, or an enemy with whom there can be no compromise, thereby reducing the moral inhibitions to inflict mass casualties.[53] Whereas secular terrorists appeal to a larger constituency that they purport to represent, the religious, millenarian, and nihilist groups frequently are alienated from society with no constituency but the group members themselves and, hence, may be less constrained by the public reaction to mass casualties. Some of these groups come together for only a short period of time, perhaps for a single purpose (such as disaffected splinter groups, or ad hoc collections of individuals sharing a com-

51. Brian Jenkins, "International Terrorism: The Other World War," R-3302-AF, RAND Corporation, Santa Monica, CA (1985), p. 25.

52. See Bruce Hoffman, "Holy Terror: The Implications of Terrorism Motivated by Religious Imperative," *Inside Terrorism* (New York: Columbia University Press, 1998).

53. Groups contemplating indiscriminate violence against innocent civilians use numerous techniques to overcome the moral inhibitions individuals might feel about poisoning innocent civilians. For example, they provide religious justification for such acts and indoctrinate members using various rituals that reinforce allegiance to the group, including the surrender of all worldly possessions to the group, breaking ties with the outside world, engaging in a daily regimen that wears down an individual's resistance and encourages total faith in a charismatic or dictatorial leader, and propagating beliefs that dehumanize potential victims. However, this does not always work, as demonstrated by the Aum Shinrikyo member who reportedly had qualms about loading botulinum toxin in the suitcases used in the March 15, 1995, Tokyo subway attack, leading him to substitute an inert substance instead.

mon philosophy or frustration).[54] If so, they may be less concerned about the public reaction to their acts. In some cases, they may be even less concerned about threats to the group's survival, viewing themselves as martyrs.[55]

Certain white supremacist groups within the US also resemble religious, millenarian, or nihilist groups; namely, they are alienated from the society within which they exist, they are hostile to any form of government above the local level, they often are obsessed with achieving racial or religious purification of the US, they think of others (i.e., nonwhites or non-Christians) as infidels, if not subhuman species that must be exterminated through racial or religious Armageddon, and the leaders of such groups often don religious titles to sanctify acts of violence. Although white supremacist groups have not killed as many people as other terrorist groups, there is some evidence that these groups have contemplated BCW use on a massive scale. Indicative of this inclination is the fact that *The Turner Diaries*, a novel depicting total war between white supremacists and their adversaries that includes the use of NW, has become a "bible" for many of these groups.[56]

54. Examples of such groups include the perpetrators of the World Trade Center bombing, the teenager who plotted to attack African-American churches in Los Angeles with machine guns and hand grenades in 1993, separate groups of teenagers who bombed Asian, Jewish, and African-American targets in other California cities and in Washington state during the spring and summer of 1993, and the two men, Timothy McVeigh and Terry Nichols, who bombed the Oklahoma City Federal Building.

55. Having said this, not all terrorist groups with religious affiliations use violence indiscriminately. For example, the Palestinian Liberation Organization and the provisional Irish Republican Army, to name two, may attack military or police headquarters, barracks, embassies and the like, but rarely do they turn to mass killing. These groups are more secular in nature since they rely on political, logistical, and financial support for the group to function and, hence, are sensitive to a backlash among public supporters. Moreover, the desire to survive as a group usually prevents them from using such means because of the likelihood of a harsh government crackdown.

56. See Bruce Hoffman, "Holy Terror: The Implications of Terrorism Motivated by Religious Imperative," pp. 6–9.

Finally, although the means for carrying out BCW terrorist attacks are becoming easier to acquire, most terrorist groups adhere to an operational code that relies on proven tactics and eschews unfamiliar methods due to the risk of failure.[57] This technological conservatism implies that BCW may not be favored methods of attack, especially since guns and conventional explosives meet the requirements for most terrorist acts. However, the rise of state-sponsored terrorism implies that access to BCW, as well as training in their use, may become less of a barrier to their use.[58] Iran, Iraq, Libya, North Korea, and Syria are all on the US State Department's list of states sponsoring terrorism and all of these states have CW or BW programs, if not both.

The Vulnerability to BCW Attacks

If the acquisition of BCW is becoming easier and the motives for acquiring, threatening, or using these weapons is on the rise, then it seems logical to conclude that the BCW threat is growing. However, to represent a clear and present danger, states must be vulnerable to such threats. Urban populations are quite vulnerable to chemical and biological attacks because little protection exists for civilians. In particular, there is no real-time capability to warn people that BCW agents have been released, states tend not to provide protective gear and training to civilians, there is inadequate medical treatment for potential victims, and little capability exists to decontaminate large areas. Finally, democratic societies are more vulner-

57. Bruce Hoffman, "Responding to Terrorism across the Technological Spectrum," pp. 366–90.

58. For example, during the Cold War the East German State Police reportedly trained Iraqi groups in the use of BCW agents against civilian targets in a special school near East Berlin and at training camps in the Middle East, a fact that becomes important in light of reported Iraqi plans and threats to conduct BCW terrorist attacks against the West after the 1991 Gulf War. See Purver, *Chemical and Biological Terrorism*, p. 12; and Carus, "Bio-terrorism and Bio-crimes," pp. 115–6, 122–3.

able to terrorism than authoritarian states because they are less able to use widespread surveillance and repressive tactics to eliminate such groups operating in their midst.[59]

Militaries, on the other hand, can be made relatively invulnerable to BCW effects by acquiring the necessary protective gear and medical prophylactics (such as vaccines, antibiotics, and chemical agent antidotes), training troops to operate in a contaminated environment, and having contingency plans to replace critical civilian support personnel at important military facilities. In the past, donning protective gear slowed the tempo of conventional military operations; however, as noted above, this may be less of a problem in the future with the advent of new chemical suits. Hence, BCW threats are largely threats of terror against civilian populations.

Substantial efforts are under way in the US to improve the protection provided to US military personnel, and to redress the vulnerability of civilian populations. In the area of civil defense, starting with the Nunn-Lugar-Domenici legislation of 1996 and followed by subsequent presidential budgets with increased funding, efforts are being made to develop new BCW detectors, to improve surveillance networks for infectious diseases, to improve intelligence capabilities to interdict BCW attacks by states or terrorists, to train local emergency medical, fire, police, and national guard forces in large US cities to cope with a BCW attack, to stockpile the necessary vaccines, antibiotics, and antidotes against standard chemical and biological agents, and to conduct research into new medical treatments that might prove more effective in the future. Eventually,

59. The case of Aum Shinrikyo is instructive in this regard because, according to the Japanese constitution, the police were not allowed to conduct surveillance against religious groups, which Aum Shinrikyo was classified as. Hence, prior to their release of chemical agents at Matsumoto in June 1994, it was very difficult for the Japanese police to conduct an investigation of the group. They needed hard evidence of criminal behavior and even then the investigation was slow because of difficulties in sharing information between different police prefectures.

these and other civil defense preparations may provide sufficient protection to render urban BCW attacks ineffective. However, we have a long way to go. Moreover, reducing the US vulnerability to various forms of economic terrorism involving chemical or biological agents will involve additional measures.

Future Attack Scenarios

Turning to the future, all of the different targets of attack (i.e., humans, crops, and livestock), methods of dissemination (i.e., injection/direct contact, food and pharmaceutical contamination, water contamination, animal vectors, and airborne release), and objectives for threatening or carrying out a BCW attack (e.g., impact on a battlefield, deterrence or coercion by a state, imitation of a prior terrorist act, assassination, economic terrorism, and mass killing) discussed above are possible in the future, with smaller, less sophisticated attacks probably being the most likely. Terrorist threats, in particular, appear to be a growing problem, although the evidence for this is less compelling than is commonly believed.

Instead of inventing future scenarios from whole cloth, this section will analyze what would have happened in two historical cases had CW or BW actually been used successfully. The first case involves the use of Iraqi BCW-armed Scud missiles against Tel Aviv, Israel. The second case involves the release of anthrax and botulinum toxin, as was attempted by Aum Shinrikyo between 1992 and 1994 without success. Examining these two scenarios illustrates the consequences of possible future attack scenarios that cannot be dismissed as fanciful because they nearly occurred.

After the 1991 Gulf War it was discovered that Iraq had tested Scud missiles with chemical warheads (Iraq produced mustard gas, sarin, and VX), and that Iraq had 25 Scud missile warheads loaded with biological agents (16 with botulinum toxin, 5 with anthrax, 4 with aflatoxin), and 157 gravity bombs loaded with biological agents

(100 with botulinum toxin, 50 with anthrax, and 7 with aflatoxin).[60] None of these weapons were used during the war because Hussein either was holding them in reserve to deter the defeat of his regime, or US, British, French, and/or Israeli retaliatory threats stayed his hand.

The payload of the Iraqi Al Hussayn missile, the extended-range Scud B used to attack Israel and Saudi Arabia during the Gulf War, is approximately 500 kg with a range of approximately 650 km. The BCW warheads for these missiles were unitary warheads, with the agent released by an explosive charge. Therefore, for illustrative purposes, an Iraqi payload of 300 kg of sarin, or 300 kg of wet anthrax or botulinum toxin slurry (with an 0.03 percent dissemination efficiency for particles in the 1 to 5 micron size range) has been assumed. Eighty-eight missiles were launched during the war, starting on January 17, 1991, and ending on February 25, 1991, with all missiles launched at night to avoid US air attacks against the missile launchers. The expected fatalities from a single missle carrying sarin, anthrax, or botulinum toxin are shown in table 3-1 for attacks against Tel Aviv, assuming the missiles were launched at midnight, nominal values for the lethal doses for these BCW agents, weather data appropriate for the days on which the attacks occurred, and an average population density for Tel Aviv of approximately 6,500 people per square kilometer. The results in the table show the range of outcomes, due to variations in the weather, on the days the Al Hussayns were actually launched.

Aum Shinrikyo attempted to release anthrax and botulinum toxin into the air on eight different occasions, five of which occurred during June and July, 1993. Table 3-1 also provides estimates for the fatalities that could have occurred with a spray truck driving

60. See William J. Broad and Judith Miller, "How Iraq's Biological Weapons Program Came to Light," New York Times (Feb. 26, 1998), p. A1.

TABLE 3-1

Estimated Fatalities from Hypothetical BCW Attacks

Attack scenario	Estimated fatalities
Tel Aviv	
Al Hussayn; 300 kg sarin	1,000–6,000
Al Hussayn; 300 kg anthrax (0.03% dispersal)	20,000–180,000
Al Hussayn; 300 kg botulinum toxin (0.03% dispersal)	1,000–6,000
Tokyo	
Spray truck; 100 g anthrax (10 min., 1% dispersal)	6,500–13,000
Spray truck; 0.1 kg botulinum toxin (10 min. dispersal)	2–4
Spray from Aum building; 1kg anthrax (15 min., 1% dispersal)	150,000–750,000
Bomb; 10 kg sarin	30–50
Bomb; 1 kg anthrax (0.1% dispersal)	5,000–11,000

around downtown Tokyo (average population density of approximately 14,500 people per square kilometer) at 9:00 AM spraying 0.1 kilograms of anthrax slurry or botulinum toxin slurry over a period of 10 minutes. Again, the range of estimates reflects variations in the weather during June and July, 1993. The spray nozzle is assumed to be 1 percent efficient for generating 1 to 5 micron particles. The anthrax released from the roof of the Aum building in northeast Tokyo is assumed to be one kilogram of anthrax slurry sprayed over a period of 15 minutes with a dispersal efficiency of 1 percent. Finally, for comparison, the fatalities that might have resulted had Aum Shinrikyo opted for explosive release instead of spray release, with 10 kilograms of sarin or 1 kilogram of anthrax slurry in the bomb, are also shown in table 3-1.

Clearly, the potential exists for chemical attacks to cause on the order of tens to thousands of fatalities in these scenarios and for biological attacks to cause thousands to potentially hundreds of thousands of fatalities.

Concluding Observations

The logic of the argument that chemical and biological threats are on the rise appears to be valid. However, this does not necessarily imply that such attacks are likely, especially at the high end of the casualty spectrum. First, hurdles to BCW acquisition remain, especially for BW if spray dissemination is desired, although one can debate how much of a barrier such hurdles represent. Second, considerable uncertainty surrounds the degree to which the incentives to threaten or to use BCW are increasing. States that threaten US urban populations, as well as state-sponsored terrorism, probably can be deterred—especially if these hypothetical attacks cause tens, if not hundreds, of thousands of fatalities because of the very strong response that would follow (possibly including nuclear retaliation under some circumstances). The vast majority of terrorist groups are not likely to be interested in inflicting mass casualties, although the rise of religious, nihilist, and millenarian terrorist groups represents a disturbing trend.

Third, terrorist groups inclined toward using WMD against civilians are likely to have distinct signatures—for example, they talk openly about apocalyptic ends, they must acquire the necessary scientific and technical expertise and, like states, they frequently test their capabilities before they use them—which increases the opportunity for police and intelligence organizations to detect their presence and preempt any attacks, assuming the police and intelligence organizations are alert and trained for such events.[61] For example, were it not for the ban on police surveillance of religious organizations in Japan, it is quite likely that the nefarious activities of Aum

61. For a similar argument that the threat of nuclear, biological, and chemical terrorism is exaggerated in the US debate, in part, due to the ease with which these acts can be interdicted, see Ehud Sprinzak, "The Great Superterrorism Scare," 112 *Foreign Policy* (Fall 1998), pp. 110–24.

Shinrikyo would have been discovered well before the sarin attacks at Matsumoto and Tokyo.[62]

Therefore, it seems reasonable to conclude that future BCW episodes will be small, unsophisticated attacks, perhaps for the purpose of assassination or directed against a specific target (e.g., a federal building). In addition, hoaxes will be more likely than actual use, chemical attacks probably will be more likely than biological attacks, and threats or attacks using readily available industrial chemicals, poisons, or BCW agents will be more likely than ones using exotic BCW agents. The possibility that BCW threats might also be used for economic terrorism is worrisome. Large open-air releases, despite their potential lethality or perhaps because of it, will remain unlikely.

Nevertheless, the expected outcome (probability times consequences) associated with different BCW scenarios may be comparable. Moreover, the psychological impact of BCW threats or attacks is likely to be much larger than the physical impact. Therefore, prudence demands that steps be taken to cope with the potential for BCW threats across the entire spectrum. A combination of improved surveillance and intelligence, deterrence, interdiction, and civil defense programs should reduce whatever incentives might otherwise exist to use BCW and provide some protection in the unlikely event that an attack actually occurs.

Having said this, determining the level of funding appropriate for BCW preparedness relative to all other US national security concerns, not to mention determining the level of funding appropriate for each response option, is difficult to determine in an objective way. Programs that have multiple benefits obviously are pre-

---

62. These attacks occurred after the cult engaged in numerous criminal activities (including murder), after several years of experimenting with BW, and after tests of sarin gas against sheep located on a ranch the cult owned in Australia. See David E. Kaplan and Andrew Marshall, *The Cult at the End of the World.*

ferred—for example, improved infectious disease surveillance networks that have public health benefits and improve the ability to detect a biological attack early, or to detect an accidental release or intentional test of a biological agent thereby making covert programs more difficult to conceal; medical research into advanced antibiotics and vaccines that have public health as well as civil defense benefits; and research on advanced BCW agent detectors that have arms control verification, export control, and civil defense applications. The current US counter-terrorism annual budget is approximately $10 billion, of which approximately $3 billion has been added over the past few years to cope with WMD. Whether this is too much, not enough, or about right is hard to say with any confidence.

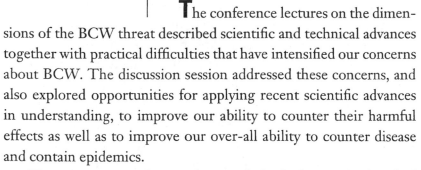

Commentary

The conference lectures on the dimensions of the BCW threat described scientific and technical advances together with practical difficulties that have intensified our concerns about BCW. The discussion session addressed these concerns, and also explored opportunities for applying recent scientific advances in understanding, to improve our ability to counter their harmful effects as well as to improve our over-all ability to counter disease and contain epidemics.

There is some good news along with the bad news. As Stanford University developmental biologist Dr. Lucy Shapiro emphasized during the conference discussion, the basic research that has advanced our ability to genetically engineer living organisms and create new pathogens has also made it possible to design compounds to destroy them or neutralize their effect. In addition we are developing and fielding more sensitive sensors able to detect and identify the presence of tiny quantities of threatening agents, as well as the onset of dangerous epidemics, more rapidly and reliably.

The implication of this is that there is a need for a coordinated effort in research and development across the government and in cooperation with the biotech industry and the large pharmaceutical houses. Progress in developing and designing new antibiotics is needed to stay ahead of new variants of pathogens that are already emerging in their own campaign of survival against current drugs. These antibiotics are needed if we are to hope to be able to stay ahead in the worldwide fight against disease, and to preserve our present condition of presumptive good health.

A commitment to basic medical research, a better communication system, and a focused medical intelligence effort are all called for to attack this problem. Public health issues that have to be addressed include understanding how to implement quarantines effectively and how to contain contagious outbreaks, and what are the legal implications of government restrictions. We face a number of difficult practical challenges, such as creating a system to deal with such issues effectively, and generating informed public awareness. If we can identify the strains of anthrax that have been stockpiled by a potential foe, we can decide whether to vaccinate all categories of people, military and civilian, for their protection. A determined adversary aware of such a program could, however, with modern biotechnical techniques alter his anthrax strains to render the immunization program useless. Facing this possibility, should we or should we not go ahead and vaccinate everybody and hope for the best? The same question applies to a decision on stockpiling antibiotics. Can our intelligence give us the necessary timely information so that we can prepare against the threatening pathogens? What surge capacity should (or can) we prepare to counter surprises? The challenges we face are difficult ones, to say the least.

Part of the good news offered by Dr. Margaret A. Hamburg,

Assistant Secretary for Planning and Evaluation, US Department of Health and Human Services, during the conference discussion, is that the Centers for Disease Control and Prevention are deeply engaged in this issue and their role will be expanding. Indeed the first line of defense in terms of detection and preparing rapid and appropriate responses comes from the public health institutions through their surveillance and epidemiology activities. This will also be important in terms of an effective global epidemiological network to counter disease. Such an effort has a dual value—for maintaining good health well as for providing enhanced protection against BW. This calls for increasingly integrating public health and health care into our thinking about bioterrorism. As Dr. Hamburg indicated, emergency monies are now starting to be invested in our public health infrastructure in order to begin the important work of assessing what we can do to build an appropriate stockpile of antibiotics and vaccines. Difficult questions remain, but at least we are becoming committed as a society, and are beginning at the local, regional, and national levels, to mobilize pharmaceutical resources that may be needed, and of value, in peace as well as in conflict.

Analogous measures are needed, and are being taken, with regard to chemical threats. Detection and public health responses that are speedy and effective are also being developed for CW, with government support. Here, as well, special capacities, training, and equipment will be necessary. But these measures should be worked out in cooperation with local and state public health and safety agencies, who are and will remain first responders to chemical threats, whether deliberately or accidentally caused.

Part Two

The Role of Intelligence

Sidney D. Drell

 # Introductory Remarks

This part of the conference proceedings focuses on the challenge of BCW to the US Intelligence Community (IC). How is the threat evolving and presenting new challenges to the IC? What responses are available to it, both technically and structurally, to meet these challenges and to prepare for the threats that we face in the future? In defining the role of intelligence for achieving warning and detection of threats, what *is* in fact the proper role of the IC and how can it best interact with the policy community for maximum effectiveness?

John C. Gannon

The US Intelligence Community and the Challenge of BCW

Stepping in as the eleventh-hour substitute for a dynamic boss such as mine, Director of Central Intelligence (DCI) George J. Tenet, I fear, is a high-risk business. I can safely say, however, that Director Tenet wanted very much to attend the Hoover Institution's November 1998 conference because he believes that the United States faces a disturbing and growing challenge from biological and chemical weapons (BCW).

I can personally attest that the Intelligence Community (IC) is working hard against the BCW target. I saw this firsthand as former DCI John Deutch's Deputy Director for Intelligence, in charge of the office with administrative responsibility for the DCI's Nonproliferation Center (NPC), and now as Mr. Tenet's Chairman of the National Intelligence Council, which has senior experts helping to guide IC intelligence production on proliferation. This is, and must be, a collaborative effort drawing together knowledge and expertise from inside and outside the US Government (USG).

I want to recognize three individuals who have played critical roles in building the IC's BCW program.

First, John Lauder, a valued colleague and friend of mine for many years, is the current chief of NPC. John, who took part in a panel at the conference, is an extraordinarily able, agile, and unflappable leader—a sort of one-man confidence-building measure—and is making a big, positive difference today.

Next, Gordon Oehler, John's predecessor as NPC chief, broke paths on proliferation at CIA and in the larger IC for a generation, as a top-notch analyst admired for the rigor of his work, as an accomplished National Intelligence Officer, as the Director of CIA's Office of Scientific and Weapons Research, and as the widely respected head of NPC. Gordon, history will note, developed NPC's strategic plan, which showed a far-flung IC how to conceptualize the complex proliferation problem and how, in a practical way, to mobilize against it. I was blessed to work with Gordon when I was Deputy Director for Intelligence. No finer mind or better man has come CIA's way.

And, third, Sidney Drell. Many will be familiar with Sid as a brilliant theoretical physicist whose impressive academic career parallels a nearly forty-year run as a much-respected USG technical adviser on national security and defense issues. I also know Sid as a particularly productive member of the President's Foreign Intelligence Advisory Board (PFIAB) and the Non-Proliferation Panel. In these capacities, Sid has been more of a determined coach than a professor, prodding us relentlessly to improve our performance on proliferation.

The organizers of the conference rightly point out that throughout the Cold War, while world leaders were preoccupied with the threat of a nuclear holocaust, more and more nations — largely unnoticed— were acquiring the ability to produce BCW.

George Shultz was among the few statesmen who recognized the threat. No one argued more tenaciously and eloquently than he did for the adoption of the Chemical Weapons Convention (CWC). Indeed, one of his final acts as Secretary of State was to address the CWC conference in Paris in January 1989, where he challenged the international community to adopt the CWC. The secretary asked: "Must it take a fresh shock of human tragedy—must more places like Flanders Fields find their place in the history books through the particular ghastliness of their destruction before governments work together to restore respect for the international norms against CW use?"

Today we recognize that BCW are *not* just a wartime concern, but a clear and constant danger for us at home and abroad. Our prestige and high profile as a global power make us the world's biggest and most dispersed target. Think about it: our deployed military, our embassies abroad, our international commercial interests, and, yes, even our home towns.

The Threat as We See It

There are four key points, and one corollary, in all that I will discuss here.

1. The BCW threat is real and growing.
2. The number of potential perpetrators is increasing, particularly nonstate actors.
3. Agents of increasing lethality are being developed, with the potential to cause massive casualties.
4. The IC alone cannot eliminate this threat, nor can any other single institution or sector. Defeating the BCW threat will take a concerted, collaborative, and integrated approach across national and regional governments, law enforcement,

the military, the private sector, the world of medicine, the academic and scientific communities, and the media.

And the corollary: The conference has taken us in the right direction by educating us all to the grave BCW challenges we face and to the need to combine resources to deal with these challenges effectively.

The development, possession, and use of these abhorrent weapons are banned by domestic law and international treaty. The US and other concerned governments are working hard to slow proliferation. Nonetheless, the number of players possessing or acquiring BCW clandestinely is substantial and mounting.

More than a dozen states, including several that are hostile to Western democracies—Iran, Iraq, Libya, North Korea, Sudan, and Syria—now either possess or are actively pursuing offensive CW and/or BW capabilities for use against their perceived enemies, whether internal or external. Many of these countries are pursuing an asymmetric warfare capability and see BCW as the best means to counter overwhelming US conventional military superiority. Several states are also pursuing BCW programs for counterinsurgency use and tactical applications in regional conflicts, increasing the probability that such conflicts will be deadly and destabilizing. In the 1980s, Iraq used CW against its own Kurdish population and against Iran during the Iran–Iraq War. The BW program that Iraq initiated in 1985 rapidly escalated to production and weaponization, constituting a potential threat to allied forces during the Gulf War.

As the Iraq case so dramatically demonstrates, even a residual state BCW capability can be highly dangerous. After four and one-half years of claiming that it had conducted only "defensive research" on BW, Iraq finally admitted in 1995 that it had produced a half million liters of refined and unrefined biological agents such as anthrax. Of course, the United Nations Special Commission (UNSCOM) believes that Iraq produced substantially greater amounts—

three to four times greater. On the CW side, UNSCOM's recent discovery of VX in Iraqi warheads shows that for seven years the Iraqis have been lying to the international community when they repeatedly said they had never weaponized VX.

Beyond state actors, the number of terrorist groups seeking to develop or acquire BCW capabilities is increasing. And many such groups, like Osama bin Laden's, have international networks. That adds to uncertainty and to the danger of a surprise attack. The constraints on nonstate actors, of course, are much less than on state-sponsored programs.

The casualty figures of the Aum Shinrikyo attack in Tokyo three and one-half years ago could have been much higher if the group had not used a combination of impure sarin agent and inefficient delivery systems. As it was, twelve people were killed and more than 5,000 needed medical treatment.

Osama bin Laden and his network also have shown a strong interest in CW. We know that bin Laden's organization has attempted to develop poisonous gases that could be fired at US troops in the Gulf states. The discovery of the VX precursor EMPTA at a factory in Sudan that had known ties to bin Laden indicates how close he may have been to achieving his goal.

Adding more unpredictability are the "lone militants," or the ad hoc groups here at home and abroad (and there are plenty of them) who may try to conduct a BCW attack.

Take the Ramzi Yousef case. There are indications that Yousef was planning to use cyanide in the World Trade Center bombing and that he had planned to use chemical agents on other occasions. And with "how to" guides like the "Anarchist's Cookbook" available commercially and on the internet, loners can easily design and build their own weapons.

To add to the threat, a growing number of bad actors can choose from a widening array of new agents and new delivery systems. BCW agents, as many of you know, are becoming more sophisticated and more effective. Rapid advances in biotechnology will yield new toxins or live agents, such as exotic animal viruses, that will require new detection methods and vaccines as well as other preventive measures. We are also concerned that some states might acquire more advanced and effective chemical agents, such as Russia's fourth-generation "Novichok" agents, which are more deadly and more persistent. Gains in genetic engineering and "designer drug" chemical agents are making it increasingly difficult for us to *recognize* all the agents threatening us.

Meanwhile, advances are occurring in dissemination techniques, delivery options, and strategies for use. We are worried that several countries of concern will weaponize BCW warheads for ballistic missiles.

We see other qualitative changes that present growing challenges to our detection and deterrence efforts.

Some countries are developing indigenous programs. That limits our interdiction opportunities. Iran is a case in point. Tehran— driven, in part, by stringent international export controls—has set about acquiring the capability to produce domestically the raw materials and equipment needed to support BCW agent production.

Denial and deception techniques, meanwhile, are becoming more effective in concealing and protecting BCW programs. Concealment is simpler with BW than with CW because there is more overlap between legitimate research and commercial biotechnology. That said, in both cases clandestine BCW research can be readily conducted in supposedly "legitimate" facilities and such facilities can convert rapidly to BCW production.

Two other phenomena complicate the problems. First, scientists with transferable know-how continue to leave the former Soviet Union, some with undesirable destinations. Second, the struggle to control dual-use technologies only gets harder, with smaller forces ready to transform opportunities for human betterment into threats of human destruction.

Russia's current economic woes, of course, could exacerbate the "brain drain" problem. By importing talent and buying technology, state and nonstate actors can make dramatic leaps forward in all the areas I just mentioned—the development of new agents and delivery systems, a much earlier achievement of indigenous capabilities, and more sophisticated denial and deception techniques. In short, hostile actors can purchase the invaluable advantage of "technological surprise."

Regarding the dual-use problem: The same technology that is used for good today, can, if it falls into the wrong hands, be used for evil tomorrow. The overlap between biological agents and vaccines and between chemical agents and pesticides is, as you know, considerable. The technologies used to prolong our lives and improve our standard of living can quite easily be used to cause mass casualties. In the biological field especially, the security community and the public probably do not fully appreciate how widely available BW technology is—in part, because all societies have a legitimate need and use for it.

Intelligence is all about ascertaining the capabilities and—even more important—the *intentions* of one's adversaries. But getting at "intent" is the hardest thing to do—getting inside Kim Jong Il's or Saddam's or bin Laden's head, if you will. What a chilling thought! Dual use goes to the very crux of the "intent" challenge.

What US Intelligence Does to Counter the BCW Threat

Let me now describe some of what US Intelligence is doing to counter the BCW threat, in addition to seeking closer collaboration with many of you.

The IC's efforts to counter the BCW threat are, speaking broadly, composed of three interrelated elements—One: Assessment and warning. Two: Deterrence and protection. Three: Monitoring arms control regimes.

First, the ultimate objective of our intelligence mission is to save American lives and protect America's vital interests. The IC's greatest responsibility is to warn the president and other decisionmakers and our war-fighters, so that they can make timely and effective decisions. For example, the National Intelligence Council, which I am privileged to lead, is very concerned about the BCW threat and is working to keep policymakers informed on this critical issue.

Second, the IC intensively focuses its intelligence assets—both human and technical—on deterring the activities of actors who possess, or seek to develop or acquire, key components needed for CW and BW. Our efforts set back Libya's CW program about ten years by focusing international attention on the Rabta and Tarhunah facilities and by preventing Libya from obtaining needed chemicals, equipment, and experts. Now, thirteen years later, Libya, after spending a great deal of money, has only a small amount of agent and two facilities it dares not use for their intended purpose. If Qaddafi had been left undisturbed, he could by now have had thousands of tons of a variety of chemical agents and the ability to produce much more at will. We are justifiably proud of this achievement, but we recognize all too well that a tactical success does not lessen the strategic BCW threat we face.

The IC also provides the information required for the Department of Defense and the military to protect our forces from the effects of enemy use of CBW agents. We have provided intelligence on evolving chemical and biological agents, their means of delivery, and their expected effects.

Third, we have provided policymakers with evidence that parties might be engaged in prohibited activities under various international control regimes, including the Australia Group export control regime, and the Biological and Chemical Weapons Conventions. Moreover, our intelligence input has helped negotiators draft tighter and more verifiable agreements.

What About Tomorrow?

Consider our warning challenge. America is no longer an insular nation protected by two large oceans. The battlefield of the future could be Main Street, USA. Our enemies—be they states launching BCW-tipped missiles or terrorists concealing small vials of virus—can bring the BCW threat to our own shores and heartland. Warning time may be all but eliminated.

Another big question we must revisit is: Who now do we warn? If we have evidence of an imminent domestic attack, we need to warn not just the president and senior policymakers, we also need to get the information—and get it fast—to police and fire chiefs, hospitals, and pharmaceutical companies that would produce vaccines. In fact, if time were of the essence, one could argue that first-responders—the local authorities—should be alerted at the same time as we warn the president. We must pursue and develop stronger and tighter links with first-responders, the public health community, law enforcement, and private industry.

We have already taken some important steps in this direction. For the first time, the DCI's Counterterrorist Center, in concert with the FBI, is providing terrorism threat-related products to state and local officials. John Lauder, the NPC Chief I lionized a short while ago, recently attended a meeting at the FBI in which first-responders from all over the Washington metropolitan area gathered to discuss BCW incident response. It was the first time a senior nonproliferation official sat side by side and exchanged ideas with police and fire chiefs. We need to work more with federal and local authorities to put some mechanism, some pipeline, in place that has enough bandwidth to get the right information quickly to the right people at all levels in time to avert the worst.

As a country, we have only started to develop strategies for limiting the damage and managing the consequences should a BCW attack occur. It is good that we have begun. We are light years ahead of other countries on this. But we are far from prepared.

With regard to the IC's deterrence and disruption function, let me tell you: The current expectation that US Intelligence will be able to thwart future BCW attacks is exceedingly high. Our fear is *not* that someday, somewhere, an attack will succeed and the IC will be accused of failure. Our fear is that people will die—a lot of people. The ominous trends I described earlier—the growing number of actors wishing us harm, and their growing ability to cloak their BCW capabilities and intentions—mean that the odds of a successful attack are increasing despite our vigilance.

The nonproliferation effort in the IC does not constitute a Manhattan Project operation. By that, I mean an operation in which leading experts from all over the country have been pulled in and assembled in one place to work on a single, definable product like building the atomic bomb. Our goal is different—effectively countering an array of constantly evolving targets. At CIA we have indeed gathered some dedicated in-house talent. Much talent also resides elsewhere in the USG and beyond, and we are working the BCW issue cross-community and with the Department of Defense and other government agencies as never before. But the talent we have is not sufficient, and additional resources alone will not solve the problem. In peacetime, it is not realistic to expect that the government can pull in America's leading engineers and scientists as we did for the Manhattan Project. The next best thing we can do—and it is critical that we do it—is to reach out and tap into that pool of expertise that resides in the public-health sector, and the chemical and biotech industries.

During last spring and summer, two distinguished officials, Admiral David Jeremiah and former Defense Secretary Donald Rumsfeld, chaired separate panels that scrutinized the IC's performance in two areas where we failed to provide adequate warning to our customers. A common theme in each report was that the IC needed to be far more aggressive in engaging outside expertise in assessing issues of highest priority to our customers. This is especially true in the scientific and technical fields where the best expertise can be found in universities and industry. The DCI recently approved a Strategic Estimates Program, to be managed by the National Intelligence Council, that has at its core a drive to bring experts into our production effort to help ensure that we get the issues and analyses right and point our collection efforts against the correct targets.

To that end, the DCI has created a senior scientist position within CIA's Nonproliferation Center, and has just hired Dr. Thomas Monath, whom many of you may know as one of the world's leading arbovirologists, to fill this part-time position. Tom remains Vice President of Research and Medical Affairs at OraVax, Inc., a biopharmaceutical firm based in Cambridge, Massachusetts. Before joining OraVax in 1992, he had a distinguished career in public service as the Chief of the Virology Division at the US Army Medical Research Institute of Infectious Diseases at Fort Detrick, Maryland, and as Medical Director of the Division of Vector-Borne Infectious Diseases at the Centers for Disease Control in Fort Collins, Colorado.

With respect to intelligence support for monitoring regimes: Almost by definition, efforts are heavily oriented toward *state* actors. I would only repeat the obvious point that international strategies for monitoring and controlling proliferation by *nonstate* actors is an area that governments and intergovernmental treaties and intelligence communities, including ours, are still trying to get their arms around. The CWC is a step in the right direction because it mandates legislation criminalizing production of CW, giving law enforcement authorities greater ability to preempt chemical attacks. That said, had the CWC been in effect at the time of the Tokyo subway incident, it probably would have had no preventive effect, because the Aum Shinrikyo assembled its CW capabilities largely through its own member scientists and network of front companies.

We need to think more about how we can exert US leadership to heighten international awareness of the growing BCW threat. I do not think that even friendly governments fully recognize how ominous the trends are. *America today is less aware and prepared for the effects of a chemical or biological attack than it should be.* As important as I think that statement is, you should know that other countries are even less aware and less prepared.

We also need to reinforce the message—and the Departments of State and Defense can play key roles here—that nonproliferation efforts do not benefit the United States alone; they benefit everyone on the planet Earth—except, of course, the proliferators. To the maximum extent possible, nonproliferation initiatives should be multinational. Even though other countries may not have the range of capabilities the US has to counter the BCW threat, they can still contribute in other ways—for instance, diplomatically or by virtue of being uniquely situated to provide key information.

Other Intelligence Dilemmas

That's the big picture. Now, let me describe some practical dilemmas that US Intelligence professionals constantly face as they work to counter the BCW threat. Some of these dilemmas are not exclusive to our BCW work; they apply to intelligence work and arms control efforts in general. I will mention the most vexing.

First dilemma: In a perfect world, intelligence always heads off the bad guys at the pass before they can do any damage. In an *almost* perfect world, we catch them red-handed with the smoking gun. But, in our *far less than perfect* world, no matter how hard we work or how many assets we bring to bear, we still may be able only to find pieces of an ominous puzzle. It is our duty to inform policymakers of what we know—even when our information is, admittedly, incomplete. Why? So that our political leaders can take prudent steps to protect American lives and defend American interests.

Second dilemma: When we *find* the smoking gun, we rarely can get the full benefit of the discovery. We must balance the policy benefits of using it against damage to sources and methods. The most compelling evidence is often the most sensitive as well. If we share this information with another government, we run serious risk of losing a human asset or compromising another important source.

Telling our story in public is even riskier, but we have been called upon to do that on several occasions in the BCW arena. Following the controversy over the Shifa pharmaceutical plant in Sudan, we released more information than we would have liked. The sad result in many such cases is that it can become more difficult to do our job in the future. This is an age-old trade-off that comes from the continuous give and take between the IC and its customers in the policy community.

Another dilemma: Our intelligence information is often unwelcome to those who selfishly resort to plausible deniability for reasons of political expediency. There have been many cases in which we tried to stop shipments of BCW-related material to proliferants, only to have the supplier country smugly reply that, since there were *some legitimate* uses for these goods and we could not *prove* that they were *solely* intended for BCW use, it would not stop the transaction.

One final dilemma: No matter what we say or do, what we say and do will be subject to controversy and scrutiny in our democracy. Make no mistake: We'd rather we had a vigorous democracy and the dilemma than no democracy and no dilemma! But our adversaries' propaganda and their denial and deception strategies for BCW exploit our dilemma in every way they can. Many countries were able to carry out illicit programs for years under a cloak of legitimacy. Libya still insists that its CW plant at Rabta is a pharmaceutical plant. The Iraqis called their CW production facility a pesticide plant and their main BW facility an animal feed plant.

We found solid evidence of CW activity at Shifa in Khartoum. Sophisticated tests done on soil samples revealed the presence of

EMPTA, a key precursor for the nerve agent VX. Perhaps if our information had been derived by less technical means, means more readily understood by the public, the case would not have been received with such skepticism. But, I emphasize, the evidence was solid. Moreover, the evidence fit into the ominous pattern we had been piecing together against bin Laden and his network. Bin Laden had attacked Americans before and he said he planned to do so again. He was seeking CW to use in future attacks. He was cooperating with the government of Sudan in those efforts. Shifa was linked to bin Laden and CW. We brought the evidence and our analyses to the president, and he took decisive action.

All these dilemmas come with the intelligence territory. Dedicated intelligence officers must confront and deal with them case by case, bringing our professional experience and our best judgment to bear, as we did in the case of Shifa.

Concluding Thoughts

Almost a decade has passed since Secretary Shultz made his impassioned plea for adoption of the CWC and challenged the international community to do better. He was right then and he is right now. We can and we must do better.

We no longer live in a bipolar world where deterrence was more straightforward and kept the nuclear and BCW threat at bay. Over the past ten years, the threat has become much greater. We face more proliferators, more elusive and sophisticated targets, and a whole new array of BCW agents.

The growing BCW threat cannot be met by US intelligence alone, but US intelligence will be crucial in meeting it. As I said at the outset, to deal effectively with the evolving BCW challenge, we all need to think together and work together in new ways. National and local governments, the military, medical world, law enforcement, private sector, the academic and scientific communities, the media, the communities you and I live in all across our country, and the world as well—all of us must contribute.

Let me close with a caveat, or, better put, an appeal for context. Woody Allen tells us that mankind today is at a crossroads. One path leads to hopelessness and despair, the other to total annihilation. Is my message simply a variation on Woody's theme? If you don't get hit by a North Korean ICBM over the next five years, chances are you will suffer a horrible, premature death when Osama bin Laden poisons your hometown water supply! Surely, we wanted to do more in the conference than set each other's hair on fire and try to put it out with a hammer! I call the BCW threat grave today at least in part because we have not collectively defined the problem and joined forces to deal with it. We are, as a result, more open to a serious incident and to surprise in general. This should make us pessimistic today. But it need not remove the possibility of a more hopeful outlook tomorrow—if we get on top of the problem. Believe it or not, after twenty years in the intelligence business, I still remain optimistic about the future of mankind and about the potential of America's people and institutions to assure that future.

My hope is that this conference will result in a set of concrete action items to get us moving in harness against the BCW threat. I want to assure you that the IC is ready and eager to do its part.

Gordon C. Oehler

Warning and Detection

A few years ago, Senator Arlen Spec-
ter displayed a chart to the US Senate that showed some ninety-six
different elements of the executive branch that were involved in
some manner with efforts to stop the proliferation of weapons of
mass destruction (WMD). His reason for showing this, clearly, was
to point out the need for greater central direction—a nonproliferation czar.

Senator Specter was right that all these government entities had
a role to play. After all, a comprehensive program to counter proliferation, including terrorist use of biological and chemical weapons
(BCW), is a very complex undertaking. It would cover everything
from preventing an opponent from acquiring WMD materials and
technologies, through preparing domestic law enforcement, medical, and emergency responders to deal with an attack in this country,

to equipping and training the US military to fight on a battlefield where WMD is used.

By any account, the costs associated with an even moderately effective biological terrorist attack, measured both in human and dollar terms, would be tremendous. For this reason, anything we can do to prevent an attack from occurring should be a top priority.

For terrorist threats originating outside the US, it falls on the US Intelligence Community (IC) to detect, warn, and sometimes disrupt terrorist planning. The IC thus has a critical (one can argue even the most critical) role to play in combating foreign terrorism. In fact, it would be fair to say that, without intelligence, there is no US Government (USG) nonproliferation or counterterrorism policy, and little hope of preventing attacks.

Unfortunately, full funding of intelligence activities does not guarantee that plans for an attack will be detected. Intelligence operations have had a mixed record over the years. But, if there is a chance that greater intelligence capabilities can offer a higher probability of threat detection, it should merit the attention of those responsible for allocating resources. It does seem to be, after all, the ultimate ounce of prevention.

Until recently, there have been two arguments for *not* expanding counterterrorism funding to cover BCW. The first is that, in the opinion of those who argued these points, the probability of a significant BW or CW attack was remote, and therefore it would be a waste of money. Second, the belief that the attack could be carried out by "two guys working out of a garage," who would stand little chance of being detected, regardless of the intelligence resources, and thus once again the additional resources would be wasted.

Neither of these two arguments has gone away. But recent knowledge and experience suggests that they are not the best bets. For the first argument, the bombings of New York City's World Trade Center, Khobar Towers in Saudi Arabia, and the US embassies in Kenya and Tanzania have shown that modern-day terrorists' objectives are simply to kill as many Americans as possible. And reporting has shown that Ramzi Yousef and Osama bin Laden were aware of the potential for BW and CW terrorism and were investigating its possible use.

Second, popular stories about the ease of manufacturing biological and chemical agents mask the major technology required for a successful attack—the weaponization of the agent. Even the Japanese cult Aum Shinrikyo, with all its wealth and scientific talent, really blew the weaponization aspect, especially in the ineffective release of biological agents. Therefore, any terrorist group that is small enough (the "two guys in a garage") to ensure secrecy will probably not have the range of talents needed to pull off a major BW attack, and will most likely make mistakes. A group that does have all the necessary skills will probably be large enough that it would be vulnerable to international counterterrorism efforts. Either way, a robust intelligence capability stands a chance to detect and stop a major attack.

On this score, much has been written lately about "stateless" terrorists, as opposed to state-sponsored terrorists. There is less of a distinction than meets the public eye. David K. Schenker, writing for the Washington Institute for Near East Policy, stated that Osama bin Laden, for instance, has had plenty of state support from Iran and Sudan.[1] Thus, here too, intelligence has more opportunities than might otherwise be thought.

The bottom line is that intelligence operations can make a powerful contribution, and that we therefore need to examine closely our intelligence capabilities. What should we expect from our intelligence agencies? Are we as effective as we could be? Is the level of funding appropriate for the level of protection we could achieve?

1. David K. Schenker, "Bin Laden and the Problem of State-Supported Terrorism," Washington Institute for Near East Policy, Policywatch No. 346 (Oct. 21, 1998).

Difficult questions to be sure, some answers to which will be suggested below.

In addition, the discussion will consider at least three areas where current weaknesses are affecting our intelligence capabilities:

- Shortcomings within the intelligence process
- Tensions with policymakers
- Shortage of technology support

Shortcomings within the Intelligence Process

To begin, intelligence efforts *are* having an effect. Perhaps the most recent example that has been publicized was the thwarting of the bomb plot against the US Embassy in Uganda.[2] This occurred shortly after the two successful terrorist bombings of our embassies in East Africa, and for obvious reasons did not receive the same level of attention. But, to be a little silly here (but not much), compare the cost of halting the Ugandan operation versus the cost to the US and the local citizens of the two successful embassy bombings in Kenya and Tanzania in August 1998.

Successes do not line pockets as much as failures do. How quick we are to find funds to fix problems after a disaster. How difficult it is to find preventive funds. That, of course, has always been the case. But this is different today. We cannot afford even one significant biological terrorist act against us before we learn this lesson.

The IC does about as well in counterterrorism activities as it does in any area of intelligence, but some recent findings still show weaknesses in over-all intelligence capabilities. For example, the Rumsfeld and Jeremiah Commission reports, which were asked to

---

2. Michael Grunwald, "CIA Halted Plot to Bomb U.S. Embassy in Uganda," *Washington Post* (Sept. 25, 1998), p. A27.

review perceived intelligence failures, both described a number of systemic weaknesses.

So, although US Intelligence has made, and continues to make, a valuable contribution to detecting and warning of BW and CW attacks—including terrorist attacks—the apparent consensus is that there is room for improvement.

Some of the weaknesses are *not* of their own making. Rather, they are due to the tough budget and recruitment environments they face. Of major concern are the significant reductions in both budgets and personnel since the end of the Cold War. It is high time we face up to the fact that the Cold War intelligence "peace dividend" is a myth. We need to admit that the Russian/East European problems have not gone away—just changed. And we also need to admit that the Soviets kept some of these problems suppressed, and that when the Soviet Union went away, these problems mushroomed for the US. Yet the budgets and personnel counts came down anyway.

Some of the weaknesses *are* of their own making. This is not intended to be critical, for good people in the IC are doing the best they can. Rather, the need is to give an idea of the constraints they are operating under so that we can better appreciate what our real capabilities for detection and warning are. Moreover, and perhaps most importantly, a better understanding of the shortcomings will lead to more involvement in developing the solutions to these shortcomings. Let us look at the shortcomings, in no particular order.

Difficulty in Hiring Skilled Technical People

In the old days, the country's high-tech research and development was done in classified programs—either in the defense or intelligence arenas. Technologists working for the CIA were at the state of the art. Research and development (R&D) budgets were sufficiently large such that high-risk development programs were common.

Today, the situation is very different. Most state-of-the-art development is done in the commercial sector. R&D budgets for working with commercial technology developers have been slashed. What programs are funded must be proven to be able to succeed before funds are allocated, ruling out high-risk, high-potential payoff developments. The centralization of the National Reconnaissance Office (NRO), where the only major pot of development money remains, removed many of the CIA's best technologists from day-to-day contact with operators and analysts in the rest of the CIA.

And finally, the explosive need for technologists in the commercial sector has led to salaries for the best scientific and technical talent that the IC cannot match. Salaries for technical intelligence personnel have seldom been equal to those in industry, but the IC has been in the past able to recruit and keep good people on the basis of the importance and excitement of the mission. But the salary differences are too great now to maintain a topflight technical staff.

Poor Understanding of the Opportunities Brought on by Technology Developments

For many of the reasons stated above, most managers in the CIA do not have a good appreciation of the technical developments shaping the world. Consequently, they do not have a vision of what the future will look like and what technologies they need to acquire to be able to operate in the future world.

Poor Ability to Deal with Foreign Languages

The end of the Cold War has placed the IC in a far more complex world, requiring attention to many more languages than before. This has, in some measure, resulted from newly emerging threats in countries that, in the past, were of little strategic interest. Perhaps an even greater reason is that, with the new independence of the former client states of the Soviet Union, these nations now demand to use their own languages for international diplomacy and international commerce. There is an urgent need for the IC to develop broad capabilities in these languages.

Poor language capabilities have long been a shortcoming and a criticism of the IC. Very few analysts in the Directorate of Intelligence, for example, can understand the newspapers and other native language materials of the countries they are responsible for studying.

The problem is not that foreign language capabilities are not appreciated—in fact salary bonuses are available to persons who learn and maintain critical language skills. The problem instead is that virtually no foreign language materials are available to the analysts through the medium they spend the majority of their time surveying—the computer terminals on their desks. With the voluminous quantities of official reporting they face each day in English over their desktop terminals, coupled with the inability of CIA's document storage, retrieval, and word-processing capabilities for most of the world's languages, there is little incentive or ability to reach much beyond English.

This shortcoming hurts most in long-term research and cultural understandings. The Foreign Broadcast Information Service (FBIS) does a reasonable job in mining the major foreign newspapers, radio, and television broadcasts for items of current importance. But the bandwidth to the analysts is limited by the translation bottleneck.

The solution requires a number of steps—most importantly is that the data information systems need to be updated to handle foreign language storage, retrieval, and presentation on the analysts' desktops. Next, the providers of information to the analysts need to open the spigot and start creating foreign language research databases. Finally, the IC needs to develop or acquire simple tools to allow analysts to find their way around these databases. Only then, when the analysts have the ability, ease, and the need to work with foreign language materials in parallel with English, will language skills finally improve.

Structural Impediments to Surging on Rapidly Emerging Problems

The intelligence target during the Cold War changed in an evolutionary way at best. Today's problems can change in very revolutionary ways. What might be a problem of major concern today could go away next week. Problems can and do crop up overnight in regions where collection priorities had been low. This has led to considerable interest in how the CIA, for example, can better surge in reaction to these fast-changing events.

However, surging in the CIA hasn't been easy. The reasons are complex, but basically come down to how work tasks are assigned. In short, analysts are given accounts and are expected to handle everything from understanding and tasking collection resources, gathering all relevant information, analyzing the data, and reporting to the customer.

But if we limit our "surge" pool to those who are familiar with the problem *and* the intelligence process *and* the IC's collection capabilities *and* the production process *and* the customers' preferences, then it is easy to see why surging is so difficult and done so occasionally. In fact, previous studies of surge capabilities usually come to the conclusion that we need to create a pool of retirees, who are kept fully cleared and available on call.

There is one other clue that helps point to the solution—over the past ten years, whenever the CIA was faced with a new and high-priority problem, it responded by creating a center or a task force to deal with it. This is proof that existing structures are incapable of dealing with the complex and rapidly changing nature of today's important problems.

Task forces and centers are first of all task-oriented. But more than that, task forces and centers make more use of teams than mainline organizations because their size, composition, and often agency or community representation responsibilities tend to force teamwork. The authorities and flexibilities of task forces and centers allow bringing in specialists to address specific aspects of the problem. These lessons need to be learned in the mainline organization. Thus, the solution is to avoid assigning accounts to individuals. Create teams where persons with expertise in one area can contribute even if they are not steeped in the broad range of intelligence skills.

Overemphasis on Tactical Support to the Military

The past few years have seen a major shift in emphasis toward intelligence support to the tactical commanders in the military. This has not come without costs. All imagery analysts, for example, have been transferred to a new agency, the National Imagery and Mapping Agency, placed in the Department of Defense, and led by a senior military officer. Perhaps of greater concern, though, has been the "Defensification" of the National Reconnaissance Office (NRO). Because highly classified intelligence reporting cannot be distributed directly to tactical commanders, there is a real tendency to downgrade the classification of sensitive intelligence products and to fund only systems that will collect low-classification information. This has transformed the NRO from the spy agency it once was into more of a data-collection agency today.

The recent failure to detect preparations for the Indian nuclear tests is a good example of the problem. Knowledge of our imagery-collection capabilities has been spread widely. This made it easy for the Indians to spoof our imagery analysts. The problem here is not that overhead imagery is widely used, but rather that we have failed to keep up the spying end of intelligence collection. Where was the collection system that did have access to the needed intelligence and that was truly clandestine? Again, we can show that lots of bytes of data were collected, but they did not answer the mail. What suffers from this overemphasis on tactical military support is the traditional, long-lead-time weapons capabilities and plans and intentions intelligence collection that can only come from clandestine systems.

Inability to Take Advantage of Modern Information Management Tools

The IC is facing all of the same problems in modernizing its information management systems as is industry—funds siphoned off for Y2K remediation, transition from legacy systems on mainframes, network maintenance, and more. But, the IC has one additional burden—an overbearing security environment. This has placed major barriers to sharing information across agency boundaries and even within agencies.

The recent spy cases involving Aldrich Ames and Harold Nicholson have only served to heighten computer security concerns. Both Ames and Nicholson downloaded information from computer systems for passing to the Russians. And even though they both had proper access privileges to the databases, this is somehow viewed as a computer security problem. The reaction is to further restrict communications and increase data ownership privileges.

Perhaps a bigger problem is the restrictions on the types of applications and programming languages. Many of the modern developments in software that are driving commercial packages have security vulnerabilities. Nevertheless, these applications and languages are coming into widespread use on public networks because of the enhanced capabilities they provide. No doubt a good case can be made for the security risks. But what of the risks and costs of not keeping up with modern software developments? These costs, at a minimum, include a loss of efficiency by the users and a continuing need to develop custom software, with its attendant high life-cycle costs. More serious is the inability to respond rapidly to new ways of handling information and, probably worst of all, a less than attractive information management environment when we need just the opposite to recruit and retain the best qualified people we can get to fight the chemical and biological terrorist problem.

Tensions with Policymakers

If our intelligence agencies correctly gather, analyze, and report a potential attack or terrorist incident, our problems are not necessarily over. Failures—usually still called intelligence failures—can occur if there is not a knowledgeable and willing customer for the intelligence product. In other words, there needs to be a great deal of trust between the administration and its intelligence services. Even then, the relationship can sometimes be difficult.

One reason for a less than totally efficient coupling between intelligence agencies and any administration is that intelligence information is most tenuous early in the threat's development. And although this gives an administration the most lead time, most decisionmakers would prefer more definitive information before acting. But by the time the more definitive information is gathered, it is often too late to take any action.

As an example of this, the IC's performance was questioned after Saddam Hussein's invasion of Kuwait in August 1990. Recall that the Iraqis had moved much materiel to the border in the two weeks before the invasion. This movement was of course monitored carefully by the IC, but the question was whether this was a bluff or whether Saddam really intended to invade. During this review of the IC's performance, a senior official noted that, if there was a failure, it was not made in the two weeks before the invasion, because the US could not have responded with military forces that quickly. Ideally, warning should have come much earlier. But if the IC had predicted an invasion back in the March time frame, when the US could have reacted militarily, the administration would have no doubt dismissed the report.

Another possible source of friction between an administration and its intelligence agencies comes from congressionally mandated sanctions. One can argue that sanctions legislation and the administration's actions to circumvent this legislation create an environment that can lead to intelligence failures.

No administration wishes to have its negotiating flexibility diminished by legislation that calls for the automatic imposition of sanctions. But rather than working with Congress to improve the legislation, administrations have chosen to believe sanctions can be avoided simply by arguing that the quality of the intelligence data never quite meets the thresholds requiring action. This has a perverse effect on the entire intelligence/policy process. When the IC brings data relating to sanctions to the table, the administration assumes the role of a defense attorney for the accused, rather than that of an objective customer. At a minimum, this can create an adversarial relationship between the IC and arguably its most important customer, and it leads to a demoralized community less willing to bring controversial issues forward. It can also lead to senior IC officials' taking the part of their executive branch customers, arguing against the strength of their own analysts' judgments, often by championing more benign alternatives.

President Clinton recently acknowledged this approach to avoiding mandated sanctions by stating that automatic sanctions lead to enormous pressure to "fudge the evaluation of the facts" to allow a range of responses. The transfer of M-11 ballistic missiles is a good example. The Chinese know they delivered the missiles to Pakistan. The Pakistanis know they received the missiles. The USG knows the missiles were transferred. But, because of the sanctions legislation, the American people were told something different.

This same effect may well be driving some public statements regarding terrorism. Osama bin Laden's organization is represented as a "stateless" terrorist group. But FBI filings in court papers make a very different case, as David Schenker has observed.[3]

---

3. David K. Schenker, "Bin Laden and the Problem of State-Supported Terrorism."

The way to fix this problem is for the administration and Congress to look carefully at sanctions legislation and change those laws that force an administration to "fudge the evaluation of the facts." We need to have honest dialogs on terrorism and proliferation issues. Anything else is unfair to the American people, encourages bad behavior by our adversaries, and can lead to a breakdown in our detection and warning abilities.

Shortage of Technology Support

Even if we have good intelligence capabilities and informed customers who are willing to act, we need to have the tools to stay a step ahead. With most of the high-technology developments occurring in the commercial sector, we can get caught in the position of competing on the basis of who has the most money. And governments, even the USG, often come up second best. For example, drug cartels today have more money than counterdrug forces. Where airplanes, ships, or signals-collection equipment often require multiyear procurement efforts in governments, drug runners can buy the same or better equipment immediately, often expecting to throw it away after one drug shipment.

The US is only going to win if it has a competitive edge. In the past, that has often been ingenuity and technology. Today, we need to develop technologies aimed at the BCW terrorism problem. The Defense Advanced Research Projects Agency (DARPA) has continually orchestrated relevant leading-edge technology developments. One area that is showing real breakthrough potential is advanced medical treatments for persons exposed to biological warfare agents. But another area—advanced, cheap, multiagent biodetectors—is equally important but much less well funded. Both are funding-limited, not idea-limited. Detectors are needed not just to warn of soon-to-come medical casualties, but, even if the new medical treatments are available, detectors are needed to alert intelligence and law enforcement agencies. Bin Laden and others have already demonstrated the ability to mount nearly simultaneous terrorist attacks. We cannot afford to wait days for medical symptoms to appear before we try to discern what happened and who was responsible.

In Summary

The people who are working these problems are hard-working, serious professionals who are facing some significant impediments. Government agencies, to include the intelligence agencies, are not like AT&T. They cannot allocate funds from future earnings to restructure to better meet future needs. They have to restructure while their budgets are shrinking, and while they continue the day-to-day grind.

If there were simple solutions, they would have been implemented by now. Fixing the problems requires first an admission that there are serious problems. It will not be possible to solve the problems without a broad understanding of the need for a robust intelligence capability by people outside the IC, and much greater public trust in the intelligence process.

Achieving greater public trust in the intelligence process will not come easily. It will require a restructuring of the work processes in the IC to accommodate outside experts more easily. But perhaps an even more difficult obstacle is the reluctance among academics and others to become involved in intelligence matters.

The founding fathers believed that citizens of the US had certain inalienable rights. But it was clear in the documents relating to the formation of this nation that these same founding fathers believed that a responsibility came with these rights. Given the key role of intelligence in preventing BCW terrorism, greater participation in, and dialog about, our intelligence objectives and capabilities is a responsibility we all need to encourage.

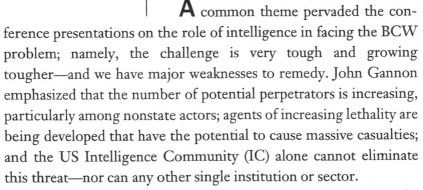

Commentary

A common theme pervaded the conference presentations on the role of intelligence in facing the BCW problem; namely, the challenge is very tough and growing tougher—and we have major weaknesses to remedy. John Gannon emphasized that the number of potential perpetrators is increasing, particularly among nonstate actors; agents of increasing lethality are being developed that have the potential to cause massive casualties; and the US Intelligence Community (IC) alone cannot eliminate this threat—nor can any other single institution or sector.

A particular concern raised in the conference discussion was the danger of attacks on the animal and plant resources of the nation. The discussion also highlighted the importance of human intelligence (HUMINT) in facing the threat of BCW. Reliance on HUMINT quite naturally presents risks—as well as opportunities—for the IC, because of the need to deal with individuals who may not be, to say the least, admirable, and who are often quite unsavory. And, whereas public exposures of failed intelligence operations are frequently embarrassing and harmful, the IC can rarely balance such negative impact by advertising the operations that are successes.

Gordon Oehler, former director of the DCI's Nonproliferation Center (NPC), highlighted three weaknesses in our current intelligence system that are limiting our capabilities. These he identified as shortcomings within the process itself, tensions with policymakers, and a shortage of technology support. They need, and are currently beginning, to receive high-level attention as US government and society are becoming more concerned with the imminence of the BCW dangers.

One very difficult problem that the IC faces was emphasized in the conference discussion and highlighted by the comments of John Lauder, current head of the NPC. It is simply that biological and chemical agents have dual uses, and these cannot readily be distinguished from one another from a distance by, for example, overhead imagery. One has to dig further inside a biological or chemical program to distinguish production of dangerous BCW agents from legitimate research for producing vaccines, antibiotics, or other pharmaceuticals to fight disease. This presents a great challenge to developing an effective intelligence system that will provide early and actionable information of growing threats.

Lauder drew an apt analogy to the game of soccer—at least as it is played by younger, less experienced players—in addressing the challenge of building a system to prepare to face the consequences of a BCW incident. Describing the importance of maintaining a strategic focus on the challenge, even when facing immediate crises that can draw all the attention to a single threat, he recalled how important it is for the players in a soccer game to protect their field positions rather than to "bunch up," converging on the ball, as is a natural tendency among young players. Translated to the BCW challenge, this means continuing long-term research into scientific understanding while developing a consequence-management system that is sufficiently flexible to face a range of potential threats.

As a way of further emphasizing the difficulty of obtaining early and effective intelligence against BCW, Lauder contrasted the required accuracy from the broadly encompassing point of view of national security today, with that required during the Cold War when sizing up the threat to NATO of deployments of Soviet ground forces in Europe. Nowadays, even if no more than several hundred pounds of a reported biological agent become unaccounted for, it could be militarily significant and a serious potential threat to national security. During the Cold War, as long as one could determine the deployed Soviet forces with uncertainties below the level of a tank army (!), it would still be acceptable for security purposes. As made abundantly clear by the problems faced by the United Nations Special Commission (UNSCOM) in Iraq, discussed at length by Ambassador Rolf Ekéus later in this book, our ability to maintain such a tight account of threatening BCW agents is limited indeed. This points up a new measure of the difficulty of the challenges to the IC posed by BCW.

Part Three

Building and Implementing BCW Control Regimes

Abraham D. Sofaer

Introductory Remarks

This part of the book combines papers delivered at the conference on the current status of legal regulation of BCW, on the drafting process of the Biological Weapons Convention (BWC) enforcement protocol, and on the manner in which UN inspections were implemented in Iraq pursuant to Security Council resolutions. The papers were delivered at separate sessions, but have been printed together as chapters in this part, as they provide a broad overview of key issues in the BCW regulatory framework.

The history and current status of BCW regulation is provided, including consideration of the scope of the Chemical Weapons Convention (CWC) and of the protocol governing CW inspections. The BWC is also discussed, along with the current effort to draft a protocol for its enforcement. Both treaties are at a turning point in their development, and face considerable resistance from several states, including the US, which has had difficulty in satisfying certain CWC obligations, particularly, in its implementing legislation.

Discussion at the conference, including that of Jonathan Tucker, broadly espoused the proposition that a norm of nonuse of BCW is rapidly evolving, and should be encouraged so as to create a principle of customary law, applicable not only to BWC and CWC adherents, but also to states that refuse to ratify the treaties.

The conference was privileged to have two distinguished, international participants report on the BWC enforcement protocol and UN inspections. Ambassador Tibor Tóth, who has the lead role in negotiations concerning the BWC protocol, reported on the current status of the draft, which has thousands of bracketed provisions but which is at least now one continuous document. He expressed the hope of arriving at consensus after the long and intense negotiations scheduled for 1999. Ambassador Rolf Ekéus of Sweden provided a fascinating description of how he led the effort, while Executive Chairman of the United Nations Special Commission (UNSCOM), to establish a regime for the inspection of Iraq's BW capability, and of the striking discoveries and achievements that occurred. His account makes clear the grave loss of security that has resulted from the termination of UNSCOM operations in Iraq.

Jonathan B. Tucker

6

From Arms Race to Abolition: The Evolving Norm Against Biological and Chemical Warfare

Arms control treaties, in addition to formalizing the "rules of the road" of international security, are the embodiment of behavioral norms. According to one definition, an arms control regime is "a fabric of international legal requirements reflecting and/or establishing accepted norms of international behavior, and mechanisms to implement or operationalize these requirements."[1]

Nowhere is the normative role of arms control more apparent than in the area of biological and chemical weapons (BCW). These weapons have been morally stigmatized not merely because they are

The author is grateful to Julian Perry Robinson of the University of Sussex, England, for his insightful comments on an earlier version of this chapter.

1. J. Christian Kessler, *Verifying Nonproliferation Treaties: Obligation, Process, and Sovereignty* (Washington: National Defense University Press, 1995), p. 9.

cruel and inhumane—most weapons are—but because they are un-controllable and indiscriminate, since winds can carry toxic agents beyond the battlefield to injure and kill innocent noncombatants. Moreover, the fact that it is far easier to defend troops against biological and chemical weapons than it is to protect civilians makes their use particularly objectionable.

The behavioral norm against BCW started out from an all-embracing taboo against the use of poison weapons—a behavioral norm of great antiquity and wide cross-cultural character. During the nineteenth century, this taboo eroded rapidly under the influence of industrial chemistry, which suddenly made the large-scale military use of poisons feasible and cheap.[2] Thanks to the deeply rooted character of the taboo, however, it gradually became reestablished as the twentieth century advanced, culminating in the current emerging norm against the development, possession, stockpiling, transfer, and use of biological and chemical weapons.[3]

That is not to say that the international community has reached the end of the road with respect to biological and chemical disarmament—far from it. Although most BCW programs are shrouded in secrecy, some twenty-five countries are currently suspected of possessing or actively pursuing chemical weapons, and about half that many are assessed to have biological weapons. BCW proliferation is concentrated in regions of the world characterized by chronic insecurity and tension, such as the Middle East and Northeast Asia. Biological and chemical weapons are attractive to countries pursuing

2. Stockholm International Peace Research Institute, *The Problem of Chemical and Biological Warfare*. Volume I: *The Rise of CB Weapons* (New York: Humanities Press, 1971), pp. 125–6.

3. On the gradual reestablishment of the norm against chemical warfare, see Alva Myrdal, *The Game of Disarmament* (New York: Pantheon, 1976), pp. 227–8; and Michael Mandelbaum, *The Nuclear Revolution: International Politics Before and After Hiroshima* (Cambridge, England: Cambridge University Press, 1981), pp. 29–40.

a mass-destruction capability because they are relatively cheap to manufacture and do not demand the elaborate technical infrastructure required for nuclear weapons.

The case of Iraq shows that a determined proliferator may be willing to pay an extraordinarily high price—in both economic and political terms—to acquire and use these weapons in defiance of global norms. Indeed, Baghdad's insistence on retaining a residual BCW capability in violation of UN Security Council Resolution 687 has cost it more than $130 billion in lost oil sales as a result of the economic sanctions imposed after the 1991 Persian Gulf War. As defense analyst Brad Roberts has argued, however, "norms matter in international politics—not because they constrain the choices of the most malevolent of men but because they create the basis for consensus about responses to actions inconsistent with those norms."[4]

Today, the world community stands at a crossroads in the development of two "disarmament cum nonproliferation" treaties designed to eliminate existing stockpiles of biological and chemical weapons and to prevent their reacquisition in the future. The 1972 Biological and Toxin Weapons Convention (BWC) has been in force since March 1975, and the 1993 Chemical Weapons Convention (CWC) entered into force in April 1997. Unlike the nuclear nonproliferation regime, which distinguishes between nuclear-weapon states and nonweapon states, the BWC and CWC are "nondiscriminatory" in that their provisions apply equally to possessors and nonpossessors of chemical or biological weapons. Member states must eliminate any and all such weapons in their possession

---

4. Brad Roberts, "Implementing the Biological Weapons Convention: Looking Beyond the Verification Issue," in Oliver Thraenert, ed., *The Verification of the Biological Weapons Convention: Problems and Perspectives* (Bonn: Friedrich Ebert Stiftung, 1992), p. 104.

and are subject to the same rights and obligations, a fact that has greatly enhanced the political legitimacy of the two regimes.

Nevertheless, the biological and chemical disarmament treaties currently face major challenges. The CWC is still in the early phase of implementation; and states-parties to the BWC are engaged in an effort to strengthen that treaty by negotiating a legally binding compliance protocol that includes on-site inspection measures. Both regimes are therefore at a turning point in their development that could lead to either a significant strengthening of the international behavioral norm against BCW or, alternatively, to the weakening of one or both regimes and an acceleration of proliferation.

Before discussing the current status of the biological and chemical disarmament regimes, it is useful to trace the historical evolution of the international legal norms against BCW. In so doing, this chapter will address several broad questions. First, how have these regimes evolved over time, and what is the relationship between legal norms and actual state behavior? Second, what is the role of multilateral treaties and their associated international organizations in inculcating and enforcing behavioral norms? Finally, how can the existing norms against BCW acquisition and use be strengthened in the future?

Origins of the International Norm

Efforts to control the use of toxic chemicals in war have a remarkably long history. Such efforts may have their origins in an innate human aversion to poisons, as well as the deeply held belief that the use of toxic weapons is particularly unchivalrous. Constraints on the use of poisons in war date back to antiquity and had become an element of customary international law by the end of the classical Greek and Roman period.[5] During the Middle Ages, Ger-

5. John Ellis van Courtland Moon, "Controlling Chemical and Biological

man artillery gunners pledged not to use "poisoned globes for the ruin and destruction of men" because such weapons were considered "unworthy of a man of heart and a real soldier."[6] Among the first codified international agreements banning chemical warfare was a Franco-German treaty drawn up in Strasbourg in 1675 to prohibit the use of poisoned bullets.

During the American Civil War, it was proposed that Union soldiers should use chlorine-filled shells, but this idea was rejected. On April 24, 1863, the US War Department issued the Lieber code of conduct, Article 70 of which declared: "The use of poison in any manner, be it to poison wells, or food, or arms, is wholly excluded from modern warfare."[7] This ban, which remained official policy until the US entry into World War I, was based on a strong social consensus that wars should be fought by professional armies in a contest based on personal skill and honor, an ideal that clashed with the use of toxic weapons that kill indiscriminately.[8]

The 1874 Brussels Declaration on the laws and customs of war, signed by fourteen European countries but never ratified, prohibited the use of poison or poisonous gases as well as arms, projectiles, or materials that would cause unnecessary suffering.[9] By this time, the taboo against the use of poisons in warfare had become so widely accepted in the Western world that the inclusion of such language

Weapons Through World War II," in R. D. Burns, ed., *Encyclopedia of Arms Control and Disarmament*, Volume II (New York: Charles Scribner's Sons, 1993), pp. 567–74.

6. Tony Freemantle, "Toxic Warfare Bloomed on a Belgian Field," *Washington Times* (Jan. 5, 1998).

7. Leon Friedman, *The Law of War: A Documentary History*, Volume I (New York: Random House, 1972), pp. 158–86.

8. Lt. Mark D. Budensiek, "A New Chemical Weapons Convention: Can It Assure the End of Chemical Weapon Proliferation?," 39 *Naval Law Review* (1990), p. 15.

9. Organization for the Prohibition of Chemical Weapons [OPCW], "A Brief History of Chemical Disarmament" [www.opcw.nl/basic/briefup.htm].

was not even debated during the conference. Nevertheless, the emergence of chemical industries in the late nineteenth century led to growing concern over the potential for large-scale chemical warfare.

The International Peace Conferences held in The Hague (Netherlands) in 1899 and 1907, attended by some forty-five states including all of the major powers at the time, were the first attempts at a worldwide approach to the problems of war and peace. The treaties that emerged from these conferences helped to codify the rules of war and established new institutions for settling international disputes. The 1899 Hague Conference generated two new instruments constraining chemical warfare that were signed and ratified by twenty-five nations, including Germany and Russia but not Great Britain, Serbia, Turkey, or the United States. First, the Hague Gas Projectile Declaration banned "the use of projectiles, the sole object of which is the diffusion of asphyxiating or deleterious gases."[10] Motivating this provision was Russia's fear that the West European powers would apply their huge advantage in chemical industry to develop asphyxiating bombs that could be used against cities to kill large numbers of noncombatants, including women and children.[11] Second, Article 23(a) of the regulations annexed to the Hague Convention with respect to the laws and customs of war on land reaffirmed the prohibition of the use of poison or poisoned arms.

10. The prohibition did not cover projectiles whose explosion incidentally produced toxic gases. The US refused to sign the Hague Convention of 1899 because its delegates were not convinced that the use of chemicals in warfare would necessarily be inhumane, so they opposed a total and permanent ban in principle. In the words of Secretary of State Hay, "The expediency of restraining the inventive genius of our people in the direction of devising means of defense is by no means clear, and . . . it is doubtful if an international agreement to this end would prove effective. . . ."

11. Richard M. Price, "A Genealogy of the Chemical Weapons Taboo," 49 *International Organization* (Winter 1995), p. 83.

In 1907, the Second Hague Convention expanded the regulations on land warfare and reiterated, "it is especially forbidden . . . to employ poison or poisoned weapons."[12] The unique aspect of the emergent behavioral norm embodied in the Hague Conventions was that it did not merely involve a ban on particular uses of chemical shells (for example, against civilians) but took the form of an absolute prohibition on their use. In this way, the treaty singled out poison gas as a stigmatized category of weaponry.[13]

Chemical Warfare During World War I

Unfortunately, the Hague Conventions did not prevent all the major powers from resorting to chemical warfare during World War I (1914–1918). After the experimental use of harassing chemicals, Germany launched the first large-scale poison gas attack on April 22, 1915, at Ypres, Belgium, against French colonial and Canadian troops. Preparations for the attack were made in secret, and it came as a devastating surprise. At the specified moment, German troops simultaneously opened 6,000 cylinders that had been buried along the front lines, releasing 168 metric tons of chlorine gas. Clouds of the greenish-gray vapor settled close to the ground and were carried on a brisk wind over the French and Canadian trenches, where they induced violent nausea, asphyxiation, blinding, and agonizing pain. Two entire French divisions collapsed, tearing a gap four miles wide in the Ypres front.[14]

Although Germany's first use of chemical weapons involved cylinders rather than explosive shells and thus technically did not violate the 1899 Gas Projectile Declaration, the use of poison gas was a

12. Terry M. Weekly, "Proliferation of Chemical Warfare: Challenge to Traditional Restraints," 19 *Parameters* (Dec. 1988), p. 54.

13. Richard M. Price, "A Genealogy of the Chemical Weapons Taboo," p. 90.

14. Robert Harris and Jeremy Paxman, *A Higher Form of Killing: The Secret Story of Chemical and Biological Warfare* (New York: Hill and Wang, 1982), pp. 2–6.

clear breach of Article 23(a) of the Land Warfare Regulations. Five months later, in September 1915, the Allies retaliated with their own use of chlorine gas. As the war ground on, both sides developed protective measures such as gas masks, as well as new offensive chemical agents of ever-greater potency, some designed specifically to defeat enemy defenses.

In December 1915, the Germans introduced phosgene, a choking gas similar to chlorine but about eighteen times more powerful. Then in July 1917, once again at Ypres, the Germans unleashed mustard gas, which causes severe chemical burns and blisters on the skin, eye damage, and inflammation of the lungs if inhaled. The relatively few casualties who absorbed a lethal dose suffered a slow, agonizing death.[15] Not only was mustard gas highly persistent, making it possible to contaminate large areas of the battlefield, but it acted through the skin and thus required troops to wear protective clothing as well as gas masks. The Allies retaliated in kind with mustard gas in June 1918.

By war's end, all the major combatants had used an estimated 124,200 metric tons of some thirty different toxic agents, 90 percent of which had been dispersed by some 66 million artillery shells. Chemical warfare had inflicted roughly one million casualties, of which more than 90,000 were fatal, and many of the survivors had been blinded or scarred for life.[16] American troops were particularly hard-hit: chemical casualties accounted for 27 percent of all US dead and injured.[17]

While the large-scale employment of chemical weapons during World War I was a clear violation of the Hague Conventions, the emergent legal norm did impose some constraints on use that helped

15. Terry M. Weekly, "Proliferation of Chemical Warfare," pp. 52–53.
16. OPCW, "A Brief History of Chemical Disarmament."
17. Peter Grier, "US Was One of History's First Victims of Gas Warfare," *Christian Science Monitor* (Dec. 14, 1988), p. B4.

to set chemical weapons apart from other novel methods of warfare. The British employed poison gas only in retaliation for German attacks, and none of the warring states deliberately used chemical weapons against noncombatants, even though civilians were targeted during conventional air raids and in submarine attacks on passenger ships.[18] Nevertheless, massive chlorine gas attacks generated dense clouds that inflicted significant casualties as far as 30 kilometers behind the front-line trenches, inevitably harming civilians as well as soldiers.[19]

Although the death toll from chemical weapons in World War I was relatively low compared to the massive number of fatalities caused by conventional weapons, the publicity given to the sometimes terrible effects of poison gas gave impetus to postwar efforts to reaffirm the ban on its use. In 1919, the victorious Allies included a special article (Article 171) in the Treaty of Versailles prohibiting the use of asphyxiating or poisonous gases and liquids, and strictly forbidding Germany from manufacturing or importing them. Similar provisions were included in the peace treaties with Austria, Bulgaria, Hungary, and Turkey.[20]

During the Washington Disarmament Conference of 1921–22 involving Britain, France, Italy, Japan, and the United States, the US delegate succeeded in incorporating an absolute prohibition on chemical warfare into Article V of the Treaty on the Use of Submarines and Noxious Gases in Warfare. Although this treaty was adopted unanimously by the five participating states, it never en-

18. Price, "A Genealogy of the Chemical Weapons Taboo," p. 92.

19. Charles E. Heller, "Chemical Warfare in World War I: The American Experience, 1917–1918," *Leavenworth Papers No. 10* (Ft. Leavenworth, KS, Combat Studies Institute, 1984), p. 17.

20. United States Arms Control and Disarmament Agency (ACDA), *Arms Control and Disarmament Agreements: Texts and Histories of the Negotiations* (Washington: Arms Control and Disarmament Agency, 1990), p. 10.

tered into force because French ratification was necessary and Paris objected to the provisions on submarine warfare.[21]

The 1925 Geneva Protocol

The question of chemical weapons was discussed in a number of committees established by the League of Nations in Geneva. In May 1925, an international conference on the international trafficking in arms was convened under the auspices of the League. During the conference, the United States proposed prohibiting the export of poisonous or asphyxiating gases for military purposes, but many countries opposed this idea on the grounds that it was discriminatory. The argument was that halting trade in chemical weapons without first banning their manufacture or use would selectively benefit those states that already possessed chemical weapons or the materials and know-how needed to produce them.[22] Although a more equitable solution would have been to ban the possession of chemical weapons outright, a special committee of the conference concluded that such a solution was not acceptable to many states.[23]

As a compromise, France proposed negotiating a separate agreement prohibiting the use in war of poisonous gases, similar to the provision included in the peace treaties with Germany, Austria, Hungary, Bulgaria, and Turkey. At the suggestion of Poland, the ban was extended to cover the use of bacteriological methods of warfare.[24] (During World War I, German saboteurs had used bac-

21. Ibid.
22. Jean Pascal Zanders, "The CWC in the Context of the 1925 Geneva Debates," 3 *Nonproliferation Review* (Spring-Summer 1996), pp. 38–45.
23. Thomas Bernauer, *The Chemistry of Regime Formation* (Brookfield, VT: Dartmouth Publishing Co., for the United Nations Institute for Disarmament Research, 1993), p. 18.
24. Charles C. Flowerree, "The Politics of Arms Control Treaties: A Case Study," 37 *Columbia Journal of International Affairs* (1984), p. 271.

terial agents such as glanders and anthrax to infect horses, which then played a key role in military logistics.) The resulting treaty, the Protocol for the Prohibition of the Use in War of Asphyxiating, Poisonous or Other Gases, and of Bacteriological Methods of Warfare, generally known as the Geneva Protocol, was adopted on June 17, 1925.[25] This treaty was not a disarmament agreement but rather a law of war that prohibited certain modes of warfare. Moreover, the aspiration expressed in the preamble—that the provisions of the protocol "shall be universally accepted as a part of International Law, binding alike the conscience and the practice of nations"—was a statement of purpose, not a declaration that the prohibition on use had already achieved the status of customary international law (making it applicable to all states, including those that had not signed and ratified the treaty).

Over the next decade, the Geneva Protocol was ratified by some forty countries, including all the great powers except Japan and the United States. (Although the White House and the Senate Foreign Relations Committee endorsed the Protocol in 1926, the chemical industry and the US Army Chemical Warfare Service lobbied successfully against it, and the treaty was referred back to committee and never came to a vote on the Senate floor.) Several countries ratified the Geneva Protocol with "reservations," stating that the treaty did not prohibit the use of chemical or biological weapons against nonparties or that the prohibition on use would cease to be binding on them if their enemies, or allies of their enemies, employed such weapons first.[26] Although the legal materiality of these reservations was questionable, two factors made the Geneva Protocol, in effect, a "no-first-use" agreement. First, the doctrine of belligerent reprisal states that any violation of the laws of war is justifiable to the extent that it is intended to bring to an end some previous

25. ACDA, *Arms Control and Disarmament Agreements*, p. 15.
26. Ibid., p. 10.

violation. Second, because the Protocol was drafted as a contract among the parties, the ban would become null and void if one side in a war were to disregard it.[27]

Another flaw of the Geneva Protocol was that it prohibited the use in war of chemical or biological weapons but not research, development, production, and stockpiling of them. The primary purpose of the protocol was to delegitimate chemical warfare in anticipation of a disarmament treaty that would be negotiated later under the auspices of the League of Nations. But although a Conference for the Reduction and Limitation of Armaments duly convened in 1932–33, it failed to reach agreement because of political differences and military tensions that were to lead six years later to the outbreak of World War II.

Most of the major powers ratified the Geneva Protocol, but their experiences during World War I had led them to believe that CW had a military value that could prove decisive in future conflicts. Thus, once states had reserved the right of retaliatory use, they found it necessary to continue research and development on toxic weapons and, in many cases, to produce and stockpile them as a deterrent, thereby increasing the chances that they would be used.

The Geneva Protocol had additional drawbacks. Because its scope was explicitly limited to the conduct of warfare, legal opinions differed as to its coverage of BCW use in civil conflicts. Last but not least, the protocol had no provisions for verification or enforcement.

The Inter-War Period

The first violation of the Geneva Protocol occurred when fascist Italy employed poison gas against unprotected tribesmen during its invasion of Abyssinia—present-day Ethiopia—in 1935–36. (Abys-

27. Julian Perry Robinson, personal communication (Jan. 15, 1999).

sinia was not a party to the Protocol when Italy began using chemical weapons there, although it quickly became one in September 1935.) This violation led some military analysts to predict that the next war would see the widespread use of CW. Meanwhile, CW agents were becoming ever more deadly. In the late 1930s, German chemists discovered a new family of supertoxic chemicals known as "nerve agents," including tabun (1936) and sarin (1938), which is ten times as toxic as tabun. Before and during World War II, Nazi Germany secretly produced and stockpiled tabun in large quantities, although its existence remained a well-kept secret until April 1945. (Germany did not succeed, however, in producing sarin on an industrial scale.)[28]

Between 1932 and 1945, Japan, which was not then a party to the Geneva Protocol (it did not accede to the treaty until 1970) employed both biological and chemical weapons against unprotected Chinese troops and civilians. According to records kept by the Chinese army, Japanese chemical attacks with mustard gas and Lewisite (another blister agent) killed at least 2,000 Chinese troops and injured 35,000.[29] In addition, the Japanese military produced biological warfare agents such as anthrax, cholera, and plague at secret microbiological facilities in occupied Manchuria, performed gruesome human experiments on Chinese and Western prisoners of war, and employed BW against civilian and military targets in China.[30] New documentary evidence suggests that Japan's use of germ war-

---

28. Stockholm International Peace Research Institute, *The Problem of Chemical and Biological Warfare*, Volume I, pp. 71–73.

29. Yuki Tanaka, "Poison Gas: The Story Japan Would Like to Forget," 37 *Bulletin of the Atomic Scientists* (Oct. 1988), p. 10.

30. John W. Powell, "Japan's Biological Weapons: 1930–1945," 37 *Bulletin of the Atomic Scientists* (Oct. 1981), pp. 43–51; Sheldon H. Harris, *Factories of Death: Japanese Biological Warfare 1932–45 and the American Cover-Up* (London: Routledge, 1994).

fare was more extensive than previously believed and included massive attacks in Yunan province bordering Burma.[31]

Other incidents of chemical warfare during the inter-war period took place in peripheral conflicts, including use by British troops intervening in the Russian civil war in 1919, the Spanish in Morocco in 1925, the Italians in Libya in 1930, and Soviet forces against Muslim insurgents in Central Asia in 1934.[32] Richard Price argues that the use of CW by the European powers in colonial wars reflected the perception at the time that modern warfare between "civilized" powers—defined in terms of technological sophistication rather than race, religion, morality, or other factors—was qualitatively different from war against "uncivilized" countries. Accordingly, the use of CW became part of the hierarchical ordering of international politics into central and peripheral areas.[33]

Nonuse of Chemical Weapons in World War II

Despite the egregious Italian and Japanese violations of the norm embodied in the Geneva Protocol, the feared large-scale use of chemical weapons during World War II never came about. On September 2, 1939, at the outset of the European war, Britain, France, and Germany exchanged pledges through the Swiss government that they would honor the Geneva Protocol, while explicitly

31. Ralph Blumenthal and Judith Miller, "Japan Rebuffs Requests for Information About Its Germ-Warfare Atrocities," *New York Times* (March 4, 1999), p. A10.

32. Tony Freemantle, "Toxic Warfare Bloomed on a Belgian Field." On Spanish use in Morocco, see Rudibert Kunz and Rolf-Dieter Müller, *Giftgas gegen Abd el Krim: Deutschland, Spanien und der Gaskrieg in Spanisch-Morokko 1922–1927* (Freiburg im Breisgau: Rombach, 1990) and Olaf Gröhler, *Der Lautlose Tod: Einsatz und Entwicklung deutscher Giftgase von 1914 bis 1945* (Reinbek bei Hamburg: Rowolt, 1978).

33. Richard M. Price, "A Genealogy of the Chemical Weapons Taboo," p. 97.

reserving the right to retaliate.[34] These declarations were motivated by the fear that strategic bombing of cities with chemical weapons would be part of the employment doctrine for the new generation of heavy bombers. The distribution of gas masks to the civilian population of many European countries testified to the belief that chemical air raids were anticipated.

Throughout World War II, more than a dozen combatant states produced and stockpiled CW and fully expected their use. By 1945, over a half-million tons of CW agents had been manufactured, greatly exceeding the total consumption during World War I.[35] Yet although all of the major armies carried stocks of CW with them as they moved over the battlefield, these weapons were never employed in significant quantities. Restraint prevailed even when chemical weapons would have offered a distinct military advantage—for example, as the least costly way for US troops to advance against Japanese forces entrenched in caves and tunnels in the Pacific islands.

What explains the nonuse of CW in World War II? As Lt. Gen. Herman Ochsner, director of the German CW program during the war, observed, "Never before in the history of mankind had weapons of proven efficacy . . . remained unused in later wars of equal or even greater proportion."[36] Some scholars, notably Frederic Brown and Julian Perry Robinson, have argued that the main reason for nonuse was the lack of "assimilation" of CW into military doctrine and force structures because of institutional constraints. According to this view, resistance to chemical warfare on the part of the military estab-

34. Jeffrey W. Legro, "Military Culture and Inadvertent Escalation in World War II," 18 *International Security* (Spring 1994), p. 132.

35. Julian Perry Robinson, "Chemical Arms Control and the Assimilation of Chemical Weapons," 36 *International Journal* (1981), pp. 517–18.

36. Herman Ochsner, *History of German Chemical Warfare in World War II, Part I: The Military Aspect* (Washington: Historical Office of the Chief of the [US] Chemical Corps, Jun. 1950), p. 23.

lishments of all the belligerent states was reinforced by popular repugnance and legal restraints on CW use.[37]

Robinson has noted that a CW capability requires a great deal of preparation, including the organization of combat and logistical support units, the training of personnel, the procurement of offensive and defensive equipment, and other mission-specific allocations of manpower and materiel. Since such preparations inevitably occur at the expense of other types of military preparedness and require significant organizational changes, they must overcome bureaucratic inertia and the active opposition of competing services. The existence of explicit and well-known prohibitions enshrined in international treaties tends to reinforce these institutional constraints. Robinson argues that the Geneva Protocol, "far from being an irrelevancy, may be seen as a principal factor imposing political considerations on purely military ones in chemical-warfare decision-making. It has thus constituted a major obstacle to the assimilation of chemical weapons into national force postures."[38]

During World War II, CW did not become assimilated to the extent that any combatant could realistically contemplate their use. The British Army tended to neglect chemical warfare planning for organizational and doctrinal reasons, including a conservative approach to military innovation, and the Royal Air Force did not want its high-explosive and incendiary bombing loads cut in favor of CW.[39] Late in the war, however, British leaders seriously debated dropping poison gas on German cities in retaliation for Hitler's rocket attacks on London. In a now-declassified memo to General Hastings Ismay dated July 6, 1944, Prime Minister Winston Churchill wrote: "If the bombardment of London became a serious nui-

37. Frederic J. Brown, *Chemical Warfare: A Study in Restraints* (Princeton, NJ: Princeton University Press, 1968), chap. 5.

38. Jullian Perry Robinson, "Chemical Arms Control," p. 520.

39. Jeffrey W. Legro, "Military Culture and Inadvertent Escalation in World War II," pp. 133–34.

sance and rockets with far-reaching and devastating effect fell on many centers of government and labor . . . I may certainly have to ask you to support me in using poison gas. It is absurd to consider morality on this topic when everybody used it in the last war without complaint."[40] Nevertheless, the threatened attacks never materialized.

For Nazi Germany, chemical warfare threatened to impede operational tempo and thus ran counter to the army's new "blitzkrieg" doctrine of mechanized warfare. Although Wehrmacht generals seriously considered delivering chemical weapons against British cities with the V-1 "buzz bomb" and the V-2 ballistic missile, they concluded that conventional explosives were more efficient in terms of weight and destructive power.[41] Adolf Hitler, having been injured by mustard gas in World War I, had a strong aversion to chemical warfare and feared Allied retaliation. These factors appear to have deterred him from ordering the use of CW against Britain or Russia, even when Germany's military situation became increasingly desperate.[42] Further reinforcing restraint was the fact that German intelligence overestimated Allied preparedness and incorrectly believed that the Allies knew about nerve gas and could produce it rapidly.[43]

Jeffrey Legro has documented several incidents of low-level CW use during World War II that could have escalated but instead were ignored or intentionally suppressed. During the German invasion of Poland in 1940, Polish forces employed mustard gas during the defense of the Jaslo bridge, causing German casualties and deaths.

40. Michelle Carabine, "Churchill Had Plan to Gas the Germans," (Edinburgh, Scotland) *Evening News* (Oct. 28, 1998).

41. Herman Ochsner, *History of German Chemical Warfare*, p. 35.

42. Joachim Krause and Charles K. Mallory, *Chemical Weapons in Soviet Military Doctrine* (Boulder, CO: Westview Press, 1992), p. 93.

43. John Ellis van Courtland Moon, "Chemical Weapons and Deterrence: The World War II Experience," 8 *International Security* (Spring 1984), p. 26.

Instead of retaliating in kind, German military leaders disregarded the attack on the assumption—correct, as it turned out—that the Polish Supreme Command had not ordered the use of gas. In July 1941, the Soviet Union employed CW in several attacks, yet although twelve German soldiers suffered mustard gas wounds, the incident was officially ignored. Even in the last frenzied months of the war, when the Third Reich was disintegrating, German military leaders did not resort to chemical warfare but instead moved their stocks of CW away from the front lines to reduce the risk of unauthorized use.[44]

Although the United States had not yet ratified the Geneva Protocol at the time of World War II, President Franklin Roosevelt was morally opposed to chemical warfare and committed to the principle of nonuse—or at least not first use. Responding to reports in June 1943 that the Axis powers were considering escalation to gas warfare, Roosevelt declared, "I state categorically that we shall under no circumstances resort to the use of such weapons unless they are first used by our enemies."[45] Since the decision to initiate gas warfare rested in the president's hands, the defeat of the Geneva Protocol in Congress was not a decisive victory for chemical warfare advocates. Opposition to chemical warfare was also widespread within the War Department. Many general officers, including General Pershing, opposed the unchivalric nature of gas and were skeptical of its military value on the battlefield. These moral and institutional constraints created resistance to any rapid US initiation of chemical warfare.[46]

After Roosevelt's death on April 12, 1945, US planning for chemical warfare advanced significantly, although not to the point

44. Jeffrey W. Legro, "Military Culture and Inadvertent Escalation in World War II," p. 137–38.

45. ACDA, *Arms Control and Disarmament Agreements*, p. 10–11.

46. John Ellis van Courtland Moon, "Chemical Weapons and Deterrence," p. 8.

where sufficient logistical or organizational readiness existed to support a resort to these weapons on a large scale.[47] During the bloody battles for control of the Pacific islands, where the tactical advantages of using gas against entrenched Japanese positions were undeniable, US initiation of chemical warfare was deterred by the fear that use against Japan would give Germany an excuse to employ gas in the European theater.[48] In the final months of the war, when the German surrender had greatly reduced the price the Allies would have to pay for initiating chemical warfare, the debate was reopened. Allied strategists drew up plans to drop mustard and phosgene gas on Japanese population centers in October 1945, prior to an invasion of Japan scheduled for the beginning of November.[49]

As it turned out, the atomic bombing of Hiroshima and Nagasaki in August 1945 led to the rapid surrender of Japan and obviated the need for a land invasion. According to historian John Moon, however, "The prospect for the initiation of gas warfare remained alive until the close of the war: a largely silent, featureless presence at the councils of decision."[50] Along similar lines, historian Barton Bernstein concludes that "Had the Pacific war dragged on into the late autumn and winter, [President Harry] Truman might have been under growing pressure to use gas against the hated Japanese."[51]

Thus, although the world came close to the reinitiation of chemical warfare in World War II, restraint prevailed despite the unconstrained use of all other available weaponry—including the atomic bomb. The immediate explanation for the nonuse of CW was the

47. Julian Perry Robinson, "Chemical Arms Control," p. 521.

48. John Ellis van Courtland Moon, "Chemical Weapons and Deterrence," p. 17.

49. Kevin Sullivan, "US Planned Chemical Attack on Japan," *Guardian* (Aug. 6, 1991).

50. John Ellis van Courtland Moon, "Chemical Weapons and Deterrence," p. 23.

51. Barton J. Bernstein, "Why We Didn't Use Poison Gas in World War II," 36 *American Heritage* (Aug.–Sep. 1985), pp. 40–45.

military's lack of preparedness to wage offensive chemical warfare and the fear of retaliation in kind, potentially involving escalation to strategic attacks on cities. Yet even in situations where the United States faced no significant threat of retaliation (as in the Pacific islands), CW were not used—a fact that underlines the importance of the political and legal inhibitions embodied in the Geneva Protocol. According to Robinson, the central lesson of the World War II experience is that "the strength of the chemical arms-control regime resides in the power of the prevailing legal norms on chemical warfare to inhibit assimilation of chemical weapons; but as assimilation proceeds, the norms are threatened. An effective route to a strengthened regime should therefore lie in the creation of specific new constraints on assimilation."[52]

The Postwar Years and the Cold War

By the end of World War II, the United States had produced some 135,000 tons of chemical warfare agents, Germany about 70,000 tons, Britain about 60,000 tons, Japan about 7,500 tons, and the Soviet Union more than 123,000 tons.[53] Various countries destroyed German CW and large quantities of their own stocks by burying them or dumping them in the Baltic Sea and other coastal waters.

In 1952, British chemists working on pesticides accidentally discovered a new generation of supertoxic nerve gases known as V-

52. Julian Perry Robinson, "Chemical Arms Control," p. 525.
53. Barton J. Bernstein, "Why We Didn't Use Poison Gas," p. 44; Soviet data from Lev Fedorov, "Table: Chemical weapon production from before World War II to 1987," Problems of Chemical Safety (Russia), issue UCS-INFO.6e (Oct. 22, 1996), reprinted in Judith Perera, "Chemical Munitions in the Commonwealth of Independent States and the Surrounding Seas," in Thomas Stock and Karlheiz Los, eds., *The Challenge of Old Chemical Munitions and Toxic Armament Wastes* (Oxford, England: Oxford University Press for the Stockholm International Peace Research Institute, 1997), p. 123.

agents. These synthetic poisons are about 10 times more deadly than sarin, are highly persistent, and readily penetrate the skin, so that a mere drop is sufficient to kill a grown man in several minutes. In the 1950s, the United States and the Soviet Union began production of first-generation nerve agents such as sarin and soman. At the same time, both countries did extensive research and development on biological weapons.

During the Korean War (1950–53), North Korea, China, and the Soviet Union accused the United States of using bacteriological weapons in Korea. Although some historians have found the charges credible, new archival evidence indicates that they were the product of an elaborate disinformation campaign.[54] In 1952, the Soviet Union introduced a draft resolution in the UN Security Council calling on all countries—including the United States—to ratify the Geneva Protocol. But Washington declared that it was not prepared to rule out the use of any weapons of mass destruction unless they were eliminated through negotiated disarmament agreements with effective safeguards.[55]

In 1954, President Konrad Adenauer of West Germany committed his country not to produce or stockpile nuclear, chemical, or biological weapons as a condition of joining the Western European Union and the North Atlantic Treaty Organization (NATO). West Germany also accepted international monitoring of compliance with this obligation, including on-site inspection, which was a unique arrangement at the time.[56] Meanwhile, however, a superpower BCW arms race was developing in parallel with the nuclear competition. During the 1950s and 60s, the United States produced more than 31,000 metric tons of blister and nerve agents, and the

54. Bruce B. Auster, "Unmasking an Old Lie: A Korean War Charge Is Exposed as a Hoax," *U.S. News & World Report* (Nov. 16, 1998), p. 52.
55. ACDA, *Arms Control and Disarmament Agreements*, p. 11.
56. Thomas Bernauer, *The Chemistry of Regime Formation*, p. 20.

Soviet Union probably more than 32,500 metric tons.[57] Large-scale production of V-agents began in 1961 in the United States and 1972 in the Soviet Union. These supertoxic agents were filled into everything from bombs to rockets to land mines, spawning fears of a "chemical Armageddon" were NATO and the Warsaw Pact ever to fight a major war in central Europe. Both sides also produced and weaponized several lethal and incapacitating microorganisms, including anthrax, tularemia, brucellosis, and Venezuelan equine encephalitis, as well as botulinum toxin and various anticrop agents.

In addition to the superpower arms race, evidence emerged that CW were proliferating in the developing world. During the Yemen civil war (1962–67), the Egyptian Air Force dropped aerial bombs filled with phosgene and mustard gas on Yemeni tribesmen fighting on the royalist side.[58] The Egyptian attacks, which began in summer of 1963, were the first use of CW by an Arab state, although Egypt officially denied them.[59] Thereafter, other countries in the Middle East and elsewhere began to acquire a chemical and/or biological warfare capability, some for use as a battlefield weapon and others as a deterrent—a "poor man's atomic bomb." This quiet proliferation began to erode the traditional political constraints on BCWs.

The Separation of Biological and Chemical Arms Control

During the late 1960s, the threat of large-scale biological and chemical warfare between NATO and the Warsaw Pact, and the

57. Lev Fedorov, "Table: Chemical weapon production from before World War II to 1987."

58. "In New Detail: Nasser's Gas War," *U.S. News & World Report* (Jul. 10, 1967), p. 9.

59. W. Andrew Terrill, "The Chemical Warfare Legacy of the Yemen War," 10 *Comparative Strategy* (1991), pp. 109–19. See also Dany Shoham, "Chemical and Biological Weapons in Egypt," 5 *Nonproliferation Review* (Spring-Summer 1998), pp. 48–58.

spread of BCW to regions of chronic tension such as the Middle East, prompted a new international effort to negotiate controls on such weapons.[60] In 1966, the Eighteen Nation Disarmament Committee (ENDC), a multilateral forum for disarmament negotiations in Geneva, took up the question of biological and chemical disarmament, but it made little headway.[61]

Meanwhile, the US was coming under growing domestic and international opprobrium for its use of tear gas and chemical herbicides to augment conventional military operations during the Vietnam War (1962–75). US forces used herbicides to deprive the enemy of cover through defoliation and to destroy crops, and employed tear gas to drive enemy forces out of tunnels or bunkers and to rescue US troops or downed pilots from behind enemy lines. Beginning in 1964, the Soviet Union and its allies charged that such combat uses of herbicides and tear gas were violations of the Geneva Protocol.

Although neither the US nor North Vietnam had then ratified the Protocol, Washington, in defending its actions, did not challenge the view that the use of chemical weapons was contrary to customary international law. Instead, the US argued that the Geneva Protocol did not ban the use of nonlethal harassing agents and defoliants, since these substances were widely used for benign pur-

---

60. The Geneva disarmament negotiating forum changed in size and composition over the years. Founded in 1960, the Ten Nation Disarmament Committee had an exclusively East–West membership. It was dissolved in 1961 but reborn the following year as the Eighteen Nation Disarmament Committee (ENDC) with the addition of eight nonaligned countries. In 1969, the membership was enlarged to twenty-six and the name changed to the Conference of the Committee on Disarmament (CCD). In 1974, the body was further expanded to thirty-one members. In 1978, it was enlarged to forty members and renamed the Committee on Disarmament. Since 1984, it has been called the Conference on Disarmament (CD).

61. The ENDC was a multilateral negotiating body that convened at the United Nations in Geneva from 1962 to 1969. It consisted of five members of NATO, five members of the Warsaw Pact, and eight neutral and nonaligned countries.

poses such as weed suppression and controlling domestic riots without resort to deadly force.

In 1966, Hungary introduced a resolution at the UN General Assembly that called for making any use of chemical or biological weapons an international crime. Although the US managed to water down this resolution, chemical warfare became a recurring topic on the agenda of the United Nations and the disarmament committees that met in Geneva to negotiate multilateral arms control agreements.[62] In March 1968, some 6,000 sheep grazing in Skull Valley, Utah, were killed after eating vegetation that had been accidentally contaminated with VX nerve agent from an open-air test at nearby Dugway Proving Ground.[63] Responding to the public outcry, President Richard Nixon canceled the planned production of new chemical weapons in 1969.[64]

Beginning with the Geneva Protocol, biological and chemical disarmament had always been addressed as a single issue. By the late 1960s, however, it was clear that while time was ripe for a comprehensive ban on BW, negotiating a similar prohibition on CW—which had been used extensively in war—would be far more difficult. Thus, in August 1968, the UK proposed that the disarmament conference in Geneva should negotiate a treaty prohibiting BW as a first step, thereby separating biological from chemical arms control.[65]

The British had long recognized the folly of continuing to develop BW, which could bring strategic benefit only to relatively poor and industrially undeveloped countries by serving as equalizers against more advanced countries with superior conventional forces.

62. Charles C. Flowerree, "The Politics of Arms Control Treaties," p. 272.

63. Philip M Boffey, "Nerve Gas: Dugway Accident Linked to Utah Sheep Kill," 162 *Science* (Dec. 27, 1968), pp. 1460–64.

64. Peter Grier, "US Was One of History's First Victims of Gas Warfare," p. B4.

65. Thomas Bernauer, *The Chemistry of Regime Formation*, p. 24.

Concluding that it was better to seek the suppression of biological warfare altogether through unilateral disarmament and arms control, London had closed down its own offensive BW program during the 1960s. Another reason behind the British push for a BW ban was to bring the United States into line with the other NATO countries, which were bound by the Geneva Protocol and, in the case of West Germany, the Adenauer Declaration forswearing all weapons of mass destruction as a condition of NATO membership. As long as the United States went its own way—for example, by employing herbicides and riot-control agents in Vietnam—NATO would have a dangerously ambiguous BCW employment policy. Although the US was unlikely to change its policy on CW in the near term, movement might be possible on a treaty banning BW, in turn making it more likely that Washington would ratify the Geneva Protocol.[66]

In July 1969 the UK, with strong support from West Germany, submitted a draft Biological Weapons Convention to the Geneva negotiating forum, which had been renamed the Conference of the Committee on Disarmament (CCD).[67] In September, however, the Soviet Union and its allies introduced an alternative draft treaty banning both biological and chemical weapons. Moscow argued that the two types of weapon should be prohibited together, since a separate BW ban might intensify the chemical arms race.[68] For the next three years, a fierce debate continued in the Geneva disarmament forum over whether biological and chemical weapons should be treated together or separately, slowing progress toward a treaty. During this period, the UN Secretary-General and the World Health Organization sponsored expert studies of BCW that laid out the gravity of the threat.

---

66. Julian Perry Robinson, personal communication (Jan. 15, 1999).

67. The French were not then members of the CCD. Marie Isabelle Chevrier and Jessica E. Stern, "Chemical and Biological Weapons in the Third World," 11 *Boston College Third World Law Journal* (1991), p. 51.

68. Charles C. Flowerree, "The Politics of Arms Control Treaties," p. 274.

In 1969, UN Secretary-General U Thant called for a "clear affirmation" that the Geneva Protocol covered the use in war of tear gas and other harassing agents. That fall, twenty-one countries introduced Resolution 2603 in the UN General Assembly endorsing a broad interpretation of the protocol to include tear gas. This resolution passed in December 1969 by a vote of eighty to three (Australia, Portugal, and the United States), with thirty-six abstentions.[69] The prominence of the tear gas issue reflected the continued political salience of the international norm embodied in the Geneva Protocol.

US Renunciation of Biological Warfare

On November 25, 1969, while the UN General Assembly was still debating whether the Geneva Protocol covered the use of tear gas and herbicides, President Richard Nixon reaffirmed the US policy of "no first use" of lethal chemical weapons, extended this renunciation to chemical incapacitating agents, and announced that he would resubmit the Geneva Protocol to the Senate for its advice and consent to ratification. Nixon also declared that, after a lengthy policy review, the US had decided to renounce unilaterally its offensive BW program and to destroy its entire stockpile of BW agents. In February 1970, the President extended the ban to cover toxins, poisonous chemical substances of biological origin. Between May 1971 and May 1972, all US stocks of anthrax, botulinum toxin, and other biological and toxin weapons were destroyed.[70]

Once the US had unilaterally renounced biological and toxin warfare, it was clearly in its interest to ensure that as many other

69. ACDA, *Arms Control and Disarmament Agreements*, p. 12.

70. William C. Patrick III, "A History of Biological and Toxin Warfare," in Kathleen C. Bailey, ed., *Director's Series on Proliferation No. 4*, UCRL-LR-114070-4 (Livermore, CA: Lawrence Livermore National Laboratory, May 23, 1994), p. 19.

states as possible did likewise. For this reason, the US government decided to support the British proposal to negotiate a separate multilateral treaty banning BW. Such a treaty would demonstrate Washington's willingness to disarm and cooperate with the Soviet Union, while deflecting international attention from the more contentious issue of CW. According to Ambassador James F. Leonard, who headed the US delegation in Geneva, "When the United States moved toward the British position favoring a separate BW treaty in 1969, many saw this shift as a ploy to diffuse the tear-gas issue and with it the Vietnam question, and also as a way to postpone indefinitely any serious discussion of chemical arms control. In fact, there was considerable truth to both charges."[71]

At first, the Soviet Union and its Warsaw Pact allies flatly dismissed the British proposal for a separate BW treaty, and the neutral and nonaligned countries were also strongly opposed. As a result, the Geneva negotiations remained deadlocked from 1969 until March 1971, when the Soviet Union suddenly reversed its position and introduced a revised draft convention limited to biological and toxin weapons.[72] Once the Soviets had changed their position, the conclusion of the Biological and Toxin Weapons Convention (BWC) was rapid. Remembers Ambassador Leonard, "Superpower agreement meant something in those days. We had a joint US-Soviet draft text in a few weeks. Not long after that we were able to get the support of our allies and of many nonaligned states."[73]

In December 1971, the BWC was submitted to the UN General Assembly, which endorsed it the same day. Unfortunately, the veri-

71. Ambassador James F. Leonard, "The Control of Biological Weapons: Retrospect and Prospect," in Jonathan B. Tucker, ed., *Inspection Procedures for Compliance Monitoring of the Biological Weapons Convention* (Livermore, CA: Lawrence Livermore National Laboratory, Dec. 1997), pp. 21–2.
72. Charles C. Flowerree, "The Politics of Arms Control Treaties," p. 274.
73. Ambassador James F. Leonard, "The Control of Biological Weapons," p. 23.

fication provisions of the convention were minimal. Under Article VI, any member state could bring an alleged treaty violation to the attention of the UN Security Council, which could then initiate an investigation. This mechanism could be blocked, however, by one or more of the five permanent members of the Security Council (China, France, the Soviet Union, the United Kingdom, and the US). In order to preclude a permanent member of the Security Council from vetoing a noncompliance investigation, the United Kingdom proposed that the BWC should be accompanied by a draft Security Council resolution preauthorizing the UN Secretary-General to investigate complaints, but this idea never materialized.[74]

It is not clear who was to blame for weakening the verification provisions of the BWC. According to one view, the US pressured the British to withdraw their proposal for preauthorized investigations of noncompliance.[75] Other analysts contend that the Soviet military refused to abandon its development of BW and agreed to support the BWC only when it became clear that the treaty would not include intrusive verification mechanisms. In this way, the Soviet leadership could declare an arms control success for propaganda reasons, while the military could continue its offensive BW program without fear of disruption from on-site inspections.[76]

The BWC opened for signature in Washington, London, and Moscow in April 1972. As the first treaty to ban an entire class of weapons of mass destruction, the BWC was a historic accomplishment, but its lack of formal verification measures made it effectively toothless.

In late 1974, President Gerald Ford sought to obtain Senate consent to US ratification of the BWC and, simultaneously, of the

74. Julian Perry Robinson, personal communication (Jan. 15, 1999).
75. Ibid.
76. Milton Leitenberg, "Biological Weapons Arms Control," 17 *Contemporary Security Policy* (1996), p. 10.

Geneva Protocol. Dr. Fred Iklé, the director of the Arms Control and Disarmament Agency, testified that given the limited military utility and moral repugnance of BW, ratification of the BWC was in the US interest despite the treaty's weak verification provisions.[77] With respect to ratification of the Geneva Protocol, the US reserved the right to retaliate in kind with chemical—but not biological—weapons if an enemy state used them first.

Moving US policy closer to the broad interpretation of the Geneva Protocol, President Ford issued an executive order renouncing the use of riot-control agents (such as tear gas) and herbicides in war, with a few exemptions requiring advance presidential approval. The permitted uses of herbicides were limited to controlling vegetation within US bases or around their immediate defense perimeters. In the case of riot-control agents, the executive order permitted combat use in "defensive military modes to save lives." Examples were to avoid the use of lethal force where civilians were used to screen attacks, to defend convoys, to control rioting prisoners of war, and to rescue downed pilots behind enemy lines. Finding this clarification acceptable, the Senate gave its consent to ratification of both the Geneva Protocol and the BWC, which entered into force in March 1975. Two years later, the large-scale military use of herbicides for defoliation was banned by the 1977 Convention on the Prohibition of Military or Any Other Hostile Use of Environmental Modification Techniques (the ENMOD treaty).[78]

Negotiating the Chemical Weapons Convention

Once the BWC had been concluded, the CCD in Geneva began a renewed effort to negotiate a comprehensive ban on CW, which

77. Marie Isabelle Chevrier and Jessica E. Stern, "Chemical and Biological Weapons in the Third World," p. 54.
78. ACDA, *Arms Control and Disarmament Agreements*, pp. 211–17.

were perceived to pose a more immediate military threat. The limitations of the Geneva Protocol's ban on first use were increasingly clear: It did not prohibit some countries from assisting others to acquire chemical weapons; it did not address the development, production, stockpiling, or transfer of CW; and it did not provide for verification of compliance or for sanctions in the event of CW use.

The fact that several countries had reserved the right to retaliate in kind further weakened the normative power of the protocol. It was gradually recognized that reliance on in-kind deterrence had the negative effect of promoting the military assimilation of CW. To serve as a credible deterrent, the weapons had to be integrated into military forces and doctrines, yet doing so led to a spiral of competitive armament that made their ultimate use more likely.[79] As Julian Perry Robinson observed,

> There may be little about a retaliatory chemical-warfare capability to make it inherently distinguishable from an initiatory one, other than the prevailing intentions of its possessors; and these may change as assimilation advances. Stockpiles built up as deterrents may thus have the effect of sustaining, even inducing, the threats they are supposed to deter. . . ."[80]

Indeed, the capture during the October 1973 Arab–Israeli war of Soviet tanks and armored personnel carriers equipped with air filters and other protective systems revealed that the Soviets were surprisingly well prepared to conduct military operations in a chemical environment. This discovery lead to growing concern in the West that the Warsaw Pact was preparing to employ CW in combat. At the same time, the rapid development of the worldwide chemical industry and the resulting growth in the number of potential CW

79. Julian Perry Robinson, "Disarmament and Other Options for Western Policy-Making on Chemical Warfare," 63 *International Affairs* (1986–87), p. 67.

80. Julian Perry Robinson, "Chemical Arms Control," p. 530.

possessors increased the importance—but also the difficulty—of negotiating a comprehensive ban.

Initially, the CW talks were largely exploratory in nature. Individual countries proposed various draft treaties, including Japan in 1974 and the UK in 1976, but the talks remained deadlocked over basic questions such as the definition of a chemical weapon, the scope of the future convention, and modalities for the verification of compliance. In the autumn of 1977, the US and the Soviet Union sought to break the deadlock by commencing bilateral negotiations on a joint proposal for banning CW, while providing regular progress reports to the multilateral forum in Geneva. Although the two superpowers agreed in principle on a number of issues relating to the scope of the proposed ban, they remained far apart on verification measures. The intrusive on-site inspections needed for effective monitoring of chemical disarmament were anathema to the Soviet Union, which viewed them as tantamount to espionage. Because of the general collapse of détente, the bilateral talks ended in 1980.[81]

In March 1980 the Geneva negotiating forum, renamed the Committee on Disarmament, agreed to establish a special ad hoc working group on CW, but it made little progress. With the inauguration of President Ronald Reagan in 1981, CW were initially low on the US arms control agenda. Nevertheless, the new administration's desire to modernize the US chemical arsenal led it to pursue arms control as a means of softening political opposition to the production of "binary" CW (in which two relatively harmless chemical ingredients are combined inside a bomb or artillery shell on its way to the target and react to produce a lethal agent that is then dispersed on impact).[82] In 1981, Congress approved $20 million to equip a facility to produce binary weapons at Pine Bluff Arsenal in

81. Thomas Bernauer, *The Chemistry of Regime Formation*, p. 26.
82. David Dickson, "Approval Seen for New US Chemical Weapons," 232 *Science* (May 2, 1986), pp. 567–8.

Arkansas, but funds for actual production were not appropriated until 1986.[83]

In February 1983, the US finally moved on the CW issue in Geneva by agreeing to participate in an ad hoc working group with a mandate to draft a multilateral Chemical Weapons Convention (CWC).[84] Some thirty-nine countries participated directly in the CWC negotiations while about 37 others others sent observers. Rejecting the option of a partial ban that would later be extended, the participating states agreed that the scope of the future treaty should be comprehensive, covering development, production, and stockpiling. The Committee on Disarmament outlined the basic structure of the CWC and agreed to develop a "rolling text" in which nonagreed language was set off in square brackets. In this way, the negotiators could focus on hammering out consensus language for the nonagreed sections.

In April 1984, Vice President Bush introduced a US draft convention in Geneva that included the groundbreaking concept of "anywhere, anytime" inspections of facilities suspected of producing CW. Although the Pentagon and the Intelligence Community (IC) had qualms about opening up sensitive laboratories and defense facilities on short notice to multinational inspection teams, the highly intrusive US proposal was actually a stalling maneuver, since no one in the Reagan administration expected the Soviet Union to accept it.[85] The Soviets did reject the US draft treaty, but it became the basis for further negotiations.

Measures for on-site verification were a key issue in the negotiations because the CWC was the first arms control treaty to have a

---

83. Charles C. Flowerree, "The Politics of Arms Control Treaties," p. 281.

84. Ibid., p. 276.

85. Michael Krepon, "Verification of a Chemical Weapons Convention," in Brad Roberts, ed., *Chemical Disarmament and US Security* (Boulder, CO: Westview Press, 1992), p. 81.

major impact on the private sector, namely the multibillion-dollar chemical industry. Detailed procedures for short-notice "challenge" inspections of any facility (declared or undeclared) suspected of producing CW were extremely difficult to develop because of the need to strike a balance between addressing compliance concerns and protecting military and commercial secrets unrelated to CW. In devising measures for the on-site inspection of commercial chemical plants, the US Chemical Manufacturers Association and other chemical trade associations from Europe, Australia, and Japan played a constructive role.[86]

Although the CWC negotiations moved at a glacial pace, the thawing of the Cold War created an opening for accelerated progress. A diplomatic breakthrough of sorts occurred in August 1987, when Soviet President Mikhail Gorbachev called the US bluff and accepted its proposal for "anywhere, anytime" challenge inspections contained in the 1984 draft treaty. This surprise move created considerable consternation within the Pentagon and the IC, which were concerned about shielding their sensitive facilities from international inspections. According to one analyst, "Soon after Gorbachev's diplomatic jujitsu act in August 1987, the search began in earnest for suitable fallback positions to an unfettered right of challenge inspections."[87] The British came to the rescue with a compromise proposal for "managed access"—a set of procedures, to be negotiated between the international inspectors and the host facility, designed to minimize the compromise of classified or proprietary information unrelated to CW at even the most sensitive sites.

---

86. Kyle Olson, "Disarmament and the Chemical Industry," in Brad Roberts, ed., *Chemical Disarmament and US Security* (Boulder, CO: Westview Press, 1992), pp. 97–105.

87. Michael Krepon, "Verification of a Chemical Weapons Convention," p. 82.

Iraqi Violation of the Geneva Protocol

In the early 1980s, the failure of Western governments including the US to sanction Iraq for its massive use of CW during the Iran–Iraq War (1980–88) seriously undermined the Geneva Protocol. Iraq began using tear gas against Iran in 1982, escalated to mustard gas in 1983, and employed a nerve agent (tabun) for the first time during the Siege of Basra in 1984. That same year, at the battle of Majnoon Island, Iraq employed both mustard gas and tabun against Iranian forces with considerable tactical success. Iraq's climactic use of CW occurred in April 1988, during the decisive battle for Fao, when VX nerve agent was reportedly used for the first time.[88] Although Iraqi chemical warfare was a flagrant violation of the Geneva Protocol, which Baghdad had ratified in 1931, short-term US foreign policy and economic interests prevailed over the broader moral and legal imperative to enforce the international ban on CW use.[89] Emboldened by the lack of international opprobrium, Iraqi forces used CW to attack Kurdish villages in northern Iraq during the 1988 Anfal campaign.[90]

At the time, *New York Times* columnist Flora Lewis sharply criticized the "deafening silence" of Western governments and warned that the "complicity of the world community" in Iraq's use of chemical arms would encourage other states in the region to acquire them.[91] Unfortunately, Lewis's prediction proved accurate. Over the next several years Iran, Libya, Syria, and other states in the region

88. Julian Perry Robinson, "News Chronology, May through August 1998," *CBW Conventions Bulletin* No. 41 (Sep. 1998), p. 35.

89. Leonard A. Cole, *The Eleventh Plague: The Politics of Biological and Chemical Warfare* (New York: W. H. Freeman, 1997), pp. 93–5.

90. Eliot Marshall, "Iraq's Chemical Warfare: Case Proved," 224 *Science* (Apr. 13, 1984), pp. 130–31; Lois Ember, "Chemical Weapons: Residues Verify Iraqi Use on Kurds," 711 *Chemical and Engineering News* (May 3, 1993), p. 8.

91. Flora Lewis, "Move to Stop Iraq," *New York Times* (Sep. 14, 1988), p. A31.

moved to acquire BCW capabilities or to expand their existing arsenals.

Restoring the Norm: The Australia Group

The first attempt to shore up the international norm against chemical warfare was the establishment of the Australia Group, an informal forum of industrialized countries that cooperate in efforts to curb the spread of BCW by harmonizing their national export controls and sharing information on BCW proliferation programs. The initial impetus for this effort came in 1984, when a number of countries took steps to control the export of CW ingredients ("precursors") to Iraq, which was then using chemical weapons in its war with Iran. The following year, fifteen nations assessed the effectiveness of their actions and concluded that a more coordinated effort was needed to reduce the risk of chemical proliferation. Accordingly, they established the Australia Group (AG), which convened for the first time in June 1985 at the Australian Embassy in Brussels.[92] In December 1991, the group expanded its coverage to BW.[93]

The AG meets annually in Paris and currently has thirty-one members, including Australia, the European Union countries, Japan, and the United States.[94] With respect to CW, participating states control the export of a list of fifty-four precursors and intermediate chemicals that can be used to make CW agents, along with certain types of production equipment. For BW, AG members control the export of a list of microorganisms, toxins, and specified

92. Gordon K. Vachon, "The Australia Group and Proliferation Concerns," *UNIDIR Newsletter* No. 33/96, p. 59–61.

93. Stuart Auerbach, "19 Nations Back US Plan for Chemical Arms Curbs," *Washington Post* (May 31, 1991), pp. A1, A9.

94. Xinhua English Newswire, "Cyprus to Join in Struggle Against Chemical Weapons" (Dec. 19, 1998) (available on Westlaw at 1998 WL 19504302).

production equipment.[95] Companies must apply to their national governments for a license to ship controlled materials and equipment to specified countries that are known or suspected proliferators.

The impact of the AG on the spread of BCW is difficult to quantify. Although determined proliferators can circumvent national export controls by means of middlemen, front companies, and multiple transshipment points, trade restrictions can slow the pace of proliferation and increase the associated costs. Perhaps more important, the AG serves to symbolize and reinforce the international norm against BCW acquisition and use. As Brad Roberts points out, "How seriously would that norm be taken by potential challengers if businesses were actively competing to sell the implements of [biological and chemical] warfare even as diplomats and politicians profess opposition to such weapons?"[96] In addition, the AG provides a forum for an unusual degree of transparency and intelligence sharing on BCW proliferation issues among the "like-minded" member states. Canadian diplomat Gordon Vachon notes that AG members define their activities "in terms of a community of interest which, in their estimation, is not universally shared and therefore requires sustained effort."[97]

Restoring the Norm: The Paris Conference

In January 1989, the international community belatedly addressed the Iraqi challenge to the CW nonproliferation regime when representatives of 149 countries met in Paris for a Conference

95. US Arms Control and Disarmament Agency, "Fact Sheet: Australia Group" (Oct. 28, 1997).

96. Brad Roberts, "Rethinking Chemical and Biological Export Controls," 3 *Monitor* (Winter 1997), p. 11.

97. Gordon K. Vachon, "The Australia Group and Proliferation Concerns," pp. 59–60.

on Chemical Weapons Use.[98] In the Final Declaration, the participants solemnly reaffirmed the prohibitions in the Geneva Protocol, called on states that had not yet done so to ratify the treaty, and strengthened the role of the UN in investigating the alleged use of chemical weapons.[99] The Paris conference also stressed the need for a comprehensive international agreement banning CW, giving new impetus to the CWC negotiations. Regrettably, a US proposal to impose economic sanctions on users of poison gas was omitted from the final document at the request of several developing countries, who viewed such sanctions as a means to retard their economic growth.[100]

Also at the Paris Conference, representatives of Arab and other countries sought to establish a link between chemical and nuclear disarmament, while alleging a double standard in the nonproliferation policies of the industrialized world—particularly with respect to Israel's undeclared nuclear arsenal. These countries demanded that the process of prohibiting chemical weapons be embedded in a broader effort to ban all weapons of mass destruction.[101] As Richard Price has observed, the rhetorical linkage between chemical and nuclear weapons could potentially erode the robustness of the CW taboo by justifying their possession as a deterrent. Since the actual use of nuclear weapons is widely perceived as illegitimate, however, on balance the linkage to nuclear weapons has tended to reinforce the norm against chemical warfare.[102]

In parallel with the multilateral talks in Geneva, the US and the

98. Norman Kempster, "Libya Plant Adds Urgency to Paris Talks," *Los Angeles Times* (Jan. 5, 1989), pp. 6, 7.

99. ACDA, *Arms Control and Disarmament Agreements*, p. 14.

100. United Nations, 14 *United Nations Disarmament Yearbook* (New York: United Nations, 1989), chap. 11.

101. Pierre Morel, "The Paris Conference on the Prohibition of Chemical Weapons," 12 *Disarmament* (Summer 1989), pp. 127–44.

102. Richard M. Price, "The Genealogy of the Chemical Weapons Taboo," p. 100.

Soviet Union conducted a series of bilateral negotiations that led to the signing of the so-called Wyoming Memorandum of Understanding (MOU) by then Secretary of State James Baker and then Soviet Foreign Minister Eduard Shevardnadze in September 1989. This agreement provided for exchanges of data on the two countries' CW stockpiles and former production facilities, as well as reciprocal visits to some of these sites. Meanwhile, the Government-Industry Conference Against Chemical Weapons, held in Canberra, Australia, in September 1989, brought together representatives of governments and the international chemical industry. The main accomplishment of this meeting was to rally chemical-industry support behind efforts to achieve a global CW ban.[103]

In June 1990, Presidents Bush and Gorbachev signed the US-Soviet Bilateral Destruction Agreement (BDA), which committed the two countries to halt the production of CW, to destroy all but 5,000 tons of their respective chemical stockpiles, and to accept bilateral verification measures to ensure compliance with these provisions.[104] Although the United States had ended an eighteen-year moratorium on production of CW in 1987 by commencing the manufacture of binary munitions, it stopped the binary program when the bilateral agreement was signed. A verification protocol for the BDA was to have been negotiated by the end of 1990, but the talks bogged down and the agreement never entered into force.[105]

103. Herschel Hurst, "Australia: Chemical Weapons: A Declaration of 'War'," 16 *Pacific Defence Reporter* (Oct. 1989), pp. 16–17. See also Julian Perry Robinson, "Review: The Canberra Conference," *Chemical Weapons Convention Bulletin* No. 6 (Nov. 1989), pp. 16–22.

104. "Documentation: Agreement Between the United States of America and the Union of Soviet Socialist Republics on Destruction and Non-Production of Chemical Weapons and on Measures to Facilitate the Multilateral Convention on Banning Chemical Weapons," 21 *Bulletin of Peace Proposals* (1990), pp. 363–69.

105. Thomas Bernauer, *The Chemistry of Regime Formation*, p. 28.

The Endgame of the CWC Negotiations

Meanwhile, the CWC negotiations continued in the Geneva negotiating forum, now called the Conference on Disarmament (CD). In September 1989, President Bush declared that the United States was prepared to destroy 98 percent of its existing stocks of CW within eight years after the entry into force of the CWC if the Soviet Union was also a party, and would destroy the remaining 2 percent within the next two years if all "CW-capable" states had become parties. Although the Soviets accepted this approach, other CD delegations strongly criticized the US for seeking a discriminatory regime in which the "haves" could retain their CW while the "have nots" would be prohibited from acquiring such a capability. Several months later, the US finally abandoned its insistence on a residual "security stockpile." In May 1991, President Bush stated that the US would destroy its entire CW stockpile within ten years after the CWC entered into force and would renounce the right of retaliation in kind immediately after becoming a party to the treaty. Bush also challenged the international community to conclude the CWC by mid-1992, moving the negotiations into the "endgame" phase.[106]

A further impetus to the multilateral negotiations came from Iraq's threat during the 1991 Persian Gulf War to initiate chemical warfare against the Coalition forces. Although Iraqi President Saddam Hussein ultimately did not employ his massive stockpile of nerve and blister agents, the Gulf War transformed CW proliferation from what had been mainly a theoretical problem for the US and its allies into a concrete security challenge.

In September 1991, three South American countries (Argentina,

---

106. "Prepared Statement of Ambassador Stephen J. Ledogar," U.S. Senate, Committee on Foreign Relations, Hearing, *Chemical Weapons Convention (Treaty Doc. 103-21)*, 103rd Cong., 2nd sess., April 13, 1994, S. Hrg. 103-869, p. 34.

Brazil, and Chile) jointly renounced the acquisition, possession, and use of CW. This treaty, known as the Mendoza Commitment, did not provide for verification of compliance but was an important step in strengthening the norm against chemical warfare and preparing the ground for the multilateral convention.[107] Bolivia, Uruguay, and Paraguay later acceded to the Mendoza Commitment.[108]

The year 1992 was crucial for the CWC talks. The negotiators at the Conference on Disarmament (CD) in Geneva recognized that they had a limited window of opportunity to conclude the treaty before international political interest and consensus were lost. As a result, the CD modified its negotiating mandate to set a deadline for concluding the treaty by the end of its 1992 session. The participating states also agreed that the Ad Hoc Committee on Chemical Weapons would remain in continuous session throughout the "endgame" phase. As a further impetus to the negotiating process, in March the government of Australia introduced a "model" treaty in which the unagreed sections in the rolling text had been replaced with compromise language. The Australian paper also laid out proposals for resolving some key outstanding issues, such as monitoring of the chemical industry and the conduct of challenge inspections.[109]

In May 1992, the chairman of the Ad Hoc Committee on Chemical Weapons, Ambassador Adolf Ritter von Wagner of Germany, drew on the agreed portions of the existing rolling text, substantial elements of the Australian model treaty, and "vision" papers prepared by various friends of the chair to develop a "chairman's text" of the CWC without footnotes or bracketed language reflecting national positions. This version, drafted in consultation with a

107. Ibid., p. 29.
108. Julian Perry Robinson, "News Chronology, February through May 1992," *Chemical Weapons Convention Bulletin* No. 16 (Jun. 1992), pp. 6–7.
109. Thomas Bernauer, *The Chemistry of Regime Formation*, p. 29.

large number of delegations, included proposals for compromise language on unresolved major issues.

The introduction of the chairman's text led to a phase of intensive negotiations at the ambassadorial level in which some of the outstanding issues were resolved or brought close to resolution by June 1992. To accelerate the talks, the participating states agreed that modifications of the draft convention could be made only if they were approved unanimously—a reversal of the normal consensus rule in the CD. This new rule made any major changes in the draft almost impossible, thus locking in the chairman's text, which met the interests of the large majority of countries.[110] In August, after a final push to resolve the contentious issues involving the conduct of challenge inspections, Ambassador von Wagner prepared a revised chairman's text (WP.400/Rev. 2) that was ultimately adopted by the Ad Hoc Committee.

To address the recurring concern of developing countries about "discriminatory" export control mechanisms such as the Australia Group, the AG member states made a formal statement in which they pledged to review their restrictions on trade in dual-use chemicals and production equipment "with the aim of removing such measures for the benefit of States Parties to the convention acting in full compliance with their obligations under the convention."[111] Even so, the timely conclusion of the CWC was only achieved through the liberal use of "creative ambiguity" to paper over substantive differences. On September 3, 1992, the last day of the session, the CD adopted the report of the Ad Hoc Committee on Chemical Weapons and agreed to transmit the draft Convention to

110. Ibid., p. 30.
111. Julian Perry Robinson, "News Chronology, May through 3 September 1992," *Chemical Weapons Convention Bulletin* No. 17 (Sep. 1992), pp. 22–23.

the UN General Assembly in New York, which endorsed it by consensus.[112]

Signature and Entry into Force of the CWC

On January 13–15, 1993, the CWC was opened for signature at a ceremony in Paris, at which time 130 countries signed. The signatory states also adopted the so-called Paris Resolution, which established a Preparatory Commission (PrepCom) to work out detailed procedures for CWC implementation where the treaty text did not provide sufficient guidance, and to create a new international agency that would oversee the chemical disarmament regime, the Organization for the Prohibition of Chemical Weapons (OPCW), to be based in The Hague. Over the next four and one-half years, the PrepCom met continually in The Hague to resolve organizational and verification issues, with the bulk of the work carried out by specialized expert groups.

The CWC specified that the convention would enter into force six months after the sixty-fifth country had deposited its instrument of ratification. This threshold was finally reached with Hungary's ratification on October 31, 1996, and the treaty entered into force six months later, on April 29, 1997. Although the US had been a leader throughout the CWC negotiations, the Clinton Administration failed to make ratification a priority and Senate action was slow—particularly after the November 1994 elections, when the Republicans gained a majority in the Senate and assumed the chairmanship of the Foreign Relations Committee, which has jurisdiction over international treaties. Opposition to the CWC by the Committee's new chairman, Senator Jesse Helms, and other influ-

---

112. For a detailed description of the endgame of the CWC negotiations, see Hassan Mashhadi, "How the Negotiations Ended," *Chemical Weapons Convention Bulletin*, No. 17 (Sep. 1992), pp. 1, 28–30.

ential Republicans raised serious doubts about whether the US would be an initial party to the CWC at the time of its entry into force. At the eleventh hour, however, the White House launched an intensive and effective lobbying campaign.[113] After an extremely contentious ratification debate, the Senate finally approved the CWC on April 24, 1997, by a vote of 74 to 26, only five days before the treaty entered into force.[114] Although Russia, Iran, and Pakistan had not ratified by the date of the CWC's entry into force, they did so by the end of 1997.

Basic Elements of the CWC

The CWC is the first multilateral disarmament treaty to provide for the elimination of an entire category of weapons of mass destruction within a fixed time-frame, under a universally applied verification mechanism. The product of twenty years of negotiation, it involves a finely wrought balance between two sets of competing national interests:

- The need for sufficiently intrusive verification to build confidence in compliance *versus* the need to protect national security and industrial secrets unrelated to chemical weapons.

- The promotion of legal trade in chemicals for peaceful purposes *versus* the monitoring and control of chemicals with a potential for misuse.

113. Michael Krepon, Amy E. Smithson, and John Parachini, *The Battle to Obtain US Ratification of the Chemical Weapons Convention* (Washington: Henry L. Stimson Center, Occasional Paper No. 35, Jul. 1997).

114. John Issacs, "Arms Control in 1998: Congress Maintains the Status Quo," 28 *Arms Control Today* (Oct. 1998), p. 18.

Consisting of a preamble, twenty-four articles, and three annexes (on schedules of chemicals, implementation and verification, and the protection of confidential information), the CWC puts in place a legally binding international regime outlawing the acquisition and possession as well as the use of CW. The convention also bans the employment of riot-control agents "as a method of warfare," while permitting their continued use for domestic law enforcement. Member states must destroy any and all CW stocks and former production facilities within ten years (with the possibility of a five-year extension in exceptional cases), and they are prohibited from transferring CW to other countries or from assisting anyone in proscribed activities. An innovative provision of the CWC is that countries that refuse to join are prohibited from trading with member states in certain treaty-controlled chemicals. These provisions are designed to increase the costs and difficulties of acquiring CW for states that remain outside the regime, while imposing an economic penalty for nonparticipation.

In marked contrast to the BWC, which has no formal measures for verifying compliance, the CWC is the most ambitious arms control treaty ever negotiated in the scope and intrusiveness of its verification provisions, which fill some 140 pages of treaty text. Complicating the verification process is the fact that many industrial chemicals can be used to make CW. For example, a solvent present in ballpoint-pen ink can be easily converted to mustard gas, while ingredients for the production of fire retardants and pesticides can be used to make nerve agents. To ensure that dual-use chemicals are not diverted for illicit CW production, commercial plants that produce, process, or consume such chemicals must submit annual declarations and host routine inspections to confirm that they are being used strictly for peaceful purposes.[115]

The frequency and intrusiveness of on-site inspections under

115. ACDA, "Fact Sheet: The Chemical Weapons Convention" (Sep. 9, 1998).

the CWC are a function of the risk posed by a given facility to the objectives of the treaty. Facilities for CW production, storage, and destruction are subject to the most stringent verification provisions, followed by commercial industry facilities that produce dual-use chemicals that could potentially be diverted to CW production. In addition, as a safety net to capture clandestine CW production sites that deliberately have not been declared, all states-parties have the right to request the international inspectorate to conduct a "challenge" inspection at any facility—declared or undeclared—that is suspected of treaty-proscribed activities.

Efforts to Strengthen the BWC

With the entry into force of the CWC, attention shifted back to biological weapons. Not long after the BWC entered into force in 1975, a number of countries began to have concerns about its effectiveness. The treaty's lack of formal verification provisions (other than the feeble mechanism in Article VI for bringing alleged violations to the attention of the UN Security Council) made it little more than a gentleman's agreement. Short of the actual use of BW, there was no way to investigate violations of the basic prohibitions on development, possession, or transfer. Moreover, the dual-use nature of BW materials and production equipment, together with the fact that BWC explicitly permits the development of military defenses, complicated the determination of compliance. Finally, the discovery of recombinant-DNA technology in the early 1970s opened up the prospect of engineering microorganisms to make them more lethal, controllable, or persistent, causing some observers to reassess the potential military utility of biological warfare.

In April 1979, persistent Western concerns that the Soviet offensive BW program was continuing in secret appeared to be confirmed when the Russian city of Sverdlovsk experienced a serious outbreak of human anthrax. The US government claimed that the epidemic had resulted from an accident at a military microbiological facility in the city that was allegedly producing weapons-grade anthrax. But the Soviet leadership adamantly rejected the US allegation and insisted that the outbreak had resulted from the ingestion of anthrax-tainted meat.[116] Because the BWC lacked inspection procedures, it was impossible to verify the US allegations or the Soviet denials.

In March 1980, five years after the entry into force of the BWC, the First Review Conference to assess the treaty's implementation was held in Geneva. This meeting was marked by two noteworthy events. First, the Swedish delegation led an unsuccessful attempt to add verification provisions to the BWC by amending Articles V and VI. Second, based on the anthrax outbreak in Sverdlovsk, the US declared its suspicion that the Soviet Union was not in compliance with the BWC.[117] In 1981, the US State Department further alleged that the Soviet Union and its communist allies were using fungal toxins known as "yellow rain" against resistance forces and civilians in Laos, Cambodia, and Afghanistan. Here again, the available evidence was not sufficient to persuade international public opinion, and the accused countries refused to permit an investigation on their territory.[118]

The persistent, unresolved allegations that the Soviet Union was violating the BWC raised serious doubts about the effectiveness of the regime. In an attempt to strengthen the treaty, the Second Review Conference in 1986 approved a set of "confidence-building

116. Nicholas Wade, "Death at Sverdlovsk: A Critical Diagnosis," 209 *Science* (Sep. 26, 1980), pp. 1501–2.

117. Marie Isabelle Chevrier and Jessica E. Stern, "Chemical and Biological Weapons in the Third World," p. 54.

118. For a supportive assessment of the "yellow rain" allegations, see Robert L. Bartley and William P. Kucewicz, "'Yellow Rain' and the Future of Arms Agreements," 61 *Foreign Affairs* (1983), pp. 805–26. For a critical analysis, see Julian Perry Robinson, Jeanne Guillemin, and Matthew Meselson, "Yellow Rain: The Story Collapses," *Foreign Policy* (Fall 1987), pp. 110–147.

measures" (CBMs) that were politically rather than legally binding. These measures included the exchange of information on research centers involved in the development of military defenses against BW or equipped with high-containment laboratories, and information on unusual outbreaks of infectious disease.

The Third Review Conference in 1991, recognizing both the value of CBMs and their limitations, moved to improve and expand them. The initial set of CBMs was augmented with additional measures, including the declaration of vaccine production plants (which are easily diverted to production of BW agents), the declaration of past activities related to biological warfare, and the exchange of information on biodefense programs.[119] Unfortunately, although the CBMs are politically binding on member states, actual participation in these measures has been poor. From 1987 to 1995, only 70 of the 139 members of the BWC submitted declarations, and only 11 took part in all rounds of the information exchange.[120] Moreover, in the absence of a BWC secretariat, the national declarations are simply collated by UN staff and circulated to member states in the original languages. Because of these limitations, the two sets of CBMs have failed to achieve their stated goal of significantly enhancing openness and transparency with respect to BWC-related activities.

Revelations about the Iraqi and Soviet/Russian BW Programs

In the early 1990s, Western countries became increasingly concerned about the proliferation of BW. A key turning point came during the 1991 Gulf War. Although Iraq had signed the BWC, it had not ratified the treaty, so its legal status was murky. Western

---

119. Third Review Conference of the Parties to the [BWC], "Draft Final Declaration," Geneva, Sep. 27, 1991, BWC/CONF.III/22/Add.2, p. 7.

120. Alexander Kelle, "Developing Control Regimes for Chemical and Biological Weapons," 32 *International Spectator* (Jul.-Dec. 1997), p. 141.

intelligence assessed that Iraq had acquired a substantial BW capability, including bombs and warheads filled with deadly anthrax and botulinum toxin, and US military leaders feared that Saddam Hussein might employ these weapons against coalition forces. According to testimony by Gen. Colin Powell, then Chairman of the Joint Chiefs of Staff, "The one that scares me to death, perhaps even more so than tactical nuclear weapons, the one we have less capability against is biological weapons. And this was my greatest concern during Operation Desert Storm, knowing that the Iraqis had been working on such a capability."[121]

In April 1991, under UN Security Council Resolution 687 spelling out the terms of the Gulf War cease-fire, Iraq was required to ratify the BWC and to eliminate any stocks of weapons of mass destruction (defined as nuclear, chemical, and biological weapons and long-range ballistic missiles) and the means to produce them in the future. Compliance by Iraq would be monitored by a UN Special Commission (UNSCOM), whose inspectors were granted the authority to inspect any site in Iraq without restrictions. This comprehensive disarmament effort, backed up by an intrusive inspection regime, was a new and unique departure for the UN.[122]

Dramatic revelations about the Soviet/Russian BW program also provided a wake-up call for the international community. In 1989 and 1992, senior Soviet bioweapons scientists defected to the West and revealed that a complex of some forty ostensibly civilian research institutes and production facilities had in fact been engaged

121. Gen. Colin Powell, testimony before the US House Armed Services Committee, Mar. 30, 1993; quoted in Graham S. Pearson, "Biological Weapons: A Priority Concern," in Kathleen Bailey, ed., *Director's Series on Proliferation*, No. 3, UCRL-LR-114070-3 (Livermore, CA: Lawrence Livermore National Laboratory, January 1994), p. 44.

122. Jonathan B. Tucker, "Monitoring and Verification in a Noncooperative Environment: Lessons from the U.N. Experience in Iraq," 3 *Nonproliferation Review* (Spring-Summer 1996), pp. 1–14.

for several years in offensive BW work.[123] In January 1992, Russian President Boris Yeltsin admitted to "a lag in implementing" the BWC.[124] In April, Yeltsin issued Edict No. 390 ("On Fulfilling International Obligations with Regard to Biological Weapons"), which committed Russia, as the legal successor to the Soviet Union, to comply with the BWC.[125] Further, in an interview with a Russian newspaper on May 27, 1992, Yeltsin acknowledged that the Sverdlovsk anthrax outbreak of 1979 had been caused by "our military development" and not by the ingestion of contaminated meat.[126]

In September 1992, the US, the UK, and Russia signed a joint statement creating a "Trilateral Process" to address lingering US and UK concerns about the complete elimination of the Russian offensive BW program and to demonstrate the defensive nature of the remaining facilities. After initial reciprocal visits to selected facilities in each of the three countries, however, the governments were unable to agree on satisfactory procedures for more extensive mutual inspections, and the Trilateral Process ground to a halt.[127]

A third warning—this time about the nightmarish potential of BCW in the hands of terrorists—came in March 1995, when the Japanese doomsday cult known as Aum Shinrikyo staged a terrorist attack on the Tokyo subway with the nerve agent sarin, killing twelve commuters and injuring several hundred (although thousands of "worried well" arrived at hospitals for treatment). A

123. John Barry, "Planning a Plague?," *Newsweek* (Feb. 1, 1993), pp. 40–41.

124. Boris Yeltsin, "Statement on Disarmament by the Russian Federation President," Moscow Teleradiokompaniya Ostankino Television, First Program Network (Jan. 29, 1992).

125. "Yeltsin Commits to Germ Warfare Ban," *Washington Post* (Apr. 17, 1992), p. A28.

126. R. Jeffrey Smith, "Yeltsin Blames '79 Anthrax on Germ Warfare Efforts," *Washington Post* (Jun. 16, 1992), p. 1. For a translation of the interview with President Yeltsin in *Komsomolskaya Pravda*, see *Chemical Weapons Convention Bulletin* No. 17 (Sep. 1992), p. 9.

127. Amy Smithson, "Concerns Renewed about Russia's Bio Weapons Program," 2 *CBW Chronicle* No. 4 (May 1998).

subsequent police investigation revealed that cult members had earlier released anthrax and botulinum toxin in central Tokyo on approximately ten occasions, in an unsuccessful attempt to inflict mass casualties.[128] Disaster was only averted by the group's failure to obtain sufficiently virulent strains and to disseminate the agents effectively.

Negotiation of the BWC Compliance Protocol

The Third BWC Review Conference in 1991, in addition to expanding the number of politically binding CBMs, agreed to establish an Ad Hoc Group of Governmental Experts with the mandate to identify and evaluate potential BWC verification measures from a scientific and technical standpoint. This group of "verification experts," which adopted the acronym VEREX, met four times over the next year and a half. During this period, the group identified and evaluated twenty-one potential verification measures, both on-site and off-site, and assessed a number of measures in combination. The VEREX final report, issued in September 1993, concluded that although no single verification measure could distinguish conclusively between prohibited and permitted activities, the use of different measures in combination could strengthen the BWC regime and reduce ambiguities about compliance.[129]

Monitoring BWC compliance is particularly challenging because the equipment, facilities, and materials for cultivating biological warfare agents are essentially the same as those used for the commercial production of vaccines, antibiotics, vitamins, biopesticides, animal feed supplements, and even beer and yogurt. Such

128. William J. Broad, "How Japan Germ Terror Alerted World," *New York Times* (May 26, 1998), pp. A1, A10.

129. Ad Hoc Group of Governmental Experts to Identify and Examine Potential Verification Measures from a Scientific and Technical Standpoint, *Summary Report* (Geneva: Sep. 24, 1993), BWC/CONF.III/VEREX/8.

"dual-capable" technologies for industrial microbiology offer the potential for higher agricultural yields and improvements in public health. Yet these technologies also have a dark side, in that they enable countries to cloak the acquisition of BW under the guise of legitimate research and production.

Moreover, whereas CW agents such as sarin or mustard gas have no legitimate uses (except in small quantities for the development of protective measures), disease-causing microorganisms cannot be banned outright because the same agents that can kill or incapacitate have legitimate medical and industrial applications. Pharmaceutical companies routinely grow dangerous pathogens for the production of vaccines, and deadly toxins such as ricin, botulinum toxin, and saxitoxin play an increasingly important role in the treatment of cancer, neurological diseases, and chronic pain.[130] Recognizing these peaceful applications, Article I of the BWC prohibits the development and production of microbial pathogens and toxins "in types and quantities that have no justification for prophylactic, protective or other peaceful purposes."

The ability to produce pathogens and toxins with dual-capable equipment in small, clandestine facilities means that intrusive on-site inspections are needed to distinguish reliably between activities that are permitted by the treaty and those that are prohibited. A subjective element may also be involved. For example, preparing a vaccine against botulinum toxin involves the production of a large quantity of that lethal toxin, which is then inactivated. Since the inactivation step takes place late in the production process, assessing intent may be critical when judging BWC compliance. In general, however, the scale of production of pathogens or toxins for pharmaceutical purposes would probably be orders of magnitude smaller than for military use.

---

130. Lawrence K. Altman, "Botulinum Toxin's Promise as Drug May Rival Its Potential as Weapon," *New York Times* (Mar. 10, 1998), p. B13.

Creation of the BWC Ad Hoc Group

In September 1994, BWC member states convened a Special Conference in Geneva to review the VEREX final report and decide on next steps. This conference moved to establish a new Ad Hoc Group (AHG), made up of political representatives from interested BWC states-parties, to negotiate a legally binding Compliance Protocol that would deter violations and enhance compliance with the convention. Four issue areas were included in the AHG mandate: (1) the definition of terms and objective criteria for BWC compliance; (2) the inclusion of existing and improved CBMs; (3) the development of inspection and other measures for promoting compliance, including those evaluated by the VEREX group; and (4) concrete measures for enhancing international cooperation in the peaceful uses of biotechnology.[131] Although the Compliance Protocol will not be able to guarantee BWC compliance, the proposed measures should increase the level of transparency and raise the financial and political costs of maintaining a clandestine BW program.

Since January 1995, the AHG has met periodically in Geneva to pursue the protocol negotiations under the chairmanship of Ambassador Tibor Tóth of Hungary. Approximately 60 of the 141 member states have participated in the talks on a regular basis. The AHG met three times in 1995, twice in 1996, three times in 1997, and four times (for a total of eleven weeks) in 1998, indicating a gradual intensification of the negotiating effort. From the outset, the chairman relied extensively on working groups led by "Friends of the Chair" to discuss the four topics ("tirets") in the negotiating mandate. Although these working groups produced substantive papers, most of the discussion for the first two and one-half years was of a

131. Special Conference of the States Parties to the [BWC], *Final Report* (Geneva: Sep. 19–30, 1994, BWC/SPCONF/1, p. 10.

theoretical nature, with little emphasis on developing concrete measures and procedures. Only in July 1997 did the AHG move to a rolling text as the basis for negotiation, with words, phrases, and sections not yet agreed by consensus set off in square brackets. In July 1998, the AHG produced a fifth draft of the Compliance Protocol, which at that time was 251 pages long and consisted of 23 articles, 7 annexes, and 5 appendices. (The BWC itself is only about five pages long.) The rolling text also contained more than 3,000 items in square brackets indicating points of disagreement.[132]

Current Status of the BWC Compliance Protocol Negotiations

The Compliance Protocol will specify which facilities relevant to the BWC must be declared and how international inspectors from a future monitoring organization will carry out visits at facilities that are suspected, or merely capable, of producing biological warfare agents. Although the AHG moved fairly quickly in 1995 and 1996 to develop a framework for compliance monitoring that involved—like the CWC—a combination of declarations and on-site inspections, progress in negotiating the procedural details has been slow, with an average pace of one page of text per meeting. Nearly every aspect of the compliance regime has been debated, including what types of visits should be allowed, how the different types of inspection should be triggered, what facilities should be covered, and the mix of parameters for conducting inspections.

Concerns over the protection of trade secrets during inspections of dual-capable industrial sites have complicated the AHG negotiations. Industrialized countries that lead in the fields of biopharmaceuticals and biotechnology (such as Germany, Japan, and the US) are reluctant to permit intrusive inspections of commercial research

132. Frances Williams, "Germ Warfare Negotiations Progress Slowly," *Financial Times* (Jul. 13, 1998), p. 4.

and production facilities because of fears of industrial espionage. Since pharmaceutical companies invest hundreds of millions of dollars to develop and test new drugs and manufacturing processes, any negotiated protocol will have to include measures to safeguard proprietary information. A significant "North-South" split also exists within the AHG. Whereas the industrialized countries view the BWC Compliance Protocol as a means of achieving disarmament and preventing the further spread of BW, much of the developing world sees the Compliance Protocol as a vehicle for obtaining enhanced access to biotechnology for purposes of economic development.

The principal technical issues in the negotiation can be divided into five basic areas: (1) definitions, lists, and criteria; (2) declarations; (3) on-site inspections; (4) technical cooperation and assistance; and (5) the nontransfer of equipment and know-how for production of BW.

Definitions, Lists, and Criteria

Because many biological and toxin agents have legitimate applications in medical therapy, biomedical research, and vaccine production, and because fermentation equipment is dual-capable, the BWC focuses its prohibitions on purposes rather than specific agents or technologies. The "general purpose criterion" in Article I bans the application of biological and toxin agents for offensive military ends while permitting peaceful uses. This basic prohibition is intended to be broad enough to capture future technological developments, so that a country could not legally circumvent the treaty by developing new types of genetically engineered pathogens or toxin agents.

Russia contends, however, that Article I of the BWC does not specify which agents and activities are prohibited, and that more precise definitions are needed if future inspectors are to make objective assessments of compliance. To this end, Russia seeks, in effect, to amend Article I through the protocol by providing specific definitions of banned activities, agents, and quantities. Western countries reject the Russian approach on the grounds that making the treaty prohibitions more precise would inevitably create loopholes that would-be cheaters could exploit. A possible compromise solution would be to leave the broad prohibitions in Article I intact while developing definitions, lists, and criteria tied to specific measures in the Compliance Protocol. For example, illustrative lists of controlled agents would be required so that member states know which facilities and activities to declare.

Declarations

Disagreement still exists over which facilities relevant to the BWC should be declared and, potentially, opened to inspection. Mandatory declarations, by increasing the transparency of biodefense sites and dual-capable production facilities such as vaccine plants, would make it more difficult to divert them for illicit activities. But although the Compliance Protocol should cover all facilities of potential compliance concern, it should not impose an undue burden on the pharmaceutical and biotechnology industries. In particular, the industrialized countries are opposed to declaration criteria that would capture a large number of Western commercial facilities that are presumably low-risk, yet the developing countries do not want to declare a disproportionate share of their own sites. A formula will have to be found that addresses the concerns of both North and South.

On-Site Inspections

Nearly all countries in the AHG support the need for challenge inspections of suspect facilities and for field investigations of alleged BW use or suspicious outbreaks of disease, but they disagree on procedures for initiating these visits. Delegations face a tradeoff between making sure that challenge inspections of truly suspicious facilities and disease outbreaks are approved, and blocking frivolous requests intended as a means of harassment, espionage, or theft of trade secrets. Countries also disagree over how inspection procedures should be structured to minimize the loss of sensitive information unrelated to BWC compliance.

Further, the AHG is split over the desirability of "non-challenge" visits to declared facilities. Most European countries contend that conducting such routine inspections on a random basis would provide an effective means of checking the accuracy of declarations, deterring the clandestine production of BW agents at declared sites, and providing a baseline understanding of relevant civilian production capacity. But Japan and the US oppose random visits to declared facilities on the grounds that they could jeopardize commercial trade secrets yet would be unlikely to detect BWC violations. An emerging middle ground is the US proposal for a "clarification" process whereby the future BWC organization could investigate facilities of concern for which the declaration information is inaccurate or incomplete. If the suspect facility does not resolve these concerns in a satisfactory manner, a member state could request a clarification visit to the site.

Technical Cooperation

The developing countries in the so-called Non-Aligned Movement (NAM) are most interested in strengthening Article X of the BWC, in which states-parties undertake to exchange know-how, materials, and equipment for the peaceful uses of biotechnology. Western industrial countries contend that the Compliance Protocol is not the appropriate vehicle for providing technical assistance for economic development. They do, however, support the transfer of equipment and know-how that could enhance implementation of the Compliance Protocol itself. Possible areas of cooperation under Article X include biosafety and international public health, such as the enhanced surveillance of emerging infectious diseases that might be employed for covert biological warfare.

Nontransfer

A particularly contentious issue concerns the relationship between the obligations contained in Article III of the BWC (which prohibits member states from transferring materials or technology relevant to the production of biological weapons) and Article X (which requires states to facilitate trade and technology transfer for peaceful purposes). Several NAM countries contend that Article X requires the complete elimination of the AG and of national export controls targeted at BWC member states, on the grounds that such trade restrictions are redundant and discriminatory. The industrialized countries respond that Article III obliges them to deny exports of dual-use materials and equipment to states suspected of retaining a clandestine BW program, and that export controls are complementary to the Compliance Protocol and cannot be replaced by it.[133] Unfortunately, this issue has become highly politicized and is unlikely to be resolved until the endgame of the negotiations.

Prospects for the BWC Compliance Protocol Negotiations

Now that language has been developed for all essential elements of the Compliance Protocol, the AHG has transitioned to a phase of consolidating and refining the draft text. Although the major conceptual differences among AHG delegations mean that large portions of the rolling text are still in square brackets, broad agreement exists that the protocol should include the following basic elements:

---

133. Malcolm Dando, "Consolidating the Arms Control Regimes for Biological and Chemical Weapons," 20 *Disarmament* (1997), pp. 43–44.

1. Legally binding, mandatory declarations that provide transparency about activities of potential relevance to the BWC.

2. A clarification mechanism to ensure that all sites whose activities merit declaration are in fact declared, and that the declarations are accurate.

3. Procedures to get investigators on-site quickly for challenge visits and field investigations of alleged BW use or suspicious outbreaks of disease, with a mandate flexible enough to do their job effectively.

4. A lean and cost-effective international organization to implement the Compliance Protocol.[134]

The delegations in Geneva have a growing sense of urgency about getting the job done. At the September 1998 session of the AHG, the group agreed to hold five negotiating sessions in 1999, totaling 16 weeks, up from 11 weeks in 1998.[135] Ambassador Tóth's overall strategy is first to build a core of consensus on key issues within the Western Group, with an emphasis on resolving the dispute over nonchallenge inspections. He will then consolidate the support of the moderate NAM countries, and finally, during the endgame phase, attempt to win over the hardline NAM states by developing packages of Article X measures for technical cooperation and assistance.[136] Ultimately, delegations will have to make political compromises to resolve the hot-button issues. This process could result in the preparation by Friends of the Chair of "vision" texts

134. The Honorable John D. Holum, Acting US Undersecretary of State for Arms Control and International Security Affairs, "Statement to the Biological Weapons Convention Ad Hoc Group," Session XII (Geneva: Oct. 6, 1998), p. 2.

135. Ad Hoc Group of the States Parties to the [BWC], "Procedural Report of the Ad Hoc Group . . ." Twelfth Session (Geneva: September 14–October 9, 1998), BWC/AD HOC GROUP/43 (Oct. 15, 1998), p. 3.

136. Interview with Tibor Tóth, Chairman, Ad Hoc Group, Geneva (Sep. 24, 1998).

without square brackets. After a few more readings, Ambassador Tóth would prepare a clean "chairman's text" of the entire Compliance Protocol, opening the way to final approval.[137]

The time appears ripe for rapid progress because much of the technical work required to develop the protocol has been completed, and because concern over the proliferation of BW has reached the highest political levels. Although the Geneva negotiations have long suffered from a lack of high-level political attention, that situation has begun to change. On September 23, 1998, a meeting organized on the margins of the UN General Assembly in New York brought together ministers from fifty-seven countries, including Russia and Iran, to promote intensified work in the AHG. The ministers committed themselves to sustaining political support for the negotiations, including the "convening of a high-level meeting at the most appropriate time during the negotiating process in 1999."[138] Moreover, on October 6, 1998, John D. Holum, Acting US Undersecretary of State for Arms Control and International Security Affairs, declared before the AHG, "Nineteen ninety-nine should be the year of the BWC Protocol. You simply must—and you can—find the time, the energy, and the flexibility to finish."[139] On January 21, 1999, Holum revised his challenge by calling for the AHG to conclude the protocol in the year 2000.[140]

For that goal to be achieved, a synergy will be required between the solution of technical issues within the AHG and sustained high-level political support. It is hard to predict when the protocol nego-

137. Graham S. Pearson, "Biological Weapons Protocol Update," *Trust & Verify* (Sep. 1998), p. 3.

138. "Declaration of the Informal Ministerial Meeting on the Negotiation Towards Conclusion of the Protocol to Strengthen the Biological Weapons Convention" (New York: Sep. 23, 1998).

139. The Honorable John D. Holum, "Statement," p. 3.

140. Stephanie Nebehay, "Clinton Seeks Nuclear, Biological Arms Deals," *Reuters International* (Jan. 21, 1999).

tiations will have made enough progress for national leaders to set a firm deadline, moving the talks into the endgame phase. According to Chairman Tóth, 16 weeks of negotiations is far less time than was required for the endgame of the 1996 Comprehensive Test Ban Treaty (which took 26 weeks) and may simply be too short to wrap up the Compliance Protocol successfully in 1999.[141] Tóth also worries that the AHG talks may fall victim to outside political factors, including competing arms control priorities and the year 2000 presidential election cycles in the US and Russia. Many of the participating countries cannot handle two full-fledged multilateral negotiations simultaneously. Thus, unless the BWC protocol talks gain sufficient momentum, they could be overshadowed by the impending negotiation of a Fissile Material Cut-Off Treaty in the Conference on Disarmament and the 2000 Review Conference of the Nuclear Non-Proliferation Treaty.

For all these reasons, the window of opportunity for concluding the Compliance Protocol may close in late 2000. The consequences of failure would be grave. As British BW expert Malcolm Dando has pointed out, "Without a strengthened BWC, the international community will have less legal and institutional legitimacy in dealing with potential proliferators."[142]

Current Status of CWC Implementation

The CWC entered into force on April 29, 1997, and currently has more than 125 parties. The Organization for the Prohibition of Chemical Weapons (OPCW) in The Hague has 480 staff members from 66 countries, including some 200 inspectors trained and equipped to inspect military and industrial facilities throughout the

141. Stephanie Nebehay, "Biological Weapon Talks End for Year," *Reuters International* (Oct. 9, 1998).

142. Malcolm Dando, "Consolidating the Arms Control Regimes," p. 45.

world. As of the end of March 1999, OPCW inspection teams had conducted 439 inspections in 29 countries, including the United States.[143] Worldwide, the inspectors had visited 61 former CW production facilities, counted and checked more than 8 million chemical munitions and 25,000 containers of bulk chemical agent, and inspected 145 declared industrial facilities.[144]

Several member countries, including China, France, India, Japan, Russia, South Korea, the UK, and the US, have declared CW stockpiles or production facilities and are proceeding to eliminate them. One of the notable benefits of the CWC is that it has encouraged countries such as India and South Korea to come clean about their CW programs as a first step in treaty compliance, thereby strengthening the emerging norm against possession.[145] The picture is not perfect, however. Iran's declaration, for example, admits that it once possessed CW but denies a current CW capability.[146]

The early record of CWC implementation is also mixed. On the negative side, recent decisions by the Conference of the States Parties—the main decision-making body of the OPCW—have upset the delicate balance in the treaty between the rights of the inspectors and the rights of the inspected state, watering down the inspection regime and creating loopholes for potential cheaters. For example, although the scope of the CWC's basic prohibition covers any toxic

143. President William J. Clinton, "Text of Clinton Letter on Weapons of Mass Destruction to the Speaker of the House and the President of the Senate" (White House: Nov. 12, 1998); OPCW, "Inspections Accomplished," *OPCW Synthesis*, Issue 2/99 (Mar./Apr. 1999), p. 9.

144. José Mauricio Bustani, "Statement by José Mauricio Bustani, Director-General of the OPCW, to the First Committee of José Mauricio Bustani, the United Nations General Assembly" (New York: Oct. 19, 1998), pp. 2–3.

145. Amy E. Smithson, *Rudderless: The Chemical Weapons Convention at One and a Half* Report No. 25 (Washington: Henry L. Stimson Center, Sep. 1998), p. 15–16. Japan's one declared CW production facility was build by the Aum Shinrikyo doomsday cult.

146. Itamar Eichner, "Iran Admits to Possessing Chemical Weapons," *Yedi'ot Aharonot* (Tel Aviv: Nov. 20, 1998), translated in FBIS-NES-98-324.

chemical intended for use as a weapon, the Conference of the States Parties has ruled that analytical devices employed by OPCW inspectors can be programmed to detect only the limited number of chemicals listed in the treaty and their degradation products. As a result, a determined violator might produce an unlisted toxic chemical in a bid to circumvent the CWC.[147]

Other new rules approved by the Conference of the States Parties enable member states to confiscate and retain any piece of analytical equipment that host-country officials believe has not been satisfactorily cleared of proprietary data unrelated to treaty compliance, and to review the inspectors' notebooks. Such constraints on inspections may facilitate malicious obstructionism. According to CW analyst Amy Smithson, "These invented rights . . . offer [CWC] members means to evade detection by expropriating evidence that could document their own noncompliance."[148] Further, a widespread tendency by member states to overclassify the data contained in their declarations and inspection reports has greatly complicated the work of the OPCW inspectorate and made it practically impossible for individual countries to draw their own compliance judgments.

Another serious problem is that Russia and the US, the two most important member states with respect to the size of their chemical stockpiles, have set a poor example with their early implementation of the CWC. Russia, which possesses the world's largest stockpile of CW (roughly 41,000 metric tons), ratified the treaty in December 1997 and made its initial declaration within the required thirty-day period. By August 1998, the OPCW had conducted initial inspections of all twenty-four CW production facilities and seven storage

147. OPCW Technical Secretariat, Office of the Director-General, "Note by the Director-General: A Review of the Status of Analytical Support for OPCW Verification Activities," S/81/98 (Oct. 30, 1998).
148. Amy E. Smithson, *Rudderless*, p. 31.

facilities that Russia had declared.[149] Nevertheless, Moscow faces daunting financial, political, and environmental challenges in destroying its massive chemical stockpile within the timeframe specified by the treaty. Because of the severe financial crisis in Russia today, the government is allocating almost no money for CW destruction, and foreign assistance remains limited.[150]

According to the timetable specified in the CWC, Russia must have eliminated 1 percent of its chemical weapons (about 400 tons) by April 29, 2000; 20 percent by 2002; and all 40,000 tons by 2007. Yet Russian experts doubt that Moscow will be able to meet these treaty deadlines and believe that it will take at least 25 to 30 years to eliminate the entire stockpile.[151] For this reason, some members of the Russian State Duma (lower house of parliament) have called for Russia to withdraw from the CWC. On November 12, 1998, President Boris Yeltsin directed Prime Minister Yevgeny Primakov to seek foreign financial assistance to speed up the CW destruction process, but whether significant additional funds will be forthcoming remains uncertain.[152]

The US shares much of the blame for the early problems of CWC implementation. With or without the treaty, the US has renounced CW and is destroying the bulk of its chemical stockpile in accordance with a law passed by Congress in 1986. Yet for more than two years after the CWC entered into force, the United States was in "technical violation" of the treaty because of its failure to submit declarations for and host inspections of US chemical industry facilities. This violation was partly the result of a protracted delay

149. José Mauricio Bustani, "Statement," p. 2.

150. "Russia Short of Funds to Eliminate Chemical Weapons," *Interfax* (Nov. 10, 1998).

151. Pavel Felgengauer, "Chemical Weapons Will Have to Be Liquidated Already by Another President," *Segodnya* (Oct. 30, 1998), p. 2.

152. "Yeltsin Orders Chemical Weapons Removal," *United Press International* (Moscow: Nov. 12, 1998).

by the Republican-controlled Congress in passing the domestic implementing legislation needed to authorize OPCW inspections of
private-sector chemical plants. Although Congress finally passed the
implementing legislation on October 21, 1998, a dispute between
the Departments of State and Commerce over which agency would
have the lead role in ensuring industry compliance further delayed
the promulgation of the necessary regulations.[153] The lack of inspections of the US chemical industry throughout this period created
resentment among countries that had met their CWC obligations,
with corrosive effects on the regime. In particular, the chemical
industries of Europe and Japan became increasingly concerned at
what they saw as an unfair commercial advantage accruing to the US
chemical industry, and pressured their respective governments to
scale down OPCW inspections at their own plants.[154] The US implementing legislation also contains three unilateral exemptions and
restrictions introduced by treaty opponents that, if allowed to stand,
could seriously weaken the CWC verification regime by creating
loopholes that could be exploited by would-be cheaters.[155]

On top of these problems, Washington has been criticized for
its narrow, legalistic, and at times confrontational approach to host-
ing OPCW inspections at military sites, and for failing to deliver

153. Lois Ember, "Getting to Regulations," 77 *Chemical and Engineering News*
(Jan. 18, 1999), p. 41.

154. David Mulholland, "US Violation Endangers Chemical Weapons Treaty,"
Defense News (Sep. 28–Oct. 4, 1998), p. 6.

155. One measure would enable a US president to refuse a challenge inspection
on national-security grounds, the second prohibits the removal of chemical samples
from US territory for analysis, and the third sharply limits the number of US
chemical facilities subject to inspection by establishing an 80 percent declaration
threshold for treaty-controlled chemicals present in mixtures. If these restrictions
and exemptions are not removed in subsequent legislation, other member-states are
certain to demand the same treatment, creating loopholes for would-be violators.
Jonathan B. Tucker, "Chemical Weapons Treaty: US Signed, So It Should Comply,"
Christian Science Monitor (Jul. 29, 1998), p. 11

equipment and training it had pledged to the OPCW.[156] According to Smithson, "Unwittingly, the United States may have initiated the beginning of a domino effect of noncooperative behavior. If this trend is not reversed, it will degrade verification effectiveness over the long term."[157]

Another problem with the CWC is its lack of universality. Several known or suspected CW possessors remain outside the treaty regime, including Egypt, Israel, Libya, North Korea, Syria, and Yugoslavia. Even without universal adherence, however, the CWC should help to slow and even reverse chemical proliferation by isolating the relatively small number of countries that refuse to join, limiting their access to precursor chemicals, and bringing international political and economic pressures to bear if they continue their CW programs.

It is also true that every international regime takes time to reach its stride. In comparison with the International Atomic Energy Agency (IAEA) at the same stage in its development, the status of CWC implementation looks fairly good.[158] Yet if the CWC is to reinforce and inculcate the norm against possession and use of CW, it will require the sustained political support of all member countries, particularly the US. As OPCW Director-General José Mauricio Bustani has pointed out,

> The OPCW is earning its place in the system of international security. If properly nurtured, it will become a mature, cost-effective, global instrument to eliminate the scourge of chemical weapons from the planet for a very modest budget: $70 million—the cost of two modern fighter jets a year. But, at the end of the day,

156. "Inaction on Chemical Arms Treaty Outlined," 76 *Chemical and Engineering News* (Sep. 21, 1998), p. 33.

157. Amy E. Smithson, *Rudderless*, p. 48.

158. Ibid., pp. 20–24.

the Organization can never be better, more effective, or more exemplary than its Member States want it to be."[159]

To a large degree, the fates of the biological and chemical disarmament regimes are linked. Successful implementation of the verification provisions of the CWC will build confidence in the arms control process and give new impetus to the BWC Compliance Protocol negotiations. Conversely, the emergence of serious problems with CWC implementation could seriously undermine the ongoing efforts to strengthen the biological treaty.

Conclusions

Over the past century, the ancient taboo against the use of poison weapons, which was seriously eroded by the rise of industrial chemistry during the late nineteenth and early twentieth centuries, has gradually been reestablished. Out of the horrors of chemical warfare in World War I, the widespread revulsion against these weapons was embodied in a system of legal restraints that has proved largely effective in preventing a recurrence of large-scale use. Although World War II was fought in an unlimited manner, including the use of nuclear weapons, the major combatants refrained from resorting to their massive chemical stockpiles. Today, the Geneva Protocol banning BCW use is the oldest multilateral arms control treaty still in effect. At the same time, a new, expanded norm, embodied in the BWC and the CWC, is emerging against the development, possession, stockpiling, and transfer of BCW, although it has yet to become a part of customary international law.

While BCW nonproliferation treaties are not a panacea, they serve important national interests. The US gave up nothing to negotiate the BWC and still perceives no military advantage in pos-

159. José Mauricio Bustani, "Statement," p. 8.

sessing BW. Yet the existence of this treaty gives Washington a solid legal and political basis for denouncing the possession of these weapons by Russia, Iraq, and other proliferant states. Although treaties cannot guarantee against the future acquisition and use of BCW, they have significantly raised the political costs of doing so.

At the same time, however, the past few decades have witnessed serious challenges to the traditional system of institutional restraints, notably the large-scale use of CW during the Iran–Iraq War and the Soviet and Iraqi acquisition of large biological arsenals. It is therefore essential to strengthen the existing treaty regimes with mechanisms for monitoring compliance. Treaties that lack effective verification measures, such as the BWC, can be counterproductive by arousing mutual suspicions that erode rather than build confidence among member states.

Closely related to the verification problem is the question of enforcement. Until now, the international community has been unable or unwilling to devise legally enforceable sanctions to punish treaty violators. As a result, all arms control treaties rely primarily on the self-interest of the parties and the pressure of world opprobrium to restrain would-be violators. Unfortunately, moral restraints by themselves are not always enough. Without a credible threat of economic or even military sanctions in response to a persistent pattern of violations, arms control treaties will never play a truly effective role in containing and reversing the spread of BCW. Iraq's blatant violations of the Geneva Protocol during the 1980s and its defiance of UN Security Council-mandated inspections in the 1990s highlight the continual need to maintain, institutionalize, and enforce nonproliferation regimes—ideally with the help of specialized international organizations—if these legal instruments are to retain their effectiveness.

In addition to treaty verification and enforcement, an important prerequisite for influencing the behavior of states is that an international norm must be perceived as nondiscriminatory and not based on the narrow self-interest of any single country or group. As expert Matthew Meselson has argued, BCW should be seen as a threat to the human species as a whole and not just the US, the rich countries, or the nuclear powers.[160]

In recent years, the frightening specter of biological and chemical terrorism has captured the public imagination. This emerging threat has made it all the more essential to reinforce the existing BCW regimes. Although disarmament agreements apply primarily to states and are not designed to address the problem of subnational terrorism, the BWC and the CWC embody international norms that are accepted in practice by at least some terrorists. Were BCW to proliferate widely among states, their use by terrorists would become much more likely.

In conclusion, it is an unfortunate fact of life that every new technology developed by human beings has been exploited for both peaceful and aggressive ends. Whereas the twentieth century was the age of the atom, the twenty-first century will be the age of the gene. Biotechnology will make it possible to manipulate life processes for good or evil, potentially enabling leaders with vicious intent to commit genocide more efficiently or to modify human thought processes for purposes of manipulation. Because of the vast potential of genetic technologies both to enhance life and to destroy or control it for hostile purposes, preserving and strengthening the norm against BCW development, possession, and use will be critical for human survival in the next century.

160. Matthew Meselson, presentation at the 18th Annual Meeting of the Association for Politics and the Life Sciences (Boston: Sep. 5, 1998).

Tibor Tóth

Negotiating a Compliance Protocol for the Biological Weapons Convention

The biological weapons (BW) prohibition regime comprising contractual-legal, trilateral arms control, nonproliferation, export control, disarmament enforcement, counterproliferation, preparedness, counterterrorism, and defense measures is facing critical challenges. Earlier endeavors to fix problems produced mixed results because solutions were sought in fragmented areas of the prohibition regime in an ever-shifting manner.

The Challenges

The shift of emphasis between different areas so much characteristic of the past two decades started off in the area of contractual-legal measures soon after the entry into force of the Biological Weapons Convention (BWC) in March 1975. With the first serious problems in the implementation of the BWC in the late 1970s, it became quite apparent that the BWC could not compensate for many of the weaknesses of the 1925 Geneva Protocol, as had been originally intended. Incremental efforts to address some of the compliance flaws were undertaken practically from the very first BWC review conference in 1980. A mechanism to investigate alleged breaches of the 1925 Geneva Protocol was established by the UN Secretary-General, a set of confidence-building measures was developed from 1986 onward, and succeeding review conferences produced common interpretations of some of the provisions of the BWC. All these steps, in essence legally *non*-binding measures, were symptomatic treatment efforts that failed to remove the underlying cause of the problem in the contractual-legal area: namely, the lack of a legally binding compliance mechanism.

By the early 1990s, the emphasis had shifted to addressing compliance concerns in exchanges between the depository governments. In September 1992, as a follow-up to the decree of President Boris Yeltsin on securing the fulfilment of the Russian Federation's BWC obligations, the governments of the UK, the US, and the Russian Federation agreed on a set of trilateral measures. The steps included the agreement of the Russian Federation to visits to any nonmilitary biological site at any time in order to remove ambiguities. Such visits were to include, among other things, unrestricted access, sampling, and interviews with personnel.[1] The agreement further stipulated that "after initial visits to Russian facilities there will be comparable visits to such UK and US facilities on the same basis."[2] In addition, the three governments agreed to address a far-reaching set of further measures, including:

1. Joint Statement on Biological Weapons by the Governments of the United Kingdom, the United States and the Russian Federation (Sep. 10-11, 1992).
   2. Ibid.

- Visits to any military biological facility, on a reciprocal basis

- A review of potential measures to monitor compliance with the BWC, and potential modalities for testing such measures

- An examination of the physical infrastructures of biological facilities in the three countries to determine jointly whether there is specific equipment or excess capacity inconsistent with their stated purpose

- Consideration of cooperation in developing BW defense

- Examination of ways to promote cooperation and investment in the conversion of BW facilities, including visits to already converted facilities

- Consideration of an exchange of information on a confidential, reciprocal basis concerning past offensive programs not recorded in detail in the declarations to the UN

- The provision of periodic reports to their legislatures and constituencies describing biological research and development activities

- The encouragement of exchanges of scientists at biological facilities on a long-term basis

The US and UK made three informal visits to Russian facilities in 1992–93, and reciprocal Russian visits to the US began in 1994. Later the implementation of the visits was suspended due to serious differences about their modalities and interpretation of their outcome, casting some unfortunate shadows on the political and public relations impact of on-site measures. More recent joint statements, like the September 1998 Clinton–Yeltsin statement on the BWC, no longer contain any reference to the trilateral measures.

The repeated breaches of the 1925 Geneva Convention in the Iran–Iraq War turned world political attention to nonproliferation and export-control measures and brought into being the so-called

Australia Group (AG). The decision to take biological export-control steps in addition to the introduction of national chemical control measures in 1984 was intended by the AG's participating governments to avoid the propagation of these weapons in violation of international law and norms. By the early 1990s, the AG had undergone a horizontal expansion with its membership having almost doubled, and a vertical expansion with its biological agents and equipment lists having been consolidated. These developments highlighted the challenges faced by participants in an informal, legally nonbinding, consultative arrangement, in the wake of the proliferation of indigenous production capabilities and emergence of new suppliers, as well as a result of circumvention efforts. Participating governments concluded in 1993 that the effectiveness of the AG controls could not be established in an absolute manner, but that in their judgment

> they had clearly raised the cost of acquiring offensive CW capability by drying up some sources and diverting the delivery routes of CW proliferators. In some cases they had imposed barriers to the programs of countries with or seeking to acquire CW by forcing them to look to other alternatives, such as less efficient production routes. In other cases they might have raised the cost of acquiring CW to the point that an interest in CW was not pursued. Similar results were hoped for in relation to the Australia Group's efforts to prevent the spread of biological weapons.[3]

Participating governments recognized, however, that

> export controls on chemicals, microorganisms and equipment alone cannot be a complete barrier to the spread of chemical and biological weapons in the longer term.[4]

3. Australia Group Doc. AG/Dec93/Press/Chair/11.
4. Ibid.

The need for more complementarity between different components of the prohibition regime became even more trivial as a result of revelations of the UN Special Commission (UNSCOM) in the aftermath of the Gulf War about the achievements of the Iraqi BCW program in just a couple of years after its declared inception. In the BW area, the Iraqi achievements included the production and actual weaponization of large quantities of bacterial agents, as well as research on a variety of other BW agents. Iraq's BW program, as described by Iraq to UNSCOM, embraced a comprehensive range of agents and munitions. The program covered a whole variety of BW delivery systems, from tactical weapons to strategic weapons and "economic" weapons. A special facility dedicated to BW research and development and large-scale production was under construction, with most essential elements completed and production and storage capabilities operational at the time of the Gulf War. A number of other facilities and establishments in Iraq provided active support for the BW program. Detailed thought must have been given by the Iraqis to the doctrine of operational use for these weapons of mass destruction (WMD).[5] The magnitude of the Iraqi BW program demonstrated the understandable limitations of fragmented nonproliferation measures and justified the UN Security Council in its ensuing shift of political efforts to the area of disarmament enforcement carried out by UNSCOM.

Although UNSCOM was not able to certify that Iraq had given a full and correct account of its BW program, by the end of 1995 UNSCOM had identified the main components of the BW program and the basic characteristics for each component. The lack of detailed knowledge of Iraq's BW program did not prevent the physical elimination of major elements of the program and "the establishment of the ongoing monitoring and verification (OMV) program

5. Excerpted from Executive Chairman's 8th Report under Paragraph 8, Security Council Resolution 715 (1991), S/1995/864 (Oct. 11, 1995).

at suspect dual-capable facilities with the declared purpose of increasing the difficulty, expense, and political cost to Iraq of attempting to reacquire WMD, thereby serving to deter future violations."[6] More recent difficulties in sustaining monitoring and verification activities further illustrate the underlying rule for monitoring and verification; namely, that effective monitoring is not possible without a full understanding of former activities and that ultimately the yield of verification efforts depends on the level of cooperation of the party involved with these efforts and the degree of its openness. The remaining tools available in the absence of such cooperation and openness—economic and military sanctions based on Security Council resolutions—did have significant political and economic (in the form of lost trade opportunities) impact, which also affected the international community. These shared costs, which, in the case of economic sanctions against Iraq could be estimated for the international community to be in the order of magnitude of some dozen billion dollars, have to be taken into account when contemplating reliance in the long term solely on such *ultimate* enforcement tools.

The investments in the aftermath of the Gulf War in counterproliferation and in asymmetrical warfare readiness reportedly yielded important improvements in these capabilities in numerous countries. In the case of the US, the range of military responses was widened with encompassing military doctrinal refinements. As in the case of economic sanctions, the financial implications for preventive counterproliferation measures is a factor that cannot be ignored. It amounts to nearly $2 billion for each military buildup and presence (a total of more than $7 billion since the end of the Gulf War). Another phenomenon, which cannot and should not be easily dismissed, is the potential "anthrax-fatigue" of the public and the media.[7]

6. Ibid.
7. In November 1998, during the lead-up to the suspension of UNSCOM

The terrorist events in the Tokyo subway, at the World Trade Center, and in Oklahoma City launched an avalanche of studies, publications (both fiction and nonfiction) and scientific conferences, all dramatically describing the vulnerability of modern societies to terrorist threats. In the US, there was an acknowledgment of the need to provide assistance to federal, state, and local authorities to prepare them to provide emergency assistance, in the event of a domestic terrorist WMD incident.[8] In 1998 two Presidential Decision Directives[9] were issued to enhance the ability to prevent and respond to BCW and cyber-weapon attacks, more investments were made in domestic preparedness—including training of emergency and rapid reaction personnel, efforts undertaken to improve the public health system, and rationalization sought among the more than 150 federal offices involved in this area. All these concentrated efforts in the field of counterterrorism and domestic preparedness, not necessarily characteristic just of the US, should be seen against the background of an increase of terrorist incidents and a multiplication of potential threat scenarios.

Another recent general trend and shift of attention is the more articulated emphasis on BW defense. In the US, the more than fourfold increase in the 1999 budget authorizations for BW defense is to produce improved vaccination programs and stronger detection capabilities, as well as more funds directed toward the private sector in a situation still reportedly characterized by inadequate supplies of

---

activities in Iraq, *Newsweek* reported: "It has been a year since William Cohen strode onto the set of ABC's 'This Week' with a sack of sugar, and tried to scare the bejesus out of America. 'Call this anthrax,' the Defense Secretary intoned, pointing to a five-pound bag of Domino's that, he said, could kill hundreds of thousands. His act was part of an aggressive US campaign to portray Saddam Hussein as a world-class threat—and to justify military strikes that would at last end the impasse over Iraq's weapons programs. But the effort backfired." *Newsweek* (Nov. 16, 1998).

8. National Defense Authorization Act for Fiscal Year 1997.

9. PDD 62 and PDD 63 (May 22, 1998).

vaccines and protective equipment and by the still persistent need to fully integrate BW defense into training and planning.

Some important lessons can be drawn from the past two decades of the evolution of the BW prohibition regime:

1. The ever-shifting political attention between different areas of the prohibition regime could not result in a long-term, steady, and regime-wide prohibition strategy.

2. The fragmented approach prevented benefiting from synergies that different pillars of the regime might jointly yield.

3. The potential contribution of a global, legally binding compliance system has still not been tested.

Possible Remedies

What potential remedies can multilateral arms control offer for the challenges the BW prohibition regime is facing ?

In the field of arms control and disarmament implementation and enforcement, the verification protocol can provide multilaterally agreed, legally binding rules for the implementation of compliance measures, including visits and investigations. That would remove the heavy political burden of negotiating implementation measures on a bi- or trilateral, case-by-case basis. The verification protocol would set up a politically and financially more cost-effective system of verification implementation, with an estimated annual budget of $25–30 million.

The possible contribution of the verification protocol to nonproliferation and export control might unfold in the form of multilaterally negotiated trade rules against nonstate parties. In addition, the protocol might provide more transparency about activities relevant to nonproliferation and export control efforts in general. The potential export control benefits of the protocol will have to be measured against the background of political expectations to remove existing trade restrictions.

The potential contribution of the verification protocol to counterterrorism would materialize first in the form of a comprehensive set of national statutes, casting an information-gathering and information-processing net on relevant national activities and facilities. The implementation of compliance measures will have to be carried out in a manner integrating the national (authority) and international (organization) levels, providing concrete physical experience at the national level as well about relevant national facilities and ongoing activities.

As for defense and preparedness measures, the verification protocol might provide the framework for pooling, on a multilateral basis, various means of protection against BW, as well as expert advice and assistance in identifying how programs for the development and improvement of a protective capacity against BW could be implemented. For fighting emerging diseases, which is an important part of any preparedness strategy, the verification protocol would offer the advantages of a global approach, the only viable approach in the face of the rapid transmission patterns of emerging diseases.

Need for a Prohibition Continuum

Multilateral arms control or a legally binding verification protocol is no panacea. At the same time, it can play a useful role in addition to other ingredients of the BW prohibition regime, providing important positive synergies with other components of the regime. The development and adoption of a verification protocol would in itself demonstrate the determination of the international community to raise further legal, political, and moral barriers against BW and noncompliance with the BWC.

As the year 2000 approaches, three important anniversaries—the 100th anniversary of the Hague Convention in 1999, the 75th anniversary of the Geneva Protocol, and the 25th anniversary of the entry into force of the BWC—provide an appropriate philosophical context for reevaluating the lessons learned from the evolution of the BW prohibition regime. With the verification protocol to the BWC within reach, a more holistic approach to strengthening the regime should be applied, and the future verification protocol should become a basic pillar of a much needed prohibition continuum.

Rolf Ekéus

UN Biological Inspections in Iraq

On April 3, 1991, following the Gulf War, the UN Security Council in its Resolution 687 dictated the conditions for a cease-fire between Iraq and the victorious coalition supporting Kuwait. The cease-fire resolution was adopted under Chapter VIII of the UN Charter and thus became inherently binding on Iraq, as well as on all member states of the UN. The resolution stated that, when Iraq accepted the resolution, a formal cease-fire would enter into force between the coalition and Iraq. On April 6, Iraq submitted its acceptance to the President of the Security Council and a cease-fire was established. With this legal arrangement, a quasi-contractual relationship was established between Iraq and the Security Council.

The core element of Resolution 687 and the cease-fire arrangement was Part C of the resolution, which regulated the matter of

Iraq's weapons of mass destruction (WMD) and related delivery systems. According to this, Iraq was obliged, inter alia, to declare all its holdings of nuclear, chemical, and biological weapons, as well as ballistic missiles with a range of over 150 kilometers. Iraq had to declare all biological weapons, all stocks of agents, all related subsystems and components, and all research development support and manufacturing facilities. All these declarable items were to be eliminated under supervision and control of a special UN commission. In addition to the prohibition on Iraq's retaining WMD and related production, research and development (R&D) equipment, and material, the resolution contained a prohibition on Iraq's acquiring such items.

The UN Special Commission (UNSCOM) was to be established with the task of overseeing the elimination of the prohibited items. Furthermore, the Commission was tasked to monitor Iraq continuously in order to verify that the Iraqi government did not use its factories, laboratories, and equipment to get its hands on prohibited weapons, or to import weapons or related items.

The Story in Brief

On April 24, I took over as Executive Chairman of UNSCOM with the first tasks of assembling a team of weapons specialists and scientists, developing procedures and methods for the Commission's operations, acquiring data and information on Iraq's capabilities, and designing a watertight system for ongoing monitoring and verification (OMV) of Iraq. The Security Council had demanded that the OMV system should be developed within 45 days. It was obvious to anyone familiar with disarmament negotiations and arms control and verifications that this was a tall order. However, to accomplish this I recruited a small group—Elisabeth Borsiin-Bonnier, a Swedish diplomat and negotiator; Nikita Smidovitsch, a top Russian negotiator in the field of biological and chemical weapons

(BCW); and Pierce Corden, an American arms control expert from the US Arms Control and Disarmament Agency (ACDA), later to shoulder the responsibilities of Deputy Executive Chairman of the Commission. The group worked without interruption from June to early August 1991 and, after detailed consultations with the permanent members of the Security Council, I introduced the final product, a plan for monitoring and verification, which was unanimously adopted by the Council as Resolution 715 in October 1991.

Concerning the BW chapter of the plan, it was clear that the BW Convention (BWC) had been of little use for the drafting team, given the virtual lack of verification and compliance provisions in the BWC. Instead, the methods and structure of the Chemical Weapons Convention (CWC), still under negotiation in 1991 in the Conference on Disarmament (CD) in Geneva, were applied. All group participants had in-depth experience with these negotiations—myself as chairman of the CD's Committee on CW during the 1980s.

The central provision of the plan stated that UNSCOM should ensure through inspections and aerial overflights, as well as through information supplied by Iraq, that activities, sites, facilities, material, and other items—both military and civilian—were not used by Iraq in contravention of its obligations under the cease-fire resolution. The Iraqi obligations were, of course, not to use, retain, possess, develop, construct, or otherwise acquire BW—any stocks of agents, any related subsystems and components, or any research, development, support, or manufacturing facilities.

According to the plan, Iraq was obliged to make available to UNSCOM information on microorganisms and toxin equipment and facilities that could be used for purposes related to biological and toxin weapons affecting humans, animals, or plants.

The plan outlined in detail which facilities should be declared by Iraq, including facilities and laboratories meeting the criteria for risk groups II, III, and IV and laboratories designated as biosafety levels 3 or 4—according to the classification in the 1983 World Health Organization (WHO) bio-safety standards. In addition, all facilities at which fermentation was carried out for the production of microorganisms as toxins using vessels larger than 50 liters, as well as any site for the production of vaccines or for research, development, testing, or other support or manufacturing of the prohibited BW, had to be declared by Iraq. Iraq was to detail all scientific and technical documents prepared by sites engaged in work relating to toxins or microorganisms.

Iraq was prohibited from importing items or conducting any activities in the fields of microorganisms and toxins without giving prior notice to UNSCOM.

This highly condensed version of the plan indicates its wide scope, which would later be proved to be of the greatest significance for the success of UNSCOM in the BW field.

Early Stages

The initial declaration of Iraq, submitted on April 18, 1991, contained the simple statement that "Iraq does not possess any BW or related items" mentioned in the cease-fire resolution. On that meager basis, the first BW inspection team was dispatched by UNSCOM in August 1991 to Salman Pak, a site long suspected of being the base for weapons research activities. To the disappointment of the inspectors, it was found that only two weeks before their arrival the site had been cleaned up thoroughly. Salman Pak had been subject to air attacks during the Gulf War, but the Iraqi authorities had also moved away all equipment, leveled the ruins, and covered them with soil. However, the team managed to obtain admissions from Iraqi representatives that some research had indeed been carried out, although they maintained that the ten research papers produced had all related to protection for nonmilitary purposes and were nothing more than basic R&D. The authorities denied that there had ever been any relationship between the Salman Pak biological facility and any military establishment. Yet, already during the first year of inspections, UNSCOM's attention was drawn to the Al Hakam facility some fifty miles west of Baghdad, to which some equipment had been moved from Salman Pak. Other items like an aerosol chamber for dispersing microorganisms on large animals (dogs, sheep, donkeys, monkeys, and the like) had also been moved away from Salman Pak to a waste dump and crushed with a bulldozer. Al Hakam was a heavily protected site with barbed wire, air defense, and armed guards. It contained a number of buildings filled with pipes, valves, pumps, stainless steel tanks, and laboratories, as well as animal houses fitted with advanced ventilation and protection systems.

No documents, maps, or site drawings about the design and purpose of the Al Hakam facility were given to UNSCOM. The official explanation was that it was used solely for the purpose of producing single-cell proteins to serve as animal feed. To counter the skepticism expressed by the professional inspectors in their reports to me as UNSCOM chairman, the Iraqi government invited news correspondents and international TV crews to Al Hakam. The news media reported that the site was "obviously" an agricultural support facility. They had with their own eyes seen plenty of chickens happily consuming single-cell proteins on the grounds.

Iraq, insisting on its original official denials, did not provide any new information during 1992 and 1993. The UNSCOM teams carried out several inspections of Al Hakam, but at this stage the laboratory treatment of the samples taken at the site did not reveal any incriminating data.

During the same period, the Iraqi government, having in October 1991 immediately rejected the OMV plan as well as Resolution 715 under which the OMV had been approved, blocked all implementation of BW OMV. The tension between Iraq and the Security Council grew close to a breaking point in the autumn of 1993. How-

ever, on November 26, after intensive high-level talks between Iraqi
Deputy Prime Minister Tariq Aziz and myself, Iraq eventually
agreed to Resolution 715 and with that the OMV, including the
portion of the plan addressing BW-related issues. Subsequently, in
January 1994, Iraq provided a declaration of the items defined in the
BW OMV.

The declared sites, facilities, equipment, and laboratories—together with additional sites designated by UNSCOM—should have
constituted baseline facilities that were to be subject to continuous
monitoring by UNSCOM's OMV teams. Foremost on this baseline
were Al Hakam, the Daura Foot and Mouth Vaccine Production
facility, Al Taji Single-Cell Protein Pilot Plant, the Water Research
Center, and what remained of Salman Pak. Not surprisingly, the
Iraqi declarations turned out to be incomplete. There were failures
to declare all equipment and material subject to monitoring and to
declare movement, repair, or modification of equipment between
inspections—all of which made it impossible to establish a reliable
baseline for the OMV.

Operations

During the spring of 1994, as relations between UNSCOM and
Iraq continued on a rocky path both politically and technically, I
decided to take the unilateral step of building a baseline of all dual-
use capable facilities and items, thus identifying, even without Iraq's
support, all such items that could theoretically be used in BW production as well as in R&D. For this purpose, a team of experienced
inspectors was recruited to UNSCOM. Dr. Richard Sperzel, a US
military officer and BW specialist from Fort Detrick, Maryland, was
to lead a more or less permanent team of biologists, including: Dr.
Ron Barton of Australia, Dr. Gabriele Kraatz-Wadsack of Germany,
two British scientists—David Kelly and Hamish Killip—and Dr.
Diane Seaman from the United States. In addition, senior scientists

from France, Russia, and Sweden joined in on a more temporary basis. When BW matters sometimes turned political, Nikita Smidovitsch was called upon to lead those portions of the work. By the end of 1994, a series of systematic baseline inspections had led to the identification of some eighty facilities and laboratories for inclusion in the biological OMV baseline. The observations during these inspections, in combination with rigorous and in-depth analytical studies of documents obtained, were put to highly effective use during interviews, amounting to cross examinations of some thirty Iraqi personnel. These interviews raised serious concerns, especially about the Al Hakam facility. In addition, a picture emerged in which a hitherto secret Iraqi organization, the Technical and Scientific Import Division (TSMID), appeared to deal with BW capabilities as the Iraqi government organ responsible for imports and procurement.

In December 1994, I was able to inform the Security Council about these concerns, stating in a report (UN Document S/1994/1422) that "while access has been provided to interview the personnel in the declared program, interviewees refused to answer questions relating to the [BW] program, providing only incomplete and misleading information." I further stated that, in spite of the insistence by the Iraqis that the BW program was in its early stages and was to have been defensively oriented, the indications all pointed to an offensive program.

It is important to observe that these new findings of UNSCOM of a concealed and not declared BW activity were a result of the baseline inspections for making the OMV plan operational. The broad scope of these inspections provided the inspectors with a countrywide overview, where patterns emerged that were telling enough to experienced and trained analysts.

Beginning in December 1994, the UNSCOM BW team initiated a series of sharp inspections of suspect facilities in Iraq and also started the penetration of Iraq's procurement network. In January

1995, these activities yielded a major breakthrough, as compelling evidence was obtained about imports of complex growth media (used by bacteriologists to cultivate microorganisms and toxins). Growth media have many legitimate uses in hospitals and clinics, mainly for diagnostic purposes. Iraq admitted that TSMID had imported large quantities of the media on behalf of the Ministry of Health for use in hospital laboratories. The problem with this explanation was that hospitals only use small quantities, acquired in small packages to reduce waste due to spoilage. It was discovered that TSMID had purchased 39 tons of media—some 30 times more than needed for civilian use, packed in large 25–100 kilogram drums. Of further significance were the types of media that had been imported. They were unsuitable for health care purposes, but ideal for large scale production of biological materials, such as warfare agents. The only rational use for quantities of media corresponding to the TSMID procurement was in BW production.

When confronted with the analysis of the BW team, Iraq presented accounts of incompetent managers, loss, theft, fire, and many other reasons to explain the discrepancies. The BW team searched warehouses and pharmaceutical factories all over Iraq. Much of the media turned out to be stored at Al Hakam. Of the 39 tons, 17 were missing in the accounting. Iraq alleged that this quantity had been distributed to some provinces, which all had been overrun by rioting after the Gulf War. The media was supposed to have been destroyed by the rioters. Such explanations were obviously not credible and Al Hakam became the subject of further scrutiny. New analytical methods started to yield results and samples taken from spray dryers at Al Hakam indicated that Iraq indeed had the technological know-how and capability throughout the country to produce BW with particle sizes associated with the dispersion of biological warfare agents. With Iraq's failure to account for all these items, the only conclusion that could be drawn was that there was a high risk that the media had been purchased and in part used for proscribed production of agents for BW. With this statement, I put the Security Council on high alert.

The April 1995 UNSCOM report to the Security Council (UN Document S/1995/284) became a milestone in BW verification when, in the face of Iraq's flat denials, the Commission documented and described the outline of a complete ultrasecret weapons program as regards BW agent production. At the same time, the Commission announced that the preparatory work for establishment of baselines for the implementation had been accomplished. Thus, monitoring began in full on April 4, 1995.

Well knowing he was cornered, Tariq Aziz continued stonewalling during the following months as to the existence of the BW program, while his BW experts, mostly led by Dr. Rihab Taha, responded to the inquiries by UNSCOM's BW team with one fanciful story after another and with only remote relation to the verified facts. Only after a sort of deal had been worked out between Tariq Aziz and myself during meetings from May 29 to June 1, 1995, was it possible to regain any meaningful progress. I undertook to give a comprehensive and reasonably positive update in the UNSCOM June report to the Security Council concerning the assessment of Iraq's CW and missile programs. To that, Tariq Aziz was to add a full accounting for Iraq's BW-related capabilities and activities.

The First Disclosure

Thus, in the June report (UN Document S/1995/494), I stated to the Security Council that with regard to the CW and missile files UNSCOM was satisfied that it had achieved such a level of knowledge and understanding of the prohibited programs that it could have confidence that Iraq did not have any significant proscribed capability and that the OMV mechanism would enable UNSCOM to detect any effort to reconstitute such programs. However, investigations would continue until UNSCOM was satisfied that it had the detailed picture. The BW side was, however, another story—the investigation was blocked. Nevertheless, UNSCOM could state that it had evidence that Iraq had obtained or sought to obtain all items and materials required to produce biological warfare agents. Iraq had failed to provide any legitimate cause for such acquisitions. Since the April 1995 report, UNSCOM had found further documentary evidence of Iraq's BW activities.

The Iraqi leadership appeared to take the June report as a delivery of the UNSCOM part of the May/June deal. On July 1, it provided its response in a major presentation delivered to me and the BW team in Baghdad by General Amer Rashid and Dr. Taha. In this presentation, Iraq admitted for the first time the offensive nature of its BW program. Biological warfare agents had been produced in large quantities at Al Hakam. Anthrax and botulinum toxins had been the preferred agents. They had been produced and stored in concentrated form at Al Hakam until October 1990. The Iraqis denied that the agents had ever been weaponized and insisted that they had been destroyed in October 1990 in view of the imminence of hostilities. In a subsequent conversation, Tariq Aziz denied emphatically that any instructions had been given to weaponize the BW agents. He repeated this denial at a plenary session on August 5, 1995, in Baghdad at the same time President Saddam Hussein threatened to end all cooperation with UNSCOM if there were no progress toward the lifting of sanctions—with the deadline set for August 31. On August 5, I declared that in spite of Iraq's assurance it was UNSCOM's conviction, on the basis of evidence, that Iraq had made efforts to weaponize the agents.

To summarize developments up to August 1995, it was the crushing evidence, based on inspection efforts, and the analytical activities of the BW team—combined with political pressure exerted by UNSCOM and a united Security Council—that brought the Iraqi government to a point where it had to end over four years of systematic misrepresentation and lying at all levels. However, the confessions were not wholehearted, as the Iraqis continued in their denials of weaponization in their declaration of August 4, 1995, which supposedly contained Iraq's "full, final and complete disclosure" (FFCD).

The Defection of Hussein Kamal

This holding out was quickly demonstrated to be in vain when, to the Iraqi government's embarrassment and shock, the overlord of the Organization of Military Industrialization, responsible for all Iraqi WMD programs, Lt. General Hussein Kamal—Saddam Hussein's son-in-law and the second-most-powerful man in Iraq—defected to Jordan. General Amer Rashid informed me about the defection on August 9, and a few days later on August 13 I received a letter from the Iraqi government where it admitted that since April 1991 it had been withholding important information from UNSCOM.

Subsequently, upon my arrival in Baghdad on August 17, 1995, a shell-shocked Iraqi government and its BW specialists disclosed a far more extensive program than previously admitted, including weaponization of BW agents into bombs and twenty-five missile warheads. On August 17, the FFCD had to be withdrawn. Some supporting documents were handed over that added richly to the UNSCOM BW team's understanding of Iraq's weapons.

On August 23, 1995, I started the debriefing of Hussein Kamal in Amman, an activity that yielded a mass of new information. Following this came a period of openness from the Iraqi side, and new data were submitted. Most surprising to me, and frightening, was the scope of Iraq's R&D, fortunately unsuccessful in most cases. Iraq's ambitions appeared to have had no limits, although in the end it turned out that the Iraqi BW program had to be organized around the "traditional" agents anthrax and botulinum. The October 1995 UNSCOM report to the Security Council (UN Document S/1995/

864) contained a massive amount of new information. In its conclusions, I emphasized that UNSCOM, to fulfill its task, needed a complete understanding of the concept behind each stage of the development of all proscribed weapons. It is this approach that must constitute the basis for any final declaration to the Security Council that Iraq has accomplished its obligations under the cease-fire resolution.

After the defection of Hussein Kamal and initial disclosure of a larger BW program, Iraq settled into its usual practice of minimalistic accommodation with regard to information both on agent development and manufacturing and on weaponization. This seriously delayed the work of the UNSCOM BW team but did not prevent it from remarkable accomplishments in its inspection and analysis work—supported by robust monitoring activities encompassing some eighty sites, including university laboratories and vaccine plants.

A high point in the Commission's operations was the destruction in May/June 1996 of the Al Hakam facility. The extensive buildings, equipment, and materials—all structures—were demolished using explosives, and the remnants buried. Large quantities of equipment and growth media used for germ production at other production sites in Iraq were also brought to Al Hakam and destroyed in the process.

In March 1996, a new tool was added to the monitoring system, as foreseen in the OMV plan of 1991. It was an export/import monitoring mechanism (EXIM) adopted by the Security Council through its Resolution 1051. With EXIM, the final building block of the OMV system was in place. A number of EXIM inspectors— normally customs officers—operate in Iraq with the task of verifying notifications by countries from which exports are made to Iraq of specific items identified on lists prepared by UNSCOM. These items are dual-use capable equipment and materials. When such an item has been imported into Iraq, the EXIM team notes at which site the item ends up. The OMV team is informed and can integrate the item into its baseline data, and from there on the item becomes an element in the OMV regime.

In the spring of 1997, I stated in my last formal report to the Security Council (UN Document S/1997/301):

> A solid framework with tested procedures for effective work is in place. It is now time for Iraq to make full use of this and provide the material and data to give substance to its stated commitment of full cooperation. The remaining problems are such that they cannot be solved through a technical process only. Their solution requires a major political decision by Iraq's leadership to give up, once and for all, all capabilities and ambition to retain or acquire the proscribed weapons. The Commission is well equipped in such an eventuality to act swiftly and effectively in carrying out its obligations.

The Methods

Intrusive Inspections

An absolutely essential component to the success in the biological field of UNSCOM was the authority to perform intrusive inspections. Casual, walk-through, polite inspections are insufficient where there is a concerted effort to conceal by the entity being inspected. Physical observations coupled with on-site discussions played an important role in identifying Iraq's past biological program.

Export/Import Information

The value of supplier information to the unraveling of Iraq's concealment of the proscribed biological program cannot be overstated. UNSCOM had suspicions that Iraq had not accurately reported its past biological program activities accurately, but could gain little momentum in obtaining convincing evidence of that fact.

Iraq's responses to UNSCOM questions suggested that it was hiding information. But only when solid evidence of the import of large quantities of particular media and media components by TSMID became available did UNSCOM have tangible evidence that was easily understood. Although the media issue was only a small subset of the information that UNSCOM had about Iraq's program, it played a large role in obtaining political support from UN member states. This was of great help in persuading Iraq to admit to its biological program.

Documents

Documents are indispensable for verification purposes and therefore Iraq went to great lengths to hide them. Special document search operations were launched by UNSCOM, sometimes with spectacular success. When documents were stored in the form of electronic data, the inspection teams had to be supplemented with computer specialists who demonstrated a remarkable skill in obtaining data out of the most protected computers. The documents could be progress reports from production facilities, financial and bank documents, travel logs, drawings, personnel lists, and production or research manuals. Certain documents of special significance had to be examined for authenticity; UNSCOM was able to draw upon the expertise of leading crime laboratories for such forensic investigations.

Interviews

In the absence of documents, interviews of Iraqi personnel alleged to have been associated with weapons programs were essential. Ideally, an interviewee should be free to speak without interference and intimidation from his authorities, something that was often difficult to achieve in Iraq. Only after tense conversations with Tariq Aziz in the summer of 1996 could I outline modalities for interviews that protected the interviewee from pressure and coaching by Iraqi authorities. Interviews, even with experts who are reluctant to provide information, are indispensable to verification and monitoring. Lies are very difficult to perpetuate if many people have to be involved. Invariably, Iraq's efforts to conceal information by the lies of its senior personnel began to break down as more people were interviewed and thus brought into the attempted concealment process. The Iraqi authorities resisted the interview process by UNSCOM probably because of this factor. Where it appears a person has something to conceal, the responses to relatively innocent questions often become bizarre; that, in itself, is a clue that something is being hidden. Interviews are thus one of the most effective tools in ferreting out a hidden program, in verifying declarations, and in monitoring.

Sampling

Sampling is another important adjunct to certification. Thus, samples collected from equipment at Al Hakam and other sites prior to their destruction in June 1996 produced evidence of secret BW production. New sampling and analysis methods have proven to be effective even where an agent has not been present for some years and where equipment has been subject to vigorous cleansing efforts. Cultures of biological agents that had been inactivated (by autoclaving) and then buried among other refuse in pits in the Iraqi desert were still identifiable five years later.

Multisource Analysis

All the collected information has been subject to very careful and critical analysis by experts thoroughly knowledgeable about all information on Iraq. The ability to connect seemingly unrelated information coming to UNSCOM from many disparate sources has been critical to the success of UNSCOM's work. Long-term continuity in staffing and corporate memory in the verification process are absolutely essential.

Information

Information, including intelligence that states were ready to share, became of great importance to UNSCOM. This required professional handling and data protection of sources and, above all, trust and confidence. As stated in the October 1995 report, UNSCOM must have complete understanding of the concept behind each stage of development of all proscribed weapons. Only when a comprehensive picture has been obtained and all loose ends have been brought into conformity with the big picture can UNSCOM have the confidence to declare to the Security Council that Iraq has accomplished its obligations under the cease-fire resolution.

Lessons Learned

The above narrative about UNSCOM and BW in Iraq is a good starting point for any discussion on the verifiability of the ban on BW. True, UNSCOM enjoyed extraordinary rights in Iraq, as it was implementing, not an international treaty, but the provisions of a cease-fire agreement. The BWC is general in scope. It is not directed at any specific case or country. Parties adhere to it voluntarily. It is assumed that the parties will observe their obligations in good faith (as with any international treaty). When a state commits itself to a multilateral treaty, it assumes that the provisions of the treaty are also respected by the other parties. A violation of a treaty is therefore an exceptional event. The verification arrangements are in place to create and support confidence between the parties.

All these facts make the control activities relatively easy and demand a light hand from the inspecting authority. It can be possible to identify something of a trigger list. There are indicators and signatures to which the inspectors must have an open eye. Such indicators can be undisclosed or underdeclared production, evidence of large-scale production capability, imports of large quantities of growth media and fermenters, unexplained foreign travel by personnel, specialized equipment without reasonable civilian use, facility designs and equipment of quality superior to declared purposes, and misleading statements and explanations.

With regard to monitoring of dual-use facilities and equipment, the UNSCOM OMV plan contains many ideas and solutions. The portion on rights, for instance, states that Iraq has to accord to UNSCOM:

- Unrestricted freedom of entry and exit without delay or hindrance, and unrestricted freedom of movement without advance notice.

- The right of unimpeded access to any site or facility for the purpose of on-site inspection.

- The right to request, receive, examine, and copy any records, data, or information; and to examine, retain, move, or photograph, including videotape, any item relevant to UNSCOM's activities, and to conduct interviews.

- The right to designate any site for observation, inspection, or other monitoring activity, and for storage, destruction, or rendering harmless of those items.

- The right to take photographs, whether from the ground or from the air, relevant to UNSCOM activities, and to take and analyze samples of any kind, as well as to remove and export samples for off-site analysis.

This is a rich menu, illustrating how complex and multifarious the monitoring activities must by necessity be when dealing with a state suspected of violating the prohibition on BW.

Especially difficult for monitoring is the dual-use character of BW production facilities. Fermentation technology is such that it can have commercial as well as military applications. One clear distinguishing characteristic, however, is that agent production for military purposes is by definition aiming at much larger quantities than practically any civilian application. (Production for terrorist purposes can, unfortunately, still be small-scale.) Another is particle size, where BW particles should be small enough to remain in the atmosphere and not quickly settle on the ground. Somewhere downstream in the production chain there emerges the production of delivery systems, bombs, missile warheads, drones, and spraying devices. At this stage, the uniformed men appear and the systems have to be brought into a command structure. At the same time, testing and training will become features of the BW force. All this provides signatures and indications, which can be picked up by an alert control regime.

The greatest developments in the field of inspection activities during the period of the UNSCOM operation have taken place with regard to sampling and, especially, sampling analysis. Thus, samples taken at Al Hakam in 1991 and 1992 did not originally yield any data, but with later progress in science, it became possible in 1996 and 1997 to obtain from the same pieces of equipment samples for analysis that contributed highly significant data—and thus hard evidence of Iraq's false declarations.

Since its outset in 1991, UNSCOM has become something of a proving ground for new arms control technologies and methods. Its successes in disclosing Iraq's supersecret BW activities demonstrate that much can be learned from such experiences. Even fully recognizing the many differences between the monitoring of a treaty freely entered into and arms control through cease-fire enforcement, the UNSCOM story will remain a major source of ideas and practices in the efforts to strengthen the BWC.

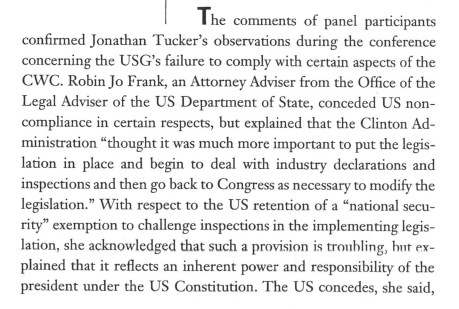

Commentary

The comments of panel participants confirmed Jonathan Tucker's observations during the conference concerning the USG's failure to comply with certain aspects of the CWC. Robin Jo Frank, an Attorney Adviser from the Office of the Legal Adviser of the US Department of State, conceded US noncompliance in certain respects, but explained that the Clinton Administration "thought it was much more important to put the legislation in place and begin to deal with industry declarations and inspections and then go back to Congress as necessary to modify the legislation." With respect to the US retention of a "national security" exemption to challenge inspections in the implementing legislation, she acknowledged that such a provision is troubling, but explained that it reflects an inherent power and responsibility of the president under the US Constitution. The US concedes, she said, that the invocation of such an exception under domestic law would violate its international duty and could subject the US to reciprocal responses. With regard to the limitation placed on thresholds for declarations and inspections of industries making mixtures of chemicals, she said this was a matter for which the Clinton Administration would seek congressional modification after the state-parties developed clearer, agreed standards. As for the in-country lab analysis provision of the implementing legislation, Frank noted this was a condition imposed by the US Senate in consenting to ratification, and therefore a legally appropriate—if regrettable—provision. The US, she assured the participants, was "committed to working with the Organization for the Prohibition of Chemical Weapons (OPCW) and other states to develop an in-country sample analysis mechanism that will ensure the analytical integrity and advance the objects and purposes of the convention." The search warrant requirement, she suggested, may be the most problematic aspect of the implementing legislation for the CWC.

Frank also commented on Tucker's observations related to the BWC. She felt that the sixteen weeks of negotiations scheduled for 1999 would enable the Ad Hoc Group under Ambassador Tibor Tóth of Hungary to develop a "protocol [that] will serve as an important mechanism for furthering compliance and transparency to countries carrying out their obligations . . . ." Even if all the elements of the protocol are not completed at the session, a great deal will have been accomplished in bringing the nations involved to approach the BWC's enforcement in a like-minded fashion. Finally, she described the background and work of the Australia Group (AG) as follows:

> [T]he AG is not a treaty regime. It is a consensual arrangement with thirty members today. . . . It is informal, unlike the Missile Technology Control Regime. . . . [T]he work of the AG and the other so-called suppliers' groups have played a critical role in de-

veloping the international community's view that one needs to take care where one exports production equipment and where one exports precursor chemicals. The group was formed in 1984 in the aftermath of use of CW during the Iran-Iraq War. . . . [T]he list of countries and companies that wittingly or unwittingly contributed to Iraq's CW and BW capability is appalling. . . . There is a developing concept of "know your end user," and the value of the AG's activities should not be underestimated in terms of norm development. . . . If a state participant does not carry out export controls in the way the AG has agreed upon as consensus, there are no sanctions except for moral suasion. Each country then implements its AG undertakings through the domestic export control regime. And so it works differently than the treaty regimes, but the end result in terms of norm development is very similar.

Michael Scharf also commented on the CWC implementing legislation. The reservation enabling the president to invoke national security to block a challenge inspection, he argued, may reflect existing domestic authority, but in practice its inclusion could have the same effect as the so-called Connolly Reservation, which reserved the right of the US to refuse to submit to any suit in the International Court of Justice (ICJ) that involved its essential national security interests. He noted:

> We never asserted that, [but] every single time we tried to bring another country to the ICJ, they asserted the Connolly Reservation against us and, as Abraham Sofaer has argued, that was one of the main reasons for terminating the US submission to the ICJ's compulsory jurisdiction. We shot ourselves in the foot by taking the Connolly Reservation. And this presidential opportunity to deny challenge inspections is going to be looked at very much by other countries like the Connolly Reservation and can be used against us when we try to enforce the CWC against them.

Scharf also questioned the wisdom of the judicial probable-cause determination for challenge searches under the CWC, noting the loss of US credibility caused by a Texas Magistrate's refusal—based on probable-cause concerns—to extradite a Hutu pastor suspected of killing many Tutsis in Rwanda.

Scharf also had several comments concerning Tucker's argument that an international norm had developed against the use of BCW. First, he noted the CWC's inapplicability to nonstate actors, such as Osama bin Laden. "[A]lthough they do get state support, and probably cannot operate without state support, the CWC does not create state responsibility for transferring precursors, technology, or expertise. . . . Germany most certainly knew, when it was allowing all of the technology, expertise and precursors to go to Iraq, that Iraq would probably use that in an aggressive way." He also observed that the CWC does not apply to "hold-out states," and even though "there is probably a customary international law prohibition on the use of CW, there is no such prohibition on the possession of CW . . . ." Most of the Arab states suspected today of possessing such weapons—Egypt, Iraq, Libya, Sudan, and Syria—have refused to sign the CWC, noting that Israel has refused to sign the Nuclear Nonproliferation Treaty. Scharf questioned the argument that BCW were not used in World War II because of a "taboo" against them. "My own research has indicated that the real reason that CW were not used in World War II was not because of a norm prohibiting them, but because of the fear of retaliation in kind . . . ." According to Scharf, that also applies to Saddam Hussein, as he "did not use CW against US troops, not because he believed in the norm . . . , but because George Bush made an implicit threat to respond . . . with NW or other devastating force if he were to do so." To be vital, Scharf maintained, the prohibition on CW requires "an expectation of consequences," just as the norm against genocide, "which everybody recognizes," must be enforced or we will continue to see genocides like the ones that have occurred in Uganda, Cambodia, East Timor, Bosnia, and Rwanda.

John Yoo also commented on the creation and utility of norms in international law. Norms imply a willingness to consent to certain conduct without the threat of sanctions, he argued, and in this sense the norm against the use of BCW is "an aspirational or moral norm," not one that meets the test of voluntariness. "[T]hese weapons were not used over a period of time because of deterrents." CW have been repeatedly used, he noted, where the victims had no capacity to respond. "So, for example, in World War II, Hitler certainly did not refrain from using CW against the Jews. And Iraq used CW against Iran." An international norm against use can be developed nonetheless, but this requires that states be convinced that nonuse (or nonpossession or any other norm) is in their interest. In the absence of consensus, Yoo asserts, lack of universal adherence should be expected.

Among the comments made by participants concerning the BWC were those of Dr. Alan Zelicoff of Sandia National Laboratories. He urged that participants in the negotiations of the BWC protocol focus on the enforcement of both Article I (including the meaning of "justification for prophylactic, protective or other peaceful purposes") and Article X (the obligation to cooperate in securing the convention's purposes). He recounted the USG's experiences with routine inspections, which he felt clearly demonstrate that "challenge inspections make good sense, but routine inspections do not." Others questioned his conclusions in this regard, and he referred interested persons to his published conclusions.[1]

Finally, in comments on the BWC Protocol, Tucker distinguished between BW and CW. These weapons "have very different characteristics, which in turn have implications for the types of measures that one would incorporate into a regime." The distinctions he noted were:

---

1. See, e.g., Alan P. Zelicoff, "Be Realistic About Biological Weapons," Letters to the Editor, *Washington Post* (Jan. 8, 1998), p. A20.

- Greater potency of BW than CW.

- Amount of material of military significance is much lower in the biological than in the chemical area.

- Number and variety of biological agents are far greater than the schedule of chemicals drawn up for the CWC.

- Inability to specify a quantitative threshold with regard to BW as compared to CW.

- Fact that BW are based on naturally occurring organisms, which cannot be used as a basis for verification to the extent possible with precursor chemicals used to make CW.

- Greater potential for legitimate use of dangerous biological substances than for chemical poisons.

- Ease with which biological agents can be destroyed, and thereby hidden, as compared to chemicals.

- Relative ambiguity of discovering dangerous biological substances, in light of their broader scope of legitimate use in comparison to chemicals.

- Enhanced danger to intellectual property posed in the biological area, because the pharmaceutical industry is concerned about protecting information, not only about the manufacturing process—as in the chemical industry—but also about the products they produce, which may mean sensitive information and also the production of microorganisms that are the "ingredients."

Further, he noted, "many companies actually genetically engineer the production organisms, which are extremely valuable to companies and they are very concerned about industrial espionage. In fact, there have been cases where visitors have put, for example, Scotch tape on the bottoms of their shoes and actually walked off with very valuable samples of microorganisms, which they were then able to reverse engineer." Tucker concluded, "the BW regime will have to take into account all of these concerns and protect this information. The technical differences between BW and CW will shape the nature of the measures needed to implement these verification regimes."

Part Four

Regulation of BCW:
Legal Constraints

Paul A. Brest

Introductory Remarks

This part of the book deals with what can be done, consistent with our Constitution and laws, to acquire information about biological and chemical weapons (BCW), to inspect biological and chemical facilities, to prevent violations of BCW commitments, and to deter and punish crimes involving such weapons.

The sense of concern and urgency we all properly feel about BCW must be seasoned with the realization that anxiety is at the source of all great challenges to constitutional order. However real and substantial is the threat posed by such weapons, measures may be advocated and adopted to control them and their use that may diminish or even jeopardize our constitutional rights and freedoms. The US has on several occasions been confronted by activities deemed threatening to its security, and has regularly fashioned responses that in retrospect have generally been acknowledged to have been excessive, unnecessary, unjust, and unwarranted by the threat posed. To name a few: the Alien and Sedition Laws of 1798; the Espionage Act of 1917; the Sedition Act of 1918; the Smith Act of 1940; and the Internal Security Act of 1950 (McCarran Act).

Our discussion should be far more than theoretical, moreover. The Chemical Weapons Convention (CWC) requires an inspection regime that allows warrantless searches, and it delegates to foreign officials powers that some have argued would violate the Constitution if implemented without necessary US oversight. The Biological Weapons Convention (BWC) will soon have a proposed compliance protocol, and it is likely to raise similar issues, including the threat to trade secrets and discoveries in medical research facilities. The horrendous bombings of New York's World Trade Center and the federal building in Oklahoma City led to legislative provisions in the Anti-Terrorism and Effective Death Penalty Act of 1996 that many have argued violate various constitutional provisions, including the First, Fourth, and Fifth Amendments. These genuine tragedies and the threat they represent were used as the driving force for securing legal powers that, as former San Jose Police Chief Joseph McNamara—now a Research Fellow at the Hoover Institution—wrote in a May 5, 1995, *Wall Street Journal* op-ed piece, have little or nothing to do with either the bombings or the threat. As he noted, "[I]t would be ironic if antiterrorist legislation helped destroy the protections of our Constitution and turned the delusions of paranoids into reality." In fact, after these words were written, the law was revised, and its controversial provisions are now vigorously defended by the USG and others as both necessary and proper to deal with the threat terrorism poses to US security.

In addition to the relatively conventional constitutional problems posed by the CWC, the anticipated protocol of the BWC, and antiterrorism legislation, we will also consider here the constitutional and statutory limits on the use of the US military in dealing with the BCW threat. The *posse comitatus* prohibition, and the Robert T. Stafford Disaster and Emergency Assistance Act of 1974, among other laws, reflect a reluctance to rely upon the military to enforce law within US territory. Congress has modified these rules in emergencies, as in the legislation authorizing the internment of Japanese-Americans during World War II, a far from reassuring departure. Should Congress authorize a broader military role within the US to deal with the BCW threat? And to the extent Congress is silent on these issues, what authority has the president to authorize the military to act domestically, and should he do so?

John C. Yoo

BCW Treaties and
the Constitution

The effort to regulate and eradicate bi-
ological and chemical weapons (BCW) has come to rely on broad
multilateral agreements for their success. Both the Chemical Weapons Convention (CWC),[1] and the Biological Weapons Convention
(BWC),[2] commit state-parties to renounce, among other things, the
development, acquisition, production, or possession of the weapons
in question. State-parties also agree to destroy existing weapons and
production facilities in their jurisdictions. Multilateral agreements

1. Convention on the Prohibition of the Development, Production, Stockpiling
and Use of Chemical Weapons and on Their Destruction, Jan. 13, 1993, Sen. Treaty
Doc. No. 21, 103d Cong., 1st Sess. (1993), reprinted in 32 *International Legal Materials* 800 (1993) (CWC).

2. Convention on the Prohibition of the Development, Production and Stockpiling of Bacteriological and Toxin Weapons and on Their Destruction, Apr. 10,
1972 (BWC). The treaty can be found at http://www.acda.gov/treaties/bwc1.htm.

seek to establish stability by enabling each nation to destroy their BCW with the assurance that other nations will undertake the same obligations.

Verification is critical to the success of these multilateral agreements. Unlike earlier arms control agreements, which placed numerical limits upon weapons stockpiles or limited the use of weapons in wartime, the CWC and BWC seek to impose absolute bans not just on use, but on development and production as well. The ease with which BCW can be manufactured and concealed, however, poses novel difficulties for a verification regime. Such weapons, moreover, often can be created by dual-use facilities that can double as civilian sites engaged in the legitimate production of chemicals and pharmaceuticals. Furthermore, the multilateral nature of the treaties requires a verification regime that allows multiple state-parties with disparate resources to measure compliance by each other. In contrast, earlier arms control agreements, such as nuclear weapons treaties between the US and the Soviet Union, forced the parties to rely upon their own national technical means of verification to ensure compliance.

To overcome these challenges, the CWC has adopted the most intrusive verification mechanism yet seen in an international agreement. It requires state-parties to provide annual, detailed reports on facilities that might produce CW, it subjects sites involved in the chemical industry to on-site inspections, and it allows state-parties to demand "challenge" inspections of any location in another party's jurisdiction. The CWC creates a new international organization, the Organization for the Prohibition of Chemical Weapons (OPCW), to monitor compliance with the treaty and to conduct inspections. State-parties interested in amending the BWC to improve its effectiveness are likely to demand similar verification mechanisms.[3]

3. See, e.g., Speech of John D. Holum, Director of the United States Arms

It is the intrusiveness of these verification procedures that produces difficulties under US constitutional law. The Constitution establishes certain guarantees that protect the rights of individuals and private organizations (such as corporations) and that limit the powers of the national government. The CWC and BWC's inspection regimes pose potential threats to these rights and limitations on governmental power, unless they are modified in certain respects to be consistent with the Constitution. This chapter will review the CWC's verification procedures, discuss the constitutional difficulties with these procedures and the manner in which Congress responded to them in implementing the Convention, and then raise some broader theoretical issues concerning the tension between the needs of arms control and the requirements of US constitutional law raised by the CWC.

The CWC establishes the most intrusive verification procedures ever contained in an arms control treaty. This is fitting, because the goals of the CWC can be achieved only if signatory nations can trust that other nations will obey the prohibition on CW. This is indeed a difficult task, because as many others have noted, CW are easy to manufacture and, as we have learned in regard to Iraq, can be concealed without too much difficulty.[4] As then-Vice President Bush, before the Conference on Disarmament in Geneva, explained:

[T]hese insidious chemical weapons are virtually identical in appearance to ordinary weapons: plants for producing chemicals for weapons are difficult to distinguish from plants producing chemi-

---

Control and Disarmament Agency, Before the Fourth Review Conference of the Biological Weapons Convention, Geneva, Switzerland, Nov. 26, 1996, http://www.acda.gov/speeches/holum/bwcrev.htm.

4. See David C. Gray, "Then the Dogs Died: The Fourth Amendment and Verification of the Chemical Weapons Convention," 94 *Columbia Law Review* 567, 574 (1994) (noting that some chemical weapons can be made simply by mixing two common chemicals together in a vat).

cals for industry and, in fact, some chemicals with peaceful utility are structurally similar to some chemicals that are used in warfare. So verification is particularly difficult with chemical weapons.[5]

As a result of the ease of manufacture and storage of CW, the verification procedures must be correspondingly intrusive and broad.

In order to achieve its ambitious goals, the CWC creates a verification mechanism that reaches not just manufacturers of CW, but also producers and users of industrial chemicals, of which there were reportedly at least 10,000 sites in the US in 1993.[6] Under the so-called challenge procedures, potentially any facility or location in the nation—whether involved in the chemical industry or not—might be subject to search. According to the treaty, challenge inspections can reach "any facility or location in the territory or in any other place under the jurisdiction" of a signatory nation.[7] Many if not most of these factories, industrial sites, and other locations will not be under the direct control of the US Government (USG), but instead will be in the hands of private commercial enterprises and companies.

The CWC's verification procedures are designed to detect different classes of chemicals. CW, of course, are the first priority. The CWC defines these substances as "any chemical which through its chemical action on life processes can cause death, temporary incapacitation or permanent harm to humans or animals."[8] The treaty calls for these weapons and their production facilities to be destroyed within ten years. On-site inspection and monitoring by the

5. Address by Vice President George Bush to the Conference on Disarmament: Chemical Weapons Convention, Apr. 18, 1984, quoted in Edward Tanzman, "Constitutionality of Warrantless On-Site Arms Control Inspections in the United States," 13 *Yale Journal of International Law* 21, 23 (1988).

6. US Congress, Office of Technology Assessment, The Chemical Weapons Convention: Effects on the United States Chemical Industry (1993) (OTA).

7. CWC, art. IX, para. 8.

8. CWC, art. II.

Technical Secretariat will occur through the storage and incineration of these weapons. As these sites and facilities either will be wholly owned by the USG or by defense contractors that have waived any Fourth Amendment rights as part of their contract, these verification procedures are not likely to present any serious constitutional difficulties.

The CWC classifies other chemicals into four categories; each category is subject to inspections of varying levels of intrusiveness. Schedule 1 chemicals, while not prohibited, are closely controlled because of their potential danger. These chemicals usually have been used or developed as CW in the past, and they have few commercial uses. The CWC limits the use of these chemicals and the amount that may be produced and stored by any signatory to 1,000 kilograms. Any facility that manufactures more than 100 grams of these chemicals may be searched on-site and is subject to on-site monitoring.

Schedule 2 chemicals are not as dangerous as Schedule 1 chemicals, but nonetheless are considered to pose a "significant risk" because they can be used as weapons or can help produce them. Although Schedule 2 chemicals are not subject to production limits, any facility that produces them also may be the object of an on-site inspection by the Technical Secretariat of the OPCW. The Office of Technology Assessment estimated in 1993 that there were 200 to 300 facilities in the US that were capable of producing Schedule 2 chemicals.[9] On its website, the OPCW now lists a "working estimate" of the total number of Schedule 2 plants "worldwide" as a number over 300.[10]

Schedule 3 chemicals are those that might be used as chemical weapons or as means to produce them, but also are used commercially in large quantities. Facilities that manufacture or use more

9. OTA, p. 15.
10. See "Verification of the Chemical Industry," at http://www.opcw.nl.

than 230 tons of Schedule 3 substances are subject to on-site inspection, and the Technical Secretariat is empowered to choose these facilities at random. The OTA estimated in 1993 that approximately 1,000 sites in the US produced or used Schedule 3 chemicals.[11] On its website, the OPCW now lists a "working estimate" of the total number of Schedule 3 plants "worldwide" as a number over 400.[12]

The final category of chemicals, labeled as "Other," includes all other organic chemicals (except petroleum) not included in the first three schedules. Facilities that produce more than 200 metric tons of these chemicals may be searched on-site, according to random targeting by the Technical Secretariat.

Inspections of CW sites, Schedule 1 facilities, and Schedule 2 facilities are to be governed by facility agreements between the state-party and the OPCW. These agreements will detail the nature and scope of inspection procedures. Inspection procedures for Schedule 3 and Other sites will be promulgated by the Technical Secretariat, but in any case the Secretariat is prohibited from conducting more than twenty on-site inspections of these facilities in any single state-party in any single year.

Details of the procedures are left to future development, but several prominent features of the CWC describe how the searches are to be conducted. Inspection teams from the Technical Secretariat must enter the state-party through a specified point of entry and must notify the state-party concerning the site to be searched and the type of inspection. According to the Verification Annex of the CWC, the inspection team enjoys "the right to unimpeded access to the inspection site,"[13] and the state-party has an obligation to grant the team access to the facility to be searched. Inspection teams may

---

11. OTA, p. 15.
12. See "Verification of the Chemical Industry," at http://www.opcw.nl.
13. CWC, Annex 2, pt. II, para. 45.

interview facility personnel, collect samples, inspect documents and records, take photographs, and bring testing equipment into the facility.

In cases in which a nation is suspected of operating a hidden or undeclared CW facility, the CWC relies upon challenge inspections. Each signatory has the right to demand an on-site inspection of any location within the jurisdiction of another signatory nation. The inspected nation must receive notification of a search at least 12 hours before the arrival of the inspection team; within 36 hours after the team arrives it must be brought to the facility, and it must be given some access for inspection within 120 hours after notification.[14]

The challenging nation must provide its reasons for the demand to the Executive Council of the CWC, but a three-quarters majority of the Council is required to block a challenge request.[15] There are no other limits on the number of challenge searches that one nation may demand of another. However, the CWC contains a provision that a signatory's obligation to provide access in response to a challenge is subject to "constitutional obligations," which apparently means that a signatory can raise a warrant requirement as a defense to a challenge inspection.[16] But this is by no means clear from the text of the treaty, nor is it clear how this warrant requirement would operate.

For the USG, the CWC's verification regime raises three discrete constitutional issues. First, on-site searches of chemical facilities or other private sites under both the routine and challenge inspection provisions of the CWC raise concerns under the Fourth Amendment to the Constitution, which generally requires that the government acquire a search warrant before conducting a search.

14. Ibid., pt. IX, X.
15. Ibid., pt. IX, para. 17.
16. David C. Gray, "Then the Dogs Died: The Fourth Amendment and Verification of the Chemical Weapons Convention," p. 590.

Second, the possibility that members of the CWC inspection teams may steal or inadvertently reveal the intellectual property of private chemical firms raises problems under the Fifth Amendment's prohibition on government taking of property without just compensation. Third, the Constitution contains structural provisions that seek to establish accountability by restricting the exercise of public power upon private citizens to officials of the USG.[17]

The Fourth Amendment and On-Site Inspections

Legal scholars have written extensively on the Fourth Amendment challenges for the CWC's verification provisions.[18] I will merely summarize the issues involved and provide my evaluation of whether doctrines providing for warrantless searches are applicable

17. For a fuller discussion of this issue, see John C. Yoo, "The New Sovereignty and the Old Constitution: The Chemical Weapons Convention and the Appointments Clause," 15 *Constitutional Commentary* 87 (1998).

18. See, e.g., Ronald D. Rotunda, "The Chemical Weapons Convention: Political and Constitutional Issues," 15 *Constitutional Commentary* 131 (1998); Robert F. Greenlee, "The Fourth Amendment and Facilities Inspections Under the Chemical Weapons Convention," 65 *Univ. Chicago Law Review* 943 (1998); Jonathan P. Hersey and Anthony F. Ventura, "Challenging Challenge Inspections: A Fourth Amendment Analysis of the Chemical Weapons Convention," 25 *Florida State Univ. Law Review* 569 (1998); David C. Gray, "Then the Dogs Died: The Fourth Amendment and Verification of the Chemical Weapons Convention;" Edward Tanzman, "Constitutionality of Warrantless On-Site Arms Control Inspections in the United States;" David A. Koplow, "The Shadow and Substance of Law: How the United States Constitution Will Affect the Implementation of the Chemical Weapons Convention," in Benoit Morel and Kyle Olson, eds., *Shadows and Substance: The Chemical Weapons Convention* (Boulder, CO: Westview Press, 1993), pp. 155–79; David A. Koplow, "Arms Control Verification: Constitutional Restrictions on Treaty Verification in the United States," 63 *New York Univ. Law Review* 229 (1988). I also have relied upon Wayne R. La Fave and Jerold H. Israel, *Criminal Procedure*, 2d ed. (St. Paul, MN: West Publishing Co., 1992). Many of these issues involving arms control and the Constitution were first identified by Louis Henkin, *Arms Control and Inspection in American Law* (New York: Columbia University Press, 1958).

to the CWC. The Fourth Amendment to the Constitution declares that:

> The right of the people to be secure in their persons, houses, papers, and effects, against unreasonable searches and seizures, shall not be violated, and no Warrants shall issue, but upon probable cause, supported by Oath or affirmation, and particularly describing the place to be searched, and the persons or things to be seized.

In interpreting this language, the Supreme Court has established a number of requirements. First, the Fourth Amendment restricts only searches conducted by the government, not those undertaken by private parties, unless the federal government significantly participates in, supervises, or facilitates the search.[19] We will return to this issue below. Second, the government action must rise to the level of a "search" under the Fourth Amendment. Generally, the federal courts will not consider a search to have occurred unless the individual who is the subject of the government action "has exhibited an actual expectation of privacy" and that this "expectation be one that society is prepared to recognize as 'reasonable.'"[20] If the individual or business enjoys an expectation of privacy, then the government's search must be reasonable.

In most cases, a court will not consider a search to have been reasonable unless law enforcement has received a warrant. When the government wishes to conduct a search for violations of criminal law, then it must receive a criminal warrant; when it conducts inspections for infractions of administrative regulations, then it must acquire an administrative warrant.[21] The Fourth Amendment guarantees that private citizens will not be searched at the whim of law

19. See Burdeau v. McDowell, 256 U.S. 465 (1921); Lustig v. United States, 338 U.S. 74 (1949); Elkins v. United States, 364 U.S. 206 (1960).
20. Katz v. United States, 389 U.S. 347, 361 (1967).
21. Camara v. Municipal Court, 387 U.S. 523 (1967).

enforcement; instead, a neutral judicial officer must be convinced that a warrant is appropriate. Furthermore, the search and seizure provision ensures that warrants will not issue in an arbitrary fashion. The judicial officer may not authorize a search unless probable cause exists, which can only be established if law enforcement presents evidence under oath establishing that the search is reasonable.[22]

In recent years, however, the Supreme Court has identified various areas in which a warrant is not required for a legal search. It has been motivated both by an examination of the "traditional protections against unreasonable searches and seizures afforded by the common law at the time of the framing,"[23] and by a growing recognition that the Fourth Amendment's text requires only that a government search or seizure be reasonable in order to meet constitutional standards.[24] In criminal cases, a warrant is generally necessary to show reasonableness, but, as Justice Antonin Scalia wrote for the Court in 1995, "a warrant is not required to establish the reasonableness of *all* government searches."[25]

The Supreme Court has recognized a number of exceptions to the general warrant requirement. The Court has held, for example, that a warrant is unnecessary for searches pursuant to arrest, for searches under exigent circumstances, for searches by consent, and for seizures of objects in plain view.[26] In recent years, the Court has expanded the grounds for warrantless searches in the drug-testing context and in random checks for illegal immigration, contraband,

22. Camara, 387 U.S., pp. 534–35.
23. Wilson v. Arkansas, 115 S. Ct. 1914, 1916 (1995).
24. Vernonia School Dist. 47J v. Acton, 115 S. Ct. 2386, 2390–91 (1995). See also Akhil Reed Amar, Fourth Amendment First Principles," 107 *Harvard Law Review* 757 (1994).
25. Vernonia, 115 S. Ct. 2391.
26. Chimel v. California, 395 U.S. 752 (1969) (warrantless search incident to arrest); Warden v. Hayden, 387 U.S. 294 (1967) (warrantless search due to exigent circumstances); United States v. Matlock, 415 U.S. 164 (1974) (consent); Coolidge v. New Hampshire, 403 U.S. 443 (1971) (plain view).

and drunk drivers.[27] The general principle at work here, the Court recently declared in the *Vernonia School District* case, is that a warrantless search can be constitutional "when special needs, beyond the normal need for law enforcement, make the warrant and probable-cause requirement impracticable."[28]

The exception most relevant for the CWC and BWC covers inspections and regulatory searches of businesses. These cases have arisen in the context of regulatory schemes that require businesses to adhere to certain public health and safety codes. In the first such case, *See v. City of Seattle*, the Supreme Court reaffirmed that the owner and the operator of a business had a right to be as free from unconstitutional searches and seizures as any other private citizen. Said the Court: a "businessman, like the occupant of a residence, has a constitutional right to go about his business free from unreasonable official entries upon his private commercial property."[29] But the Court also cautioned that business premises could be searched reasonably in more situations than private homes. In *Colonnade Catering Corp. v. United States*, the Court upheld a warrantless inspection of a liquor licensee's business due to the "long history of the regulation of the liquor industry."[30] In 1972 the Court permitted a warrantless inspection of a firearms and ammunition dealer, on the ground that the search was a crucial part of the regulatory scheme, that a warrant requirement could frustrate the inspection, and that the dealer had chosen to participate in a "pervasively regulated business" with the knowledge that his records would be subject to effective inspec-

27. See, e.g., Vernonia School Dist 47J v. Acton, 115 S. Ct. 2386 (1995) (random drug testing of high school athletes); Skinner v. Railway Labor Executives' Assn., 489 U.S. 602 (1989) (drug testing of railroad personnel); Treasury Employees v. Von Raab, 489 U.S. 656 (1989) (drug testing of federal customs officers); United States v. Martinez-Fuerte, 428 U.S. 543 (1976) (automobile checkpoints); Michigan Dept. of State Police v. Sitz, 496 U.S. (1990) (drunk drivers).

28. 115 S. Ct. at 2391 (quoting Griffin v. Wisconsin, 483 U.S. 868, 873 (1987)).

29. See v. City of Seattle, 387 U.S. 541 (1967).

30. Colonnade Catering Corp. v. United States, 397 U.S. 72 (1970).

tion.[31] If the reasonableness of a search depends on the defendant's expectation of privacy, the Court reasoned, then participation in a heavily regulated industry, with its pervasive rules and inspections, creates reduced privacy interests.

This last rationale—that warrantless inspections are constitutional in heavily regulated industries through some theory of implied consent—could have created a dangerous bootstrapping justification for warrantless searches. If participation in a heavily regulated industry amounted to consent to a search, then the imposition of an administrative scheme that called for pervasive inspections and regulatory searches itself could provide the grounds for the Fourth Amendment exception. The Supreme Court distanced itself from the implications of this approach when, in *Marshall v. Barlow's Inc.*, it held invalid warrantless OSHA inspections of almost any factory, plant, or workplace in the nation.[32] Finally, in a later case, *Donovan v. Dewey*, the Court commented that any implied consent was fictional and could not provide the basis for a warrantless search.

In the past fifteen years the regulated industry exception to the warrant requirement has become settled. In the past two cases in this area, *Donovan v. Dewey*,[33] and *New York v. Burger*,[34] the Court formulated a test which stresses that the regulatory scheme must establish a warrant-like process that constrains the discretion of the inspecting authorities. In *Burger*, the most recent case, Justice Blackmun for a 6–3 Court upheld a warrantless inspection of an auto junkyard because of five factors: (1) the duration and extensive nature of the regulatory scheme indicated that the business was "closely regulated"; (2) a substantial government interest supported

---

31. United States v. Biswell, 406 U.S. 311 (1972).
32. Marshall v. Barlow's Inc., 436 U.S. 307 (1978).
33. 452 U.S. 594 (1981).
34. 482 U.S. 691 (1987).

the regulatory scheme; (3) warrantless searches were necessary to further that scheme; (4) the scheme "provides a constitutionally adequate substitute for a warrant"; and (5) the inspection is "carefully limited in time, place, and scope."

Applying this framework to the CWC, it appears that there would be little difficulty in inspecting actual chemical weapon production, destruction, and storage sites. Many of these locations will be under the direct control of the USG and others will be owned or operated by defense contractors with whom the government already has reached agreement for warrantless inspection.[35] But whether the warrantless search exception includes private industries that produce Schedule 1, 2, or 3 chemicals is not plainly obvious, nor is it clear whether industries involved in "Other" chemicals or nonchemical industrial storage locations—under the challenge provisions, any location in the US may be searched—would qualify as closely regulated businesses under *Burger*.

At this moment, it is difficult to determine whether the Supreme Court would find that the chemical industry is sufficiently regulated to satisfy the initial prong of the *Burger* test. The Court has never suggested that the entire chemical industry is so regulated. Indeed, in a case involving the warrantless search of a Dow Chemical plant, the Court appears to suggest that the chemical industry generally is not to be considered a closely regulated business for Fourth Amendment purposes.[36] On the other hand, the chemical industry is subject to a number of comprehensive environmental regulatory schemes, under such federal statutes as CERCLA and RCRA, among others.

35. See David C. Gray, "Then the Dogs Died: The Fourth Amendment and Verification of the Chemical Weapons Convention," p. 622 and n. 343.

36. Dow Chemical Co. v. United States, 476 U.S. 227 (1986); see also Edward Tanzman, "Constitutionality of Warrantless On-Site Arms Control Inspections in the United States," pp. 49–53 (noting that "the pervasive regulation exemption to the warrant requirement may require expansion to encompass special on-site inspections").

But although these laws provide that the EPA has a right of entry to inspect the production or disposal of hazardous chemicals,[37] this does not release the agency from the duty of obtaining a warrant if an owner or operator of a business refuses to allow access to inspectors.[38] These warrants, even if granted on a lesser showing than probable cause, still must be issued by a federal magistrate or judge.

Furthermore, these statutes do not regulate all the locations and sites that might possibly be searched under the CWC's provisions, particularly those facilities falling into the "Other" and the challenge inspection categories. Indeed, under the challenge procedures, it is entirely possible, if not likely, that a location to be inspected would not even be part of the chemical industry, but instead might be an unrelated site simply suspected of harboring an illegal CW facility. How the Supreme Court would resolve a constitutional attack on a warrantless search of a non-CW plant, therefore, is unclear; in my judgment the available law and evidence does not indicate a positive result.

Moving to the other *Burger* factors, it appears that the second and third elements of the test—that the regulatory scheme must serve an important government interest and that the search serves a need of that scheme—are easily met in this situation. No one can doubt that eliminating CW is a significant governmental interest; and it is equally clear that warrantless inspections further that interest not only by detecting and deterring violations, but also by en-

---

37. Comprehensive Environment Response, Compensation, and Liability Act of 1980, 42 U.S.C. § 9604(e)(3)(4) (1988); Resource Conservation and Recovery Act of 1980, 42 U.S.C. § 6927(a); see also David C. Gray, "Then the Dogs Died: The Fourth Amendment and Verification of the Chemical Weapons Convention," n. 3, p. 625, and n. 351.

38. See, e.g., Koppers Industries, Inc. v. United States Environmental Protection Agency, 902 F.2d 756 (9th Cir. 1990) (EPA sought search warrant from federal magistrate after company refused investigators entry).

hancing mutual trust among the CWC's signatories that the treaty is being enforced.

The fourth *Burger* factor—requiring a warrant-like procedure—presents a more difficult obstacle for the CWC. The law at issue must inform the business operator that inspections will be made on a regular basis and that they are conducted pursuant to some objective criteria, rather than at the discretion of a government official. This requirement both provides the business owner with notice and limits the discretion of the government.[39] Although an administrative warrant mechanism might partially satisfy the fourth *Burger* factor, it is unclear whether the involvement of the OPCW might undermine the constitutionality of these domestic procedures. Under the CWC, for example, there are few, if any, standards that guide the Secretariat's decision to search, at least as to Schedule 3 and Other facilities, nor do any rules guide what locations may be chosen for a challenge inspection. In some cases, neither the Secretariat nor the challenging nation bear any legal obligation (enforceable under US law) to explain its reasons for selecting a particular target for inspection. It is difficult to see how the CWC constrains the discretion of the Secretariat or a challenging nation. Nor is it clear how many of the possible facilities that could be inspected will receive sufficient notice of the search, its scope, and its reasons. This situation may change, however, as the CWC's institutions develop internal rules and criteria for inspections.

Even if a court were to conclude that the CWC's verification procedures met all of these requirements, Congress need not be satisfied with the most minimal protections for individual constitutional rights. *Burger* establishes the farthest that government officials can go in the context of warrantless searches. Congress may demand a higher level of protection for Fourth Amendment rights. In the Civil Rights Act of 1964, for example, Congress chose to

---

39. Burger, 482 U.S., p. 711.

outlaw intentional racial and gender discrimination by private employers when the Court had not prohibited that activity. So, too, in this case can Congress prohibit the government from engaging in warrantless searches even when the Constitution permits them.

The Fifth Amendment and the CWC

On-site inspections of production facilities within the US raise another significant constitutional issue. The Fifth Amendment to the Constitution declares that private property shall not "be taken for public use, without just compensation."[40] As the Supreme Court has noted, intellectual property, such as patents, copyrights, trademarks, and trade secrets, are a form of property that falls under the protection of the amendment.[41] Therefore, the government can fall afoul of the Takings Clause if it takes patented information in the course of its activities for the purpose of providing it to competitors, or even if it inadvertently reveals a trade secret in a manner that reduces its value by making it publicly available.[42] The Fifth Amendment is not a prohibition on action, but only a remedial provision. It does not completely bar the government from taking property, but it does require the government to pay fair compensation when it does. The inspection regime created by the CWC disrupts the balance struck by the Constitution between government power and private property. Under the CWC, inspectors will have the right to enter US commercial facilities and examine their manufacturing and research and development processes. Although the inspectors will be officials of the OPCW, they will also be citizens of other nations. As they will possess technical expertise in CW and the chemical

40. U.S. Const. Amend. V.
41. Dow Chemical Co. v. United States, 476 U.S. 227 (1986); Ruckelshaus v. Monsanto, 467 U.S. 986 (1984).
42. Ibid.

industry, they most likely will come from backgrounds in government, the military, the chemical industry, or academia. Thus, their activities will pose a threat of industrial espionage, especially with respect to inspectors from cultures that place a lower value upon intellectual property than does the US. US chemical companies will find it difficult both to prevent such illegal thefts and to receive a remedy for them. The CWC allows a state-party to demand an inspection of "any facility or location" within another state-party, which has the "obligation to provide access" to the inspectors. Private parties subject to the inspection have no right, under the CWC, to block or even question a search—that right belongs only to the national government. To be sure, the CWC provides the state-party with the right to "prevent disclosure of confidential information and data, not related to this Convention."[43] The CWC, however, nowhere defines what information is and is not "related to this Convention," who has the ultimate authority to decide this question, and what rights of appeal and review exist for determinations of this question. Due to the dual-use nature of certain chemical research and manufacturing processes, scholars have observed that "virtually all relevant intellectual property" will fall within the scope of an inspection, regardless of its commercial value.[44] Indeed, the CWC appears to recognize the possibility of the theft of commercial secrets in urging that the OPCW take "every precaution" to protect the civil and military secrets it encounters.[45]

Unfortunately, the CWC's effort to address the problem of intellectual property theft seems weak. If a state-party is concerned that certain members of inspections teams named by OPCW pose a threat to trade secrets, it can declare that it will not accept those

43. CWC, Art. IX, para. 11(c).
44. Ronald D. Rotunda, "The Chemical Weapons Convention: Political and Constitutional Issues," p. 146.
45. CWC, Art. VIII, para 5.

inspectors.[46] It is assumed that the OPCW will not use those inspectors when selecting a team to carry out an on-site visit. Once an inspection is announced, however, a state-party "shall not seek to have removed from the inspection team for that inspection any of the designated inspectors or inspection assistants named in the inspection team list."[47] Furthermore, a state-party may not even be able to strike all of the inspectors that it suspects from the initial list. If the Director-General of the OPCW, for example, believes that a state-party's decisions on inspectors "impedes the designation of a sufficient number of inspectors or inspection assistants or otherwise hampers the effective fulfillment of the tasks of the Technical Secretariat," then he may refer the issue to the Executive Council of the CWC.[48] If the executive council overrules the objection, then a state-party will have to accede.

These procedures do not address the concerns raised by the Takings Clause, moreover, because they fail to provide a mechanism for just compensation for the loss of intellectual property. As a result, the CWC also does not grapple with the difficult questions concerning the procedures and the nature of a remedy for such a taking. Consider, for example, a hypothetical incident in which a member of an inspection team from Country A, who also works for Company A in that country, takes part in on-site monitoring and verification within the US as provided for by the CWC. In the process of conducting an inspection of a chemical plant owned by Company B in the US, this inspector obtains a trade secret by observing the manufacturing process of Product C. The inspector then returns to Country A, a large developing nation, and provides the intellectual property to Company A, which is a competitor of Company B. Company A uses the information to make its production

46. CWC, Verification Annex, Part II, para. 2.
47. Ibid., para. 5.
48. Ibid., para. 7.

processes more efficient, and as a result is able to compete more effectively with Company B, which is forced to lower its prices in the US and abroad for Product C simply to maintain market share.

Without any compensation mechanism, the difficulties for Company B of receiving any remedy are profound. Even stating a prima facie case is difficult. Unless it has its own proof, such as testimony or physical evidence from its own officials, Company B will have difficulty even alleging that the inspector stole its trade secret. It cannot force a court to subpoena the inspector to testify, because the CWC grants inspectors immunity, similar to that accorded diplomats, from domestic legal process. Such immunity, of course, makes sense because it prevents state-parties from fabricating legal charges to inhibit proper searches. It also creates problems, however, for parties seeking just compensation. Even if Company B could convince a US court to issue compulsory process to be served upon the inspector, the court could not force an inspector outside the US to obey its demand for information. Because inspectors enjoy immunity, moreover, no method exists to ensure that they tell the truth, as they would remain immune from US perjury and contempt sanctions.

The CWC also provides no guidance on what burden of proof ought to rest with Company B to prove the loss of intellectual property. Assume that Company B has no hard evidence that the inspector stole the trade secret for manufacturing Product C. All Company B may be able to point to as proof is the sequence of events: the CWC inspection occurred, shortly thereafter Company A experienced a dramatic improvement in its production efficiency, and then prices for Product C dropped swiftly in Country A. It is doubtful whether such evidence alone would be enough to establish a prima facie case, let alone to carry the burden of persuasion at trial. Legitimate reasons might exist to explain Company A's sudden success, such as a research breakthrough of its own, a decision to gain market share at the expense of profits, or simply an effort to increase production levels, even at an operating loss, to maintain employment. Allowing Company B to state a prima facie case without evidence of the inspector's actions might have the broader effect of allowing US companies to force their overseas competitors into costly and slow litigation, just because the companies can show that a search had occurred, followed by price cutting by foreign competitors. No doubt, foreign countries would protest, if not retaliate against, a legal process that could interfere with legitimate commercial competition in the marketplace.

Finally, the possibility exists under the CWC of conflicting national policies. Under our Constitution and laws, the inspector's actions would violate either the Takings Clause, if he were a government official, or intellectual property laws, if he were a private citizen. Other nations, however, may not recognize the policies behind either the Constitution's bar on public appropriation of private property or US protection for inventions. An inspector might hail from a country that does not require the government to reimburse its citizens for takings of property, or that has such a legal principle but rarely enforces it. The inspector's nation might not have enacted intellectual property laws that protect inventors' rights as rigorously as US laws do. Some developing countries have chosen to seek quicker economic progress by reducing the ability of inventors to monopolize the benefits of their creations. Thus, even if an inspector's theft of intellectual property violates the laws of the US, it may not transgress the laws of his own nation, which might make that nation reluctant to cooperate with US efforts to investigate such a theft.

The CWC's Implementing Legislation

Because the CWC did not adequately address these Bill of Rights issues, Congress was left with the responsibility of adapting the treaty to constitutional requirements. Once ratified by the Senate, treaties such as the CWC may create binding international obligations upon the US, but they do not automatically take effect as domestic law unless they specifically so state.[49] Rather, such a treaty requires further legislation that implements the treaty's requirements. Passed by the normal lawmaking process, including the House as well as the Senate and the President, the implementing legislation should also shape our treaty obligations in a manner that renders them consistent with the Constitution. Due to the Fourth and Fifth Amendment concerns discussed above, the CWC's implementing legislation required significant political and legislative efforts.

As a result, implementing legislation was delayed in Congress for more than a year after ratification, but was passed at the end of the 105th Congress. As part of the end-of-year omnibus law that funded the federal government's budget, the Chemical Weapons Convention Implementation Act of 1998 enacted the regulation of Schedules 1, 2, 3, and Other chemicals and the facilities that produce them, as called for by the CWC.[50] The legislation also implemented the on-site verification regime set out by the treaty, and made violation of the CWC or efforts to impede its operation a crime under federal law.[51] Most importantly, for our purposes, the Act created procedures for the issuance of warrants and the payment of just compensation for the loss of intellectual property.

Under the Act, a warrant must issue before CWC officials may conduct an inspection of a regulated facility. For facilities that are subject to regular monitoring and verification inspections, because they fall within one of the CWC schedules, the Act follows *New York v. Burger* and does not require a criminal search warrant. In-

49. See, e.g., Louis Henkin, *Foreign Affairs and the United States Constitution* (New York: Oxford University Press, 1996), p. 198.

50. Chemical Weapons Convention Implementation Act, Pub. L. No. 105-277, 1998 H.R. 4328 (1998).

51. Ibid.

stead, it establishes an administrative warrant procedure that requires the government to show: (a) that the CWC is in force in the US; (b) that the facility is subject to routine inspection under the CWC; (c) that the purpose of the search is to verify that the facility's activities are consistent with the information it has provided; (d) the items to be searched; (e) that the site was selected according to CWC procedures; and (f) the time and duration of the search, among other things.[52] The USG must provide to the court all the information about the inspection provided by the Technical Secretariat, and it must seek the consent of the facility owner for the search.[53] If the facility owner refuses, then the government may apply for the administrative warrant provided for by the statute.

Noticeably absent, however, from the procedures governing routine inspections are the warrant elements of the Fourth Amendment. For example, the 1998 Act does not require that the government provide evidence, under oath, that probable cause exists in order to receive a warrant.[54] The legislation's silence on this point makes the CWC vulnerable to constitutional challenge. As we saw above, the Fourth Amendment permits warrantless administrative searches, such as those contemplated by the drafters of the CWC implementing act, only of those facilities that participate in industries that are subject to ongoing, pervasive regulation. To date, the Supreme Court has displayed a reluctance to find that the entire chemical industry is such a regulated industry,[55] and it also has refused to allow a regulatory scheme to bootstrap itself into the status

52. Ibid., § 305(b).

53. Ibid., § 305(a), § 305(b)(1)

54. Even if it did, the government would likely rely upon evidence provided by the Technical Secretariat to show probable cause, rather than upon information developed by domestic law enforcement. It is unclear how reliable US judges will consider such information, which is also involved in the administrative warrant process, given that it will have been developed by sources that lie outside the US justice system.

55. See Dow Chemical Co. v. United States, 476 U.S. 227 (1986).

of pervasive regulation.[56] In other words, the CWC's implementing legislation has failed to solve the warrant issue for routine searches, and at some point the federal courts will have to address whether the CWC has transformed the chemical industry into a pervasively regulated one subject to warrantless search, where before the CWC it was not such.

If the courts do not consider the chemical industry to be pervasively regulated, then US judges will have to decide whether the national security concerns promoted by the CWC themselves are sufficient to justify a relaxation of the Bill of Rights. As noted before, the courts have found that other areas of pressing concern, such as exigent law enforcement situations, deserve reduced scrutiny of government activity. Some have proposed that national security interests also should justify reduced Bill of Rights restrictions on governmental action,[57] although the Supreme Court has refused to recognize a "blanket" national security exception to the Fourth Amendment or the First Amendment.[58] While the executive branch may possess a national security power to act against noncitizens free from the restrictions of the Constitution, it has no such power against US citizens, certainly not on US soil.[59]

Challenge inspections receive stricter constitutional scrutiny under the implementing legislation. Unlike routine inspections, challenge inspections require that the Technical Secretariat and the federal government obtain a criminal search warrant in order to enter the chemical facility of an owner who has withheld his or her

56. See Marshall v. Barlow's Inc., 436 U.S. 307 (1978).

57. See, e.g., Katz, 389 U.S., p. 364 (White, J., concurring); Robert F. Greenlee, "The Fourth Amendment and Facilities Inspections Under the Chemical Weapons Convention," pp. 968–74.

58. See, e.g., Dennis v. United States, 341 U.S. 494 (1951), pp. 524–25 (Frankfurter, J., concurring) (First Amendment).

59. See, e.g., Reid v. Covert, 354 U.S. 1 (1957) (plurality opinion) (Bill of Rights applies to federal government's actions toward US citizens abroad).

consent.[60] The government, therefore, must produce evidence of probable cause, on oath, and it must describe with particularity the places, persons, and things to be searched.[61] The legislation requires that the government provide all appropriate evidence it has obtained from the Technical Secretariat or other sources concerning why the facility was selected, and the reasons why the other state-party has provided for the challenge. Although the law provides sufficient constitutional protections for facilities and locations under the Fourth Amendment, it is unclear whether the legislation will raise a fatal obstacle to the implementation of challenge searches. It seems likely that in at least some cases federal judges will refuse to issue warrants. State-parties, for example, that request challenge inspections may be reluctant to provide sufficient information to justify their demands, perhaps because doing so may compromise intelligence sources or methods. Without such information, however, a federal judge may be unable to find that probable cause exists sufficient to issue a criminal warrant. Even if a state-party provides such information, a federal judge may not find it reliable, as it comes from outside the US law enforcement system. Ironically, the government may find it easier to obtain criminal warrants in the case of routine inspections, where it has access to more information it can share with a court, than in the case of challenge inspections.

Congress more effectively addressed the Fifth Amendment issues raised by the CWC. Under Section 103 of the Act, Congress made the USG liable for any damages caused by the actions of the OPCW or the Technical Secretariat, either due to the theft of trade secrets or due to a tort.[62] Aggrieved companies or individuals may bring a cause of action for recovery of damages, caused by the OPCW or Technical Secretariat, in federal court against the US,

---

60. Pub. L. No. 105-277, § 305(b)(4)(A).
61. Ibid.
62. Ibid., § 103(a)(4)-(b).

which waives its sovereign immunity from suit.[63] The Act requires that the plaintiff carry the burden of proof to establish a prima facie case that members of the OPCW or a Technical Secretariat inspection team, under color of their CWC authority, have taken "proprietary information" or have divulged such information without authorization. The cause of action applies even in those cases in which the inspection teams are legally entitled to obtain the intellectual property under the CWC, but disclosed it without authorization. Apparently, even public or unintentional dissemination of proprietary information may give rise to a damages suit. The statute, therefore, goes beyond the typical scenario of an inspection team member who might steal information intentionally for a foreign company or nation. It still leaves unanswered, however, several of the difficult questions identified earlier, such as proving a prima facie case when inspectors remain immune from judicial process, showing causation, and calculating damages. Nonetheless, Section 103 is a striking innovation, because it makes the USG financially and legally responsible for the actions of an unaccountable third party.

Putting aside the compensation provision, the 1998 Act also stands as a remarkable development in our economic sanctions policy. When we consider the subject of international economic sanctions, we tend to think of the embargoes and trade measures that the US often imposes upon nations such as Iraq, North Korea, and Cuba under laws such as the International Emergency Economic Powers Act.[64] The 1998 Act's provisions, however, seem designed for use against friends as well as enemies. It orders the US to seek "recoupment" of any damages it must pay under its compensation provisions from any members of the OPCW or Technical Secretariat responsible for the loss of intellectual property. Furthermore, the US is to impose sanctions on any company or government that

63. Ibid., § 103(c).
64. 50 U.S.C. § 1701 et seq.

"knowingly assisted, encouraged or induced" the foreign citizen "to publish, divulge, disclose, or make known in any manner or to any extent" not authorized by the CWC any "United States confidential business information."[65]

These sanctions can be harsh. If a company has participated in the theft of US intellectual property, the executive branch must impose three types of sanctions. First, it must forbid the export of military goods and technology to the company. Second, it must use its votes in international financial institutions to oppose any loans or other assistance to the business or the foreign citizen responsible. Third, it must prohibit any US bank from making loans or extending credit to the company, and it must block the movement of the company's assets out of the US, which are to be used to defray the costs of compensating the US plaintiff.[66] If a foreign government has taken part in the theft of confidential business information, then the executive branch must impose similar sanctions upon that nation, and it also must terminate any economic, military, or financial assistance that the foreign nation receives from the US.[67] If the US does not receive repayment, the President may decline to impose the sanctions only if he determines that the waiver of sanctions is necessary to protect our national security.[68] Finally, following the example set by the 1996 Helms-Burton Act, the 1998 Act requires the Secretary of State to deny visas to any person who has participated in the theft or disclosure of confidential trade secrets, who "traffics" in such information, or who is a corporate officer, principal, or shareholder with a controlling interest in a company that was involved in the disclosure of information (so long as the US owner

65. Pub. L. No. 105-277 § 103(e)(2)(A)(ii); ibid. § 103(e)(3)(A).
66. Ibid., § 103(e)(2)(B).
67. Ibid., § 103(e)(3)(B).
68. Ibid., § 103 (e)(4)-(5).

has a proven claim for the loss of the information).[69] Like Helms-Burton, the 1998 CWC Implementation Act imposes sanctions on friendly nations and their companies in an effort to create incentives for them to take actions upon third parties that are in the interests of the US.[70]

As with the Helms-Burton Act, the 1998 Act's sanctions are sure to generate political controversy and international legal difficulties under the GATT. Our trading partners, in particular, may claim that the use of trade sanctions amounts to a violation of the GATT obligations of national treatment and most-favored-nation status, although the Act may fall within GATT's national security exception.[71] Regardless of the resolution of these issues, however, the 1998 implementation act will continue to provide a compensation remedy for those US citizens who suffer a taking or a tort due to the actions of CWC inspectors and officials. Congress thus was able to bring our international obligations under the CWC into line with the requirements of the Fifth Amendment's Takings Clause. We cannot be as sanguine about the Act's provisions relating to the Fourth Amendment's prohibition upon unreasonable government searches and seizures, because in some areas the Act appears to establish insufficient protections for constitutional rights of privacy.

Although Bill of Rights concerns are important, they obscure a deeper, perhaps more important, structural issue: the exercise of governmental authority upon US citizens by international officials. Under different lines of authority, the Supreme Court has identified separate provisions of the Constitution that seek to guarantee basic accountability for the actions of the government. In short, the Con-

---

69. Ibid., § 103(f)(1)-(4). Compare with Title IV of the Cuban Liberty and Democratic Solidarity Act of 1996, Pub. L. No. 104-114, 110 Stat. 785 (1996).

70. For a criticism of Helms-Burton, see John C. Yoo, "Federal Courts as Weapons of Foreign Policy: The Case of the Helms-Burton Act," 20 *Hastings International and Comparative Law Review* 747 (1997).

71. For a similar analysis of Helms-Burton, see ibid., pp. 758–62.

stitution requires that every exercise of public power upon a private citizen must be undertaken by an official who is either elected by the people or appointed by their elected representatives. These principles, however, are arguably undermined if the national government may vest public power in officials who lie outside the US governmental system. If the President and the Senate authorize an international organization to conduct searches on US soil, under color of federal law, they will have delegated public authority outside the governmental system established by the Constitution. Such maneuvers, however, may be necessary in order to secure the neutrality and independence of verification required by recent international agreements. In this respect, the CWC may be an example of a tension that will become only sharper as the US seeks further multilateral solutions to problems that are global in scope.[72]

The CWC's signal innovation in the area of verification is its creation of an independent international agency, the OPCW and its Technical Secretariat, for the execution of routine and challenge inspections. The CWC is a watershed in the development of arms control because of its reliance upon its own verification methods, rather than upon national governments. This has the effect of enabling international law to reach through the state into the lives of private citizens. Traditional international agreements place obligations upon the national governments of state-parties, which then assume the responsibility of enforcing treaty terms upon their citizens. The CWC seeks to sidestep national governments by conducting inspections of privately owned facilities and locations. Members of the Technical Secretariat choose the sites to be inspected, according to standards that they develop, and they conduct the searches, accompanied by US officers only in an observer capac-

---

72. For a more complete analysis of this problem, see John C. Yoo, "The New Sovereignty and the Old Constitution: The Chemical Weapons Convention and the Appointments Clause."

ity. Members of the Technical Secretariat are not accountable to any US official, they are not appointed or elected by US officials, they cannot be removed by US officials, and they do not take orders from any US officials.

The independence of the CWC's verification mechanism is perhaps the critical component of the treaty. Its clear intention is to address the problem posed by state-parties that cannot be trusted to carry out faithful verification of their own activities or to obey the treaty's requirements. The creation of the independent verification regime is also designed to build trust between the state-parties by vesting implementation in a neutral, impartial entity that is not controlled by any one nation or alliance.[73] Reassurance through verification helps alleviate fears of cheating, by engaging state-parties in repeat encounters in which they can learn to cooperate and thereby make policy choices that increase overall security. This result, however, might not be possible without an independent, neutral verification process because the large stakes involved in national security issues might create obstacles to cooperation.

Although desirable from the perspective of international policy, it is precisely this independence and neutrality that produces constitutional problems. Vesting verification in an impartial international organization may build assurance and trust, but it also creates tensions with fundamental constitutional principles of government accountability and popular sovereignty. Two constitutional provisions—the Appointments Clause and the Executive Power Clause—promote these values, and it is these clauses that pose obstacles for the future of international agreements like the CWC and the BWC. Recent Supreme Court decisions interpreting these clauses indicate that individuals who exercise significant federal authority must be

73. See generally, Abram Chayes and Antonia Handler Chayes, *The New Sovereignty: Compliance with International Regulatory Agreements* (Cambridge, MA: Harvard University Press, 1995).

appointed as officers of the USG. Requiring that all officers of the US undergo appointment and remain subject to presidential control renders all who exercise national power answerable to the people's elected representatives, who ultimately are responsible to the people themselves. Efforts to vest federal power in officials who do not undergo appointment according to constitutional requirements and/or who are not subject to presidential control come into conflict with constitutional principles of government accountability.

Turning first to the Appointments Clause, the Constitution establishes procedures for the creation and the filling of offices within the federal government. Under Article II, Section 2, Clause 2 of the Constitution, the President

> Shall nominate, and by and with the Advice and Consent of the Senate, shall appoint Ambassadors, other public Ministers and Consuls, Judges of the supreme Court, and all other Officers of the United States, whose Appointments are not herein otherwise provided for, and which shall be established by Law: but the Congress may by Law vest the Appointment of such inferior Officers, as they think proper, in the President alone, in the Courts of Law, or in the Heads of Departments.[74]

By its text, the Clause classifies all officers of the US into two categories: principal officers and inferior officers. Principal officers, such as ambassadors, federal judges, and cabinet officers, must be nominated by the President and confirmed by the Senate. If Congress so chooses, inferior officers may avoid this cumbersome process by undergoing appointment by the President, the courts, or cabinet secretaries. According to the Supreme Court, inferior officers are distinguished from principal officers because the former are limited to certain discrete duties, are subject to removal by a higher execu-

---

74. U.S. Const. Art. II, § 2, cl. 2.

tive branch official, and are of limited tenure and jurisdiction.[75] Even though yet a third category of employee (such as secretaries, groundskeepers, and the like), without which the federal government could not function, is unmentioned in the Clause, it too has been recognized by the Supreme Court.[76]

At first, one might think that the Appointments Clause is an eighteenth-century anachronism. In a series of recent cases, however, the Supreme Court has identified a broad principle of government accountability underlying the Clause. According to the Court, the Appointments Clause pursues two goals. First, the Clause prevents Congress from arrogating to itself the power to appoint federal officials who enforce federal law. Thus, in *Buckley v. Valeo*, the 1976 case that struck down parts of the federal campaign spending laws, the Court declared that the Appointments Clause prohibited Congress from appointing members of the Federal Elections Commission.[77] In *Morrison v. Olson*, the 1987 case that upheld the independent counsel law, the Court permitted Congress to vest the appointment of the independent counsel in the federal courts, so long as the President retained ultimate removal authority.[78] In *Printz v. United States*, the 1997 case that invalidated the Brady handgun law's background checks, the Court emphasized that Congress could not vest federal power in officials who were not removable by the President.[79] Allowing Congress to vest executive power outside of the executive branch, the Court wrote, would undermine the independence and effectiveness of the presidency.[80]

Second, the Appointments Clause embraces broader concerns

---

75. Morrison v. Olson, 487 U.S. 654, 671–72 (1988).
76. Buckley v. Valeo, 424 U.S. 1, 126 n. 162 (1976).
77. Ibid.
78. Morrison v. Olson, 487 U.S. 654 (1988).
79. Printz v. United States, 117 S. Ct. 2365 (1997). See also Edmond v. United States, 117 S. Ct. 1573 (1997).
80. Printz, 117 S. Ct., p. 2378.

about the scope of national power and those who exercise it. If the Clause, for example, were limited only to certain types of federal officials, such as cabinet officers, then it would still permit the delegation of authority to officers outside the federal government. The Supreme Court, however, has answered this question by declaring that anyone who exercises significant federal authority must undergo the process outlined in Article II, Section 2 of the Constitution.[81] By requiring the appointment of such officials, the Constitution prevents the national government from blurring the lines of responsibility between the people and their agents. It ensures that anyone who wields the power of the state is appointed by, and therefore controlled by, democratically elected officials, who themselves are monitored and controlled by the people. As Chief Justice Rehnquist wrote for the Court in a 1991 case, "The Clause is a bulwark against one branch aggrandizing its power at the expense of another branch, but it is more: it preserves another aspect of the Constitution's structural integrity by preventing the diffusion of the appointment power."[82]

In divining this principle from the Appointments Clause, the Court has been guided by the original understanding of the provision and the history of its drafting and adoption. Historical evidence—too detailed to review here—suggests that the Framers sought to provide for the appointment of government officials in a manner that was open and accountable to the public.[83] Shaped by their revolutionary experience with Great Britain, the Framers wanted to avoid the diversion of public authority to individuals who were not accountable to the electorate, but instead were appointed

---

81. Buckley v. Valeo, 424 U.S. 1, 126 (1976).
82. Ryder v. United States, 115 S. Ct. 2031, 2035 (1991) (quotes and citations removed).
83. See John C. Yoo, "The New Sovereignty and the Old Constitution: The Chemical Weapons Convention and the Appointments Clause," pp. 105–11.

by a distant government in which they had no representation.[84] "Those who framed our Constitution," the Court observed in a recent Appointments Clause case, "addressed these concerns by carefully husbanding the appointment power to limit its diffusion."[85] With a centralized appointment process, the people would know whom to turn to when the government acted improperly. "By limiting the appointment power," the Court has said, the Framers "could ensure that those who wielded it were accountable to political force and the will of the people."[86]

Two other structural elements of the Constitution reinforce the Appointments Clause's promotion of government accountability. First, the Constitution creates a unitary executive branch that requires that all officials who enforce federal law remain subject to the President, who is the only member of the government elected by the entire nation. A vigorous debate continues in legal circles, between "formalists" and "functionalists," about how far Congress may go in shaping the organization and powers of the presidency.[87] Formalists believe that the Constitution creates only three types of government power—executive, legislative, and judicial—that are to be exercised by the three branches suited to those powers. Functionalists are willing to provide more flexibility to the political branches in arranging, allocating, and sharing government powers. This division in academia mirrors confusion in the Supreme Court's recent separation of powers cases, which have wavered between formalist[88] and functionalist approaches.[89]

84. Ibid.
85. Freytag v. Commissioner, 501 U.S. 868 (1991).
86. Ibid., p. 884. See also Weiss v. United States, 114 S. Ct. 752, 757 (1994).
87. See, e.g., Martin S. Flaherty, "The Most Dangerous Branch," 105 *Yale Law Journal* 1725 (1996); Steven G. Calabresi and Saikrishna B. Prakash, "The President's Power to Execute the Laws," 104 *Yale Law Journal* 541 (1994); Lawrence Lessig and Cass R. Sunstein, "The President and the Administration," 94 *Columbia Law Review* 1 (1994).
88. INS v. Chadha, 462 U.S. 919 (1983) (invalidating legislative veto); Bowsher

An effort to transfer power outside of the federal government, however, raises constitutional difficulties under either theory of the separation of powers. A formalist would argue that the power to execute federal laws, such as conducting searches or enforcing treaty provisions, is an executive one. Therefore, those powers can be exercised only by the President or those removable by him, in other words the members of the executive branch. A functionalist, too, would object, because the leading functionalist case—*Morrison v. Olson*—held that the President ultimately must have removal authority over all officers who exercise federal law, even if the Court recognized that Congress possessed some power to condition the removal power.[90] Further, functionalists believe that the strict separation of powers can be relaxed only to further other governmental values, such as public accountability, which are undermined by the transfer of federal authority outside of the national government.

A separate but related constitutional principle, known as the nondelegation doctrine, also enforces accountability in government. Ever since the New Deal, the Supreme Court has permitted the legislature to delegate significant administrative and rulemaking powers to the executive branch.[91] According to the nondelegation doctrine, however, Congress may not delegate such authority without providing intelligible guidelines and standards for its use.[92] Such standards prevent Congress from wholly abdicating its constitutional responsibility to formulate policy, and they ensure that Con-

---

v. Synar, 478 U.S. 714 (1986) (invalidating Gramm-Rudman-Hollings budget deficit legislation); Metropolitan Washington Airports Authority v. Citizens for the Abatement of Airport Noise, 501 U.S. 252 (1991); Plaut v. Spendthrift Farm, Inc., 115 S. Ct. 1447 (1995).

89. Morrison v. Olson, 487 U.S. 654 (1988); Mistretta v. United States, 488 U.S. 361 (1989).

90. Morrison, 487 U.S., p. 692.

91. See Yakus v. United States, 321 U.S. 414 (1944).

92. See, e.g., Mistretta v. United States, 488 U.S. 361 (1988).

gress will remain responsible to the electorate for its legislative decisions. The nondelegation doctrine also seeks to preclude the executive branch from exercising lawmaking power without standards both to guide its discretion and to review its performance. It prevents Congress and the President from colluding in transferring public policymaking authority to persons insulated from the electorate. Delegating authority outside of the national government overrides these safeguards, because Congress cannot enforce its standards through the usual legal and political methods that are used against the President and administrative agencies. Such delegation also risks the capture of government policy by private interests. Because of these concerns, the Supreme Court in the New Deal period struck down laws that attempted to delegate to private industry the power to promulgate regulatory codes and standards.[93]

These principles of government accountability, and their expression in the Supreme Court's modern reading of the Appointments Clause and other provisions, create significant difficulties for the CWC. Simply put, the CWC requires the vesting of federal power in officials who are not members of, or responsible to, the federal government. Members of the Technical Secretariat and the OPCW are not appointed pursuant to the Appointments Clause, are not members of the executive branch, and are not removable by the President. Their decisions of where, why, and how to search a location within the US therefore are not those of officers of the US, nor are their choices and methods subject to review by US officials. Within the borders of the US, they operate with the authority of federal law behind them—it is illegal, for example, for facility owners to interfere with the inspectors' freedom of access. No legally enforceable criteria constrain CWC officials in their selection of

---

93. Carter v. Carter Coal Co., 298 U.S. 238 (1936); A.L.A. Schechter Poultry Corp. v. United States, 295 U.S. 495 (1935). See also Larkin v. Grendel's Den, 459 U.S. 116 (1982).

locations to search; in fact, some of the searches are to be conducted at random. Finally, they are immune from the ultimate check on government action that is provided by the national political process. Congress cannot use its oversight or funding powers to affect CWC inspections, nor can public criticism be brought directly to bear against an inspection policy over which the President has no control.

These constitutional problems become almost inevitable once the decision is made that CWC inspectors must be both independent and vested with legal authority. The purpose of this chapter, however, is to identify and discuss this tension, not to solve it.[94] How this problem is resolved will have a significant impact on the nation's ability to conduct its foreign policy in the future. The CWC's reliance upon an international organization, rather than on state-parties, to conduct verification will serve as a model for future multilateral agreements, including the BWC, which will contain similar provisions for on-site verification. If upheld, these procedures and legal structures are likely to spread beyond the arms control arena to other international regimes, such as those involving the environment, labor, and human rights, that attempt to regulate, not just state behavior, but the conduct of private parties within the state. As the US decides whether to promote a world of multilateral solutions to international problems, it will have to address how its Constitution will affect its ability to live up to its national commitments.

---

94. I have made an effort elsewhere to discuss potential solutions: John C. Yoo, "The New Sovereignty and the Old Constitution: The Chemical Weapons Convention and the Appointments Clause," pp. 123–29. In short, a solution might involve decoupling the CWC's international verification purposes from its domestic law enforcement and prosecution objectives.

Legal Authority for a Domestic Military Role in Homeland Defense

In recent years, Congress and the executive branch have begun to address the threat of a terrorist attack on our homeland using weapons of mass destruction (WMD). These efforts have focused primarily on limited contingencies. We have in place certain legal authorities intended to address the use of the military for assisting civilian agencies in responding to technical and logistical aspects of such attacks.

However, there has been much less focus on an actual or threatened WMD attack on a massive, orchestrated scale—an attack more akin to war than terrorism. Such attacks are less likely than biologi-

The thoughts collected here reflect the early stages of a larger project into Homeland Defense being conducted under the auspices of Fred C. Iklé. The author is grateful to Dr. Iklé for permission to share this preliminary work and to the Hoover Institution for the opportunity to air these preliminary thoughts.

cal and chemical weapons (BCW) terrorism.[1] But they merit study, because the threat of such an attack is not fanciful, and because an orchestrated WMD attack on our homeland could present a major discontinuity in the geopolitical world.

Many commentators believe that the military would have to play the key role in domestic responses to such an orchestrated WMD campaign. Yet a recent Department of Defense (DoD) Science Board Study, key executive branch and congressional offices, and independent private inquiries indicate that the legal authorities for a domestic military role in dealing with such contingencies are less well, and less widely, understood.

A lack of clear authority (or clear understanding of that authority) may obfuscate agency responsibilities for planning and response to an orchestrated WMD attack. An effective response to such threats is critical not only for reducing casualties when an event occurs, but for dissuading an aggressor from acquiring such capabilities, and for enabling the US to conduct an active foreign policy against aggressors armed with such weapons.

Clear legal authority, debated and enacted before a crisis begins, is also the surest way to minimize threats to civil liberty that may arise when a crisis spins out of control. If significant domestic use of the military is needed to save lives in a future BCW attack on the US, we do not advance civil liberties by pretending otherwise. The time to study and debate these issues—and to set clear legal guidelines—is now, before a crisis comes.

Recent Events and Perceptions of the New Threat

Recent events have focused the public, Congress, and the Clinton Administration on homeland defense in general, and in particu-

---

1. Issues related to missile defense and to the legality of retaliatory or preventive military strikes against an aggressor are beyond the scope of the present discussion.

lar on the possibility that the US may one day need to respond to an attack within our borders that employs WMD against one or more targets. The conventional explosive attacks on the Oklahoma City federal office building and the World Trade Center in New York City have heightened awareness of domestic vulnerabilities. The sarin gas attack on a Tokyo subway station by a Japanese domestic group, recent popular literature, and reports on Iraqi capabilities have focused the public on the growing availability and devastating capabilities of WMD.

Both Congress and the executive branch have acknowledged publicly the potential dangers of domestic use of WMD. Congressional findings in 1996 stated that the threat posed to US citizens by nuclear, biological, and chemical weapons delivered by unconventional means is significant and growing.

In November 1997, Secretary of Defense William Cohen stated:

> We have begun to treat the threat of chemical and biological weapons as a likely—and early—condition of future warfare. . . . Most ominous among these threats is the movement of the front line of the chemical and biological battlefield from foreign soil to the American homeland, which compels us to increase our domestic preparedness.[2]

The Legacy of a Century Without a Focus on Homeland Defense

The focus on homeland defense is a change for modern US citizens. With the exceptions of threats to coastal shipping during WWI, relatively brief fears of invasion in WWII, and investments in air defense during the early Cold War years, homeland defense

2. William S. Cohen, "In the Age of Terror Weapons," *Washington Post* (Nov. 26, 1997), p. A19.

has not been a significant mission of our armed forces for over a century. In the later Cold War years, homeland defense consisted primarily of being capable of massive retaliation. In those years, we became complacent about a level of risk to civilians that once seemed shocking and intolerable. Shamefully, the legacy of that era breathes still.

As a result of this history, we have built up a series of legal and policy myths that hamper serious efforts at homeland defense at the national level. To quote Deputy Secretary of Defense John Hamre:

> [F]or the first time, our Government is now seriously talking about homeland defense. . . . It's deeply rooted in American Constitutional democracy that's evolved over the last hundred years, 125 years, that the Department of Defense only deals with threats outside of the borders of the United States. If it's inside the borders of the United States, it is a law enforcement problem. I believe that's an artificial distinction.[3]

Perhaps it is not surprising then that the primary response to this threat to date has been to strengthen our laws and capabilities with respect to limited domestic threats. We address such threats largely within the framework of local crisis response and law enforcement. Such limited threats seem more likely and more immediately addressable. They also fit well within our recent experience and natural predilections for a military with only a limited domestic role.

However, the assumption that such threats will remain largely localized is a dangerous one. Legal authorities under which DoD supports local first responders, the Federal Emergency Management Agency (FEMA), and law enforcement may not be suffic' ~t in a crisis generated by a widespread, orchestrated attack.

---

3. Remarks to the Defense Special Weapons Agency (DSWA) Annual Conference (Jun. 11, 1998).

Appreciating the Nature of the Threat and Its Consequences

The threat of a broad-based WMD attack is real and growing. A Fall 1997 Defense Science Board study determined that there is evidence that the transnational threat will escalate in the future and that the threat will entail extensive campaigns and greater use of WMD. As stated in the study's Final Report:

> Today, most US experiences have, or appear to have, involved isolated events or limited campaigns. But around the world, cases of multiple events, some of them quite serious, are prevalent. At this level, the threat can serve to limit DoD options or constrain operations and can have a serious impact on the economy and national cohesion. But if a transnational actor or nation state successfully wages an orchestrated campaign of these sorts against the US, it could lead to mission failure, disengagement from overseas missions, and possibly national upheaval. America's position in the world could be altered.[4]

Underestimating the Impact of Foreign Capabilities

Whether or not an orchestrated WMD attack on the US actually occurs, the prospect of facing adversaries with such capabilities will likely inhibit, or even cripple, aspects of US foreign policy. An activist US foreign policy will remain a major stabilizing influence in the world. Such a policy will require a willingness to exert our influence overseas through military operations, either alone or in coalition with others, and through forward presence. Such operations become problematic when an orchestrated WMD campaign can threaten unprecedented US domestic casualties.

4. Defense Science Board 1997 Summer Study Task Force on DoD Responses to Transnational Threats, vol. 1, *Final Report*, p. 20.

We need only recall the extent to which the US sought to avoid direct confrontation with the Soviets during the Cold War to appreciate how different US foreign policy might appear in a world in which multiple aggressor states possess a credible capability for a devastating homeland attack on the US. Or consider the debate that preceded the US decision to confront Iraq in Operations Desert Shield and Desert Storm. This debate centered on the risks to US troops and interests in the Middle East. There was relatively little concern over a retaliatory strike by Iraq against the US homeland. If in the future we were concerned that Iraq, or numerous other aggressor states, had the capability to cause enormous homeland casualties, our willingness to confront such aggressors would be greatly inhibited.

In short, we are likely to see WMD used in the post-Cold War world much as nuclear weapons (NW) were commonly used in the Cold War era—to deter or inhibit unwanted actions. Such weapons in the hands of regional aggressors may well deter the US from taking actions otherwise in its interests overseas. This is a real and viable possibility so long as WMD remain, and are perceived to remain, offense dominant. For this reason, if no other, it is enormously attractive for an aggressor to obtain the asymmetric, leap-ahead capabilities that WMD offer. And it is important for us to counter them.

Moreover, the use of WMD may impose real military costs, in addition to psychological ones. A recent DoD report, *Assessment of the Impact of Chemical and Biological Weapons on Joint Operations in 2010*, noted that continental US military facilities, particularly ports and airports used for force projection, "can no longer be considered immune to attack, including potential attacks with chemical and biological agents." In particular, the report noted the crippling effect such attacks might have on our ability to project power overseas:

We could not predict the US public reaction to [chemical or bio-
logical] attacks on CONUS military and civilian facilities necessary
for the projection of forces to a theater of operation. Specifically,
we could not predict the availability of a civilian/contractor work-
force to return to previously contaminated areas and resume work.

Overestimating Nuclear Deterrence

The threat of nuclear retaliation by the US, effective during the
Cold War, is not necessarily a reliable means of deterrence against
aggressor states or transnational actors in the post–Cold War era.
Deterrence has often been an effective counter to WMD threats.
However, there may be no certainty as to who the aggressor state or
actor is; or the actor's calculations may differ from those of the
former Soviet Union in Cold War days.

Nuclear, biological, or chemical weapons may in the future be
delivered through clandestine means. It may not be certain whether
the culprit was a foreign state with which the US is locked in a
confrontation, or a third party anxious to see such a foreign state
suffer from a US strike. The aggressor may calculate that we will
not act against it where reasonable uncertainty prevails.

Where there is relative certainty as to the actor, a transnational
actor may offer no suitable target for NW. Even where an aggressor
state is clearly to blame, a possible nuclear threat may be insufficient
to deter a foreign leader who sees his own survival at stake and
WMD as his only potential leverage for achieving a negotiated set-
tlement. A US policy constrained by the inability to topple such a
figure would itself be an undesirable outcome.

Finally, substantial destruction of an aggressor through a nuclear strike (as, for example, where the capital contains a high per
centage of the aggressor state's GDP and leadership) may be considered too disruptive to regional power balances. Use of NW against

an ethnic group may be considered politically intolerable. Some note that the US public, long accustomed to the prospect of using NW against the Soviets when our own survival was at stake, may be less willing to contemplate raining destruction upon the population of a third-world state. This is particularly true where our own pre-war rhetoric vilifies the dictator, not the people he represses. Each of these factors were considerations at one time or another in advance planning related to the Gulf War.

Bureaucratic Pressures that Minimize the WMD Threat

Bureaucratic pressures may also reinforce a reluctance to acknowledge or confront more strenuously the risks of an orchestrated WMD attack. First, in an era of decreasing budgets and broadening commitments, supporters of an assertive foreign policy and strong military are not eager to divert resources to domestic threats. Second, supporters of the military are loathe to encounter the potential political risks they fear may come with an increased domestic role. Civil libertarians fear domestic use of the military. Finally, other bureaucratic actors are not readily willing to cede a major role to the DoD. These bureaucratic pressures tend to inhibit even preliminary planning that might lead to undesired bureaucratic outcomes.

The Need for Real World Planning

The threat of an orchestrated WMD campaign requires that we view homeland defense as more than a local challenge or a law enforcement problem. In the words of Deputy Secretary of Defense Hamre:

[As] those of you who have been involved in any analysis associated with a terrorist act that might use chemical or biological weapons know, it is startling how soon this becomes a national security problem. It's within minutes [that] a chemical or biological terrorist act transcends the capabilities of local law enforcement or emergency responders. This will be a homeland defense issue, a national security issue if it ever were to happen. *Over the next 16 to 18 months, we will be wrestling through all of the tough but essential details of . . . starting to develop real world plans to defend this country.* [Emphasis added.][5]

Many commentators believe that the DoD must play a significant or even leading role in any "real world" attempt to address the problems posed by a broad-based WMD campaign. In their view, the DoD's leading involvement is critical at every stage of an effective response to such an attack. Research, development, procurement, and deployment of the sensors and countermeasures necessary for a national defense are likely to require expertise and skills resident at the DoD. Training, organization, discipline, coordination, and prioritization of defenses in a nationwide crisis are similarly likely to require expertise and skills resident at the DoD. DoD vaccination programs may render DoD personnel the only responders capable of working in large numbers.

In a recent issue of *Foreign Affairs*, former Assistant Secretary of Defense Ashton Carter, former CIA Director John Deutch, and former National Security Council staff member Philip Zelikow describe the present structure for dealing with a WMD attack. This present structure, they state, is adequate for limited terrorist threats or WMD attacks, but not for large-scale ones. For that, they say, the DoD is needed:

5. Remarks to the DSWA Annual Conference.

If the US Government learned that a large-scale attack of weapons of mass destruction was imminent, however, this usual structure would be pushed aside. . . . The operational command structure would need to . . . set up interdiction on ground, at sea, and in air; mobilize thousands of soldiers; and move thousands of tons of freight. None of these actions can happen quickly unless plans have already been drawn up and units designated to carry them out, with repeated training and exercises that create the readiness to bring the plans to life. In this situation, the Defense Department would take the leading role.[6]

Consider just one aspect of dealing with such a crisis: coordination. Today's military commanders refer to it as the "C2 Furball," roughly understood as the "Crisis/Coordination Mess." Karl von Clausewitz called it the "fog of war." Military operations are not often good at disentangling the "furball," but in general, to paraphrase Winston Churchill, they are significantly ahead of everyone else. This is particularly true of the efforts being made for tomorrow's military to have real-time visibility and control of assets, total situational awareness, precision logistics, and networked sensors.

For the DoD to accept a more significant role requires political direction and a change of culture within it. There will need to be efforts to expose some of the myths surrounding existing legal authorities. And, perhaps, some new authority will need to be provided.

Evaluating the adequacy of current laws for domestic military responses to an orchestrated WMD attack on our homeland is complicated because we do not really know today what the military would be needed to do. We do not know in part because no one has done the detailed planning and gaming needed to make such a determination. While civilian medical, law enforcement, and emer-

6. Ashton Carter, John Deutch, and Philip Zelikow, "Combating Catastrophic Terrorism," 77 *Foreign Affairs* 80 (Nov./Dec. 1998), p. 90.

gency authorities will carry an enormous portion of the burden in response to an orchestrated WMD attack, only thorough planning and gaming will give us confidence as to whether such civilian responders can carry the burden alone, or even the primary burden. Such preparation will require a much clearer political mandate, and the clear legal authority that makes such a mandate sustainable. For that reason, as well as others, the laws governing the use of the military in response to such an attack merit scrutiny.

Primary Legal Authorities for a Military Role in Preparing for, Preventing, and Responding to a WMD Attack

Limited WMD Attacks

Most discussions of a domestic military response to a limited WMD attack begin with the Stafford Act, recent legislation regarding WMD defense, and the Posse Comitatus Act.

The Robert T. Stafford Disaster and Emergency Assistance Act of 1974, as amended (Stafford Act),[7] is the principal federal authority for the provision of disaster relief and emergency assistance to state and local governments. Together with various executive branch directives and regulations, the Stafford Act guides the military's relief efforts in support of civilian authorities. As a general matter, the Stafford Act authorizes the President to declare an event a "major disaster" or an "emergency" upon the request of a governor of a state. In certain instances, however, when necessary to preserve life and property, the Act authorizes the President's limited use of DoD resources without awaiting invitation.

Many of the functions of the President under the Stafford Act

---

7. 42 U.S.C. § 5122 et seq.

have been delegated to FEMA. FEMA is charged with coordinating all federal assistance to state and local governments through the Federal Response Plan (FRP). The FRP identifies emergency support functions to be performed in a major disaster or emergency, and assigns responsibility for each such function to specific federal departments and agencies, including the DoD.

An annex to the FRP published in 1996 specifically addresses the federal government's response to nuclear, biological, or chemical attacks within the US (FRP Annex). The FRP Annex implements Presidential Decision Directive (PDD) 39, "US Policy on Counterterrorism" (Jun. 21, 1995) and succeeding authorities.

In accordance with the PDDs, the FRP Annex divides prime responsibilities of Crisis Management[8] and Consequence Management[9] between the Federal Bureau of Investigation and FEMA, respectively. Various other federal agencies, including the DoD, are expressly instructed under presidential directive to support technical operations required as part of the federal response.

Under the Defense Against Weapons of Mass Destruction Act of 1996,[10] and various authorities in Title 10 of the US Code, the DoD may provide training and advice, facilities, equipment, and

---

8. "Crisis Management includes measures to identify, acquire, and plan the use of resources needed to anticipate, prevent, and/or resolve a threat or act of terrorism. The laws of the United States assign primary authority to the Federal Government to prevent and respond to acts of terrorism; State and local governments provide assistance as required. Crisis management is predominantly a law enforcement response. Based on the situation, a Federal crisis management response may be supported by technical operations, and by Federal consequence management, which may operate concurrently." Terrorism Incident Annex to FRP (Unclassified).

9. "Consequence Management includes measures to protect public health and safety, restore essential government services, and provide emergency relief to governments, businesses and individuals affected by the consequences of terrorism. The laws of the United States assign primary authority to the States to respond to the consequences of terrorism; the Federal Government provides assistance as required." Terrorism Incident Annex to FRP (Unclassified).

10. 50 U.S.C. § 2301 et seq.

maintenance services to civilian agencies preparing to respond to a crisis. The DoD may also provide personnel to operate equipment in defined circumstances.

The FRP Annex specifically notes that "[a]s required under the Constitution and laws of the United States, DoD will coordinate military operations within the United States with the appropriate civilian lead agency(ies) for the technical operations."[11] With respect to biological or chemical threats, the FRP and the law prohibit the military from conducting arrests, search and seizure of evidence, or any direct participation in the collection of intelligence for law enforcement purposes, except under limited circumstances.[12] Interestingly, in emergency situations involving nuclear materials the military is authorized, without such qualification, to conduct arrests, searches, and seizures.[13]

The National Emergencies Act of 1974, 50 U.S.C. §§ 1601–1651 (NEA), provides the President with the authority to declare national emergencies and thereby activate certain statutory emergency powers. Such powers appear at various places throughout federal law. A number may prove useful as authority for specific actions in response to a WMD attack.

However, rather than an extension of presidential emergency power, the NEA was passed in the wake of Vietnam and Watergate in an attempt to harness, and more closely regulate, presidential emergency powers. Certain sections of the NEA repealed emergency powers relevant to a response to nuclear, biological, or chemical attack. For example, the NEA repealed 18 U.S.C. § 1383. This law had given the President authority to declare a military zone in any part or all of the US. Once such a military zone was created,

---

11. Terrorism Incident Annex to FRP (Unclassified).
12. 10 U.S.C. § 382.
13. 18 U.S.C. § 831.

people within it could be jailed for one year for violating any "executive order of the President."

There are other acts that potentially give the President broad authority for domestic military responses to an orchestrated WMD attack. Among the statutes worth considering in this context are those at 10 U.S.C. §§ 331–333. For example, 10 U.S.C. § 333 empowers the President to use the military as he deems necessary to suppress any unlawful combination, or conspiracy or domestic violence that opposes or obstructs the execution of the laws of the US or deprives the citizens of states of rights secured in the Constitution. Two of these statutes were used during the school desegregation campaign in the 1960s. In this context, they were held to allow preventive deployments of troops. Whether these statutes were intended for, or could be applied to, actions necessary to prepare for, prevent, or respond to a WMD attack of ambiguous or foreign origin is not yet clear.

Responses to Orchestrated WMD Attacks

What happens if a massive, orchestrated WMD event requires actions that exceed the scope of authorities offered under the Stafford Act, other leading statutes, and the FRP? What is the President's power to use the military to defend the country from an orchestrated WMD attack more akin to war than terrorism?

It would seem self-evident that the nation has the power in wartime to defend itself as best befits the situation. Yet the President's emergency use of the military without specific statutory authority, particularly in a domestic context, rapidly brushes up against a number of Constitutional and statutory issues:

1. Does Congress's right to declare war and raise armies give it ultimate authority over how war is conducted and whether the military may be used?

2. Do the President's authority to execute the laws and his role as Commander in Chief give him inherent war powers, particularly in the realm of self-defense, that allow him to use forces domestically? To what extent do Congressional authorization of and appropriation for forces give the President implicit authority to use those forces in the national defense?

3. Does the doctrine of Posse Comitatus prevent the President from using the armed forces domestically to defend against attacks and, in the process, restore law and order?

The unseen galaxy around which the Stafford Act revolves is the Posse Comitatus Act, 18 U.S.C. § 1385. Enacted after the Civil War, it prohibits the use of military personnel to "execute the laws" except "under circumstances authorized by the Constitution or Acts of Congress."

"Execution of the law" occurs when the armed forces perform tasks assigned to an organ of civil government or assigned to them solely for purposes of civil government. Courts have asked three questions in interpreting these standards:

1. Is there direct active use of the military to execute the law?

2. Has the use of the military pervaded the activities of civilian officials?

3. Have citizens been subjected to the exercise of military power which was regulatory, prescriptive, or compulsory in nature?

Posse Comitatus is a statutory, not a Constitutional, doctrine, which may itself be modified by statute. If Posse Comitatus is seen as an impediment to an effective response, the law can be amended.

As noted earlier, specific authority for military assistance that would constitute an exception to the restrictions of the Posse

Comitatus Act has recently been provided for emergency situations involving nuclear, biological, or chemical weapons of mass destruction. However, this authority may not be enough for responding to an orchestrated WMD campaign. Nor is it clear if other acts that give the President authority to use the military domestically would be applicable in the event of a WMD attack of unknown or foreign origin.

Moreover, Posse Comitatus simply may not apply to particular domestic uses of the military in a war or warlike situation as a matter of statutory interpretation. Waging war, including defensive aspects of war, may be viewed as different from "executing the laws" under the statute; or a Constitutional exception, specifically recognized in the text of the statute, may apply. DoD regulations note that the Act *does not apply* to cases in which the military takes action for the primary purpose of furthering a military or foreign affairs function of the US (DoD Directive 5525.5). DoD regulations also cite two Constitutional exceptions for using the armed forces during civil disturbances when duly constituted authorities are unable or unwilling either to prevent loss of life or to protect federal property and functions (32 C.F.R. § 215.4(c)).

Constitutional scholars debate the founding fathers' concept of the inherent powers of the President to wage war. The debate turns largely on two Constitutional clauses little debated at the Convention: the Commander in Chief provision, and the Congressional power to "declare," as opposed to "make" war. Whatever the outer margins of this debate, the majority of scholars seem to agree that the Constitutional Convention did not intend to deprive the President of his right to respond to a sudden attack at home.

In addition, while some scholars would argue that the Convention did not intend for the President to wage undeclared war, all agree that this interpretation, if ever valid, was not in practice followed from the time of Washington and Adams on. We are indebted to Abraham Sofaer's work for covering this history and the Supreme

Court decisions upholding the President's right to conduct undeclared wars.[14]

Taken together, it would seem that the President has, at a minimum, the power to use the military to wage defensive war, declared or undeclared, when the US is suddenly and unexpectedly attacked. The question of whether particular conduct falls within the concept of waging war may need to be explored, depending on the particular uses to which the President would want to apply the military in response to an orchestrated WMD attack.

There is authority stemming from at least as early as the quasi-war with France in 1798 for the proposition that Congress may restrict the *manner* in which the President wages war. But it would be questionable whether Congress could remove from the President entirely the right to use authorized forces. This would vitiate, not restrict, his role as Commander in Chief. Moreover, such limits may require a much clearer Congressional expression of intent to limit the President's wartime powers than that presented by the Posse Comitatus injunction.

Traditionally, this problem has been considered from three aspects: has the President been prohibited from selected actions by Congress; is Congress silent on the President's right to exercise a given power; or has Congress authorized the actions required? The severity of the emergency and the necessity for the Presidential action are usually strong undercurrents in the analysis. In the case of an orchestrated WMD attack, the necessity should seem acute.

Chief Justice Rehnquist's recent book, *All the Laws But One*,[15] endorses a doctrine of necessity. While not directly addressing the Posse Comitatus issues, the Chief Justice writes that it is "neither

---

14. See Abraham D. Sofaer, *War, Foreign Affairs, and Constitutional Power: The Origins*, vol. I (Cambridge, MA: Ballinger, 1976).

15. William H. Rehnquist, *All the Laws But One: Civil Liberties in Wartime* (New York: Knopf, 1998).

desirable nor is it remotely likely that civil liberty will occupy as favored a position in wartime as it does in peacetime."[16] He notes former Attorney General Francis Biddle's observation that the Constitution has not "greatly bothered" any wartime President.[17]

Martial Law

Under certain circumstances during time of war, military authorities can promulgate and administer martial law. In its strictest sense, martial law can only exist when the civil arm of government becomes powerless because of invasion, insurrection, or anarchy. Such power does not arise from threatened invasion; the necessity must be actual and present and the invasion real, such as effectively closes the courts and deposes the civil administration. It can never exist where the courts are open and in the proper and uninterrupted exercise of jurisdiction.

Once martial law is declared, subject to applicable Constitutional limitations, military authorities may act as reasonably necessary for the purpose of restoring and maintaining public order. Although it has been stated that martial law supersedes all civil authority during its existence, the power of the military under martial law over civilian persons is limited by the reasonable necessities of the occasion. In practice, martial law may run well beyond a declared emergency. Martial law declared in New Orleans in 1814 and in Hawaii in 1944 ran well beyond the actual emergency. Although the circumstances underlying these two examples may not be duplicated in the US of the twenty-first century, they give some cause for concern.

In short, in addition to any inherent or Constitutional basis, martial law may be argued to be outside the Posse Comitatus pre-

16. Ibid., p. 224.
17. Ibid., p. 191.

scription. Nonetheless, relying on a declaration of martial law seems a poor way to plan. Such reliance has all the downsides of not planning at all, and few of the benefits that may come from a clear assignment of responsibilities in advance.

Conclusion

Clear legal authority for an effective military role in response to WMD attacks on our homeland is an important element of preparing to deter or minimize the consequences of such events. Such authority, debated in advance of a crisis, is also our best guarantee against unwarranted interference with civil liberties during a crisis. To protect our freedom, to minimize casualties, and to retain our ability to conduct an active foreign policy in the next century, we must confront now the practical and legal issues that may lie between us and effective responses to the post–Cold War threat of orchestrated BCW attacks on our homeland.

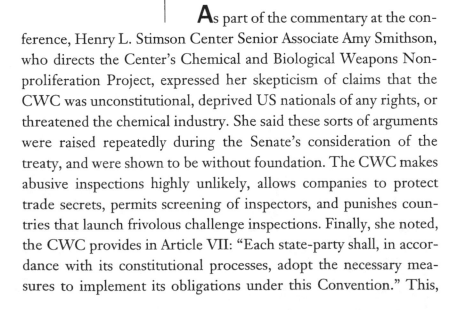

Commentary

As part of the commentary at the conference, Henry L. Stimson Center Senior Associate Amy Smithson, who directs the Center's Chemical and Biological Weapons Nonproliferation Project, expressed her skepticism of claims that the CWC was unconstitutional, deprived US nationals of any rights, or threatened the chemical industry. She said these sorts of arguments were raised repeatedly during the Senate's consideration of the treaty, and were shown to be without foundation. The CWC makes abusive inspections highly unlikely, allows companies to protect trade secrets, permits screening of inspectors, and punishes countries that launch frivolous challenge inspections. Finally, she noted, the CWC provides in Article VII: "Each state-party shall, in accordance with its constitutional processes, adopt the necessary measures to implement its obligations under this Convention." This, she maintains, should enable Congress to ensure that no violation of the Constitution occurs.

Stanford Law Professor Professor Pamela Karlan provided a perspective on the dangers posed by BCW-related activities by focusing on the Fourth Amendment of the Constitution. She analyzed how the necessary searches, seizures, and other related activities could be accomplished consistent with the Fourth Amendment, given its flexibility—including:

- Greater freedom to search pervasively regulated industries than private homes

- Possibility of consent searches

- Warrantless stops without probable cause

- Permissible use of dogs and other sensing devices

- Wide range of lawful surveillance techniques that require no warrant

- Use of undercover agents

- Relative ease of obtaining warrants

She noted also the significance of the forms of remedy normally available for Fourth Amendment violations: suppression of the evidence obtained in criminal trials, and damages for searches without probable cause. The President, or Congress, or law enforcement officers are thus able to violate this aspect of the Constitution in perceived emergencies—so long as they are not seeking to make criminal cases with any evidence seized but are interested in protecting the public in an emergency, and so long as they are prepared to pay the price in damages that may be imposed. Karlan suggested that other legal problems might similarly be exaggerated by some commentators, given the flexible and practical manner in which these constraints have been interpreted and applied.

Ronald Lee, Associate Deputy Attorney General, US Department of Justice, commented on the role of law enforcement in dealing with the BCW threat. In all such incidents, he said, law enforcement personnel will have a major role, whether the incidents are domestic or transnational. BCW incidents pose special challenges, however, with regard to time, space, and information. Unlike incidents involving conventional weapons—say, when a bomb goes off and thus triggers an investigation—BCW incidents will likely force law enforcement to reach backwards in time from the realization that a BCW incident has occurred in order to investigate the incident. Dealing with the scene of such incidents will be very different from "traditional" conventional-weapons situations, given the special risks involved. Public health concerns clearly will play a much larger role. Information and expertise pose a particular challenge, which law enforcement should meet not only by enhancing its understanding of the issues but by enlisting the help of the medical, public health, and scientific communities to a degree not previously known, and on a continuing basis. These relationships will create a "network analogy" for how law enforcement relates to other participants, rather than the normal hierarchical model of law enforcement. The ultimate objective of these arrangements must be to maximize each player's ability to help the others prevent and respond to BCW incidents. Finally, Lee emphasized that this task must be performed with fidelity to the Constitution and US values. With regard to the possibility of utilizing the military to deal with major incidents, he noted that:

> the statutes that have evolved allow for limited reliance by the civilian authorities on military assistance, reflecting a very careful balancing and assessment of what the best way is to meet threats without sacrificing what we view as our core of values. It is true that

we have to reexamine these values when we are forced to think about larger threats such as WMD. But in our reexamination we must also . . . balance the need to have effective measures to supplement civilian authorities versus the traditional idea that in a crisis the military should not have the lead role.

Part Five

Preparing for
BCW Attacks

Thomas P. Monath

Introductory Remarks

This part of the book addresses the difficult area of consequence management for biological or chemical attacks on the US. We all share the view that our civilization is extremely vulnerable and that the impact of such an attack—particularly in the case of BW—would be much larger and a much more serious event than anything we have experienced in the past.

The expansion of BCW programs, with increased capabilities and long-range delivery systems, and the escalation and increased sophistication of terrorist groups around the world, have mandated a call to action with respect to the civil defense issue. In order to meet this challenge, it will be necessary to marry elements of our national security forces with the public health infrastructure in unprecedented ways. This process has only recently begun and is certainly far from complete.

The basis for the federal response was established in 1995 with Presidential Decision Directive 39, which established the framework for coordination among federal agencies in case of a terrorist BCW attack. This framework was extended in PDD 62 in May 1998. The lead agency for management of all the human-health-related consequences of a terrorist BCW attack is the US Department of Health and Human Services (HHS)—specifically, the Public Health Service (PHS).

One of the most vexing issues in the consequence management of a BW attack is the prevention of disease among persons exposed but not yet ill. In the case of a transmissible agent, the contagion is spread throughout the population both contiguous to the event and, most troublesome, by persons dispersing during the incubation period. Since all BW agents have a range of incubation periods, determined by the dose of the inoculum and by innate immunity of the host, which is quite individual, the recognition of an incident after the first cluster of cases would invariably be followed by a period of opportunity for intervention with drugs and vaccines. Although our military forces are relatively well prepared at this point to deal with such contingencies, we are very far from solutions at the civil defense level.

In April 1998, during a meeting at the White House, in which the president asked a group of scientists—including myself and other conference participants—for advice on the BW threat, the focus of discussion centered largely on the issue of domestic preparedness for BW attack, most especially the shortfall in drugs and vaccines. To meet these deficiencies, the panel recommended to the president a federal investment of $600 million over five years in the areas of antiviral drug discovery and antibiotic and vaccine research and development, plus $420 million for national stockpiling of drugs and vaccines. Shortly thereafter, in May, President Clinton acknowledged the need to stockpile drugs and suggested an immediate investment of $300 million.

Then, in June 1998, the US Senate Committee on Appropriations, the Subcommittee of Labor, Health and Human Services—the education-related agencies subcommittee—held hearings on preparedness for epidemics and terrorism. Although recognizing the vital role of federal health agencies, the hearings emphasized the lack of critical resources provided to the PHS to carry out its mission and the fact that insufficient emphasis was given by lead agencies, including the Centers for Disease Control (CDC) and the National Institutes of Health (NIH), to the problem of bioterrorism. The American Society of Microbiologists testified at that meeting and recommended that Congress invest new federal funding of $200 million to address the bioterrorist threat, and an additional $175 million in the area of emerging infections and enhanced labs.

I was heartened recently to learn that in fact some new money—$120 million—has been given to the CDC to address some of the areas I have mentioned. I believe that is great for a start; however, it represents a sum that is far short of what may be required.

At a recent strategic exercise sponsored by the US Marine Corps, participants voted on the likely use of biological agents by terrorist groups and universally agreed on five as leading candidates—of which four were conventional biological agents: plague, tularemia, smallpox, and anthrax. In the case of two of these agents, anthrax and smallpox, it is noteworthy that the emergency response to an incident would require mass immunization with vaccines that are either unavailable now to the civilian population or available in only extremely limited supply.

All in all, we have only begun to wrestle with the issue of emergency preparedness for terrorism.

Richard J. Danzig

Two Incidents and the NEW Containment

Defense against biological weapons (BW) employment and improving national consequence management (CM) capabilities are now commendably high priorities for our national leadership.[1] Presidential Decision Directives, Congressional legislation, and the Secretary of Defense's advocacy show that our government is serious about addressing this threat.[2] Now that

1. Consequence Management is defined by the Federal Emergency Management Agency (FEMA) abstract, approved by the National Security Council, attached to Presidential Decision Directive (PDD) 39 (Jun. 21, 1995). The definition states that it "includes measures to protect public health and safety, restore essential government services, and provide emergency relief to governments, businesses and individuals affected by the consequences of terrorism. The laws of the United States assign primary authority to the States to respond to the consequences of terrorism; the Federal Government provides assistance as required."

2. See PDDs 39, 62 and 63 (both May 22, 1998); Nunn-Lugar-Domenici

commitment on the part of US policymakers has been demonstrated, the question is: How do we turn this aspiration into reality? National will and funding must be translated into an active and practical defense and, perhaps more importantly, a viable CM program.

BW present insidious challenges to the defender and unique advantages to a potential attacker. They differ from traditional weapons because they are instruments of nonexplosive warfare (NEW). Elsewhere, I have suggested that this class of weapons, consisting of biological, chemical, radiological, and information weapons, has special characteristics that require defenses we do not yet have.[3] Traditional defenses against more conventional attacks, such as massing troops or building walls, do not help, and indeed may be counterproductive against NEW weapons. Further, BW have unique properties that set them apart even from the other NEW weapons. We are therefore compelled to treat BW as a category separate from its traditional grouping amongst the trinity of weapons of mass destruction (WMD).[4]

The most attractive means of providing an effective defense against BW would be to prevent an attack in the first place. Improved intelligence efforts can obviously contribute in this regard. State actors may also be deterred by the threat of massive retaliation.

Our planning assumption, however, should be that intelligence is not likely to be consistently available and deterrence may not always be effective, particularly against nonstate actors. We need therefore to complement these efforts with a strong system of consequence management. To be effective, such a system must differ-

---

domestic preparedness legislation; multiple public statements by Secretary of Defense Williams S. Cohen, including an extensive interview in a PBS television documentary on BW. "Plague War," *Frontline* (WGBH Boston: 1998).

3. Richard J. Danzig, "The Next Superweapon: Panic," *New York Times* (Nov. 15, 1998), p. 15.

4. Nuclear weapons (NW), biological weapons (BW), chemical weapons (CW).

entiate a BW attack from the threat posed by other WMD. These differences have broad ranging implications for the design and implementation of a CM program.

The following two scenarios develop this point and demonstrate some of the special challenges inherent in coping with a BW attack. An analysis of how the US might respond to these situations, given present capabilities and challenges, will show that we would be wise to enlarge and refine our national investment in robust CM.

The Ambiguity of Attack

I will set my first scenario in an indefinite time—I will call it "the year 18." Imagine a situation such as the US experienced at the time of Desert Storm. Assume that in the year 18 there is a country, "X," that has invaded another country, and the US has responded by mobilizing its armed forces. This involves gathering our active duty troops and reservists at various places in the US for staging.

In one of those places, Fort Riley, Kansas, the troops begin to get sick. The sickness presents itself at first as a typical flu-like experience. It is, by and large, ignored by troops as they go about their business, because they realize the gravity of their work. By ignoring the illness in its early stages, and emphasizing the higher value of what they are pursuing, they become more ill and more prone to infecting other people. Ultimately, there is a serious outbreak at Fort Riley. The doctors treat the sickness like they treat the flu— with aspirin, bed rest, decongestant, and the usual remedies.

In a few days many people get sicker; a significant number of people die. Post-mortem examinations reveal that their lungs have filled with a transuded fluid (a liquid that does not suggest the presence of bacteria, but is indicative of a viral infection). Then abruptly, the illness goes away. Mobilization continues and troops are sent overseas. But a few weeks later, just as suddenly, the disease breaks out again, and more people die. It infects our troops abroad, allies and, to some degree, even the troops of country X.

The disease then reappears in the US. For example, at Fort Drum, New York, well over 10 percent of the soldiers on duty are incapable of functioning because of the illness. As the illness spreads to the civilian population, they begin dying by the tens of thousands. Within a couple of months, deaths in the US exceed one million.

What is the impact of this national trauma on decisionmakers? It is quite likely that they will think about biological weaponry and retaliation. Let us suppose that it can be shown that X, in this case, has experimented with BW and has developed a variety of BW techniques, although it has not exhibited capabilities directly related to this particular illness. As the illness spreads and deaths mount, the pressure for nuclear retaliation against X will rise. The arguments for using NW in this circumstance will be very extreme and strong. The desire for retaliation will be intensified further when the FBI arrests two people who clearly are agents of country X, attempting to introduce a different biological agent into the US.

Imagine yourself in the role of a decisionmaker. Are you on the brink of nuclear warfare? Now, take a step back. I have modeled the year 18—the time in which this scenario is set—after an actual year: 1918. I have just described the "Spanish Flu" epidemic in the US as it was experienced in 1918. In that year, after an initial outbreak at Fort Riley, illness spread to US troops overseas, then to the allies, and eventually a more virulent form returned to the US. Ultimately, deaths in the US reached 600,000 in 1918.[5] That equates to about

5. In the spring of 1918, what became known as the "Spanish flu" began to ravage the US. It is believed to have started at Fort Riley. By the time it completed its rampage, the virus had swept US military bases and civilian populations, crossed the Atlantic, attacked populations on both warring sides, and returned to the US in a more virulent state. In addition to US deaths, the pathogen is estimated to have killed 20 million people worldwide. "Influenza 1918," *The American Experience* (WGBH Boston: 1998).

1.4 million in today's population. Biological attack was not merely a remote suspicion in 1918—during World War I German agents infected horses with glanders disease in New York before they were shipped to France.[6] It is uncertain what effect the glanders disease attack had on the Allies' logistical efforts, but the human cost of the naturally occurring influenza virus was devastating.

That scenario may seem to be very dated and unfair, but an influenza outbreak is a very realistic example; it could easily happen again. Dr. Joshua Lederberg, for example, has emphasized the importance of preparing against a flu recurrence and he has pointed out that we are not dramatically better prepared scientifically than we were in 1918.[7] Of course, we know about viruses now; we did not know about viruses then. We have antibiotics now. But antibiotics deal with bacteria; bacterial infection is only an opportunistic second-order effect of viral infections.

Of course in today's world a sample of the virus would soon be sent down to the CDC to be carefully assessed and, when that analysis was complete, it would become apparent that we were dealing with a new and more virulent form of virus. But when the change in the virus's sequencing and its degree of mutation were determined, it would still be unlikely that we would be able to resolve whether we were confronting a man-made change in sequencing or a natural occurrence. Bear in mind that if retaliation, especially nuclear retaliation, were being contemplated, a very high degree of certainty would likely be demanded. The years of forensic work that went into determining culpability for the bombing of Pan Am Flight 103

---

6. After the war, it was determined that German operatives employed US stevedores to commit various acts of sabotage, including infecting horses awaiting export to France and England with glanders disease. Jules Witcover, *Sabotage at Black Tom: Imperial Germany's Secret War in America, 1914–1917* (Chapel Hill: Algonquin Books, 1989), pp. 93, 127–127.

7. Dr. Joshua Lederberg, a Nobel Prize winner, is a noted microbiologist and geneticist. He is a consultant to the DoD on various CM issues.

over Lockerbie, Scotland, provide an inkling of the standard of proof required for a determination of biological attack. The difficulties that arose in Hong Kong in 1997, when a new variant of influenza (H5N1) was discovered, illustrate the massive epidemiological effort needed to address a previously unknown pathogen. Scientists ultimately determined it to be derived from an avian, or bird-based, flu transiting to become a human-based flu in a way that was previously unprecedented.[8]

In another context, we know that natural occurrences can be thought of as biological attacks. In 1977, when Rift Valley Fever broke out in Egypt, Egyptian newspapers alleged that the disease was the result of an Israeli plot. In fact, on first examination, there was strong reason to believe that this was not a natural occurrence. The disease is named Rift Valley Fever because it is known to occur almost exclusively in Africa's Great Rift Valley. Prior to the 1977 outbreak in Egypt, Rift Valley Fever had been largely confined to Kenya and South Africa, with rumors of an outbreak in Sudan. When US doctors and scientists began to investigate in-depth why this outbreak occurred, it turned out that a previously unfamiliar phenomenon had caused it. The building of the Aswan Dam altered the migration route of the animal population that carries this illness.[9] So, a "natural," or at least nonmalicious, epidemic can readily be confused with a man-made occurrence. We will return to this point, but first, let me bring you back from the brink of nuclear war to consider a second scenario.

8. Dr. William Atkinson, Centers for Disease Control, personal interview (Nov. 9, 1998).

9. James M. Meegan and Charles L. Bailey, "Rift Valley Fever," in *The ARBO Viruses: Epidemiology and Ecology*, ed. Thomas P. Monath (Boca Raton: CRC Press, Inc., 1989), pp. 51–76.

Mass Disruption

Once again "X" has invaded another country in a Desert Storm-like scenario.[10] The US mobilizes and begins a bombing campaign to try, as in Desert Storm, to soften the aggressor. Suppose the White House receives a written threat from a terrorist group in the US, along with a vial of anthrax. The letter states that the authors regard the bombing of country X as an immoral act—not because it is an act of warfare, but because it kills civilians. Because the bombing campaign is killing X's civilians every day, the letter's authors say they intend to retaliate by killing civilians in the US until the bombing campaign is halted. They will do it by biological attacks on four unnamed US cities, with an unspecified agent, but they are enclosing anthrax to show their seriousness and credibility. They also provide a code to authenticate future communications.

Shortly after that, the US receives information from country X about a terrorist group that is preparing to wage biological attacks on US cities. The government of country X says that it regards this as anathema. However inappropriate our bombing campaign is in their view, they assert that they are entirely opposed to a biological attack and regard it (like the US bombing campaign) as contrary to all legitimate rules of warfare. Since they regard this terrorist threat as immoral, they are providing the US with all of their information about this group. Unfortunately, this information is extremely limited and is of very little help.

The president summons various experts in the BW field to advise him. They are confronted with some serious difficulties. One dilemma relates to the limited preparations available to counter this threat. Another relates to how to employ the resources that are on hand when a threat is clear but its character and location are unde-

10. I am grateful to Lewis Libby for originally suggesting a version of this scenario to me.

fined. The difficulty is accentuated when a second message is received from the terrorist group, validated by its code. It indicates that they have selected one city among the four and want to make its name known to decisionmakers. That city is San Jose, California.

At this point does the president say anything to the citizens of San Jose? Does the US take preparatory action? What should it consist of? Assume that an intelligence assessment is made that, among other things, the threat here is credible. Suppose the president asks: "Should I be stockpiling antibiotics?" In 1998 he would be told that the population of San Jose is 900,000; that there are 1.8 million people in the surrounding county, and that the antibiotic supply for the entire nation would last approximately three weeks if given exclusively to the citizens of San Jose. The president would then have to decide whether he wants to do this or to take partial measures that might provide a modicum of help to more people.

If he does treat San Jose, what does it mean in terms of preparations and resources in the unnamed cities? If he makes a public announcement, what is the effect on San Jose and, for that matter, on the bombing campaign? What is the psychological effect on the people?

Obviously, serious difficulties arise. They are all too realistic. Note that at this point, our national security apparatus and, to the extent this situation becomes known, the public, are likely to be severely stressed. And that is so even if an attack never occurs.

Conclusions

What are the implications of these two tales? In the context of a dinner speech (which this chapter was originally delivered as, on November 17, 1998), I will limit myself to five points that I think are of particular importance.

First, biological warfare can be richly ambiguous. It blurs distinctions. Definitively determining whether an outbreak is an attack or naturally occurring disease can be a tough challenge. Even if an incident is known to be an attack, it would be extremely difficult to demonstrate who initiated it. Distinctions between state and non-state actors are critical, but often insidious. Moreover, distinctions between home and abroad are no longer operable—the traditional notion of a "Fortress America" immune from foreign attack rapidly deteriorates.

A great deal of this ambiguity, however, can be resolved by superior intelligence work—not just in thwarting an attack, but also in responding to one. The ability to determine whether we are dealing with a man-made weaponized virus or a natural one relies not only upon epidemiology but also on a detailed understanding of the capabilities of a potential adversary. Intelligence may earn its weight in gold by persuading policymakers that they are or are not dealing with a state actor.

Note that in neither of the two incidents that I described was there an actual biological attack. Yet it is easy to imagine the potential tumult and chaos that might arise if San Jose were to learn of the threat against it. Of course, the president could have decided not to tell San Jose about the threat, but then if the government of X or the terrorist group did inform the public, the outrage and turmoil could well be even greater. This would be even more likely if it were simultaneously revealed that the president knew about the threat but chose to remain silent. The difficulties and ambiguities of these circumstances—about what is happening and whether you are being attacked, whether a pathogen is natural or man-made—give rise to wholly different consequences than in many other forms of warfare. They need to be incorporated into our thinking.

A second point relates to nuclear deterrence. Discussions about nuclear deterrence seem to me to usually assume that biological attack would take place in some binary manner—we would know whether we were or were not intentionally attacked. Asserting a credible nuclear deterrent is vastly more difficult in ambiguous circumstances. Of course, the threat of nuclear retaliation may have some significant role to fulfill. You can subdue the inclinations of states to use terrorist groups as cat's paws, but in my view it would be foolish to overrely on deterrence. It would not help the US terribly much in the scenarios just related.

Third, note that in these scenarios the duration is different from that in other types of potential terrorist attacks. Biological attack is not an incident; it is an extended series of events, even in the circumstance of a single attack. In the example that I have just given, an attack that never materialized had consequences that appeared over a period of weeks. As a result, the consequences are extremely complex.

This leads to a fourth point—the crucial arena of activity is consequence management. It is unlikely that all BW attacks will be thwarted or deterred. What is more believable is that success will come by managing the consequences of an attack and limiting its effects. By doing this reasonably well, the propensity for individuals or groups to engage in copycat incidents will be reduced. That is why this presentation is called "Two Incidents and the NEW Containment." In the end, what we should be striving to do is not so much to contain in the historical sense of preventing an opponent from getting at us, as trying to contain the effects of an attack if one occurs.

CM cannot be mastered by the single silver bullet of the multivalent vaccine, by the ability to find an effective nuclear deterrence, or by some prevention device or detector. It is, in very substantial measure, an issue associated with panic, mass psychology, intelligence and public health. During the sarin attack in Tokyo in 1995, medical facilities confronted an influx of "worried well" (hypochondriacs and those who were unsure about their exposure to the agent). These healthy but burdensome patients outnumbered truly sick patients by a ratio of 4 to 1.[11] They overwhelmed the available medical

11. Dr. Fred Sidell, "U.S. Medical Team Briefing," in *Proceedings of the Seminar*

infrastructure and personnel. The skills required to deal with such a situation are unique and demanding. They are not common to the military psychology or to the existing bureaucracy. They require new ways of thinking and responding.

In the second scenario, intelligence could have helped enormously in CM. Intelligence is not merely a means of thwarting an attack; in combating biological incidents it is a crucial means of cueing a response. It identifies the likely extent of an attack, what kinds of prophylactic steps to take, and where to concentrate CM efforts. Knowing where to focus our efforts allows a husbanding of limited resources—vaccines and antibiotics, equipment, personnel, and the like. That focus improves the ability of government to help a larger number of people and it lessens the likelihood of a president's having to make the hard decisions described above of helping one city or population over another.

A proactive effort to build national CM capabilities, through a robust public health program, is far more than a traditional one-way investment in civil defense. Resources put toward BW civil defense are not sterile investments in 1950s-style bomb shelters. They are investments in public health, the benefits of which are manifold. Developing new vaccines and stockpiling them protects mankind from both natural and man-made threats. Educating the public on BW threats improves awareness about, and thus aids in prevention of, naturally occurring disease.

This brings us to a fifth and final point. The kinds of issues raised by these scenarios cross every type of traditional boundary. Our hardest problems are often encountered in overcoming bureaucracy and precedent in attempting to work across these boundaries. These scenarios have touched upon how the US would respond with

---

on Responding to the Consequences of Chemical and Biological Terrorism (Jul. 11–14, 1995) (Bethesda: Department of Health and Human Services, 1995), pp. 2–33.

our intelligence apparatus, our military forces, FEMA and the Public Health Service, and federal and local law enforcement authorities. The complexities of coordinating such an effort are enormous. They present multidisciplinary challenges. The influenza DNA discussed earlier is going to have to be analyzed at CDC; the results will need to be presented to and understood by the press. Discussion among people who do not normally talk to one another will need to take place, and those engaged in such conversations will have difficulty understanding each other—and sometimes be uncomfortable in dealing with one another.

If the events described above occurred today—as well they could—we would have a world that has benefited enormously from the progress made over the past several years. We have first responders trained in some significant measure in San Jose.[12] We have the beginnings of antibiotic stockpiles. We have units like the CBIRF (US Marine Corps Chemical-Biological Incident Response Force) in place. We have a higher degree of attention paid to the work done at USAMRIID (United States Army Medical Research Institute of Infectious Diseases) and the CDC. We have even begun to understand and establish the relationships needed between different US domestic agencies, the Department of Defense, and a variety of state and local officials and organizations. Most significantly, we have a coordinator in the White House and serious presidential interest.[13] But the fact is that the US is still vulnerable to severe injury, because even now we are far from where we need to be.

In a variety of ways our sophisticated society's machinery is much more cumbersome than a potential attacker's organization,

12. As a result of the 120-city Domestic Preparedness Training Program introduced under Nunn-Lugar-Domenici.

13. Richard Clarke was appointed by President Clinton to be the National Coordinator for Security, Infrastructure Protection, and Counter-Terrorism. See PDDs 62 and 63.

giving an adversary the advantage of asymmetry. Having said that, obviously we need to play the hand we are dealt. Despite a seemingly bleak picture, solace can be found in the belief that a nation that has done such a good job of overcoming so many other challenges throughout its history can also address this one in a satisfactory way.

Robert F. Knouss

The Federal Role in Protection and Response

Terrorist violence is not a new threat in the US. Since World War II, examples of these events dot our history. The bombing of the US House of Representatives in the 1950s, the violence of the antiwar protests in the 1960s and 1970s, and in this decade the catastrophic events at the World Trade Center and the Alfred P. Murrah Federal Office Building were shocking terrorist events. Now we are concerned about a new type of mass-casualty-producing threat—the use of weapons of mass destruction (WMD). Substantial attention is being given to this new attempt to disrupt our society, both to preventing such an event from affecting our citizens here and abroad and to dealing with its consequences should we fail in our prevention efforts.

The US Department of Health and Human Services (HHS), and particularly the Public Health Service (PHS), is responsible for dealing with the health effects of terrorist acts. The most challenging would be those involving the release of a biological, chemical, or radiological/nuclear device. At present, we are engaged in a comprehensive program of research and local, state, and federal systems development to be ready to respond should the need arise. Before the details of our approach are discussed, it may be helpful to describe the systems already in place to meet the needs after catastrophic events that create sudden and overwhelming demands on local health systems. These events may be the result of natural disasters, such as earthquakes, floods, and hurricanes; technological disasters, such as nuclear power plant explosions; or major transportation accidents, such as commercial airline crashes.

Early in the 1980s, the need to be prepared to deal with substantial numbers of US casualties led to the creation of the National Disaster Medical System (NDMS). This is a system capable of handling both those wounded in a military conflict abroad, who have to be returned to the US for definitive care, and those requiring medical care as a result of a catastrophic disaster domestically. In each circumstance, the NDMS could be used should the first-line medical resources be overwhelmed—military and Department of Veterans Affairs (VA) hospitals in the event of an armed conflict, and local civilian facilities in the event of a domestic disaster. Today, over 2,000 private sector hospitals, committing approximately 100,000 beds, voluntarily participate in NDMS. These hospital resources are coordinated and their participation facilitated by seventy-two Federal Coordinating Centers around the country that are managed by the Departments of the Army, Navy, and Air Force, and by the VA.

NDMS is a partnership of four federal agencies—HHS, the VA, the Department of Defense (DoD), and the Federal Emergency Management Agency (FEMA). Its "Board of Directors," so to speak, is made up of the Assistant Secretary for Health and Surgeon General of HHS, the Assistant Secretary of Defense (Health Affairs) of DoD, the Undersecretary for Health of the VA, and the Director of

FEMA. The Director of the Office of Emergency Preparedness (OEP) in the PHS, of HHS, coordinates the day-to-day activities of the NDMS.

The NDMS is capable of providing emergency and primary care at the disaster site, and if local health resources are overwhelmed, of evacuating victims to participating hospitals away from the disaster area. HHS has now organized about sixty primary care response teams with over 6,000 health care volunteers around the country as part of NDMS. The most active are twenty-four Disaster Medical Assistance Teams (DMATs), each of which is capable of fielding a team of thirty-five physicians, nurses, pharmacists, emergency medical technicians, and administrative personnel within twelve to twenty-four hours. They can be self-sufficient for up to three days, carry their own medical supplies, and can provide service under austere conditions at the disaster site, or at transportation points.

Specialized DMATs have been created to address the unique needs of pediatric and burn victims, to provide crisis intervention and other mental health services, to assist medical examiners in identifying victims, and to provide decontamination, triage, and initial care to victims of the release of biological and chemical weapons (BCW). Ten teams, called Disaster Mortuary Teams (DMORTs) provide assistance to medical examiners in identifying victims. Over the past several years, they have assisted in such places as Oklahoma City — when the Murrah Federal Building was destroyed; in the Midwest—when extensive floods dislodged caskets and human remains from cemeteries; and in Guam—when a Korean Air flight crashed on its final landing approach. Four teams, called National Medical Response Teams (NMRTs), are prepared to respond rapidly in the event of the threat or actual release of WMD and can provide on-scene extraction, decontamination, antidote administration, and other primary care services. One of these teams is committed permanently to the Washington, DC, metropolitan area and was prepositioned for response, should it have been needed, during the presidential inauguration and other high-visibility events.

The NDMS forms the backbone of health and medical response under the Federal Response Plan (FRP), an interdepartmental, federal action plan for responding, under FEMA's coordination, to presidential disaster declarations. The twelve emergency support functions (ESFs) under the FRP include such critical functions as mass care, urban search and rescue, transportation, communications, and public works, to name only a few. For each function, a lead agency is designated and is assisted by other federal agencies.

HHS is responsible for leading ESF 8, which addresses health and medical services. Four functions characterize the services that are included under ESF 8: (1) preventive health services (i.e., public health services), (2) medical services, (3) mental health services, and (4) environmental health services. NDMS is used to meet the most resource-intensive medical and mental health services. Both the FRP and the NDMS will be called upon to manage the health consequences of the release of WMD in the US.

Until the sarin attack in the subway system in Tokyo by the Japanese cult Aum Shinrikyo, the release of BCW in the US was not a principal concern of domestic preparedness. In fact, when the same cult was thought to be preparing a sarin attack in the US in 1995, resources were hurriedly prepositioned to be able to respond, should it have been necessary. Since that time, two Presidential Decision Directives (PDDs) have addressed what needs to be done to respond to this new challenge. PDD 39[1] assigned FEMA the lead role for consequence management. Because human health would be most adversely affected in a terrorist attack using WMD, HHS has been

---

1. "US Policy on Counterterrorism," PDD 39 (June 21, 1995) (portions remain classified).

assigned a central role, which is described in PDD 62.[2] (See also PDD 63.[3])

BCW are substantially different and require different types of responses, a fact that is frequently overlooked in response planning. CW fall into several different categories and include: organophosphate nerve agents, such as sarin; vesicants, such as mustard; pulmonary agents, such as phosgene; and cyanide. Other CW have less deadly consequences. Although they are all chemical agents, their effects and treatment differ substantially. In general, however, their effect is more localized than that of biological agents. Even so, potentially thousands of people could be affected.

In the Tokyo attack, the immediate effects were localized: twelve people died and hundreds were exposed and suffered symptoms. An estimated 5,500 sought medical care in area and regional hospitals; most were "worried well," who overwhelmed the health care system. Unfortunately, the local emergency response system was unprepared. First-responders became victims themselves. Unsuspecting hospitals were contaminated by victims seeking care and the causative agent was not correctly identified by most health care providers until hours after the weapon's release.

Given the lessons learned in the Tokyo incident, preparations for the Atlanta Olympics provided the opportunity for HHS to plan the resources and systems needed to respond to the release of a BW or CW by a terrorist, whether foreign or domestic. Of principal concern at the time were releases of organophosphates, cyanide, or toxins. In addition to training local and national teams, decisions were made about: the pharmaceuticals and equipment to use; how to establish on-scene triage and initial care; how to transport victims safely to local hospitals; the best way to control access to local hospitals to prevent their contamination; how to assure adequate re-

2. "Combating Terrorism," PDD 62 (May 22, 1998).
3. "Critical Infrastructure Protection," PDD 63 (May 22, 1998).

sources at local and regional hospitals for the care of those exposed; and what to do to manage mass fatalities, should that have been necessary.

Key to our preparations was our coordination with local public safety and health systems. During a situation involving chemical agents, the first on the scene will likely be public safety or emergency medical services (EMS) personnel, who have been called because people suddenly begin experiencing severe symptoms, including eye or skin irritation, blurred vision, runny nose, muscle spasms, convulsions, and unconsciousness. Unless the first-response personnel are trained, have access to the necessary protective equipment, and have the appropriate pharmaceuticals to initiate therapy on the scene, lives that could have been saved will be lost. A special team in the Atlanta area, called the COBRA team, was trained to provide on-scene decontamination and initial care prior to safe transportation to local hospitals. These hospitals were also prepared to initiate decontamination of self-referrals, as well as offer definitive care to those brought in for emergency treatment.

The model that was used in Atlanta was based on the prototype team that has been developed in the Washington, DC, metropolitan area, consisting of fire, EMS, and other public safety and health personnel, called the Washington Metropolitan Medical Strike Team (WMMST). WMMST was the idea of the Arlington, VA, Fire Chief, who was concerned that an incident in his jurisdiction, which includes the Pentagon, would find his department unprepared to respond. As a result, beginning in 1995, the PHS began elaborating his concepts and helping turn his ideas into a multijurisdiction response team that can respond within ninety minutes to offer on-scene victim extraction, decontamination, antidote administration, and initial care. Local fire/EMS resources are also being upgraded to provide a more rapid first response; some local hospitals, particularly in downtown Washington, DC, are installing permanent decontamination equipment.

Since September 1997, the PHS has been supporting the development of medical strike teams and the accompanying medical response system (including local hospitals) in an additional twenty-five cities, all of which have also been selected for participation in the Nunn-Lugar-Domenici legislation's sponsored program of domestic preparedness, administered by DoD. Most of these cities were selected because of their size, others because of their remoteness (Anchorage and Honolulu, for example), and still others because of special events, such as the Summit of the Eight (in Denver). Eventually, these systems will be established in the 120 largest cities in the country. Their importance is that the response to the release of a WMD begins in the affected community; essentially, the response must be local at first, then regional, and eventually national. Rapid response time is critical if it is to be effective, particularly in a chemical attack using a nerve agent such as sarin.

More daunting is the challenge presented by the release of a biological agent. Rather than having immediate effects, BW may first become apparent days after their release. Of special concern are weaponizable agents, such as smallpox, anthrax, plague, and tularemia, which can affect literally millions of people.

From a planning perspective, however, it is useful to consider population impacts of various sizes. Most frequent is the small, isolated event, such as has occurred when, for example, a lab worker intentionally has contaminated coworkers' food. Less frequent has been the kind of event in which larger populations may be exposed, as in the case that occurred in the late 1980s in Oregon, when a cult group spread salmonella on a restaurant salad bar and caused food poisoning in hundreds of people. These events are distinguishable from major events by the objectives of the terrorists, the types of organisms used, the potential human effects, and the number of victims. But they nonetheless are acts of bioterrorism.

Policymakers at the national level are most concerned today about the use of organisms that may have a more widespread population impact. For this type of terrorist act, the threat agents are more limited in number and are concentrated on those that can affect one million or more people. The list of most likely organisms includes those mentioned above—namely, smallpox, anthrax, plague, and tularemia.

Some experts consider smallpox to present the most ominous threat. Although eradicated from natural circulation, the virus is still officially kept in two government laboratories—one in the US, at the Centers for Disease Control and Prevention, the other at a Russian state laboratory called Vector—awaiting a decision by the World Health Organization about its destruction. Nonethess, some fear that the virus may be covertly harbored in other state laboratories and possibly by terrorist groups. Should it ever be released in the general population, it could rapidly spread person to person because it is not treatable with available antivirals and few would still be protected by immunization campaigns that ceased in the early 1970s. In addition, some fear that weapons have been made from genetically altered smallpox by rogue researchers or laboratories. Smallpox, as with other biological agents, could be released silently, without warning. In the days before the first symptoms developed, those infected could spread the virus, creating a public health emergency of enormous proportions until those potentially exposed could be effectively vaccinated.

Anthrax, on the other hand, continues to occur naturally, yet its spores can be formed into a weapon that can be released in the air over an extensive area. Theoretically, the spores from an airborne release could be inhaled by millions of unsuspecting people. In those who inhale a sufficient quantity of spores, respiratory anthrax could develop in as few as two days. The data from an accidental release in Sverdlovsk, Russia, in 1979, indicate that those exposed might remain at risk of developing the disease for as long as six to seven weeks.

Once symptoms develop, respiratory anthrax is almost always

fatal, even with aggressive antibiotic therapy. On the other hand, prophylactic treatment with antibiotics to which the bacteria is sensitive provides a potential means for protecting an exposed individual from the disease. Although usually sensitive to penicillin, resistant strains may be used in weapon development, necessitating the use of powerful antibiotics such as ciprofloxacin until sensitivities have been established. An effective vaccine has been produced by a Michigan public health laboratory and is under license to the DoD, which has made the decision to vaccinate the forces it considers at risk. In exposed, unvaccinated populations, vaccination could be initiated simultaneously with prophylactic antibiotic therapy.

Plague has presented a serious threat to urban populations for millennia and is suspected of having been used centuries ago as a BW. In aerosolized form, plague produces a difficult-to-diagnose pneumonia. Infected fleas may also be released, producing the bubonic or septicemic form of the disease as the presenting clinical manifestation of an attack. Unlike anthrax, which is not spread person to person, plague is contagious in the pneumonic form. For those who are symptomatic, streptomycin and gentamicin are the antibiotics of choice. Doxycycline may be used for prophylaxis.

Tularemia, usually a tickborne infection, is highly infectious when aerosolized. As few as ten organisms can produce disease of the respiratory tract. The same antibiotics can be used for treatment and prophylaxis of tularemia as are used for pneumonic plague.

Other organisms, such as those that produce Q-fever or a variety of viral encephalitides, or hemorrhagic fevers, are not thought to be as desirable as weapons for producing mass fatalities.

Because of the huge populations that may be exposed, effective strategies are required to counter the threat that BW present. In the case of smallpox, if the virus were introduced into human populations, up to an estimated 40 million people might be at risk of infection, as the virus would spread rapidly. Models predict that aerosolized anthrax could infect millions. Over a megalopolis, anthrax could put as many as 10 million people at risk. Both plague and tularemia might threaten up to one million.

A strong public health infrastructure and a well-informed provider community are required to detect the release of BW. Epidemiological surveillance systems must be strong enough and sensitive enough to detect a release, distinguishing naturally occurring disease from intentional releases. Laboratory networks need to be strong enough and capable enough to rapidly identify the causative organism and its sensitivities to treatment. Public health professionals will have to be knowledgeable enough to be able to determine the likely population at risk, particularly after an aerosol release or when person-to-person spread may occur.

The elements of an effective response involve four essential functions: (1) a mass prophylaxis campaign to assure that those at risk are provided necessary vaccinations or pharmaceuticals, (2) a mass treatment capability for those who become symptomatic, (3) a system for managing potentially large numbers of casualties, and (4) a system for assuring that the environment does not continue to present a risk for the population after an attack has occurred.

Both mass prophylaxis and mass care require development of systems for stockpiling necessary vaccines and drugs. New vaccines are needed against smallpox and anthrax. Drugs that are used daily in the treatment of infectious diseases can be dynamically stockpiled by creating an inventory "bubble" in supply lines that already exist. Even so, distribution systems will be required to make these supplies rapidly available to the exposed populations. In addition, the capacity of the health care system in the affected areas will have to be rapidly expanded, and arrangements made for transporting patients to hospitals at locations distant from the original targets. Both the NDMS and federal health care capacity will have to be mobilized to assist in meeting the potentially overwhelming health care demands.

Following such an attack, preplanned systems will have to be mobilized to assist in the sensitive disposition of those who succumb.

Depending on the agent that is released, special precautions may be required to assure that those who die do not present a continuing threat to those who survive. The environment will have to be rendered safe for habitation. Some agents, such as nitrogen mustard, may persist for decades, presenting a long-term health hazard.

All these elements are challenges to the current public and personal health care systems. We are now at the beginning of the effort to prepare for the challenges that would be presented by the release of WMD, particularly BW that could adversely affect the health of millions of people and paralyze a major population center, not to minimize its effects on the nation as a whole. This effort requires years, and our plans must remain in a state of continual development as new threats and countermeasures emerge.

The impact of the terrorist use of WMD is very high, but the probability that such an event will occur in any specific community is very low. This contrast between impact and probability creates a challenge for local communities, which are aware of the need for preparedness but have limited resources. As a result, local communities must develop a system that meets the needs present during a WMD incident but is based on the more probable scenarios that exist during more routine emergencies.

Federal assistance to local communities includes providing training, equipment, supplies, and pharmaceuticals. Improving the local ability to respond is an important phase of the overall plan. Additionally, this plan includes the federal community—HHS, the DoD, FEMA, the VA, the DoJ, the Environmental Protection Agency, and other responders. But our involvement, coordination, and preparedness must be enhanced. A robust federal response to a terrorist incident will be rapid, but not immediate. For this reason, local communities must be capable of sustaining their own response for at least 12 to 24 hours.

In order to decrease this response time, existing response networks, like NDMS and the National Guard, are being enhanced,

resulting in the strategic positioning of specialized federal responders throughout the country. In addition, other federal assets must be
made available to enhance the surveillance and communication networks between local, state, and federal counterparts. This coordinated, interagency, and intergovernmental effort is envisioned to
produce a comprehensive and effective response system, one absolutely essential to protect the well-being of our citizens. One can
only hope that it will never have to be used.

Ariel E. Levite

Toward a National Defense Strategy

The threat of biological and chemical weapons (BCW) is indeed growing, both as a potentially serious domestic terrorism threat, as well as weapons of choice in confrontations and war in interstate conflicts. The exposure to BCW threats and attacks may obviously have considerable, at times even grave, political, economic, military, and social implications. There is a great diversity of contexts and scenarios in which BCW may be employed in peace, in crisis, and in war. They may be employed covertly or overtly, by states or nonstate (and possibly even stateless) entities, using different types of chemical weapons and/or a growing range of biological agents.

The author bears sole responsibility for the views expressed in the chapter, which do not necessarily reflect the positions of the Government of Israel.

The severity of consequences resulting from the employment of BCW could range from the relatively harmless and meaningless to (in extreme cases) the absolutely catastrophic, depending on certain key factors and circumstances. This remarkably wide range of consequences is coupled with considerable diversity in scenarios of application plus a multilayered and deeply rooted uncertainty over many key features of the threat and the response. Taken together, they present an especially demanding set of defense and preparedness problems and challenges. Civilian and military planners wishing to prepare for dealing with the threat effectively, let alone cost-effectively, thus face a truly daunting task.

The importance of this task of preparing to deal with the BCW threat is underscored by its promise. Effective preparations against the CW and even the BW threat—unlike the nuclear weapons (NW) threat—are, in principle, practicable. Moreover, they could dramatically reduce the vulnerability to threat and the consequences of its realization. Toward this end, this chapter first reviews the basic pillars of response to BCW threats, then proceeds to discuss six building blocs of an effective BCW defense, and finally highlights a few acute dilemmas associated with building effective BCW defenses.

The Basics

A coherent response to the BCW threat in both peacetime and wartime must be multilayered, comprising a package of measures that include an elaborate nonproliferation (denial) effort reinforced by arms control arrangements. But it must be complemented by an effective and equally elaborate counterproliferation strategy consisting of:

- Intelligence
- Deterrence

- Passive defense
- Active defense
- Offensive options

All the layers of the response are necessary, since each has its unique virtues and limitations. None will do by itself, and the critical challenge is to coordinate and harness them to be mutually reinforcing in a cost-effective manner.

Passive defense, although only one layer of the package, is nevertheless an especially critical and cost-effective pillar of the overall response. It serves two principal goals:

- Enhancing the deterrence against BCW attack by denial, namely through diminishing the prospects that an attacker will attain his desired results.

- Minimizing the consequences of an attack were it to take place.

If and when applied in a sophisticated manner, passive defense measures may also serve a third function, that of strengthening public confidence in the capacity of government (at its different levels) to handle such threats competently, both before and after an event. At times, fulfilling this function may assume critical (but possibly transient) importance for maintaining law, order, and an acceptable quality of life.

Passive defense measures, in turn, must include three layers, namely:

- Routine, peace-time precautionary measures and preparations.

- Crisis management capability to manage and defuse a crisis or incident.

- Consequence management capability to diminish the ramifications of an event in which BCW have actually been used, as well as to restore life back to normal conditions as rapidly as possible.

The Building Blocks of Sound Defenses

The key to sound defense against BCW lies in marrying successfully information, capabilities, and training and reaping the significant synergetic effects inherent in such a successful combination.

Information

The first order of business is to make an effort to know and understand, ahead of time, the threat. It is essential to know in advance that you are actually or potentially threatened by BCW. And it is of paramount importance to be able to identify ahead of time the agents that could be involved in such an attack (or, at least, their biological or chemical families), the weapons and methods likely to be used for their dissemination, and to be aware of the likely doctrine for employment, its likely time and target(s), and the like. Such information is necessary in order to make the problem concrete. Otherwise, it is impractical to raise awareness, secure budgets, channel resources into research and development (R&D), acquisition and force development, training and readiness, and to guide operational planning as well as concrete preparations.

Adequate advance preparations can offset some of the risks associated with lack of intelligence-derived knowledge in one or more of the above-mentioned categories. But there are limits to what can be done against ill defined or poorly understood threats. In the absence of concrete threat indicators, it is excessively costly and politically controversial to build up, let alone maintain over time, significant dedicated capabilities and a high level of readiness. Yet all these advance preparations are necessary to deal effectively, and everywhere within one's jurisdiction, with all theoretically possible BCW threat scenarios. Moreover, even if this approach were somehow to prove miraculously viable, in many cases the application of those general purpose capabilities could, at best, produce suboptimal results.

One illustration of the value but also of the limitations of a general early warning is provided by the incident in which the Japanese cult Aum Shinrikyo disseminated sarin in the Tokyo subway. Thanks to some advance preparations based, at least in part, on a general level of early warning (probably generated on the basis of earlier incidents involving the Aum Shinrikyo sect), four different Tokyo hospitals proved able to deal quite successfully within a matter of just a few hours with upward of 5,000 CW casualties (most of whom were "worried well"). At the same time, the chaos and contamination that nevertheless occurred in the hospitals demonstrates also the upward limit of what is likely to prove possible in the absence of preparations to meet a specific threat.

It is also clear that advance warning makes it possible not only to prepare defenses but also to take preventive action against the threat. This preventive action could take the form of either a sustained effort by law enforcement agencies to foil a concrete BCW terrorism threat, or a determined action to reinforce deterrence or take preemptive measures against possible BCW use by state actors. Both forms of information-triggered actions have been practiced in recent years in the Middle East. The US, UK, and Israel have repeatedly made efforts to dissuade BCW use by Iraq (in 1991 and 1998), and the US has attacked a suspected CW facility in the Sudan.

The task of generating actionable information requires, in the case of the BCW threat, a sustained and especially intimate dialogue between the intelligence community and law enforcement agencies, on the one hand, and the emergency preparedness and medical community on the other. Such an intense process should sensitize the generators of information to the key questions and parameters that affect the advance preparations (related to the need to prepare for a smallpox threat, for example). Just as importantly, it might help overcome organizational, bureaucratic, and political obstacles that stand in the way of putting in place prudent precautionary measures against BCW threats.

Situational Awareness

The second building block of a sound BCW defense has to be an efficient, reasonably reliable and, perhaps most importantly, rapid ability to detect signs of a BCW attack and identify its nature and location. This type of knowledge can be initially generated by one of the following sources:

- Intelligence
- Technical detection and identification systems; joint or separate sensors (local kits as well as remote standoff systems), as well as a rapid diagnostic capability
- Epidemiological monitoring
- Agricultural disease monitoring (both plants and livestock)

In general, arriving at the desired level of situational awareness ultimately requires harnessing all of these sources. This, in turn, means that a considerable effort has to be invested, inter alia, in all of the following areas:

- Raising routine awareness and understanding of the prospects and possible manifestations of a BCW attack. This must be done for all the sectors and communities that might be the first to encounter symptoms or indicators of an attack, be they in the intelligence, military, law enforcement, emergency services, and the medical community, or in the agricultural sector.

- Identifying and disseminating knowledge about different types of clearcut or even possible indicators of a BCW attack, in a sufficiently concise, comprehensible, and easy to use manner, to be employed by all the first-responders.

- Expediting the development of cheap and reliable rapid diagnostic kits, and handing them over to all likely first-responders, coupled with an intensive training in sample collection and handling (to meet both scientific and legal requirements).

- Structuring and streamlining the information flow from all possible sources of indicators to all relevant consumers. The latter may, in many cases, require collection beyond, and cooperation with agencies lying beyond, one's national borders.

- Collecting benchmark information on routine occurrences of human, livestock, and plant diseases to facilitate detection of unusual outbreaks.

- Placing certain sensors in sensitive facilities and installations that might be particularly vulnerable to a BCW attack.

Delineating the Affected Area

The third building block of a defense package should be the ability to delineate rather quickly and reliably the affected area, both the transient and the more permanent danger zones. This requirement is very demanding, since it must factor in terrain, wind, and climate conditions, as well as the specific qualities of the agent and the method of dissemination. It naturally presents an especially daunting task in urban areas. Yet this capability is of critical importance, since its potential for reducing uncertainty has a profound impact on both the scope of advance preparations that are required to handle BCW scenarios, as well as on the ability to conduct reasonably orderly and efficient crisis management and consequence management operations.

Here it must be emphasized that some capabilities in this realm are, and could be, of a dual-use nature. They could and should serve the purposes of handling both hazardous materials (HAZMAT) incidents, as well as BCW attacks.

Decision Making and Public Affairs

Fourth comes the requirement for a legally based, coherent, integrated, and rapidly implementable (practically anywhere) capability to handle crisis decision making, and especially public affairs policy. Although this requirement is traditionally viewed as an integral part of crisis management it nevertheless poses some especially acute problems that merit treating it, at least analytically, as a separate category.

Events involving threatened, suspected, let alone confirmed, use of BCW agents are likely to be characterized, at least initially, by a combination of all the following features:

- Huge uncertainty and confusion
- Severe time pressure
- Considerable complexity given the diverse possible implications and the interplay of inconsistent, possibly contradictory, considerations
- Intense media interest
- Public anxiety

Much depends on the speed and efficiency with which the requirements for handling crisis decision making and public affairs can be met. This is likely to have an equal, or even greater, impact than the specific agent release on the scope and consequences of the crisis that ensues following a chemical, and especially biological, attack. The difference between a relatively confined and limited incident (to which all but the most extreme cases of BCW attacks can be reduced) and chaos lies, to a large extent, upon carefully developed and well rehearsed decision-making processes, coupled with an elaborate and well coordinated public affairs campaign.

Manuals and training for crisis decision making and public affairs can make a dramatic difference in the outcome of the incident. Yet the unique features of BCW attacks as described above present formidable challenges for decision making and public affairs. These will, in all likelihood, remain extraordinarily difficult to meet. But certain decision-making aids, most prominently in the areas of detection, identification, and delineation of BCW attacks, can considerably enhance the chances of success.

Crisis Management

Crisis management capability more broadly defined constitutes the fifth building block of a sound defense package. It has to address, in addition to the challenges in the above-mentioned domains, many practical issues of an interdisciplinary nature, requiring very different skills and areas of specialty. In addition, in all but the very small localized events, it is essential to mobilize and coordinate the work of diverse organizations of very different character, jurisdiction, and affiliation, in order to:

- Freeze the situation in the immediately affected area.

- Arrest, seize, or otherwise neutralize the perpetrators (in case of domestic use or blackmail incident).

- Neutralize unexploded ordnance.

- Maintain law and order throughout the wider area (including the prevention of hospital flooding, and the imposition of curfew and/or closure, and conduct of small-scale evacuation, if necessary).

- Administer standard and dedicated medical first aid to exposed people.

Naturally, the capability to do these things in a timely and efficient manner is heavily predicated on availability of early warning and information, advance preparations of capabilities, and training.

Consequence Management

This element is the sixth and final building block of a defense package. Consequence management (CM) deals with many of the challenges associated with crisis management, albeit under a somewhat less severe time pressure and (hopefully) a better situational awareness. Assuming that an incident has broad, widespread, and/or enduring characteristics (lasting more than a few hours), this phase assumes considerable importance and brings in new challenges of a rather sensitive nature. It may then require both the administration of longer-term medical treatment (ranging from the dissemination of supplies and medications, the provision of care, and the management of surge production of scarce medical supplies), to mass evacuation, wide area decontamination, and restoration of normalcy in all (or in spite of) immediately affected areas and domains.

Dilemmas

As a conclusion to this short discussion, it is important to highlight several especially acute dilemmas associated with building a solid defense package against BCW.

Awareness versus False Alarm

Awareness of the risks and prospects of BCW attacks is obviously one prerequisite for securing resources for BCW defense as well as for enhancing readiness of the first-responders in general, and the medical community in particular. Yet, at the same time, as has become painfully apparent of late, this growing awareness means heightened sensitivity that carries with it the risk of generating false alarms, some of which are far from being cost-free. Over time it also runs the increased risk of reducing sensitivity through what is known as the "cry wolf" syndrome.

The dilemma is further complicated when we take into consideration also the impact of exposure on the prospects of a "self fulfilling" prophecy. Increased media and public attention to the threat and its potential consequences may actually serve to enhance the appeal of BCW to would-be terrorists.

Transparency versus Secrecy in Precautionary Measures

Related to the earlier dilemma is the trade-off between transparency and secrecy. The public's right to know is firmly grounded in democratic values, and transparency regarding threat assessment and the response to it is also most helpful in coordinating and mobilizing support for defensive preparations. Yet transparency regarding these matters may also compromise sources and methods of intelligence collection and, worse still, may expose vulnerabilities in the response system that, in turn, could be exploited by terrorists or other aggressors. Moreover, while certain defensive preparations may only be conducted publicly (such as mass population pre-exposure vaccination against a leading single threat agent), these run the risk of rechanneling the threat to other (or more therapy-resistant) strains of agents against which one is less well prepared.

Disclosure versus Secrecy in Crisis Management

Incidents involving the use of BCW threats are difficult if not impossible to conceal. Furthermore, disclosure may actually prove essential in mitigating some of the more adverse consequences of such attacks, by providing the public with guidance on how to behave to minimize exposure and suffering. Still, huge uncertainty is likely to prevail, at least initially, over the nature, scope, and implications of such an attack and, by implication, also over the desired remedial course of action. Early disclosure may also cause panic and lack of confidence, due to the inevitably partial, contradictory, or inconsistent information the authorities will be able to provide at that time. Panic and chaos may then ensue, and their consequences could well prove difficult to control, especially if the public loses its trust in official statements

This lesson has already been evident in the case of epidemics, diseases such as "mad cow" disease, and similar clusters of events. The opposite course of action, however, may prove just as harmful. Attempts at suppression of information, even if legally sound and carried out for perfectly legitimate reasons, are likely to backfire if and when discovered, thus eroding media and public confidence. Later they may also open the door for controversy and accusations over political and personal accountability and legal liability for damage and/or loss of life.

Defense versus Deterrence

Another dilemma concerns the impact of defensive preparations to withstand BCW attacks based on the likelihood that such attacks will materialize. It centers on the possibility that investments in BCW defenses could possibly prove counterproductive by making such attacks more likely. This dilemma has to do with the possibility that investments in diminishing the adverse consequences of BCW attacks somehow indicate that they are considered, or are made to be (by virtue of the diminished damage they may cause), so to speak, "tolerable." This, in turn, may undermine one's deterrence posture (based on "deterrence by punishment") against BCW use, since the credibility of the threat of harsh retaliation derives its legitimacy from the catastrophic consequences to which it responds.

This dilemma is obviously reminiscent of the earlier debate in the nuclear context on "deterrence by denial" versus "deterrence by punishment" and the trade-offs between them. But it assumes, perhaps, a more real meaning in the BCW context, insofar as BCW defenses indeed possess a much greater inherent potential for reducing casualties and damage than does civil defense against nuclear attacks. It becomes, however, even more difficult to address here, as there is also a distinct possibility that BCW defenses may actually have a net beneficial impact on one's deterrence posture. Such potential is grounded in depriving a would-be aggressor of high expectations for success in attaining the desired impact in his attack.

Efficiency and Affordability versus Social Justice

The last cluster of dilemmas has to do with some inevitable tension between moral and ethical considerations, on the one hand, and practical considerations on the other, in designing and applying BCW defenses. Several such dilemmas present themselves in this context, all having in common the difficulty of making judgments on the scope and direction of BCW defenses exclusively on the basis of efficiency considerations.

One particularly vexing issue in this context is whether all segments of any given society should be accorded the same level of protection, even if the protection of some is, inherently, much more costly or difficult to achieve than that of others. This issue naturally assumes greater prominence because the overall resources available for BCW defenses are bound to be both finite and insufficient. This dilemma holds true, for example, when contemplating extending some forms of BCW passive defenses (both physical and medical) to certain most vulnerable segments of society (the sick, elderly, very young, pregnant women, and the like) as well as to certain religious groups whose beliefs prevent them from accepting some forms of protection and/or treatment. Similar dilemmas arise when considering the expansion of the protection package (for example, in active defense) to the entire territory of a nation even when some of it may be believed to be less exposed to the BCW threat than others.

Some of these dilemmas are quite common in other areas of public health and national defense. Painful choices often have to be made regarding the right balance among ethical, political, and practical considerations in determining policy. Yet the BCW context may prove to be an area where certain painful choices are inevitable, and these choices carry an especially grave potential for triggering controversy that will be particularly difficult to contain. This fact is due to the dramatic manifestations of exposure to BCW, and the very high costs (both routine pre-exposure, and ad hoc post-exposure) as well as the uncertain effectiveness and adverse side effects associated with certain forms and applications of BCW defenses.

In many areas the ability to extend the BCW protection to more demanding parts of society is constrained more by priorities in resource allocation than by technical feasibility. This constraint, in turn, raises difficult issues of prioritization and proportionality both within the domain of BCW defenses as well as between this domain and other domains of social expenditure. The availability on the commercial market of certain elements of the BCW protective package, from antibiotics and vaccines to some types of protective gear, also brings to the fore another dimension of the social justice dilemma, insofar as the rich may enjoy a higher level of protection than the poor. This is likely to become an issue wherever a government elects to leave certain areas of BCW protection partially or wholly to the discretion (and by implication, also to the funding) of its individual citizens.

Conclusion

BCW have two formidable qualities. They present a potentially most serious threat of both an immediate and enduring nature. Yet, this threat can be significantly diminished through a comprehensive defense package. These two qualities, when taken together, combine to turn defense against BCW into a formidable national and international challenge. This is all the more so given the growing prospects of BCW use not only by state actors but also by state-sponsored and independent terrorists throughout the world.

Considerable diversity exists in BCW agents and in the possible threat scenarios involving their application. Scientific and technological gaps also exist in our ability to assess the threats, especially but not exclusively in real time. Thus, when attempting to confront the BCW threat we must confront an inherent uncertainty over the threat, exacerbated by significant constraints, and many practical as well as ethical dilemmas, in devising the response. Consequently, no single or simple solution to the threat is viable. A comprehensive response package to the threat thus becomes a necessity, and its devising and implementing requires formidable effort. Only some of the considerations and challenges that underlie the design of such a package have been discussed here.

Frances E. Winslow

The First-Responder's Perspective

Public administrators and political scientists must raise a variety of issues regarding biological and chemical weapons (BCW) terrorism, and the federal government's plans for responding to a terrorist event in a US community. First, we recognize that the goal of terrorism is to make the government appear inept, so the goal of a response planning effort must be to be prepared to respond effectively. For example, a sudden attack on an unprepared community could easily overwhelm normal systems for managing multiple casualties. Patient distribution could become one of the first services to be disrupted, as local hospitals with high in-patient census reports refuse to accept more critical patients likely to require in-patient care. Although existing multiple casualty plans provide a basis for operation during a terrorist attack, the sheer numbers of potential patients guarantee that the system would be overwhelmed quickly.

What facilities would be capable of managing the numbers of infected or affected patients? Would it be better to send the stable patients with existing medical problems out of the area, and keep all of the infected or chemically affected victims in one place? Would this help to slow the spread of secondary infections, or raise the quality of health care available to the injured? Would the patients be willing to stay in an area filled with sick people, or would those still able to travel self-evacuate?

Enforcement of the quarantine laws arises as a potential Constitutional issue. Quarantine laws in the US date back to the age of rampant childhood infectious diseases, before inoculations were routinely administered. These laws were enforced in an era before the existence of the civil rights movement. Would enforcement of quarantine laws now be viewed as an infringement of the civil rights of the patient? Would keeping sick persons in an area where services were already overwhelmed violate their right to travel, their right to seek medical care of their choosing? How much force could be used to enforce quarantine laws and regulations?

State Department of Health Services officials and county and city health officers in California are empowered to protect and preserve the public health, and to order and enforce quarantines—including creating quarantine regulations, declaring quarantine locations, and controlling "bodies" of living and deceased persons.[1] Would local law enforcement officials be expected to assist in the maintenance of a quarantine on an entire community or region? Could, and would, National Guard forces be used? Under the federal Posse Comitatus Act,[2] military forces cannot be used for do-

1. See *California Health and Safety Code* §§ 100170, 101030, 101040, 101375, 101470, 101475, 120130, 120135, 120140, and 120145.
2. 18 U.S.C. § 1385.

mestic peacekeeping within the US. Would that law have to be changed? What biological or chemical agents would justify the use of deadly force to prevent a victim from leaving the infected/affected area? Would, for example, a biological agent such as smallpox or plague justify the use of deadly force?

All these questions raise a second public policy issue: the use of scarce financial resources to plan and prepare for a potential biological or chemical terrorist attack. In California funds available to public agencies to address any new threat must come from the scarce tax dollars available after Proposition 13 passed to limit real property tax increases.[3] This means that any new initiative requires that another existing activity be diminished or eliminated from the public budget. Local elected officials view the numbers of demands for services, and evaluate the threat of a terrorist attack on a particular community as not very large. With the exception of a few internationally famous cities and the capital, most cities have a greater potential for natural disaster than for a terrorist attack. Is it prudent for local officials to divert money from social programs or other services to provide for training of police, fire, and medical personnel to respond to such an unlikely event?

In 1996 the US Congress passed the Nunn-Lugar-Domenici legislation (formally known as the Defense Against Weapons of Mass Destruction Act of 1996),[4] which created the Domestic Preparedness Program. This provided resources to the twenty-seven largest cities to form Metropolitan Medical Task Forces, also known as MMTFs. The MMTF is a multiprofession organization trained to respond to an event involving weapons of mass destruction

3. Proposition 13 was an initiative passed by California voters on June 6, 1978, taking effect less than a month later, on July 1, to rein in what were perceived to be runaway real property tax increases; however, it has also had the effect of significantly restricting the tax revenue base of California's 58 counties. See California Constitution, art. 13A, §§ 1 and 5.

4. 50 U.S.C. § 2301 et seq.

(WMD)—nuclear, biological, or chemical. The team includes police, fire, medical, coroner, and emergency services resources. Six federal agencies were named as partners in the effort to recruit, train and equip these MMTFs. The federal partners were the Department of Defense (DoD), the Department of Health and Human Services/Public Health Service (PHS), the Federal Bureau of Investigation (FBI), the Environmental Protection Agency (EPA), the Department of Energy (DoE), and the Federal Emergency Management Agency (FEMA). Congress provided funds to the DoD to give terrorism awareness and response training to a total of 120 preselected communities, of which the twenty-seven largest were to have MMTFs.[5] In addition to offering classes in the twenty-seven communities, the DoD also left behind a cache of "training equipment," response equipment that could be used for classes and drills. The equipment has a value of about $300,000 for each city. DoD then gave funding to PHS to provide equipment and pharmaceuticals to the MMTFs on a contract. This contract required these twenty-seven cities to develop plans, design equipment and pharmaceutical caches, and design and implement training cycles for sustaining the MMTF. PHS funding was $350,000 for the average city, although exact amounts varied.[6]

After one year of operation, the MMTF communities, and about ninety others, had the opportunity to apply for a grant from the Department of Justice (DoJ). The size of these grants was determined by the size of the community, with the midrange being $250,000. Grants could be used for personal protective equipment for first-responders, detection equipment for the WMD agents,

5. The twenty-seven Metropolitan Medical Response System cities are: Anchorage; Atlanta; Baltimore; Boston; Chicago; Columbus, OH; Dallas; Denver; Honolulu; Houston; Indianapolis; Jacksonville; Kansas City, KS/MO; Los Angeles; Memphis; Miami; Milwaukee; New York City; Philadelphia; Phoenix; San Antonio; San Diego; San Francisco; San Jose; Seattle; Washington, DC; and Winston-Salem.
6. The smaller cities got $300,000, and the largest cities got $500,000.

communications equipment, or other approved purposes. The requirement was that this equipment would constitute an enhancement of existing capability that would take the recipient community to a high level of readiness for terrorist events.

Although total federal funding of an average of $900,000 from three sources sounds like significant support for the MMTFs, these funds included no reimbursement for local training costs, such as overtime for those attending the classes or training facilities usage charges. There was no funding to cover the substantial commitment of staff time required to coordinate the training with DoD contractors, write the local plans, develop the equipment and pharmaceutical caches, design and sustain training, oversee the applications for the grants and the execution of the contracts, or participate in the multi-agency committee structure essential to the development and maintenance of a multi-agency team.

In order to justify the use of scarce local resources to prepare for an unlikely event, local officials have tried to create a dual-use system. In many ways a WMD event is just a major multiple-casualty incident, or a major hazardous materials event. Equipment, supplies and training that are applicable to either WMD events or related conventional events have a greater and more immediate benefit to the community. The training to use this dual-use equipment is more easily justified, even though it requires the diversion of funds from other activities to terrorism-response planning. The selection of pharmaceuticals that can be used in existing medical programs as well as to combat WMD effects enables low-cost support of the program. These pharmaceutical caches may be placed into use in the current public hospital system, and used and replaced regularly, so that the drugs do not have to be discarded at the end of their shelf-life of five years or less.[7]

---

7. For example, San Jose's cache is now part of the Santa Clara County Valley Medical Center's clinic system resource base, guaranteeing that fresh replacement

The dual-use concept is often the only way to obtain the support of financially conscious local government administrators and elected officials, yet it was resisted by both DoD and PHS in the early months of the Domestic Preparedness Program. Their concern was that terrorism-response funds would be siphoned off to supplement existing programs that communities should support on their own. Conversely, they were not sensitive to the high cost to local agencies of participating in the program. In fact, the City of San Diego actually refused all funds and all participation in the Domestic Preparedness Program, even though it was one of the twenty-seven selected communities at the beginning of the program. San Diego determined that the cost of participation was not justified by the benefit the community would receive.[8]

Ultimately, because of the persuasive powers of regional PHS administrators, the dual-use concept was accepted for many applications. Thus, pharmaceuticals that can be used in AIDS clinics were allowed to be the antibiotics of choice for the MMTF, rather than the more exotic items originally suggested. Decontamination tents that can be used for WMD victims can also be used for the victims of a conventional hazardous materials accident. However, the requirement to purchase some single-use items, such as the Mark I kits and the unproved "Smart Ticket" biodetectors, remained.

A third significant policy issue for the local public administrators and locally elected officials is the proper role of local authority vis-à-vis federal authority in the event of a WMD event in a community. Unless there has been a threat or an announcement of attack by a

---

pharmaceuticals flow into the system as existing stocks are used. The long-term issue is to retain this supply as "overstock," and not to allow it to substitute for preexisting designated quantities, which would defeat the original purpose of the stockpile.

8. Ultimately San Diego's MMTF was assembled using San Diego County personnel and DoD resources from various commands in the San Diego metropolitan area. Recently, the San Diego Fire Department has also begun to participate.

terrorist group, the community many not know that a terrorist event has occurred until hours, or even days, afterward. In the first hours, the event will be managed by local officials as though it were a conventional event, such as a hazardous materials accident, explosion, or naturally occurring epidemic. Local police, fire, and medical professionals will handle the event until they realize it is a terrorist event. Then they will notify the FBI, who will mobilize the federal resources necessary to handle the investigation of the event. While the local FBI agent in charge may arrive within a few hours of being notified, it may be half a day or more after the onset of the event. Other federal resources may have to travel from the East Coast, and take several days to arrive.[9]

What then are the proper roles of the local police department, the FBI, the National Guard, or the active-duty military in such an event? The local police department will be the first-responder to a criminal event. They maintain certain responsibilities for local civil conditions, regardless of the presence of federal officials. What responsibilities can be turned over to federal officials, and what responsibilities must be shared? The National Guard, a state resource at the command of the governor, is seeking a peacetime role that will maintain force readiness.[10] Terrorism response would seem to be a reasonable readiness activity, yet Guard unit members have to be mustered from their regular jobs to their reporting areas, and deployed from there, a 24-hour minimum time requirement. What useful role can they play that far into the event? What training, knowledge, or equipment do they have that could help? Since ter-

9. For example, resources from the US Army Medical Research Institute of Infectious Diseases (USAMRIID), the US Marine Corps Technical Escort Unit, and Centers for Disease Control and Prevention forensic personnel.

10. See "National Guard Report to the Congress of the United States of America: Weapons of Mass Destruction Study" (Oct. 12, 1998); and the National Academy of Public Administration's report, "The Role of the National Guard in Emergency Preparedness and Response" (Oct. 1996).

rorism may be an act of war against the US by a foreign power, would the active-duty military, or military reserves, have a role in the response or investigation of the event?[11] These are some of the many issues that remain unresolved regarding federal, state, and local roles.

Fourth, the education of the public about WMD events is a public policy question for local public administrators and elected officials. Should public education be undertaken in advance of any warning or threat? Would advance public education limit panic in the event of a terrorist attack? The March 1979 Three Mile Island incident, the worst commercial nuclear accident in the US, suggests that advance education is usually ignored by the general public. A precautionary evacuation suggestion by the Governor of Pennsylvania, which applied to only a small segment of the population, led to a mass exodus by large numbers of residents who would never have been in any danger. If public information comes from sectors with high credibility, such as fire or medical officials, would that information be better received? We have no useful model for anticipating the public's response. WMD events are not similar to natural hazard events, but more closely related to wartime events, where information is usually limited for national security purposes.

Fifth, the threat of terrorism, and terrorist events, both pose psychological hazards to the general population of a potentially threatened area. Some people are frightened by the realization that such an event is even possible. Those with previous experiences of war, severe community disruption, or large-scale natural hazards may suffer greater symptoms than those without previous traumatic experience.[12] After an actual event, even those community members

---

11. Again, it would be necessary to consider the impact of the Posse Comitatus Act, 18 U.S.C. § 1385.

12. The "echo effect," the name given to the phenomenon of enhanced stress reaction in previous victims, has been documented in victims of natural disasters and violence. See Joseph A. Flaherty, et al., *Psychiatry: Diagnosis and Therapy* (Norwalk,

not directly affected physically may suffer from trauma related to the community impact of the terrorist event.[13] Therefore, it is critical for local officials to consider how best to manage the public's education, how best to prepare the community to weather such an event. A postevent response plan is essential, as critical incident stress defusings in the first days, and critical incident stress debriefings in the first weeks, will be essential to the mental recovery of the community.[14]

Legal liability issues also arise regarding the public perception of a WMD event. The accidental release in July 1993 of chemicals from a sulfuric acid manufacturing plant in Richmond, CA, points to a problem that may also occur after a WMD event. People went to the hospital whether they were directly affected or not. Statistics have suggested that approximately 5,000 people lived close enough to the release site to have justified medical evaluation at a hospital. However, about 20,000 sought medical attention, including many whose goal appeared simply to be participation in the "Toxic Cloud" class-action litigation—which ultimately included some 60,000 claimants and settled for $180 million—rather than remediation of actual symptoms.

An important part of the Domestic Preparedness Program is the ability to respond effectively to an attack on the community. If the attack is a chemical attack, the victims will need to be treated with appropriate pharmaceuticals quickly, and for some time into the

---

CT: Appleton & Lange, 1993), pp. 156, 167, et seq.; American Psychiatric Association, *Diagnostic and Statistical Manual of Mental Disorders: DSM-III-R* (3rd ed. rev.) (Washington: American Psychiatric Association, 1987).

13. Notable documented community impact events include the Aero Mexico plane crash in Cerritos, CA, in 1988 and the explosion of the Alfred P. Murrah Building in Oklahoma City in 1996.

14. For a description of treatment techniques see Joseph A. Flaherty, et al., *Psychiatry: Diagnosis and Therapy*, pp. 169–70; Jeffrey T. Mitchell and George S. Everly, Jr., *Critical Incident Stress Debriefing* (Ellicott City, MD: Chevron Publishing Corp., 1995).

future. The selected MMTF communities have been given about $100,000 each for pharmaceuticals, but this cache is only adequate for initial emergency treatment. If there are 1,000 patients, much more support will be needed within hours of the event.

If the attack is biological, vaccines and drugs will both be critical. Recent legislation has provided some $120 million for the federal government to use to stockpile drugs and vaccines in a national cache that can be deployed as needed. The development of this cache is a critical link in the preparedness chain. In addition, medical equipment, such as ventilators, is essential to treat patients suffering from chemical or biological agent exposure. Each city or region cannot fund the development of a cache of ventilators individually; a national, mobile supply is essential. Although the National Disaster Medical System (NDMS) provides an avenue to definitive care outside of the affected area, support equipment is needed to sustain the patient in transit to the NDMS location. Furthermore, current military air ambulance protocols limit the types of treatment that patients can be undergoing while being transported by them. This restriction further limits the access of some patients to definitive medical care outside of the affected community.

Another gap between local and federal responders is the planning gap. The local governments in California operate their emergency response on the Incident Command System (ICS) and the Standardized Emergency Management System (SEMS). These systems dictate who is in charge at every phase of an event. In addition, response is built on a suite of complementary supporting plans. These include the community's Emergency Operations Plan, the Multiple Casualty Incident Plan, the Hazardous Materials Response Plan, and the MMTF Operational Plans. In MMTF cities these plans have been harmonized to support the WMD response at each phase. However, the six federal partner agencies do not seem to have well integrated plans for their levels of response to an event. DoD provided training, but seems to have no ongoing role with MMTF communities. PHS provided planning guidance and a supply cache. The MMTF plan must integrate with the NDMS, through which advanced medical care can be obtained for disaster victims. The FBI is designated the lead agency in crisis and consequence management, as of the fall of 1998. It plans to send personnel to establish a joint operation with the local agencies, but the timing of FBI assistance is unpredictable in any given event. EPA and DoE have specialized roles related to the agents used as weapons. It is assumed that their role will be advisory to the medical and recovery aspects of the emergency response, but no written plan is available.[15] FEMA's role, formerly consequence management, has become problematic. It has informed the MMTF cities that there is no funding authority under the Robert T. Stafford Disaster and Emergency Assistance Act of 1974[16] to financially support the local agencies' response to a terrorism disaster, although they do provide financial support during natural and technological disasters.[17]

Local government will most likely have to manage the first hours of a terrorist event without the participation of the federal partners, due to geographical dispersion of federal assets. The crisis management will actually begin with the local first-responders: hazardous materials team, emergency medical services including decontamination and transportation, paramedic care, law enforcement, and hospital resources management. Patient care will begin with

15. Terrorism amendments to the Federal Emergency Response Plan issues in 1997 need to be more broadly discussed. Local governments, especially MMTF communities, need to be trained and exercised in these new plans with their regional federal partners, if the plan is to be useful. FEMA currently provides a self-study course on its website, and a series of five model tabletop exercises for five different terrorist scenarios. However, the briefings and tabletops at the regional level that were advertised in FEMA's April, 1997 PTE newsletter need to be carried out in proximity to every MMTF city.

16. 42 U.S.C. § 5122 et seq.

17. Upon inquiry by DoD personnel during the January 1998 San Jose chemical tabletop exercise, this was the response of the Washington staff of FEMA.

decontamination, triage, on-scene treatment, and transportation into the hospital system.

The hospital system continues to be the weak link at the local level. Although fire department personnel and emergency medical services personnel are aware of and trained for their crucial roles in a WMD event, members of the hospital community have not yet accepted an active role in community preparedness. Physicians typically do not attend WMD training. The chief executives of hospitals see such an event as a money loser, and have no interest in devoting today's scarce revenues to planning for an event that is unlikely to occur in their communities. Managed health care organizations see no reason to spend money on staff training or facility preparedness for high-probability natural hazards, and low-probability WMD events hold no interest for them either.

Actually managing the general public during a response will also be a challenge for local officials. In a chemical event, most victims will still be ambulatory, and they will flee. Rapid response, mass decontamination, and rapid treatment for generic "chemical exposure" is most likely all that most of the victims will stay for. Most will leave the scene before the first responding units of police and fire can arrive, carrying possible contamination on their shoes and clothing into other parts of the metropolitan area.

Biological attacks, unless announced, are even more insidious. Victims will not know they have been exposed to a biological agent until a significant number of people get sick at the same time, and until the epidemiology ties them together. With a large dispersion of the victims over a two- to five-day period, victims could be in different countries, even on different continents, before an attack is identified. These factors make effective epidemiology crucial to the discovery and containment of a biological attack, especially if an infectious agent is involved. Most infectious-disease-reporting requirements give doctors ten days to report an illness, if it is recognizable as a reportable disease. Furthermore, this information may not be aggregated in a meaningful way for weeks. A nationwide computer network would speed the aggregation of information. Additional funding for the Centers for Disease Control and Prevention has enabled the development of such a system. The timelines for reporting should be revised to make disease reporting, at least of the most contagious diseases, a very prompt event.

The MMTF program results in the need for ongoing training efforts. Some elements of the MMTF system, such as physicians and hospitals, have yet to accept initial training. First-responders must receive reminders of the safety rules for responding to WMD events, including an awareness of potential secondary devices on the premises. All MMTF members require updating and refresher training to sustain the team's response capabilities. Equipment damaged or consumed in training will have to be repaired or replaced. Some equipment and single-use pharmaceuticals will eventually have to be replaced. Currently, the federal programs assume that local officials will have to fund all these activities. The reality is that unless there is an actual event in the US before these materials expire, it is unlikely that local officials would choose to spend money that way.

Recovery from a WMD event will bring its own challenges. Some public site in the community will most likely have been the site of the terrorist event, a horrifying occurrence with which people will not want to continuously associate. That site may have to be removed from the view of the community. Who will reimburse the property owner? How will the community be made whole? What will the site be used for in the future? A few examples of actual events suggest that the recovery process will be slow and expensive for the community at large.

In July 1976, in Philadelphia, the American Legion held their convention at the Bellevue Stratford Hotel, one of the city's oldest and most prestigious hotels. An infection that was apparently passed through the heating, ventilation, and air conditioning system made many legionnaires sick, and twenty-nine people died. This unknown disease came to be called Legionnaires' Disease (Legionellosis), and the hotel was forever associated with the sickness. Soon it had few patrons, and was forced to close, even though all health inspections showed that there was no remaining infectious disease problem. Eventually the hotel was bankrupted by the disease and remained vacant for several years. It was eventually rehabilitated with a new name and a new facade to completely remove any mental association with Legionnaires' Disease.

In Santa Cruz, the Pacific Garden Mall and the Cooper Building were destroyed by the 1989 Loma Prieta Earthquake. The rubble of the buildings was removed, but members of the community made a moving videotape about the pain they felt at the loss of these landmarks. The videotapes were sold to raise money to create a memorial on the site of these landmarks, even though new buildings were erected in their place.

The bombing of the Alfred P. Murrah Federal Building in Oklahoma City in April 1995 was one of the greatest acts of domestic terrorism in US history. The federal government has demolished the remains of the building. There are plans to maintain that area as a park, a memorial to the hundreds, including little children, who lost their lives. Oklahoma City will not soon forget this terrible event that touched the lives of everyone in the community in some way.

These examples suggest that a post-terrorist event recovery will be long and expensive. The loss of the attack site as a viable public facility is likely. Clean-up of the premises and disposal of the building material will be problematic. Even moving the debris may prove to be politically volatile, especially if other local jurisdictions are involved in a transportation plan. Psychological harm, environmental impacts, and economic effects can only be guessed at.

The Domestic Preparedness Program has provided a paradigm for communities to use to prepare for WMD events. However, no community can truly prepare for such a horrifying event. The federal partners, especially PHS and the FBI, have effectively assisted the selected cities in developing their MMTF systems, including realistic and achievable plans. Congress must now make a commitment to provide the financial assistance necessary to sustain the process at the local government level if a strong capability is to be maintained into the twenty-first century.

Commentary

The speakers in this part of the conference emphasized different aspects of the challenge. In addressing the conference, Secretary of the Navy Richard Danzig described two scenarios—one real and one fictional—to illustrate the difficulties and complexities of the BCW problem. The real-life situation was the worldwide outbreak of the "Spanish Flu" in 1918; the imaginary one is a hypothetical threat of a BW attack against a US city, posed by a terrorist group in response to a "Desert Storm-like" US military campaign against an "aggressor" country. Secretary Danzig highlighted the inherent ambiguities and uncertainties as to what actually occurred in the past and could occur now or in the future, emphasizing the enormous difficulties that are faced in determining the appropriate responses to an outbreak of disease or to the threat of deliberate delivery of biological agents.

Secretary Danzig's talk triggered a lengthy discussion of the difficulties of determining, in a timely manner, whether one is dealing with man-made or natural pathogens in a BCW incident; it turns out that it does not matter all that much whether the threat is from a naturally occurring disease or from a BCW attack deliberately launched by an enemy. From this it follows that investments in defense in order to better manage the consequences of a BCW attack are also sound investments in a stronger public health system.

Drawing on his long government experience, Dr. Robert Knouss discussed recent policy decisions of the president and actions undertaken by the Public Health Service and its parent agency, the US Department of Health and Human Services, to prepare for effective response to terrorists who might unleash BCW in the US. He described in detail the various stages of the preparation, including a mass prophylaxis campaign, development of mass treatment capability, assistance to manage large numbers of potential casualties, and assistance to restrict and remove risks following BCW attacks.

Ariel Levite spelled out the basic elements—and the dilemmas—that need to be addressed by a BCW counterproliferation strategy. These start with efforts at denial, reinforced by arms control arrangements, and include a multilayered strategy based on the "building blocks" of intelligence, deterrence, passive and active defenses, and—finally—offensive options.

Frances E. Winslow described the problems of preparing for and responding to BCW attacks in order to minimize casualties and effectively manage consequences. Her comments provided the pragmatic perspective of a first-responder to BCW planning needs.

In the discussion at the conference, several additional points were highlighted. Dr. Donald Prosnitz of the Lawrence Livermore National Laboratory emphasized the critical importance of information should a BCW event occur. Progress is being made in sensor technology to enable improved detection and warning, as well as to treat the effects of a BCW incident. But there is an additional, human aspect of great importance on which Dr. Prosnitz concentrated, and that is simply this: What does one tell people, and how does one meet their greatest personal and family fears and keep them under control, in case of such an incident? A parent will ask immediately, for example, what should I do? How should I react in order to protect my family?

One knows from past examples of biological- and chemical-spill incidents that the magnitude of mass reactions can be much worse than reality when there is ineffective communication or an absence of trust between officials and the affected population. The pneumonic "plague epidemic" widely reported to have broken out in India in September 1994 eventually led to some fifty-three deaths, of which no more than a dozen cases were actually pneumonic; moreover, such a fatality rate was not much different from normal background occurrences. Reports in the media, however, told of hundreds of thousands of people fleeing the cities and hoarding medicines in a panic that was fanned by lack of reliable information and the public's absence of trust in government. The release of sulfuric acid in an industrial accident in July 1993 in Richmond, CA, caused some twenty people to be admitted to a local hospital for painful stinging in their eyes. Yet, some 60,000 people participated in a $180 million legal settlement, about 20,000 of them having actually shown up at hospitals—whether in panic or to (cynically) make a claim—after the accident. The release of poisonous gas from a Union Carbide pesticide factory in Bhopal, India, in December 1984 led to the truly terrible death of 3,800 people, and the injury and continued suffering of tens of thousands more—but more than 630,000 claimed to be affected. These illustrations have been repeated in other incidents around the world in which there have been enormous multipliers working to magnify the population's reaction in relation to the true severity of a biological or chemical event. One of the obvious challenges we face is to prepare to make as much information as possible available, swiftly and accurately, to help avoid hysteria among people in and around an area that suffers a BCW incident.

Physician and infectious-diseases specialist Dr. Lucy Tompkins of the Stanford University Medical Center underlined another significant issue: The medical profession must be prepared to identify unusual disease symptoms in the event of a BW attack. Such symptoms may often appear to be innocuous, but will mask potentially deadly diseases. This is a markedly different situation from what doctors are generally prepared for in their training and work experience. For example, many initial symptoms of infections from biological agents are nonspecific, often resembling nothing more than a mild case of the flu. It is vital to know whether the flulike symptoms are communicable or noncommunicable; for example, a person infected with smallpox is highly contagious but one infected with anthrax is not. A rational response system requires a tight link between the responding physicians and the epidemiologists, who are the ones with the advanced specialization and responsibility to decide on the appropriate response to a virulent outbreak of disease or a BCW attack. This issue has, of course, already been clearly recognized, and an effort is under way to create centers that will forge the necessary links in communication. Such preparation is of critical value, and the effort needs continued, strong encouragement. There is also a need for continuing provision of appropriate protective gear and equipment—filters, masks, and suits, among other items—and emergency training.

Dr. Alan Zelicoff of the Sandia National Laboratories emphasized the importance of two types of activities: investigations of allegations of use and of unusual outbreaks of disease. He described a project in which US and Russian scientists are investigating the incidence of a dangerous disease, Hepatitis C, "the prevalence of which is really not known even today.... [T]he virus mutates rapidly and turns up in all sorts of types when you look for it in various portions of the world." For a modest amount of expense, and the with powerful tools of computer science and epidemiology, he was able to ascertain that the prevalence of this disease in rural New Mexico is at a level some three times higher than expected ("a public health disaster"). The data have proved valuable to Russia and the US in revealing the environmental risk factors associated with the disease. He summed up:

> So I think we've achieved several obviously important things. First is, we can actually do this work virtually over the internet. Second, it costs virtually nothing. This is about a $20,000 project with the Russians. Third, we've both learned something about a public health risk that was not known before. Fourth, this kind of work can all be done cooperatively without any political barriers whatsoever, because of mutual interest in the results. It demonstrates the measure of the disease monitoring that we can take forward to Geneva as a viable concept for the Biological Weapons Convention.

Part Six

Deterring the Use of BCW

Condoleezza Rice

Introductory Remarks

One Sunday in November 1998, "Meet the Press" viewers watched as Secretary of Defense William Cohen told them that Iraq's Saddam Hussein was trying to develop a massive biological and chemical weapons (BCW) capability. Cohen sat, a familiar yellow bag of Domino sugar in front of him, and noted that just that amount of anthrax could effectively poison the water supply of the city of New York. Cohen wanted to garner public support for air strikes against Hussein in retaliation for his refusal to permit UN inspections of suspected production sites for BCW. Cohen did something else, entirely, however—he reminded the people of their vulnerability to biological and chemical attacks, a vulnerability that today seems absolute.

Anthrax and e-coli attacks have been material for television movies and disaster novels for decades. But in recent years, it has begun to dawn on national security experts, lawmakers, and political leaders that the threat of BCW is real and growing. Perhaps the end of the Cold War and, with it, the lifting of the "Sword of Damocles" of nuclear annihilation has refocused our energies on other apocalyptic scenarios. It may be that the sense of order that the Cold War brought—albeit a tense one—has disappeared, leaving a feeling of chaos, which refocuses on the fact that threats can come from small states and terrorists just as easily as from one powerful adversary. The consequences of terrorism on US territory have been brought into stark relief by the Oklahoma City and World Trade Center bombings. It is not hard to imagine the horror had those incidents involved not "simple" car bombs but weapons of mass destruction (WMD).

To date, there has been more heat than light on the subject of the BCW threat. It is all too easy to let one's imagination run so far and so fast that the standard problems of security—how to deter and what to do if deterrence fails—appear insurmountable. This book is an important contribution in the effort to bridge the gap between the problem and its potential solutions.

Clearly, answers will come from a multitude of disciplinary perspectives. The November 1998 Hoover Institution conference on BCW brought scholars with training in science, medicine, and public health, who can help to determine the contours of the threat and potential responses, together with other experts who understand the tools of security policy. Because the US may face new questions about how it organizes against the BCW threat—some that raise important issues regarding civil liberties and constitutional protections—specialists in international and constitutional law also participated in the conference. The wide range of knowledge and expertise required to address the threat underscores its complexity.

To be sure, the best solution is to prevent the use of BCW. First on every list is to check the proliferation of WMD and their means of delivery. Here, the collapse of the Soviet Union and the weakness of the successor Russian state is a real problem. Russia possesses the most sophisticated BCW capability in the world. That some of that stockpile and/or knowledge about how to build/develop it will leak or may already have leaked to rogue states seems a virtual certainty. It goes without saying that efforts to prevent the further spread of these technologies should be pursued with vigor.

Some people hope that the international treaties and conventions, and perhaps even norms, against use of BCW will provide protection against this horrific threat. But such treaties are far more difficult to verify than the nuclear arms limitation templates on which they are often based. Biological and chemical agents are easier to produce and easier to hide. Moreover, most of the culprits who would be likely to use BCW are unlikely to be restrained by norms of nonuse.

Nonproliferation efforts and international treaties and conventions may prove inadequate to the growing BCW threat. The remaining options are not attractive, for they raise difficult questions and unpalatable answers. What is left is to deter BCW use by active defense and coercion, to use better and probably more intrusive intelligence, and to prepare for the worst should deterrence fail.

The threat of retaliation is clearly an option—but what should we threaten? The debate between Richard Haass and Scott Sagan concerning the threat of retaliation with nuclear weapons (NW) in deterring BCW goes to the heart of the matter. Such threats would likely be more effective against states or state-sponsored terrorists than against those rogue terrorists acting more or less alone. The question, however, is whether explicit nuclear threats in retaliation for BCW use are tolerable, given the long-standing norm of nonuse of NW against nonnuclear states. It may be an unpalatable policy but one of the few available to a US president should deterrence fail.

There is also the possibility of active defense. Suitcases, rental trucks, and vials of BCW agents dropped into a water supply may indeed be the preferred means of delivery by terrorists. But the horror would be far greater and the consequences infinitely more widespread if ballistic missiles were available to a BCW perpetrator. Thus, the recent emphasis on ballistic missile defense against nuclear attack could be important for the BCW problem too, and ought to be pursued with all WMD in mind.

The most troubling questions, however, are not those of deterrence or defense but the ones that ask who we are as a people. Barriers to effective response may lie in our culture and treasured traditions and values of openness and individual protections. No one would suggest that the US become "Fortress America" in order to diminish the BCW threat, no matter how grave. It would not work and would change dramatically who we are and what we are trying to protect. Yet, improved intelligence in countering this threat does raise uncomfortable questions. For instance, we have turned squeamish and apologetic in recent years about our association with tough actors in places like Guatemala and Nicaragua during the Cold War. The human assets likely to be involved in BCW intelligence may be even more unsavory. Can we stomach those associations?

Moreover, within our own domestic context, efforts at "preventive" and "preemptive" intelligence may well be needed. That raises issues of civil liberties and constitutional protections that cannot be cast aside.

Finally, should deterrence fail, the US is simply ill-prepared to deal with the consequences. We need to devote attention to the challenges that our decentralized federal system poses for a coordinated response to a serious incident. The importance of proper civil defense measures and means of recovery cannot be underestimated as a counter to blackmail and panic. The role of the armed forces on the territory of the US is also at issue and must be reassessed.

In a democracy such as ours, there is no substitute for open and honest dialog about the impact of what we do on our laws and our values. Without that, no leader can pursue a coherent strategy confident of the support of the people.

Remaining sober and realistic about both the threat and potential responses is absolutely critical to any progress toward a coherent BCW policy. This is a problem tailor-made for hyperbole and over-reaction. But the threat is serious and the policy challenge is very difficult indeed. This conference volume provides a starting point for a comprehensive look at the problem. And that examination is long overdue.

Richard N. Haass

Strategies for Enhanced Deterrence

15

Much of the intellectual effort devoted to biological and chemical weapons (BCW) understandably focuses on nonproliferation—on steps that can and should be taken to prevent, or at least slow, the development or acquisition of BCW capability by nation-states and others. A partial list of such efforts includes:

- Export controls and supplier clubs

- Intelligence sharing and covert operations that disrupt procurement and development efforts

- Arms control arrangements that establish both the norms that ban possession of capabilities and the monitoring and verification arrangements that increase confidence that prohibitions are being respected

- Sanctions against both providers and recipients of proscribed technologies

- Diplomatic activity that aims to remove sources of insecurity or disagreement

- Security assurances and conventional arms transfers that seek to reduce the desire or perceived need to acquire weapons of mass destruction (WMD)

The results of these efforts can best be described as "working but not succeeding." The BCW threat is not going away and appears to be getting worse. BCW offer a less difficult and less expensive production option than either advanced conventional weapons or nuclear weapons (NW). They are also easier to conceal. And they can be used in both traditional settings (battlefields) and against civilian targets as a form of terrorism. Indeed, it is possible that US advantages in other forms of warfare may have the result of increasing the desirability of this option to states and other actors.

As a result, there exists a range of strategies to deal with this problem quite different from measures associated with traditional nonproliferation policies. These efforts focus on the postdevelopment or postacquisition phase of the BCW challenge. Initiatives can aim to prevent the use of BCW capabilities, or they can seek to minimize the actual impact of the use of BCW capabilities. This chapter focuses on three issues: (1) enhancing deterrence to reduce the likelihood of BCW use; (2) employing preventive and preemptive strikes to reduce the ability to employ BCW; and (3) improving defense, to increase the odds that deterrence might succeed and to lessen the impact of BCW attacks if deterrence fails. Taken collectively, these efforts should not be seen as an alternative to traditional nonproliferation policies but instead as a complement to them.

Enhanced Deterrence

Deterrence of BCW use, as is the case with deterrence more generally, involves the attempt to persuade another actor that the costs and/or risks of a particular activity being contemplated outweigh its expected benefits—and therefore that the party in question should not go ahead with it. In the case of BCW, it means increasing the costs of developing or otherwise obtaining the capability—and increasing the costs yet again if BCW were ever used. Deterrence succeeds if others come to calculate that they should not become BCW-capable—and that if they do, employment should not follow on from deployment.

The US has a compelling interest in keeping regional wars limited to conventional arms. The calculus of intervention—the basic assessment of projected costs and benefits—changes if it includes chemical, biological, or nuclear agents. Use of unconventional (non-explosive) weapons by adversaries requires US personnel to adopt measures, from special equipment to changed tactics, that detract significantly from performance and slow operations. In addition, use of unconventional munitions by foes greatly increases the danger of casualties.

US policy in this realm is complicated by the reality that we have forgone deterrence in kind—deterring through a threat to retaliate with BCW if they are used against the US or an ally. It is not simply that we have eschewed first use of BCW; it is that we no longer have the option of any use.

One issue worth raising is whether this situation is wise. Regardless of whether it *was* in the US interest to forfeit the right to possess any BCW, it is fair to ask whether it remains so today and for the foreseeable future. The answer here is "yes." The US has a strong interest in promoting a world in which BCW proliferation is kept to an absolute minimum. Given the superiority of our conventional forces and the reality that terrorists will be tempted to target US populations and assets, given both who we are and what we do, such weapons are far more likely to be used against us. At the same time, BCW offer little of value to us militarily while we possess alternative means to deter their use by others and limit their impact if deterrence fails.

There are several alternatives to "deterrence in kind" that merit examination. Conventional escalation is one possibility. In principle, the US could threaten to attack a set of high-value targets with conventional forces that would otherwise remain off limits. In particular, target lists could be expanded to include nonbattlefield targets closely associated with the leadership.

There are, however, multiple problems with depending on conventional escalation to deter (or respond to) BCW use. First, conventional escalation is an expensive proposition. Second, by promising more of the same, psychological impact is lost. And third, it is not always the case that a discreet set of targets will exist for this purpose. The target list in Desert Storm, to choose but one example, was already so extensive that it is not obvious that a US threat to broaden coalition attacks would have had much additional military or political significance.

Economic sanctions are another possibility. In theory, sanctions could be threatened as a means to deter BCW use—and then implemented if BCW are used.[1] Here, too, there are questions. The threat of sanctions may not be enough to deter use if a country believes its vital national interests are at stake. The threat of comprehensive sanctions failed to dissuade either India or Pakistan from testing nuclear warheads in May 1998; it is doubtful that sanctions would

---

1. See Jessica Stern, "Would Sanctions Improve the Enforceability of the Chemical Weapons Convention?" in Benoit Morel and Kyle Olson, eds., *Shadows and Substance: The Chemical Weapons Convention* (Boulder, CO: Westview Press, 1993), pp. 233–49. For a more general discussion of economic sanctions in the post-Cold War world, see Richard N. Haass, ed., *Economic Sanctions and American Diplomacy* (New York: Council on Foreign Relations, 1998).

have persuaded Iraq to not employ chemical weapons against Iran when it felt threatened by massive infantry attacks. Also unclear is whether most countries will agree in advance to supporting sanctions against anyone using BCW. Such multilateral support is needed for sanctions to be effective, but many governments are likely to want to reserve judgment, depending on the particular circumstances and their own interests.

There is also the question of an exit strategy. What would it take for sanctions to be lifted after they were applied in the wake of failing to deter BCW use? Would anything less than regime removal be acceptable? The difficulty with such an objective is that sanctions tend not to work if goals are overly ambitious. There is also the reality that using sanctions to destabilize a country that possesses WMD could lead to a loss of control over the weapons, be it out of choice or chaos.

Yet another potential path to enhancing deterrence is through the private and/or public communication of clear warnings to potential adversaries of the consequences for them of using unconventional weapons against US or allied friendly forces. On the Korean peninsula, where South Korean forces provide a natural potential army of occupation, a message could be transmitted to the North that any use of BCW on its part would result in the war's not being terminated until there is a change in regime in Pyongyang. Indeed, this latter message could be generalized—that is, the US could go on record making clear that it is committed to both the removal of any regime that uses BCW and to the arrest and trial for war crimes of any individuals (regardless of whether they are part of a government or some organization) associated with BCW use. The difficulties here would come in lining up international support for such a posture, and in actually removing the leadership should a North Korea or an Iraq or some terrorist organization use BCW. This could require the most intrusive and expensive form of military intervention and occupation.

The question also arises as to the utility of NW in this context, both to deter BCW use and to retaliate if deterrence does not succeed. History provides little insight. The fact that Iraq did not use BCW during the 1990–91 Gulf War tells us little. Fear of possible US nuclear retaliation, hinted at in George Bush's January 1991 letter to Saddam Hussein, may have played a role. But more mundane factors may have been at work, including the fact that the pace of the battle might have gotten ahead of Iraqi preparations. Also unclear is how the US or Israel would have responded to Iraqi use of BCW. On the US side, conversations about such a possibility were inconclusive; my own view is that US behavior would have reflected the scale and impact of any Iraqi BCW use, and that nuclear retaliation would have received consideration as an option in such circumstances.

The lack of clear evidence has not stilled the debate over a potential role for NW in BCW deterrence. There are those who argue against such a role lest continuing US reliance on NW for this or any purpose undermine efforts to reduce or eliminate the existence of NW worldwide. There are also arguments put forward suggesting that US threats to use NW would have little deterrent effect— and that if deterrence failed, we would not want to use or need to use NW to adequately retaliate, given our interest in discouraging NW use and the adequacy of conventional military options and other foreign policy tools.[2]

On the other side of the debate are claims that NW have such a

---

2. For two advocates of a policy of "no first use of WMD" that preserves a US nuclear option, see Robert G. Joseph, "Nuclear Deterrence and Regional Proliferators," 20 *Washington Quarterly* (Summer 1997), pp. 167–75; David Gompert, Kenneth Watman, and Dean Wilkening, "Nuclear First Use Revisited," 37 *Survival* (Autumn 1995), pp. 27–44. For two who see this option as unnecessary and/or undesirable, see Victor A. Utgoff, *NW and the Deterrence of Biological and Chemical Warfare* (Washington: Henry L. Stimson Center Occasional Paper 36, October 1997); George Bunn, "Expanding Nuclear Options: Is the US Negating its Non-Use Pledges?," 26 *Arms Control Today* (May/Jun. 1996), pp. 7–10.

tremendous psychological impact—and destructiveness—that threat of their use would surely give pause to any potential BCW user. NW would also be useful following BCW use, be it to prevent additional attacks by an adversary or to discourage copycat attacks by others. Moreover, there is no proof that assigning such a role to NW would have any appreciable impact on efforts to stem the global spread of NW. Countries appear to make such decisions based on their own political and security needs and not on the number of US NW or the role assigned to them. Adopting such a posture would also not preclude the US from reducing its stockpile of NW—or from reducing the alert status of those NW it retained.

Another perspective is that nuclear deterrence of BCW use could be facilitated by the US adopting a policy of "no first use of WMD." Under such a policy, nuclear use would be considered only if an adversary broke the WMD threshold by BCW or nuclear use.

Adopting such a policy would not be without its diplomatic complications, however. It would require changing strategy for both NATO and Korea, where the US is on record as threatening nuclear use in the face of an overwhelming conventional attack. South Korea is unlikely to welcome such a policy switch given the bellicose nature of the North, and most NATO members will want to avoid a debate over what for many is a theological issue. Such a "no first use of WMD" policy would also require modifying so-called "negative security assurances," by which the US has pledged not to use NW against a non-NW state party to the Nuclear Non-Proliferation Treaty and not allied with an NW state.

The US ought not to eschew the possible use of NW as a means of bolstering deterrence. This said, there is no need at this time to invite a difficult domestic and international debate by actively and explicitly ruling in nuclear response as a general proposition. The existence of NW inherently gives them a role in deterring or countering BCW use without our having to make this explicit. Current US policy, as suggested by former Secretary of Defense William

Perry and then again by NSC official Robert Bell, thus seems about right in not ruling out the potential use of NW in the face of BCW attacks.[3]

Preemptive and Preventive Strikes

Preventive uses of force are those that seek either to stop another state or party from developing a military capability before it becomes threatening or to hobble or destroy it thereafter. For the target country, preventive attacks are the proverbial bolt out of the blue. An example is Israel's attack against Iraq's Osirak nuclear reactor complex in 1981. A more recent example is the summer 1998 US attack on a pharmaceutical factory in Sudan that was believed to be producing chemical agents. The Desert Storm coalition's attacks against Iraqi unconventional warfare capabilities inside Iraq also involved preventive employment of force; the capabilities targeted were not yet in a state of development to affect the course of this battle.

Similarly, preventive action is often discussed as a possible course of action to destroy North Korea's nuclear capability. A preventive strike would be a serious option if North Korea were on the verge of developing a significant NW capability. Gaining formal international authority for an attack would be extremely difficult, if not impossible; more important would be gaining the support (or at

3. Speaking in 1996, Perry suggested the possibility of US use of NW against Libya given its BCW program. Bell made his comments in the context of conditioning US support for the African Nuclear Weapon Free Zone. Both are discussed in George Bunn, "Expanding Nuclear Options: Is the US Negating its Non-Use Pledges?" pp. 7–10. One context in which moving to an explicit role for NW in deterring BCW use might make sense is if efforts by the new German government and others to have NATO adopt a "no first use of NW" posture appear to be succeeding. Were this to occur, US advocacy of a "no first use of WMD" posture might prove to be both an acceptable compromise and preferable to NATO's adopting a blanket "no first use" stance.

least the acquiescence) of those states most likely to be affected adversely by any North Korean response—namely, Japan and especially South Korea.

Preventive attacks have several inherent shortcomings. To begin with, they can be difficult to conduct successfully. A good deal of information is needed just to know what exists and to assess its significance—information that can be hard to come by. Such programs tend to be surrounded by walls of secrecy and may use tunnels, camouflage, and other devices to divert suspicion. Even more precise information (information that is instantly outdated if something is moved) is needed to target a capability. Also necessary is the capacity to carry out the mission, which tends to demand surprise, great accuracy, and the ability to penetrate formidable protective barriers. In addition, an attack on a nuclear or biological research or weapons facility may cause harm to innocent civilians in the area. Perhaps most important, it is impossible to know in advance how the object of the attack will respond; a preventive attack, even if successful, might be the beginning rather than the end of the confrontation. It is in part for this reason that the US has thus far refrained from attacking North Korean nuclear facilities; even if successful, such an attack could trigger a large conventional conflict.

Closely related to preventive uses of force are preemptive actions. The difference is one of timing and context. Preemptive uses of force come against a backdrop of tactical intelligence or warning indicating imminent military action by an adversary; they may constitute actions or attacks before the other side acts or attacks—or even after hostilities have begun—but before the targeted forces have been introduced into battle. Israel's air strikes against its Arab neighbors in June 1967 are an example. Preemptive and preventive strikes are similar in that they can raise political problems with skeptical publics, both domestic and those of neutrals and allies. It is important to be able to demonstrate the necessity of acting, to make the case that the costs and risks of striking were less than those of holding back, and to prepare for any possible retaliation.

There are also diplomatic problems to consider. The notion of preventive self-defense—"legitimate anticipation" in the words of one legal scholar—is not universally accepted in principle and is difficult to apply in the specific.[4] The international community has long embraced the norm of the right of self-defense and is beginning to recognize a second norm of humanitarian intervention. It is, however, a long way from accepting a third norm that would legitimize preventive or preemptive strikes to destroy the nascent unconventional weapons capabilities of states deemed by some to be rogues.

Defense against BCW

If preventive and preemptive uses of force are in essence examples of "offensive defense," also to be considered are those measures that constitute active and passive defense. Such measures can reduce the vulnerability of the US homeland, US military forces around the world, and other US assets overseas. Despite their considerable economic cost, defensive measures make sense in two ways: They reduce the impact on ourselves if BCW are used against us, and they alter the calculation of possible gains from BCW use by the would-be attacker, thereby reducing the attractiveness of the option, something that serves our interest in deterrence.

There is a full range of defense efforts to undertake, including hardening and other steps to reduce the physical vulnerability of critical buildings and installations to BCW attacks. Also relevant in this context are measures that enhance the capacity to cope with attacks—consequence management—including vaccination production, storage, and distribution, as well as decontamination. All of

4. See Michael Walzer, *Just and Unjust Wars* (New York: Basic Books, 1977), pp. 74–85.

these endeavors apply domestically as well as to US facilities overseas. Continuing to improve coordination among the various branches of the federal government, between federal, state and local levels, and between the public and private sectors, is critical. For US military forces overseas, there are additional measures to be undertaken, including procuring and deploying detection mechanisms, providing special equipment for individuals and unit protection, and deploying theater defenses against ballistic missiles carrying BCW (and nuclear) payloads.[5]

One last approach to defense needs to be raised. According to its proponents, the US can reduce its vulnerability to BCW attacks (be it as an act of terror or warfare) by being more selective when it comes to its involvement in the world, thereby avoiding provoking others to attack US citizens, interests, and assets.[6] This thinking is flawed because adversaries will attack regardless, both for what the US is as well as what it does; it is misguided because a world in which the US plays a less active role is one likely to be more characterized by a diffusion of military power—including BCW and other WMD—as friends and foes alike take steps to meet the perceived necessity or opportunity to react to US retreat.

A Net Assessment

The defensive steps discussed just above promise reduced vulnerability, not invulnerability, for the US in the face of an increased BCW threat. At home, they also raise matters of law enforcement

---

5. For an introduction to the emerging threat and US options, see Richard A. Falkenrath, Robert D. Newman, and Bradley A. Thayer, *America's Achilles' Heel: Nuclear, Biological, and Chemical Terrorism and Covert Attack* (Cambridge, MA: MIT Press, 1998).

6. For discussion, see Richard Betts, "The New Threat of Mass Destruction," 77 *Foreign Affairs* (Jan./Feb. 1998), pp. 40–41; Samuel P. Huntington, "The Erosion of American National Interests," 76 *Foreign Affairs* (Sep./Oct. 1997), pp. 28–49.

(some of which may involve trade-offs in the coin of compromising privacy and civil liberties), financial cost, and general inconvenience for the society to consider. For the military, preparing for BCW is also expensive and performance-degrading. As noted, though, the benefits such defensive steps offer are twofold: They reduce exposure against all would-be users and they improve the calculus of deterrence against nation-states in particular.

Deterrence is also bolstered by keeping open the option of nuclear retaliation and by a commitment to remove from power and arrest anyone involved in a decision to use BCW. Possibly of use, but difficult to implement for technical and diplomatic reasons alike, are preventive and preemptive strikes, although capabilities for both options should be developed and carried out if particular circumstances warrant. Less promising are policies based on conventional escalation and economic sanctions, and postures based on either deterrence in kind or retreat should be ruled out. The net result is that the challenge of BCW use is something that can only be reduced and managed, not prevented or eliminated. Given the potential costs and impact of such use, this is a judgment that should generate more concern than satisfaction.

Scott D. Sagan

Why the US Should Not Use Nuclear Threats

Should the US threaten to use nuclear weapons in retaliation for the use of biological or chemical weapons by its adversaries? The US government has a clear policy on this issue: It is deliberately unclear about its plans. In March 1996, Secretary of Defense William J. Perry explained: "For obvious reasons, we choose not to specify in detail what responses we would make to a chemical attack. However, as we stated during the Gulf War, if any country were foolish enough to use chemical weapons against the United States, the response will be 'absolutely overwhelming' and 'devastating.'"[1] The purpose of this policy—which has become known as the "calculated ambiguity" doctrine—was underscored by

---

1. Prepared statement by the Honorable William J. Perry, before the Senate Foreign Relations Committee on the Chemical Weapons Convention (Mar. 28, 1996).

Secretary of Defense William S. Cohen in November 1998: "We think the ambiguity involved in the issue of nuclear weapons contributes to our own security, keeping any potential adversary who might use either chemical or biological [weapons] unsure of what our response would be."[2] The doctrine's proponents, both inside and outside the US government, claim that such a threat to respond asymmetrically—retaliating with tactical or strategic nuclear weapons (NW)—is an unfortunate necessity. Without the nuclear option, the US, which has eliminated all biological and chemical weapons (BCW) in its own arsenal, would be unable to deter new US adversaries—so-called "rogue nations"—from using their newly acquired BCW.

The calculated ambiguity doctrine is deeply controversial, however, for it raises important questions about the effectiveness of both US deterrence strategy and US nonproliferation policy, and creates a strong tension between the goals of enhancing deterrence against particular adversaries and promoting global nuclear nonproliferation. Is a threat of nuclear retaliation credible as a deterrent against states that possess BW and/or CW? Are such nuclear threats harmful to US and global efforts to stop the further proliferation of NW? These are critical issues for the future of international security. In the Persian Gulf today, or on the Korean Peninsula tomorrow, or in Iran or Libya in the future, the US may enter into a severe conflict with an adversary that possesses BW and/or CW, and deterring the use of such weapons will be essential to stability in a crisis or US victory in a war. Yet, reinforcing the global nuclear nonproliferation regime is also of critical importance for regional and global security. The US and other NW states have made legally binding commitments, most recently during the 1995 nuclear Non-Proliferation

2. Dana Priest and Walter Pincus, "US Rejects 'No First Use' Atomic Policy: NATO Needs Strategic Option, Germany Told," *Washington Post* (Nov. 24, 1998), p. A24.

Treaty (NPT) extension conference, that they will neither use nor threaten to use NW against any nonnuclear state who is a member in good standing of the NPT.[3] Efforts to back away from such promises, critics argue, undercut these global commitments and legitimize NW threats, and thereby encourage nonnuclear states to follow the US lead and develop the bomb to deter their dangerous neighbors.

In this chapter, I argue that the US nuclear policy of calculated ambiguity is misguided, because—contrary to widespread opinion—it increases both the likelihood that the US NW will be used deliberately in future conflicts and heightens the risk that adversaries' BCW will be used by accident or in an unauthorized manner. The risk of US nuclear use will be raised because, as will be demonstrated below, the US cannot make its nuclear threats credible without also increasing the likelihood that a US president will feel compelled to use NW if deterrence fails. Explicit or implicit US nuclear threats also increase adversaries' fears of US attacks that directly target adversaries' political leaders in their command bunkers. Such fears of "nuclear decapitation strikes" unfortunately also encourage such leaders to predelegate authority to use other weapons of mass destruction (WMD) to lower level military officers, which in turn increases the risk of BCW use by accident, through unauthorized use, or by responding to a false warning. In short, the US should refrain from making asymmetric deterrent threats against states with BCW capabilities, not because such nuclear threats will not be credible,

---

3. There is only one declared exception to this official government commitment. On April 5, 1995, Secretary of State Warren Christopher, on behalf of the US government, stated that the US "will not use nuclear weapons against any nonnuclear-weapons states party to the treaty on the Non-Proliferation of Nuclear Weapons *except* in the case of an invasion or any other attack on the United States, its territories, its armed forces, or other troops, or a state toward which it has a security agreement carried out or sustained by such a nonnuclear weapons state in association or alliance with a nuclear-weapon state." Department of State, Statement of Secretary of State Warren Christopher (Apr. 5, 1995).

but precisely because they *are* credible. These risks, on top of concerns about the negative effects of US nuclear threats on potential nuclear proliferators, lead me to conclude that a new US doctrine—explicitly eschewing the option of nuclear retaliation in response to nonnuclear attacks—is advisable.

To develop this argument, I will first outline the existing debate on the subject, showing that the arguments of both supporters and opponents of the US calculated ambiguity doctrine contain logical inconsistencies and inadequate evidence. Second, I will present the existing evidence about the effectiveness of US nuclear threats against Saddam Hussein during the 1991 Gulf War. Third, will I explain how an asymmetric deterrence doctrine increases the risk of US NW use and other states' accidental use of BCW. Fourth, I will show how such nuclear threats, even if they are effective as deterrents in particular cases, can have a harmful impact more broadly on the domestic debates about the utility of NW inside potential proliferant nations. Finally, in the conclusions, I will present both the policy recommendations that flow from this argument and some more general lessons about the development of deterrence theory in the coming decades.

The Existing Debate

The current debate on this issue—in Washington, at NATO meetings, and in the scholarly community—has been unfortunately narrow in framework and exceedingly thin on empirical evidence. Two conventional wisdoms exist concerning nuclear threats and BCW use: the deterrence hawks' position and nonproliferation doves' position. The proponents of these two schools take polar-opposite positions on both of the key questions concerning asymmetric deterrence.

Deterrence hawks argue that NW threats—whether they are clearly articulated or presented with calculated ambiguity—are effective, indeed sometimes necessary, for deterrence in military crises with BW- and CW-armed states.[4] Deterrence hawks also maintain that such threats are not harmful to global nuclear nonproliferation efforts, because states are seen to pursue NW programs purely based on their regional security concerns and are therefore not influenced by US nuclear doctrine.[5]

Nonproliferation doves argue both that nuclear threats are not effective as deterrents against anything other than another state's NW and that such threats have or will soon have horrendous effects on the nonproliferation regime. Threats to use NW in response to a BW or a CW attack are inherently incredible, it is argued, since it is simply inconceivable that a US president would order nuclear retaliation except as a response to nuclear attack against the US homeland or US troops deployed overseas.[6] Moreover, many nonproliferation doves argue that explicit threats are unnecessary, since "existential deterrence," the impossibility of knowing for sure that retaliation would not occur, would still exist. US nuclear threats are

4. Prominent examples include Richard K. Betts, "The New Threat of Weapons of Mass Destruction," 77 *Foreign Affairs* (Jan./Feb. 1998), p. 31; Richard N. Haass, "It's Dangerous to Disarm," *New York Times* (Dec. 11, 1996), p. A21; Keith B. Payne, "Post-Cold War Requirements for U.S. Nuclear Deterrence Policy," 17 *Comparative Strategy* (Jul.-Sep. 1998), pp. 265–66; and David Gompert, Kenneth Watman, and Dean Wilkening, "Nuclear First Use Revisited," 37 *Survival* (Autumn 1995), pp. 27–44.

5. For example, Franklin Miller, the Principal Deputy Assistant US Secretary of Defense, has argued that US doctrine does not impact proliferant states, since "any proliferant is going to develop nuclear weapons based on their own desires to either dominate their region or respond to their neighbor's development programs." As quoted in Brian Hull, "Overkill Is Not Dead," *New York Times Magazine* (Mar. 15, 1998), p. 84. See also David Gompert, Kenneth Watman, and Dean Wilkening, "Nuclear First Use Revisited," p. 39.

6. Adam Yarmolinsky and Mark P. Schlefer, "Two Wrongs . . . ," Letters to the Editor, 77 *Foreign Affairs* (May/Jun. 1998), pp. 157–58; George Bunn, "Expanding Nuclear Options? Is the U.S. Negating its Non-Use Pledges?" 26 *Arms Control Today* (May/Jun. 1996), pp. 7–10; George Bunn and Wolfgang K.H. Panofsky, "The Doctrine of the Nuclear Weapons States and the Future of Nonproliferation," 24 *Arms Control Today* (Jul.-Aug. 1994), pp. 3–9.

TABLE I
Two Conventional Wisdoms

	Deterrence hawks	Nonproliferation doves
Deterrence effects	Nuclear threats are effective—indeed sometimes necessary—to deter BCW.	Nuclear threats are both ineffective and unnecessary to deter BCW.
Nuclear nonproliferation effects	US nuclear threats do not encourage proliferation, since states proliferate in response to regional security concerns, not US declaratory policy.	US nuclear threats encourage proliferation by legitimizing NW and suggesting that other states may need NW to deter BCW.

also seen to encourage nuclear proliferation by legitimizing expanded roles for NW, and thereby providing an additional rationale for acquisition by new nuclear proliferators. As George Bunn has argued:

> If the United States, having the most powerful and technologically advanced conventional forces in the world, insists that it must have nuclear weapons to retaliate against a chemical attack, what about much less powerful countries much closer to likely sources of chemical weapons? How can they be persuaded that they do not need *nuclear* weapons to counter their potential antagonist's use of chemical weapons."[7]

The two conventional positions are presented in Table 16-1.

There are, however, a number of reasons to be concerned about the current state of this debate about US nuclear doctrine. First,

---

7. George Bunn, "Expanding Nuclear Options," p. 10. See also Thomas Graham, Jr., and Douglas B. Shaw, "Nearing a Fork in the Road: Proliferation or Nuclear Reversal?," 6 *The Non-Proliferation Review* (Fall 1998), pp. 70–6.

there are logical inconsistencies in both positions. The hawks, for example, maintain both that specific US nuclear threats—or even hints about such retaliation plans—will strongly influence potential aggressors, and also insist that US nuclear threats in general will have no influence on other potential proliferators. Yet, it is by no means clear how US doctrine could be so influential in one case but not the other. The doves maintain both that explicit asymmetric threats are incredible, and that the mere existence of NW—existential deterrence produced by the impossibility of knowing what a nuclear power will do if attacked—will continue to have a useful deterrent effect. It is unclear, however, how one ambiguous threat can have absolutely no credibility while the other ambiguous threat has attached to it some irreducible amount of credibility.

Second, observers should always be suspicious of debates in which both parties insist that their position is the best solution to all dimensions of the problem. It is common, of course, for all individuals and groups to avoid value trade-offs by insisting that their preferred policy will not create any costs at all. Avoiding analyses of trade-offs, however, is very problematic in this case, since the available evidence suggests that both schools of thought are half-right. The logic and evidence presented below suggest that the hawks are right about the effectiveness of asymmetric retaliation; US NW can be credible threats against BCW use. The evidence also suggests, however, that the doves are right about the negative effects on nuclear nonproliferation; the broader impact of the US policy will encourage other proliferators to develop similar doctrines and the forces to support them. If both schools of thought are half-right, then it is essential to assess the trade-off between two important goals: the short-term deterrent benefits derived from nuclear threats against the harmful long-term damage to the nonproliferation regime. This has not yet been done, and indeed the bifurcated nature of the current debate discourages analyses of trade-offs between these two important policy objectives.

Finally, the debate has simply not focused on what is arguably the most important question: Will the US asymmetric deterrence policy increase or decrease the likelihood that NW will be used in combat for the first time since 1945? As I argue below, the US cannot make its nuclear threats credible without also increasing the risk that its NW will actually be used in the event of a biological or chemical attack. There is, therefore, some increase in the likelihood of US nuclear use as an inescapable by-product of our effort to gain the benefits of asymmetric deterrence. This increased risk, however, is the most important reason *not* to maintain the current US government policy. This observation leads to the final conclusion: The US should not threaten to retaliate with NW despite the possibility (indeed, because of the possibility) that such threats are credible deterrents against new states with BCW.

The Gulf War Revisited

The term "calculated ambiguity" was coined by former Secretary of State James A. Baker III, who used it to describe what he believed to be the Bush Administration's successful effort to deter the Iraqi use of BCW with hints of US nuclear retaliation during the 1991 Gulf War.[8] Baker is far from alone in holding this view. Indeed, the current US government policy concerning asymmetric deterrence has been strongly influenced by the official estimates within the intelligence agencies that the fear of US nuclear retaliation was the major reason why Saddam Hussein did not use the BCW in his arsenal during the Desert Storm campaign.[9]

8. James A. Baker III with Thomas M. DeFrank, *The Politics of Diplomacy: Revolution, War and Peace, 1989–1992* (New York: G. P. Putnam's Sons, 1995), p. 359.
9. The CIA reported soon after the Gulf War that: "We now believe that Saddam decided to withdraw his chemical ordnance from the Kuwait theater because he concluded that the potential benefit of chemical warfare was outweighed by the

Because so much of the support for the asymmetric deterrence policy stems from this particular interpretation of the Gulf War experience, it is important to review the evidence about US threats and their effects. Unfortunately, the existing evidence does not support either the widespread view that Saddam Hussein was definitely deterred from using BW and CW by US nuclear threats, or the less common view of critics that Saddam could not use his unconventional weapons because of the physical disruption of Iraq's command and control system during the war.[10] Indeed, a close look at the evidence can lead to only two firm conclusions. First, we simply do not know what effect, if any, the US nuclear threats had on Iraqi behavior. Second, the publication of US leaders' memoirs from the period, revealing how reluctant they were even to contemplate nuclear retaliation, makes it less likely that ambiguous nuclear threats can be used easily in future crises.

What US nuclear threats were made during Desert Storm, and what was the intent of senior US officials? We now know, from numerous officials' memoirs, that the senior leaders of the US government had decided that they would not use NW even in response to an Iraqi use of unconventional weapons, but that they would present the opposite impression to Saddam Hussein for the sake of

---

risk of retaliation by the United States and others. We believe Saddam decided the advantage his forces would accrue from chemical warfare was not worth the gamble of the United States or United Kingdom retaliating with attacks Baghdad could neither match nor absorb. Similar considerate [sic] probably influenced Saddam's decision not to use chemical-filled Scud missiles against Israel." From declassified CIA report "Iraq and the Gulf War, 1990–1991" (Declassified Jul. 2, 1996. Original publication date unavailable. At http://www.gulflink.osd.mil/declassdocs/cia/19960702/070296_cia_70086_70086_01.html). See also *Gulf War Air Power Survey (GWAPS) Summary Report*, p. 81.

10. For thorough examinations of the Gulf War threats, albeit with conclusions that differ significantly from my own, see William M. Arkin, "Calculated Ambiguity: Nuclear Weapons in the Gulf War," 19 *Washington Quarterly* (Autumn 1996), pp. 3–18, and Avigdor Haselkorn, *The Continuing Storm: Iraq, Poisonous Weapons, and Deterrence* (New Haven, CT: Yale University Press, 1999), pp. 51–85.

deterrence. As President Bush and national security advisor Brent Scowcroft note in their joint memoirs:

> What if Iraq used chemical weapons? We had discussed this at our December 24 meeting at Camp David and had ruled out our own use of them, but if Iraq resorted to them, we would say our reaction would depend on circumstances and that we would hold Iraqi divisional commanders responsible and bring them to justice for war crimes. No one advanced the notion of using nuclear weapons, and the President rejected it even in retaliation for chemical and biological attacks. We deliberately avoided spoken or unspoken threats to use them on the grounds that it is bad practice to threaten something you have no intention of carrying out. Publicly, we left the matter ambiguous. There was no point in undermining the deterrence it might offer.[11]

In his memoirs, Baker similarly recalled the deliberations of the senior Bush Administration officials:

> The President had decided, at Camp David in December, that the best deterrent to the use of weapons of mass destruction by Iraq would be a threat to go after the Ba'ath regime itself. He had also decided that US forces would not retaliate with chemical or nuclear weapons if the Iraqis attacked with chemical munitions. There was obviously no reason to inform the Iraqis of this.[12]

The official US threats to use NW were therefore deliberately kept ambiguous throughout the war.[13] President Bush, for example, wrote in his letter of January 9, 1991, to Saddam Hussein:

11. George Bush and Brent Scowcroft, *A World Transformed* (New York: Knopf, 1998), p. 463. See also Colin L. Powell with Joseph Perisco, *My American Journey* (New York: Random House, 1995), p. 486.

12. James A. Baker III, *The Politics of Diplomacy*, p. 359.

13. Vice President Dan Quayle told the press on February 1, 1991, that "I just can't imagine President Bush making the decision to use chemical or nuclear weapons under any circumstances." Yet he also quickly returned to the chosen refrain: "But you never rule options—any options—out." White House transcript, CNN Newsmaker Saturday, Feb. 2, 1991, as cited in Arkin, "Calculated Ambiguity," p. 6.

[T]he United States will not tolerate the use of chemical or biological weapons, support of any kind of terrorist actions, or the destruction of Kuwait's oilfields and installations. The American people would demand the strongest possible response. You and your
country will pay a terrible price if you order unconscionable actions
of this sort.[14]

Secretary of State Baker later recalled that at his January meeting with Tariq Aziz "in hopes of persuading them to consider more
soberly the folly of war, I deliberately left the impression that the
use of chemical or biological agents by Iraq could invite tactical
nuclear retaliation."[15] He reports that he therefore told the Iraqis:

[I]f the conflict starts, God forbid, and chemical or biological weapons are used against our forces, the American people would demand
vengeance. We have the means to exact it. With regard to this part
of my presentation, this is not a threat, it is a promise. If there is
any use of weapons like that, our objective won't be only the liberation of Kuwait, but also the elimination of the current Iraqi
regime, and anyone responsible for using those weapons would be
held accountable. . . . War will destroy everything you fought to
build in Iraq and it will trigger, thanks to your unwillingness to
withdraw from Kuwait, a conflict that will turn Iraq into a weak
and backward country.[16]

14. Lawrence Freedman and Efraim Karsh, *The Gulf Conflict, 1990–1991: Diplomacy and War in the New World Order* (London: Faber and Faber, 1993), p. 255.
  15. James A. Baker III, *The Politics of Diplomacy*, p. 359.
  16. Ibid. Secretary of Defense Richard Cheney made an additional public statement, emphasizing the Israeli, not US, possibility of retaliating with NW. "I assume
he knows that if he were to resort to chemical weapons that that would be an
escalation to weapons of mass destruction, and that the possibility would then exist,
certainly, with respect to the Israelis, for example, that they might retaliate with
unconventional weapons as well, and I think the uncertainty that's there may have
discouraged him, and maybe he's saving it, that he'll attempt to use it down the road.
We have to assume that he may, at some point, use chemical weapons and we have
to be prepared for that." Transcript, CNN's "Evans and Novak" (Feb. 2, 1991).

In a press conference in Saudi Arabia, General Norman Schwarz-kopf also attempted to plant fear in Saddam Hussein's mind about possible US nuclear responses to Iraqi escalation: "If Saddam Hussein chooses to use weapons of mass destruction, then the rules of this campaign will probably change—and I think that's as it should be."[17]

What were the effects of such ambiguous US nuclear threats? According to senior Iraqi sources, the US statements were critical to Saddam Hussein's decision not to use BCW during the war. For example, General Wafic al-Samurrai, a high-level defector, later claimed that Saddam was convinced that the US would retaliate with NW if the Iraqis used BW or CW in the war:

> Some of the SCUD missiles were loaded with chemical warheads, but they were not used. We didn't use them because the other side had a deterrent force. I do not think Saddam was capable of taking a decision to use chemical weapons or biological weapons, or any other type of weapons against the allied troops, because the warning was quite severe and quite effective. The allied troops were certain to use nuclear arms and the price will be too high and too dear.[18]

When evidence gathered by United Nations Special Commission (UNSCOM) inspectors in 1995 forced senior Iraqi officials to acknowledge that Iraq had developed biological warheads to fit on SCUD missiles during the Gulf War, these officials also stated that the reason why such weapons were not used was the US nuclear threat. According to Rolf Ekéus, then UNSCOM's Executive Chairman: "Iraqi officials claimed they decided not to use the weapons after receiving a strong but ambiguously worded warning from

17. CENTCOM Transcript, news briefing by General Norman Schwartzkopf, Riyadh, Saudi Arabia (Jan. 30, 1991).

18. General Wafic al-Sammurai, as quoted by Senator Thad Cochran during the February 12, 1997, Hearing of the International Security, Proliferation, and Federal Services Subcommittee of the Senate Governmental Affairs Committee.

the Bush Administration on January 9, 1991, that any use of unconventional warfare would provoke a devastating response."[19]

There are, however, three important reasons to be suspicious about these Iraqi self-reports about Saddam being deterred by US threats. First, as Ekéus has noted, when these statements were made, it was in Saddam Hussein's *strategic* interest to portray himself as the victim of Western nuclear threats; such a portrayal might engender international public sympathy and encourage support from those governments opposed to US policy toward Iraq.[20] Second, it may have been in Saddam Hussein's *domestic* interest to maintain that the US nuclear threat, rather than the more direct US promise to remove him from office, was what prevented him from using BCW. As one unidentified Arab diplomat has noted: "The regime had to explain to its military commanders why it was pulling back from the brink, so it looked a lot better to say that it was sparing the Iraqi people from nuclear holocaust than to admit that the leaders were worried about their own skins."[21] Third, it is crucial to remember that the January 9, 1991, Bush letter, to which the Iraqis referred, did not threaten a devastating response only in retaliation to Iraqi use of BCW; Bush also listed Iraqi support for terrorist activities or the destruction of the Kuwaiti oil fields as actions that would cause the US public to "demand the strongest possible response." It is therefore not self-evident that US deterrent threats were effective in January 1991, since two of the three actions to be deterred were actually taken by Iraq during the last days of the Gulf War.

In short, the evidence is inconclusive about the effects of US nuclear threats in the Gulf War. Ambiguous US threats produced ambiguous results. What is clear is that all the key US decision-

19. R. Jeffrey Smith, "UN Says Iraqis Prepared Germ Weapons in Gulf War," *Washington Post* (Aug. 26, 1995), p. A1.

20. See William M. Arkin, "Calculated Ambiguity," p. 9.

21. Joseph Fitchett, "Nuclear States See Vindication: Threat of Annihilation Deterred Iraq, They Say," *International Herald Tribune* (Sep. 12, 1995), p. 2.

makers from the Bush Administration have acknowledged that they were *not* planning to order the use of NW if Iraq used BW or CW. This fact is likely to encourage future US leaders, if they choose to rely on nuclear threats in crises, to make them more explicit.

Threats and the Commitment Conundrum

When a state's leadership says that it might use NW in a specific situation, what effect, if any, does this have on the credibility of threats—that is, the subjective estimate by adversaries that the state in question will actually use NW? This is a crucial, but rarely analyzed, question. Under the logic of expected utility theory, deterrence is a product of capability and credibility; deterrence will succeed if the potential costs of punishment times the probability that the deterrent threat will be implemented exceeds the expected gains from the conflict. Given the terrible destructive power of NW, a little credibility can go a long way. But even with devastating potential costs, the credibility of a threat must not be zero in order for deterrence to be successful.

What happens when a state leadership underlines that it has such a destructive capability and claims that it might use it under specific circumstances. Table 16-2 presents five factors that logically can influence an adversary's calculations about the credibility of threats. What is interesting about the list is to observe that the strength of most of these factors could be estimated in advance—that is, their influence on the probability of a state's taking a particular action can be conceived of as being largely independent from the declarations of the state during the crisis. Statements about possible nuclear use might be deliberately designed to alter an adversary's perception of one's own interests at stake or military effectiveness estimates, for example, but the strategy is an obvious one and therefore such signals could easily be dismissed as calculated deceptions.

TABLE 16-2
Factors Influencing Credibility

---

1. Perceived interests at stake. Are they vital or not?

2. The potential costs of counterretaliation. If you follow through on your nuclear threat what could happen in response in a counterretaliatory strike?

3. Reputation. What is your general reputation for following through on threats?

4. Legitimacy. What is the international legitimacy of the action? Would implementing a threat give you international opprobrium or international prestige?

5. The cost of not following through. What are the perceived costs to one's international or domestic reputation, if one does not follow through on threats if actions occur despite one's efforts?

By this logic, it is table 16-2's fifth factor, and only the fifth factor, that should be significantly changed when a leader makes an existential threat more explicit. Such threats increase the capability to deter precisely because they increase the likelihood that a leader will feel compelled—for reasons of both domestic interests and international reputation—to follow through on deterrent threats if his or her bluff is called.[22] (The fact that in February 1991, 45 percent of the US public supported the use of NW to limit US military casualties during the Gulf War provides some indication of the political jeopardy a US leader might face if his or her deterrent bluff was called, and he or she failed to use NW in retaliation.[23]) Unless one assumes that these threats will be 100 percent effective, however, then one has to balance the benefits of deterrence against the risks that one might feel compelled to use NW in response to BCW attacks. In short, risk is the consequence of commitment: A state

22. For a discussion of this point in a different context, see James D. Fearon, "Domestic Political Audiences and the Escalation of International Disputes," 88 *American Political Science Review* (Sep. 1994), pp. 577–92.

23. Robert C. Toth, "American Support Grows for Use of Nuclear Arms," *Los Angeles Times* (Feb. 3, 1991), p. A1.

can't get the extra "umph" of deterrence without accepting some extra risk of having to implement that threat if deterrence fails.

To the degree that the US government values the fifty-year-old tradition of nonuse of NW, however, this is a risk that should be avoided if at all possible. The calculated ambiguity doctrine thus presents a conundrum: US nuclear threats both *decrease* the likelihood that BCW will be used and *increase* the likelihood that NW will be used *if* deterrence fails. The net effect is thus very difficult to predict. One reason why both Bush and Clinton Administration officials have tried to keep US nuclear threats ambiguous is to escape the commitment conundrum. This tactic attempts to minimize this risk of precommitment to nuclear responses—responses we would not want to take in the event that BCW are used. The US, however, cannot have it both ways: The strength of the nuclear deterrent threat is related to the degree to which foreign leaders believe that the president would feel compelled to follow through on such threats if his or her bluff were called. It should also be noted that ambiguity is not a natural condition for military planners, who are responsible for developing war plans, standard operating procedures, and training exercises. It is not surprising therefore that since the calculated ambiguity doctrine was announced, senior US military officers have sought to turn its hints of possible nuclear use into firm policy statements of US intent. Perhaps the most dramatic example of such an effort was the declaration by then-Commander in Chief of the US Strategic Command, General Eugene Habiger, to a group of Washington reporters in March 1998: "We now have a policy that's articulated that says nuclear weapons *will be used* in response to the use of rogue states using weapons of mass destruction."[24] The purposes behind such misstatements of US policy are

---

24. General Eugene Habiger Interview with the Defense Writers' Group, Washington (Mar. 31, 1998) (emphasis added). Another participant responded: "I don't think they really said that, did they? They've suggested that?" Habiger then

rarely clear. Such declarations could be inadvertent "clarifications" of ambiguity; they could be deliberate, but individual, trial balloons to see how others in the bureaucracy react; or they could be part of a concerted effort to push the administration toward a firmer stance on this nuclear doctrine issue. What is clear, however, is that such misstatements are picked up by the US and foreign press as if they are US policy on the issue. In the Habiger case, for example, it was his statement that US policy says that "nuclear weapons will be used"—not his later effort to reflect US doctrine more accurately— that was picked up by reporters and presumably by foreign governments as well.[25] Similarly, when a "senior American official" told the *New York Times* in November 1998 that "if he [Saddam Hussein] tries to use weapons of mass destruction, he should know that we will obliterate Iraq," efforts to correct the statement to reflect US policy were not widely reported.[26]

Hidden Dangers of Accidental BCW Use

An additional hidden risk produced by US nuclear threats is that they increase the likelihood that foreign leaders with BW or CW would feel compelled to delegate authority to use such weapons to officers lower down the chain of command in order to ensure that retaliation would occur in the event that they themselves were destroyed in a US nuclear attack. Our analysts are unfortunately insensitive to this problem, in part because they often simply assume that some of the leaders we worry about most would never delegate au-

---

amended himself: "Suggested it. I'm not saying, I'm suggesting it. Let the record reflect, I suggested it." Nevertheless, only his initial statement was picked up in the press.

25. See for example Bill Gertz, "China's Nukes Could Reach Most of US," *Washington Times* (Apr. 1, 1998), p. A1.

26. Steven Erlanger, "US Set to Give Up Arms Inspections for Curbing Iraq," *New York Times* (Nov. 8, 1998), pp. A1, A12.

thority for the use of BW or CW to subordinate officers, because of their fears of coups or insubordination. Dictators who fear their own military, it is assumed, would ensure that they retained personal command and control over WMD.

The evidence on this issue with respect to Iraq, however, points in the opposite direction. For example, even a leader as concerned about his own military officers as Saddam Hussein was nevertheless compelled by military necessity to predelegate authority to use CW to his military officers in the field during the Iran-Iraq War in the mid-1980s.[27] Even more alarming is the emerging evidence that Saddam Hussein appears to have predelegated authority to use BW, and possibly CW, to senior officers in a special SCUD unit during the Persian Gulf War. Saddam's speeches clearly show that he was worried about a nuclear decapitation threat and sought, at a minimum, to deter it through declarations that predelegation existed for a retaliatory strike in retribution for an attack on Baghdad. Saddam, for example, told a group of visiting US senators in April 1990 that he had ensured that others would retaliate in his place if necessary:

> I repeat now, in your presence, that if Israel strikes, we will strike back. I believe this is a fair stand. A stand known in advance is what helps peace, and not otherwise. For if Israel realizes it will be struck, it might refrain from striking. Then, if the West truly wants peace, such behavior is for the sake of peace. This behavior, furthermore, only disturbs those who want Israel to strike at Iraq with Iraq retaliating. I also have said: If Israel uses atomic bombs, we will strike at it with the binary chemical weapon. I reiterate now that if Israel does this, we will do that. We have given instructions to the commanders of the air bases and missile formations that once they hear Israel has hit any place in Iraq with the atomic bomb, they will

27. Timothy V. McCarthy and Jonathan B. Tucker, "Saddam's Toxic Arsenal: Chemical and Biological Weapons and Missiles in the Gulf War," in Peter R. Lavoy, Scott D. Sagan, and James J. Wirtz, eds., *Planning the Unthinkable: New Proliferants and the Use of Weapons of Mass Destruction* (forthcoming, 1999), p. 121.

load the chemical weapons with as much as will reach Israel and direct it at its territory. For we might be in Baghdad holding a meeting with the command when the atomic bomb falls on us. So to make the military order clear to the air and missile base commanders, we have told them that if they do not receive an order from higher authority and a city is struck with an atomic bomb, they will point toward Israel any weapons capable of reaching it.[28]

During the war, Saddam appears to have tried to remind the US of this policy statement. In a rare wartime interview, the Iraqi leader told Peter Arnett of CNN:

ARNETT: You have unconventional weapons like [words indistinct] chemical weapons. Will you use chemical weapons in a land war in Kuwait?

SADDAM: We will use weapons that match those used against us by our enemy. I believe that by now you are [word indistinct] that we have done all we had previously said.

ARNETT: The multinational [word indistinct] said they would not use chemical weapons against you. Would that mean that if they do not use them, you do not use them?

SADDAM: I said that we will use weapons that are equivalent to those used against us.[29]

Most US intelligence analysts during the Gulf War, and scholars looking back on the events today, find it very difficult to believe that Saddam Hussein would in reality delegate his authority to make such critical decisions to anyone else. Yet the evidence emerging on the Gulf War SCUD operations is perfectly consistent with the

28. "Saddam Hussein Addresses U.S. Senators," Baghdad Domestic Service (Apr. 16, 1990), in FBIS-NES-90-074 (Apr. 17, 1990), p. 7.
29. "'Mother of Battles' Airs Saddam CNN Interview," Baghdad Mother of Battles Radio Network (Feb. 2, 1991), in FBIS-NES (Feb. 6, 1991), p. 21 (emphasis added).

possibility that predelegation occurred. UNSCOM investigators have uncovered evidence that the twenty-five biological SCUD warheads and fifty chemical warheads were moved out of central storage locations and hidden in secret locations outside of the capital. A small number of SCUD missiles were kept in a special, highly alert, "reserve" force, and though not all BCW warheads were co-located with these reserve force SCUDs, there are some reports that BW warheads were mated to a handful of these missiles. Finally, Iraqi military documents suggest that these SCUD missiles were managed by special units under a separate command and control system, which is the form of predelegation one would anticipate if Saddam did not trust his regular commanders.[30]

For a leader to predelegate the capability and authority to use BCW may be a reasonable response to the fear of a decapitation attack, but it inevitably raises the risks of accidental uses of such weapons. The research on similar problems with NW during the Cold War identifies two fundamental and related dangers: the risk of unauthorized use by a "rogue commander" or mistaken launch of WMD after a false warning of an attack by an adversary.[31] Similar problems are likely to emerge among new proliferators. Two incidents from the Gulf War dramatically illustrate these dangers. First, on January 28, 1991, when the US bombed a large ammunition bunker outside of Basrah, the explosion was so large that both the Soviets (using their infrared satellite monitors) and the Israelis (who were receiving downlinks from the US satellites) contacted Washington to ask if US forces had just detonated a nuclear weapon.[32] Second, on February 7, 1991, when the US used a "Daisy Cutter"

30. The paragraph is based on McCarthy and Tucker, "Saddam's Toxic Arsenal," pp. 141–47, although the interpretation of these revelations is my own.

31. See Bruce G. Blair, *The Logic of Accidental Nuclear War* (Washington: Brookings Institution, 1993), and Scott D. Sagan, *The Limits of Safety: Organizations, Accidents, and Nuclear Weapons* (Princeton, NJ: Princeton University Press, 1993).

32. *GWAPS*, Vol. II, Part I, p. 281.

BLU-82 bomb, an SAS British commando behind the lines saw the explosion, which was so large that he announced on the radio, "Sir, the blokes have just nuked Kuwait."[33]

Given the existence of these incidents from the Gulf War, it should not take too much imagination to think through similar, realistic scenarios in which the special security officers in charge of BCW might believe that the conditions under which their predelegated orders to use their weapons had in fact come into effect. At an operational level, this kind of risk produced by an adversary's predelegation of authority raises difficult questions about US military targeting policies, especially concerning attacks against an adversary's command, control, and communication capabilities. At a more general level, such risks raise questions about whether the US should threaten the use of NW at all against enemies armed with BCW. If such a policy further encourages predelegation, then it is not clear whether the net effect of US threats would raise or lower the probability of these states' using BCW.

Effects on Proliferation Decisions

What are the effects of the US calculated ambiguity doctrine in terms of the proliferation decisions of third parties? Proponents of calculated ambiguity are certainly correct to argue that other states do not develop NW *solely* because of US threats against other states, or because US nuclear doctrine serves to "legitimize" NW possession. Yet, this is not the right criterion by which to evaluate the effects of US policy. Nonproliferation efforts should not be based on the false assumption that foreign governments behave as a single unitary actor in making crucial decisions about weapons procure-

---

33. ITV News Bureau, Ltd. "A Psy-Ops Bonanza in the Desert" (Apr. 18, 1991); Douglas Waller, "Secret Warriors," *Newsweek* (Jun. 19, 1991), p. 24.

ment.[34] New and potential proliferators often have fierce domestic debates on national security issues and the major influence that US nuclear threats can have is to give ammunition to hawks in those particular states and to decrease the legitimacy of other actors' anti-nuclear positions. It is impossible to measure such effects with accuracy. Indeed, it is usually difficult to find any direct evidence on this issue, since nuclear proliferation decisions are so often made in secret. Analysts should nevertheless not assume that US influence is nonexistent just because final proliferation decisions are made in secret meetings outside our view.

Examining the case of India provides a good example of the indirect, but nonetheless negative, effect of US nuclear policy on a potential proliferator. The US threats against Iraq during the Gulf War were widely reported in the Indian press and became a heated subject of domestic debate. The US nuclear threats, for example, prompted Rajiv Gandhi to issue his first public criticism of the Chandra Shektar government's strong support for the US-led coalition. Gandhi stated that "ever since the outbreak of hostilities in the Gulf my worst apprehension has been of the use of nuclear weapons" and declared that India would be left with "hardly any option but to convert our nuclear weapons capability into nuclear weapons capacity" in the event of US use of NW against Iraq.[35] Responding to the press reports of Bush's threats, Indian General K. Sundarji wrote that "this only confirms for the rest of the world that the possession of nuclear weapons is indeed the only coinage of power that the world recognizes as ultimate."[36] Spokesmen for the

---

34. Scott D. Sagan, "Why Do States Build Nuclear Weapons?: Three Models in Search of a Bomb," 21 *International Security* (Winter 1996), pp. 54–86.

35. "Cong-I Cautions Government on Gulf Issue," *Indian Express* (Feb. 12, 1991), p. 1. See also "Rajiv Fears Use of N-Arms," *Hindustan Times* (Feb. 12, 1991), p. 20.

36. General K. Sundarji, "The Threat of Nuclear Strike Is Real," *Hindu* (Feb. 3, 1991), p. 4.

Bharatiya Janata Party (BJP) quickly joined the debate, claiming that Gandhi and the Congress Party "just did not have the guts and the vision to go nuclear." For the BJP, the US policy simply proved that Indian restraint on nuclear tests was counterproductive: "We have wasted years enough. Let us not waste any more."[37]

Even in societies in which decisions about proliferation take place almost entirely in secret, behind a veil, it would be unwise to discount the potential effects of US nuclear doctrine on domestic debates. Iran is perhaps the most important case in point. Although there are undoubtedly many important actors in Iran who favor the acquisition of NW, there are other officials who either are primarily interested only in acquiring nuclear power, and still others who are undecided about whether Iran should develop NW quickly or only keep the nuclear option open for an uncertain future.[38] When the US threatens NW use in response to any Iraqi BW or CW attack, however, it logically provides extra support for the arguments of the more hawkish elements in Teheran since Iran also faces a similar threat from Iraq today and in the coming decade.

Conclusion: Trade-offs and Debate

This chapter has developed a new set of arguments about a set of poorly understood risks that are the hidden consequences of the current US calculated ambiguity doctrine. These risks exist even if the US threat to use NW deters some adversary from using BCW in a conflict with the US. Any final policy judgment on this issue, of course, must take into account both the great uncertainties involved in predicting the crisis and wartime behavior of adversaries, as well

---

37. "Ling-I Statement on Nuclear Arms an Ad-hoc Reaction" *Indian Express* (Feb. 13, 1991), p. 9.

38. See Peter Jones, "Iran's Threat Perceptions and Arms Control Policies," 6 *Nonproliferation Review* (Fall 1998), pp. 39–55.

as the difficult set of value trade-offs that often exist between the goal of deterrence of biological and chemical attacks and the goal of preventing further nuclear proliferation. Given this set of complexities, it should not be surprising that reasonable people adopt different policy prescriptions.

What is not reasonable, however, is for the US to continue to maintain the calculated ambiguity doctrine without a vigorous debate about all of the policy's costs and benefits. Given the horrible consequences that will result from any adversary's using BCW, even a small decrease in our current ability to deter such attacks is a cost that the US should be highly reluctant to pay. But reluctance to accept one set of obvious costs should not lead us to ignore other, more hidden, dangers. The first step toward a better debate on the subject would be for scholars and policymakers to accept that there is a set of much harder choices to be made about this doctrine than is widely recognized. As difficult as it may be to accept, wisdom here must begin by contemplating the possibility that some reduction in deterrence of the BCW threat may be a price worth paying to avoid the even greater harm of NW use by ourselves and others.

Michael P. Scharf

Enforcement Through Sanctions, Force, and Criminalization

In spite of the dreadful effects of biological and chemical weapons (BCW), nations regularly disregard treaties that forbid the use of such weapons and continue to develop, produce, and stockpile threatening quantities of these deadly agents. BCW have allegedly been used in a wide range of conflicts, including Afghanistan, Chechnya, Eritrea, Laos, Myanmar (Burma), Sri Lanka, Yemen, and the former Yugoslavia.[1] By far the best documented case was Iraq's use of these deadly weapons in its 1980–88 war against Iran, and subsequently against Kurdish groups in north-

---

1. Burns H. Weston, Richard A. Falk, and Hilary Charlesworth, *International Law and World Order: A Problem-Oriented Coursebook* 462 (3rd ed.) (St. Paul, MN: West Publishing Co., 1997); Miriam E. Sapiro, "Investigative Allegations of Chemical or Biological Warfare: The Canadian Contribution," 80 *American Journal International Law* 678, 677, n. 3 (1986) (citing reports of UN investigators).

ern Iraq.[2] In the aftermath of the 1990–91 Persian Gulf conflict, inspections by UN teams revealed an enormous CW inventory[3] and documents seized from the Iraqi Defense Ministry indicated that Iraq possessed a substantial BW capability at the time of the Gulf War.[4] Some twenty other countries are currently suspected of possessing similar weapons of mass destruction (WMD).[5]

For a variety of reasons, the proliferation of BCW has recently begun to pose a much greater and more immediate threat to international security than in prior years. First, the globalization of industry has greatly eased access to the technology, expertise, and raw materials of BCW. Second, BCW have been mated to missile delivery systems with particularly destabilizing implications. A state's ability to threaten attack with BCW against an enemy's population centers has encouraged leaders in the developing world to think of chemical and biological weaponry as "the poor man's atom bomb."[6] Unlike nuclear weapons programs, which require sensitive materials that are difficult and expensive to produce plus specialized facilities for bomb fabrication, BCW can be developed with readily available dual-use equipment and substances.[7] Thus, BCW can be developed

2. Miriam E. Sapiro, "Investigative Allegations of Chemical or Biological Warfare: The Canadian Contribution."

3. Andrew D. McClintock, "The Law of War: Coalition Attacks on Iraqi Chemical and Biological Weapon Storage and Production Facilities," 7 *Emory International Law Review* 633 (1993).

4. According to US officials, documents seized from the Iraqi Defense Ministry indicated the production of anthrax, botulinum toxin, and clostridium perfingens (the causative agent of gangrene). Ibid., p. 634, n. 2.

5. Jonathan B. Tucker, "The Current Status of the BCW Regimes." Paper delivered at the Hoover Institution Conference on Biological and Chemical Weapons at Stanford University (Nov. 16–18, 1998; early draft of chapter 6, this volume), p. 1 (on file with the author).

6. Brad Roberts, "Controlling Chemical Weapons," 2 *Transnational Law and Contemporary Problems* 435 (1992).

7. Anne Q. Connaughton and Steven C. Goldman, "The Chemical Weapons Convention and Department of Commerce Responsibilities," 760 *PLI/Comm* 533, 537–38 (1997).

by most countries and even terrorist organizations that are determined to do so. Third, BCW have proliferated to states, such as Iraq and North Korea, that have repeatedly flaunted international standards and have been known to sponsor terrorism. Finally, the prohibition on the production and use of these weapons has been weakened by the international community's failure to respond to Iraq's use of them against Iran and against the Iraqi Kurds.

There currently exist two means of enforcing the international prohibition of BCW. First, the international community can induce compliance through imposition of sanctions, such as trade embargoes, freezing of assets, and diplomatic isolation. Second, when sanctions fail, states can individually or collectively respond to the threat of BCW by resorting to military force. After exploring the potential strengths and weaknesses of these approaches, this chapter examines the desirability of supplementing them with a third approach based on the criminal prosecution of persons responsible for the production, stockpiling, transfer, or use of BCW.

The Letter of the Law

Before scrutinizing the means of enforcing the ban on BCW, it is necessary to understand the scope of the prohibition. This section thus examines the question of coverage, and demonstrates that at least part of the problem is due to inadequacies in the existing BCW treaty regimes: the 1907 Hague Convention, the 1925 Geneva Protocol, the 1972 Biological Weapons Convention (BWC), and the 1993 Chemical Weapons Convention (CWC).

The laws of war were first comprehensively codified in the 1907 Hague Convention,[8] which has been authoritatively deemed to con-

---

8. The Hague Convention (IV) Respecting the Law and Customs of War on Land and the Regulations annexed thereto of 18 October 1907, reprinted in Adam Roberts and Richard Guelff, eds., *Documents on the Law of War* (2d ed.) (New York: Oxford University Press, 1989), p. 44.

stitute customary international law.[9] Article 23 of the 1907 Hague Convention prohibits the use of poisonous weapons,[10] as well as the deployment of weapons "calculated to cause unnecessary suffering."[11] Unfortunately, these prohibitions did not deter the use of gas warfare by both sides in World War I.[12] It is estimated that use of chlorine and mustard gas during that war caused over a million casualties with 90,000 deaths.[13]

9. The Secretary-General of the UN stated in his report on the Statute of the International Criminal Tribunal for the Former Yugoslavia, that "the part of conventional international humanitarian law which has beyond doubt become part of international customary law is the law applicable in armed conflict as embodied in: . . . the Hague Convention (IV) Respecting the Law and Customs of War on Land and the Regulations annexed thereto of 18 October 1907; . . . ." See *Report of the Secretary-General Pursuant to Paragraph 2 of Security Council Resolution* (1993), p. 808, para. 35, UN Doc. S/25704, 3 May 1993, reprinted in 2 Virginia Morris and Michael P. Scharf, *An Insider's Guide to the International Criminal Tribunal for the Former Yugoslavia* (1995) (2 Morris and Scharf), pp. 3 and 9. See also paras. 609–17 of the judgment of the International Criminal Tribunal in the Tadic case (IT-94-1-T) (May 7, 1997), reprinted in relevant part in John R.W.D. Jones, *The Practice of the International Criminal Tribunals for the Former Yugoslavia and Rwanda* (1998), p. 40.

10. The Hague Convention (IV) Respecting the Law and Customs of War on Land and the Regulations annexed thereto of 18 October 1907, Art. 23(a), reprinted in Adam Roberts and Richard Guelff, eds., *Documents on the Law of War* (2d ed.).

11. Ibid., Art. 23(b). The 1977 Protocol I Additional to the 1949 Geneva Conventions similarly provides:

1. In any armed conflict, the right of the Parties to the conflict to choose methods or means of warfare is not unlimited.

2. It is prohibited to employ weapons, projectiles and material and methods of warfare of a nature to cause superfluous injury or unnecessary suffering.

3. It is prohibited to employ methods or means of warfare which are intended, or may be expected, to cause widespread, long-term and severe damage to the natural environment.

Protocol Additional to the Geneva Conventions of 12 August 1949, and Relating to the Protection of Victims of International Armed Conflicts, 8 June 1977, art. 35, 1125 U.N.T.S. 3 (1977).

12. Hilaire McCoubrey and Nigel D. White, *International Law and Armed Conflict* (Brookfield, VT: Dartmouth, 1992), p. 245.

13. Burns H. Weston, Richard A. Falk, and Hilary Charlesworth, *International Law and World Order: A Problem-Oriented Coursebook*, p. 463.

In 1925, the Geneva Protocol was established to ban the "use in war of asphyxiating, poisonous or other gasses, and of all analogous liquids, materials or devices."[14] The Geneva Protocol was a direct response to the failure of the 1907 Hague Convention to prevent the use of chemical weapons during World War I. Over 145 states have ratified the 1925 Geneva Protocol.[15] The treaty was hailed as successfully preventing the use of CW by all of the European belligerents in World War II.[16] However, in subsequent years, it became increasingly evident that the Geneva Protocol was just as ineffective in preventing the production and use of BCW as was its predecessor.

When ratifying the Geneva Protocol, many states reserved the right to use BCW against nonparties and to retaliate in kind against parties who used BCW first. In addition, the Protocol does not ban the design, testing, production, or stockpiling of BCW or CW precursors, thereby providing an incentive for countries to continue producing and stockpiling these weapons, and ensuring the short-order availability of such weapons for retaliatory purposes. Moreover, the prohibition applies only to wartime use—not peacetime use—of BCW. Nor does it apply to internal use, that is, by a government against its own citizens, such as the Iraqi government's poison gas attacks on the Iraqi Kurds, which resulted in the deaths of several hundred thousand people. Further, the Protocol contains no verification regime to investigate suspected violations and ensure compli-

14. Protocol for the Prohibition of the Use in War of Asphyxiating, Poisonous or Other Gasses, and of Bacteriological Methods of Warfare (1925), 26 U.S.T. 571, 94 L.N.T.S. 65 (Geneva Protocol of 1925).

15. Theodor Meron, "The Continuing Role of Custom in the Formation of International Humanitarian Law," 90 *American Journal International Law* 238, 246 (1996).

16. Richard M. Price, *The Chemical Weapons Taboo* (Ithaca, NY: Cornell University Press, 1997). Price argues that the 1925 Geneva Protocol created a "chemical weapons taboo" which was a necessary condition for the avoidance of chemical warfare in World War II. The author acknowledges, however, that the nonuse of chemical weapons during the war was largely out of fear that the opposing side would respond by employing chemical weapons against population centers.

ance with the prohibition. Finally, the Protocol has not been enforced. The international community has not imposed sanctions for documented violations of this Protocol, such as the use by Iraq of CW against Iran.[17] Nor has the international community imposed sanctions on countries that allow the export of CW precursors to countries such as Iraq.[18] It became apparent that the Geneva Protocol was not an adequate solution to the problems posed by the frequent use of CW and the growing proliferation and stockpiling of BW.[19]

Some of the weaknesses of the 1925 Geneva Protocol were eliminated with the establishment of the 1972 Biological Weapons Convention, which entered into force in 1975.[20] The BWC was the first treaty to totally outlaw an entire category of weapons.

Under Article I of the BWC, each state-party agrees never to produce, stockpile or otherwise acquire:

1. Microbial or other biological agents or toxins whatever their origin or method of production of types and in quantities that have no justification for prophylactic, protective or other peaceful purposes; and

2. Weapons, equipment or means of delivery designed to use

17. Anne Q. Connaughton and Steven C. Goldman, "The Chemical Weapons Convention and Department of Commerce Responsibilities," pp. 536–37 (1997).

18. Paul Rubenstein, "State Responsibility for Failure to Control the Export of Weapons of Mass Destruction," 23 *California Western International Law Journal* 319, 322 (1993). Rubenstein argues that countries such as Germany that allowed the export of chemical precursors, chemical process equipment, and technical expertise to Iraq during the 1980s could be held liable under principles of state responsibility since it was reasonably foreseeable that Iraq would use them to produce chemical weapons for aggressive use.

19. Peter H. Oppenheimer, "A Chemical Weapons Regime for the 1990s: Satisfying Seven Critical Criteria," 11 *Wisconsin International Law Journal* 1 (1992).

20. Convention on the Prohibition of the Development, Production and Stockpiling of Bacteriological (Biological) and Toxin Weapons and on their Destruction (1972), 26 U.S.T. 583, 1015 U.N.T.S. 163 (BWC).

such agents or toxins for hostile purposes or in armed conflict.[21]

Article II requires each state-party to destroy existing stockpiles of BW within nine months of the BWC's entry into force.[22]

The BWC, which has been widely ratified, reflects a comprehensive repudiation of the development, production, and stockpiling of biological weaponry. Despite its symbolic importance as a norm-creating treaty, the absence of verification and enforcement provisions has rendered it "merely a paper agreement that could easily be circumvented."[23] This became apparent when, in 1979, an accident at a covert Soviet BW plant was responsible for the outbreak of an epidemic of anthrax in Sverdilovsk, USSR, which killed up to a thousand persons.[24]

In addition, the BWC is riddled with gaps and loopholes. For example, research into biological weaponry is not prohibited. In addition, the Article I limitation to biological agents or toxins "that have no justification for prophylactic, protective or other peaceful purposes" constitutes an enormous loophole since "protective" (de-

---

21. Ibid.
22. Ibid.
23. Susan Wright, "Prospects for Biological Disarmament in the 1990s," 2 *Transnational Law and Contemporary Problems* 453 (1992); Nicholas A. Sims, *The Diplomacy of Biological Disarmament: Vicissitudes of a Treaty in Force, 1975–85* (Basingstoke, Hampshire, UK: Macmillan, 1988). Sims concludes:

> Those who took the British initiative of 1968 [which included strong provisions for verification and complaint investigation] and watered it down into the Convention of 1972 gave the world biological disarmament on the cheap; a disarmament regime of minimal machinery which would cost next to nothing to sustain. It is now painfully evident that these short-term savings have been outweighed by the long-term costs of a regime lacking the means to sustain its credibility in the face of suspicious events which cannot be resolved one way or the other (p. 290).

24. Raymond A. Zilinskas, "Review of the Diplomacy of Biological Disarmament: Vicissitudes of a Treaty in Force, 1975–85, by Nicholas A. Sims," 84 *American Journal International Law* 984, 984–85 (1990).

fensive) and "peaceful" applications cannot reliably be distinguished from hostile military applications. Similarly, the obligation to destroy stockpiles for any biological agent or toxins contained in Article II does not apply to biological agents that are "divert[ed] to peaceful purposes," thereby providing states an alarming degree of discretion.[25]

In 1994, the parties to the BWC established an Ad Hoc Group of fifty interested member-states to draft a Compliance Protocol to strengthen the Convention.[26] The draft Protocol produced in July 1998 was 251 pages long and consisted of twenty-three articles, seven annexes, and five appendices—with over 3,000 provisions in brackets (indicating points of disagreement).[27] The Ad Hoc Group plans to meet for sixteen weeks of negotiations in 1999 to complete the Protocol.[28]

Given the deficiencies of the Geneva Protocol, in 1968, the international community began negotiating a comprehensive CW convention that would ban not only the use, but also the production and stockpiling of CW, and that would additionally provide the means to verify compliance and to sanction violations.[29] The objective of the CWC was to eliminate an entire class of WMD.

On April 29, 1997, the CWC entered into force.[30] Over 120 states (including the US, China, India, Iran and Russia) have ratified or acceded to the CWC.[31] In twenty-four articles and three annexes,

25. Richard A. Falk, "Inhibiting Reliance on Biological Weaponry: The Role and Relevance of International Law," 1 *American University Journal International Law and Policy* 17 (1986).

26. Jonathan B. Tucker, "The Current Status of the BCW Regimes," p. 8.

27. Ibid., p. 9.

28. Ibid., pp. 11–12.

29. Anne Q. Connaughton and Steven C. Goldman, "The Chemical Weapons Convention and Department of Commerce Responsibilities," p. 537.

30. See John J. Kim and Gregory Gerdes, "International Institutions," 32 *International Law* 575 (1998).

31. Ibid. The US Senate gave its advice and consent to the Chemical Weapons Convention on April 24, 1997, subject to twenty-eight conditions. Notable among

the CWC prohibits the development, production, other acquisition, retention, stockpiling, transfer, and use of CW and CW-production facilities.[32] It also prohibits state-parties from engaging in any military preparations to use CW and from assisting or inducing anyone to engage in an activity that is prohibited by the CWC. Under the CWC, state-parties must within ten years eliminate all CW and CW-production facilities under their jurisdiction or control.

Most importantly, the CWC establishes a permanent Organization for the Prohibition of Chemical Weapons (OPCW), whose role is to monitor implementation of the agreement through on-site inspections—including inspections of private (nonmilitary) chemical production facilities.[33] In addition, the CWC provides for challenge inspections of any facility or location, public or private, when a state-party has concerns that the facility may be in noncompliance with the CWC. Because of its extensive verification procedures, the CWC is estimated to cost between $70 million and $500 million per year to operate.[34]

Although the verification provisions of the CWC have been her-

---

these is Condition 28, which requires the president to certify that proper search warrants would be obtained for any US facility subject to inspection when consent of the owner was withheld. This condition responded to concerns that US businesses could be subject to unreasonable searches and seizures by the Convention in contravention of their Fourth Amendment rights.

32. Convention on the Prohibition of the Development, Production, Stockpiling and Use of Chemical Weapons and on Their Destruction (1993), *Sen. Treaty Doc. No. 21*, 103rd Cong., 1st Sess. (1993), reprinted in 32 *International Legal Materials* 800 (CWC). For an analysis of the CWC's negotiating history, see Walter Krutzsch and Ralf Trapp, *A Commentary on the Chemical Weapons Convention* (Norwell, MA: Kluwer Academic Publishers, 1994), and Thomas Bernauer, *The Projected Chemical Weapons Convention: A Guide to the Negotiations in the Conference on Disarmament* (Geneva: UN Inst. for Disarmament Research, 1990).

33. Under Article III of the CWC, parties must disclose to the OPCW the location of their production facilities and chemical weapons stockpiles.

34. Raymond A. Zilinskas, "Review of the Diplomacy of Biological Disarmament: Vicissitudes of a Treaty in Force, 1975–85, by Nicholas A. Sims."

alded as "the most intricate and intrusive ever designed for a disarmament regime,"[35] the CWC is not without its flaws. In particular, the CWC does not provide mandatory sanctions against violators. Furthermore, it does not apply to numerous "holdout" states that continue to refuse to join.[36] Nor does it apply to nonstate actors, such as terrorist or paramilitary groups, which are increasingly likely to resort to such weapons. Moreover, it only regulates CW and their precursors in terms of tons, while technological advances are resulting in agents that are lethal in quantities up to 100,000 times smaller than tons.[37] And it permits any state-party to withdraw from the regime for "the supreme interests of the country" on only ninety days' notice.

The CWC's most significant weakness is the result of ill-conceived action by the US Congress. In enacting implementing legislation, Congress included three "poison-pill" provisions introduced by treaty opponents that could eviscerate the CWC's verification regime.[38] One provision authorizes the US president to refuse a challenge inspection on "national security grounds," the second prevents the removal of samples from US territory for analysis, and the third sharply limits the number of US chemical plants subject to inspection. Other countries are likely to treat these as equivalent to reservations and assert them to frustrate verification.[39]

35. Peter H. Oppenheimer, "A Chemical Weapons Regime for the 1990s: Satisfying Seven Critical Criteria," p. 1.
36. Most of the Middle Eastern countries did not sign and have not ratified or acceded to the CWC, citing Israel's refusal to sign the Nuclear Non-Proliferation Treaty. Ibid.
37. Ibid.
38. Jonathan B. Tucker, "The Current Status of the BCW Regimes," p. 7.
39. The result would be similar to the effect of the US "Connally Reservation" to the compulsory jurisdiction of the International Court of Justice, which provided that US acceptance of the World Court's jurisdiction would not apply to "disputes with regard to matters which are essentially within the domestic jurisdiction of the United States of America as determined by the United States of America." Barry E. Carter and Phillip R. Trimble, *International Law: Selected Documents* (2d ed.) (Boston:

Means of Enforcement

None of the treaties on BCW provide for the imposition of mandatory sanctions against violators. The parties to these treaties can individually or collectively impose sanctions, but embargoes are ineffective unless they are universally enforced. Thus, the UN Security Council may increasingly be called upon to respond to violations of the BCW conventions.

The UN Charter charges the Security Council with the responsibility of determining the existence of any threat to, or breach of, the peace. Articles 41 and 42 of the Charter authorize the Council to restore international peace and security, by force if necessary. The Security Council may call upon UN members to impose sanctions and to use force to ensure compliance (for example, to interdict vessels violating an embargo). The Council can also freeze assets of responsible leaders,[40] and ban their travel.[41] Further, the Security Council can call upon or authorize states to use military force in response to a violation of the international prohibition on BCW. The Security Council can even authorize the capture of persons responsible for serious violations of international law.[42]

Little, Brown, 1995), pp. 305–6. One of the reasons given for the US withdrawal from the compulsory jurisdiction of the International Court of Justice in 1986 was that every time the US attempted to bring a case against a country before the International Court of Justice, the country used the reservation against the US via reciprocity to successfully defeat the International Court's jurisdiction. See Statement of the Legal Adviser, Abraham D. Sofaer, to the Senate Foreign Relations Committee (Dec. 4, 1985), reproduced in Barry E. Carter and Phillip R. Trimble, *International Law: Selected Documents*, p. 324.

40. S.C. Res. 841, U.N. SCOR, 48th Sess., 3238th mtg., U.N. Doc. S/INF/49 (1993) (freezing the assets of the de facto military regime in Haiti and their major civilian supporters).

41. S.C. Res. 1137, U.N. SCOR, 52nd Sess., 3831st mtg., U.N. Doc. S/RES/1137 (1997) (imposing travel restrictions on Iraqi leaders).

42. See S.C. Res. 837, U.N. SCOR, 48th Sess., 3229th mtg., p. 83, U.N. Doc. S/INF/49 (1993) (authorizing the "arrest, and detention for prosecution, trial and punishment," of Somali warlord Mohamed Farrah Aidid, who was responsible for the murder of 24 UN Peacekeeping troops in 1993).

In the aftermath of Iraq's invasion of Kuwait, the Security Council adopted a series of resolutions to impel Iraq to destroy its arsenal of BCW. After Iraq invaded Kuwait, the Security Council imposed sweeping sanctions and authorized the use of force against Iraq.[43] At the conclusion of the Persian Gulf conflict, the Security Council adopted Resolution 687 (1991), which imposed on Iraq the terms required for an end to all UN actions, including the lifting of sanctions.[44] To avoid the possibility of a future Iraqi threat using BCW,[45] Resolution 687 required Iraq to "unconditionally accept the destruction, removal, or rendering harmless, under international supervision, of . . . all chemical and biological weapons and all stocks of agents and all related subsystems and components and all research, development, support, and manufacturing facilities."[46] The preamble of Resolution 687 invokes inter alia the Geneva Protocol and the BWC as its basis for imposing this requirement.

Resolution 687 required Iraq to divulge the locations, amounts,

---

43. See S.C. Res. 660, U.N. SCOR, 45th Sess., 2932nd mtg., U.N. Doc. S/RES/ 660 (1990) (demanding withdrawal of Iraqi troops from Kuwait); S.C. Res. 661, U.N. SCOR, 45th Sess., 2933rd mtg., U.N. Doc. S/RES/661 (1990) (imposing economic sanctions); S.C. Res. 665, U.N. SCOR, 45th Sess., 2938th mtg., U.N. Doc. S/RES/665 (1990) (authorizing use of force to enforce the embargo); Res. 678, U.N. SCOR, 45th Sess., 2963rd mtg., U.N. Doc. S/RES/678 (1990) (authorizing invasion of Iraq by coalition forces).

44. S.C. Res. 687, U.N. SCOR, 46th Sess., 2981st mtg., U.N. Doc. S/RES/687 (1991).

45. In a letter to the leaders of the House and Senate regarding Iraq, President Clinton stated in relevant part:

Sanctions against Iraq were imposed as a result of Iraq's invasion of Kuwait. It has been necessary to sustain them because of Iraq's failure to comply with relevant UNSC resolutions, including those to ensure Saddam Hussein is not allowed to resume the unrestricted development and production of weapons of mass destruction.

Clinton Letter to the Leaders of House and Senate, Iraq (visited Oct. 1, 1998) http://www.usis.usemb.se/regional/nea/gulfsec/clnt201.htm.

46. S.C. Res. 687, U.N. SCOR, 46th Sess., 2981st mtg., U.N. Doc. S/RES/687 (1991), para. 8.

and types of its BCW to the UN Secretary-General. The destruction of these materials was to be performed under the supervision of the UN Special Commission (UNSCOM), which was charged with the responsibility for inspection and investigation of all known or suspected weapon sites. After a series of violations of Resolution 687, culminating in Iraq's refusal to allow the inspection teams access to sites designated by UNSCOM in December 1998,[47] the US and UK resorted to use of military force to compel Iraqi compliance.[48] The US and UK asserted that such force was permitted by Resolution 678, which authorized member states to use all necessary means to uphold and implement "all relevant resolutions" subsequent to Resolution 660.[49]

The UNSCOM inspection regime was the most intrusive and comprehensive ever imposed upon a nation. Notwithstanding Saddam Hussein's intermittent intransigence to permit UN inspections and UNSCOM's departure from Iraq since late 1998,[50] the Security Council's approach to Iraqi BCW convention violations provides a blueprint for the future.

Prior to the advent of the UN Charter, there had existed a customary right of reprisal, permitting use of military force to enforce

47. See "Standoff in Iraq: Chronology of Iraqi Violations" (Oct. 1, 1998), at http://www.foxnews.com/news/packages/iraq/violations.sm/.

48. See President Clinton's Address: Text of President Clinton's Address to Joint Chiefs of Staff and Pentagon Staff (Feb. 17, 1998), at http://paddle4.canoe.ca/CNEWSIraq/clingtonaddress.html.

49. See Frederic L. Kirgis, "The Legal Background on the Use of Force to Induce Iraq to Comply with Security Council Resolutions," *American Society International Law Flash Insight* (Nov. 1997). The governments of several other members of the Security Council, including China, France, and Russia, have disputed that Resolution 678 can be used as an ongoing authority to use force. (Ibid.)

50. See Paul Taylor, "West Found Weakened in Annual Arms Survey," *Boston Globe* (Oct. 23, 1998), p. A2 ("The study [published by the International Institute for Strategic Studies] noted that although the United States and Britain made a credible threat of force in February to compel Iraq to resume cooperation with U.N. arms inspectors, they had not acted after Bahgdad in August effectively ended the searches for weapons of mass destruction.").

international obligations in certain limited circumstances. The specific parameters governing lawful reprisals were set forth in the *Naulilaa Incident Arbitration* decision:

1. The offending state must have committed an act contrary to international law.

2. The injured state must make a demand on the offending state and that demand goes unsatisfied.

3. The force used in the reprisal must be proportionate to the offending act.[51]

If it were still good law, the doctrine of armed reprisal could be used to justify an attack on a chemical or biological weapons facility operating in violation of the BCW conventions. The practice of the UN and the opinions of the World Court (i.e., the "International Court of Justice" or ICJ), however, indicate that the right of armed reprisal is generally contrary to the UN Charter. Numerous resolutions condemning armed reprisals as inconsistent with the Charter have been adopted over the years.[52] Most notably, the 1970 Declaration on Principles of International Law Concerning Friendly Relations and Cooperation among States in Accordance with the Charter of the United Nations provides that "states have a duty to refrain from acts of reprisal involving the use of force."[53] The ICJ impliedly

51. Portuguese-German Arbitral Tribunal, 8 Trib. Arb. Mixtes 409, 2 R. International Arb. Awards 1012 (1928), translated and discussed in William W. Bishop, Jr., *International Law: Cases and Materials* 903–4 (3d ed.) (Boston: Little, Brown, 1971).

52. Rex J. Zedalis, "On the Lawfulness of Forceful Remedies for Violations of Arms Control Agreements: 'Star Wars' and other Glimpses at the Future," 18 *New York University Journal International Law and Policy* 73, 123 (1985).

53. Declaration on Principles of International Law Concerning Friendly Relations and Cooperation among States in Accordance with the Charter of the United Nations, G.A. Res. 2625, 25 U.N. GAOR Supp. (No. 28), p. 121, U.N. Doc. A/ 8028 (1970).

rejected the right of reprisal in the *Corfu Channel Case*[54] and in the *Case Concerning United States Diplomatic and Consular Staff in Tehran.*[55] The UN Charter thus generally prohibits armed reprisals, but such measures are permissible if they qualify as an exercise of self-defense under Article 51 of the Charter, as discussed below.

Self-defense is to be contrasted with reprisal. Whereas reprisals are punitive in character, the purpose of self-defense is to mitigate or prevent harm. But the two concepts overlap in the case of anticipatory self-defense. Hugo Grotius, often regarded as the father of international law, first recognized a state's right to use force to forestall an anticipated attack in 1625.[56] The contours of the right of anticipatory self-defense were fleshed out in an exchange of diplomatic notes between the governments of the US and UK during the *Caroline* incident of 1837.[57] The two countries agreed that international law permitted a military response to a threat provided that the danger posed was, in the words of US Secretary of State Daniel Webster, "instant, overwhelming, leaving no choice of means and

54. *Corfu Channel Case (UK v. Albania)*, 1949 I.C.J. at 4 (rejecting British contention that a mine-sweeping operation to clear the waters of mines laid by Albania in contravention of international law constituted a justifiable intervention in self-help to remedy the breach of a general international obligation).

55. *Case Concerning United States Diplomatic and Consular Staff in Tehran (US v. Iran)*, 1980 I.C.J., p. 3 (expressing concern in regard to the legality of the US incursion into Iran). Judge Morozov's dissenting opinion expressly characterized the incursion as violative of the Charter because it did not meet the requirements of Article 51. Ibid., pp. 51, 56–57 (Morozov, J., dissenting).

56. Hugo Grotius, *The Law of War and Peace* (1646) (Francis W. Kelsey, trans.) (Oxford: Clarendon Press, 1925), pp. 169–85.

57. In 1837, rebels in Upper Canada, with American logistical support, unsuccessfully revolted against British rule. The Canadian military identified the American steamboat *Caroline* as a vessel running arms to the rebels and sent a military force into the US to set the ship ablaze, killing an American citizen in the process. Subsequently, American officials arrested a Canadian citizen in New York for the murder, which prompted a protest by the British government. See 2 John B. Moore, *Digest International Law* (1906), pp. 409–14.

no moment for deliberation."[58] The Webster formulation of self-defense is often cited as authoritative customary law. Following the *Caroline* incident, the imminent threat of armed attack has generally been found to justify defensive military action provided the threatened nation has first exhausted all peaceful means of resolution and that the action ultimately taken was proportionate to the threat.

Scholars are divided over whether the specific language contained in Articles 2(4) and 51 of the UN Charter has overridden the customary right of anticipatory self-defense as articulated during the *Caroline* incident.[59] Article 2(4) prohibits the use of military force in the territory of another state without its consent.[60] Article 51 provides an exception to that prohibition for the case of self-defense in response to "an armed attack."[61] Those who favor a restrictive inter-

58. Ibid., p. 412.

59. Those taking the position that Article 51 prohibits anticipatory self-defense include: Louis Henkin, *How Nations Behave: Law and Foreign Policy* (2d ed.) (New York: Columbia University Press, 1979), p. 141; Philip C. Jessup, *A Modern Law of Nations: An Introduction* (3d ed.) (New York: Macmillan, 1968), pp. 166–67; Ian Brownlie, *International Law and the Use of Force by States* (Oxford: Clarendon Press, 1963), pp. 275–76; Hans Kelsen, *The Law of the United Nations: A Critical Analysis of Its Fundamental Problems* (London: Stevens and Sons, 1950), pp. 797–98; Lassa Oppenheim, *International Law: A Treatise* (H. Lauterpacht, ed.) (7th ed.) (New York: Longmans, Green, 1948), p. 156. Those taking the position that Article 51 allows anticipatory self-defense include: Abraham D. Sofaer, "Terrorism, the Law, and National Defense," 126 *Military Law Review* 89 (1989); Oscar Schachter, *International Law in Theory and Practice* (Norwell, MA: Kluwer Academic Publishers, 1991), pp. 150–52; Yoram Dinstein, *War, Aggression, and Self Defense* (Cambridge, UK: Grotius Publications Ltd., 1988), pp. 172–76; D. W. Bowett, *Self-Defense in International Law* (1958), pp. 188–89; Myres S. McDougal, "The Soviet-Cuban Quarantine and Self-Defense," 57 *American Journal International Law* 597 (1963), pp. 599–600.

60. Article 2(4) of the UN Charter provides: "All Members shall refrain in their international relations from the threat or use of force against the territorial integrity or political independence of any state, or in any other manner inconsistent with the Purposes of the United Nations."

61. Article 51 of the UN Charter provides: "Nothing in the present Charter shall impair the inherent right of individual or collective self-defense if an armed attack occurs against a Member of the United Nations, until the Security Council has taken measures necessary to maintain international peace and security."

pretation of self-defense argue that the original Charter signatories intended to supplant customary self-defense norms and rely on new UN enforcement mechanisms for maintaining peace in an effort to minimize the overall use of force.

The modern (though by no means universal) trend is to interpret the UN Charter as not requiring a state to absorb a devastating or even lethal first strike before acting to protect itself. International law "is not a suicide pact, especially in an age of uniquely destructive types of weapons."[62] It is also noteworthy that the equally authentic French version of Article 51 uses the phrase *aggression armée*— meaning armed aggression—instead of the more restrictive term "armed attack" contained in the English version.[63] The right to respond to armed aggression would include the right to respond to threats, since aggression can exist separate from and prior to an actual attack.[64] Even if that were not the uniform interpretation of the drafters of the UN Charter in 1948,[65] interpretation of the Charter must keep pace with technological developments in weaponry that render restrictive interpretations obsolete.

If scholars are divided on this issue, this division only reflects the discordant practice of the UN as evidenced in particular by its contrary responses to the Israeli preemptory airstrike against Egypt in 1967 and the Israeli bombardment of the Iraqi Osirak nuclear reac-

62. Louis R. Beres, "The Permissibility of State-Sponsored Assassination During Peace and War," 5 *Temple International and Comparative Law Journal* 231 (1992), p. 239.

63. Beth M. Polebaum, "National Self-Defense in International Law: An Emerging Standard for a Nuclear Age," 59 *New York University Law Review* 187 (1984), p. 202.

64. Ibid.

65. The meaning of "armed attack" may have appeared self-evident to the drafters of the UN Charter who had just experienced a war which began with Hitler's massive blitzkrieg assaults (accompanied by scores of tanks, planes, and soldiers) into Germany's neighboring states.

tor in 1981.[66] The UN appeared to recognize the right of anticipatory self-defense when Israel launched a preemptory airstrike against Egypt, precipitating the 1967 Six Day War.[67] Many countries supported Israel's right to conduct defensive strikes prior to armed attack and draft resolutions condemning the Israeli action were soundly defeated in the Security Council and the General Assembly.[68]

Fourteen years later, on June 7, 1981, Israeli pilots bombed the Iraqi Osirak nuclear reactor. In a statement released after the airstrike, the Israeli government justified its action as an act of self-defense since "sources of unquestioned reliability told us that [the reactor] was intended . . . for the production of atomic bombs. The

66. The UN has also taken seemingly inconsistent stands on the issue in the context of the 1986 US air raid on Libya and the 1993 cruise missile attack on Iraq. The overwhelming majority of the members of the UN rejected the US claim that the Libyan raid was justified as anticipatory self-defense as discussed below. In contrast, most members of the UN supported the claim by the US that the 1993 cruise missile attack on Iraq was justified as anticipatory self-defense in light of Iraq's attempts to assassinate former President Bush. See generally Stuart G. Baker, "Comparing the 1993 U.S. Airstrike on Iraq to the 1986 Bombing of Libya: The New Interpretation of Article 51," 24 *Georgia Journal International and Comparative Law* 99 (1994).

67. The Israeli air strike was in response to Egyptian President Nasser's having ordered Egypt's armed forces into a state of maximum alert, terminating the presence of the UN peacekeeping force in his country, and closing the Gulf of Aqaba and the Strait of Tiran to Israeli shipping. A few days later, the armed forces of Syria, Jordan, and Iraq were placed under unified Egyptian command. Israel pursued alternative means to resolve the conflict by prevailing upon other nations to intercede. But with the Arab leaders issuing increasingly bellicose threats, Israel initiated a preemptory air strike against the Egyptian airfields. See Beth M. Polebaum, "National Self-Defense in International Law: An Emerging Standard for a Nuclear Age," p. 193.

68. A draft resolution submitted by the Soviet Union calling for a condemnation of Israel was not accepted by the Security Council. 22 U.N. SCOR (135th mtg), p. 5, U.N. Doc. S/7951 Rev. 1 (1967). The same resolution was brought to the floor of the General Assembly for a vote and was defeated. U.N. GAOR (5th Emergency Special Session, Jun. 17–Sep. 18, 1967) (154th mtg.), pp. 15–17, U.N. Doc. A/L.519 (4 Jul. 1967).

goal for these bombs was Israel."[69] This time, the Security Council and General Assembly responded by condemning Israel for the strike.[70] However, the resolution condemning Israel and the explanation of votes did not declare that the threat to Israel was not credible, that the Israeli strike was disproportionate to the threat, or that Israel had failed to seek alternative peaceful means to resolve the crisis.[71] Those commentators who agree with the UN condemnation generally take the position that the Iraqi threat to Israel was not sufficiently "immediate" within the formula or the spirit of the *Caroline* incident.[72] Yet, the action of the UN, "unaccompanied by clear explanations or analysis, seem[s] to represent a mere political consensus and not a legal one."[73]

Notwithstanding the international community's condemnation

69. Beth M. Polebaum, "National Self-Defense in International Law: An Emerging Standard for a Nuclear Age," p. 205. Israel's attack on the Iraqi reactor should be viewed within the context of the following factors: (1) Since Israel was created by the UN in 1948, Iraq has sought Israel's destruction by participating in all wars against Israel and by rejecting all possibilities for peace. Iraq has remained in an official state of war with Israel throughout its existence. Ibid., p. 218. (2) A few months prior to the bombing, the Iraqi government issued public statements suggesting that its nuclear reactor was intended to be used "against the Zionist enemy." Ibid. (3) Iraq had little need for peaceful nuclear energy in light of its vast oil reserves. Ibid., p. 221. (4) Intelligence indicated that the Iraqi reactor would become operational in one to three months, after which time bombardment would endanger civilians by releasing radioactive materials. Ibid. (5) While an attempt at negotiations with Iraq would have been futile, Israel made repeated unsuccessful diplomatic efforts to persuade the French and Italian governments to cease shipments of sensitive nuclear material to Iraq. Ibid., p. 223.

70. S.C. Res. 487, 36 U.N. SCOR (2288th mtg.), p. 10, U.N. Doc. S/Res./487 (1981); G.A. Res. 27, 36 U.N. GAOR Supp. (No. 51), p. 17, U.N. Doc. A/Res./36/27 (1981).

71. S.C. Res. 487, 36 U.N. SCOR (2288th mtg.), p. 10, U.N. Doc. S/Res./487 (1981); G.A. Res. 27, 36 U.N. GAOR Supp. (No. 51), p. 17, U.N. Doc. A/Res./36/27 (1981). See also U.N. Doc. S/PV.2285-88 reprinted in 20 I.L.M. 993 (1981).

72. See Anthony D'Amato, "Israel's Air Strike upon the Iraqi Nuclear Reactor," 77 *American Journal International Law* 584 (1983).

73. Beth M. Polebaum, "National Self-Defense in International Law: An Emerging Standard for a Nuclear Age," p. 218.

of the Israeli attack on the Iraqi nuclear plant, the US took similar action on August 20, 1998,[74] against a plant in Khartoum, Sudan, said to be producing the lethal nerve agent VX and other CW components.[75] The US government justified its cruise missile attack on the Shifa plant by stating that the plant had no commercial uses, was closely guarded, and that its owner had close financial links to Osama bin Laden (a Saudi exile suspected of masterminding the August 1998 bombings of two US embassies in Kenya and Tanzania).[76]

At first, international criticism of the attack on the Sudanese plant was muted, signaling acceptance of the principle of anticipatory self-defense in the context of the destruction of CW facilities in the hands of a known terrorist.[77] However, world opinion (even among our closest allies) began to coalesce against the US when it turned out that Osama bin Laden had no financial connection to the Sudanese plant and that the plant actually produced antimalaria pills

---

74. Ibid. This was the second time that the Clinton Administration asserted the doctrine of anticipatory-self defense to justify an attack. Five years earlier, it had relied on the doctrine to justify its June 26, 1993, cruise missile attack on the Iraqi Intelligence Service Headquarters in Baghdad in the aftermath of the failed attempt to assassinate former President Bush during his visit to Kuwait. See Statement by Ambassador Madeleine K. Albright, United States Permanent Representative to the United Nations, in the Security Council, on the Iraqi Attempt to Assassinate President Bush (Jun. 27, 1993), USUN Press Release 110-(93) (Jun. 27, 1993) (on file with the author). The majority of states expressed no objections to the 1993 airstrike and seem to have largely accepted the legal justification provided by the US; the only states that publicly condemned the US action were China, Bangladesh, Yemen, Iran, and Sudan. Stuart G. Baker, "Comparing the 1993 U.S. Airstrike on Iraq to the 1986 Bombing of Libya: The New Interpretation of Article 51," pp. 99–104.

75. Colum Lynch, "Allied Doubts Grow About the US Strike on Sudanese Plant," *Boston Globe* (Sep. 24, 1998), p. A2.

76. CNN Interactive, U.S. Missiles Pound Targets in Afghanistan, Sudan (visited Sep. 16, 1998), at http://cnn.com.US/9808/20/us.strikes.02/index.html.

77. This is to be distinguished from the international community's vocal condemnation of the United States' April 1986 air raid against targets in Libya, which were conducted in response to the Libyan bombing of a German discotheque frequented by US serviceman, which is discussed below.

and other legitimate pharmaceuticals including a vaccine used to fight disease in livestock.[78] The US case was further eroded when it was discovered that the Sudanese plant had a contract with the UN to provide these medicines—a contract that had been approved by the US Representative to the UN.[79] While the US government steadfastly refused to provide its intelligence data to dispel doubt, former US President Jimmy Carter, as well as several Arab countries, demanded an independent UN investigation to determine whether chemical warfare agents could be detected in the remains of the factory.[80]

It is noteworthy that the international response to the US cruise missile attack on the Sudanese plant focused on the degree of proof required, rather than on the underlying legal right to launch antici-patory attacks against CW facilities. Yet, having failed to sufficiently prove its case, the action seriously undermined US credibility, making it more difficult to garner international support for such action against BCW facilities in the future. As a congressional critic of the attack against the Sudanese plant pointed out: "Attacking an instal-lation in another country may be justified, but you've got to be very, very sure about the threats before launching the attack. It is impor-tant to have self-defense capability, but if you overuse it, you lose it."[81]

The Sudanese bombing incident focused attention on the neces-sity requirement of the doctrine of self-defense. Because a preemp-tory attack on a BCW production or storage facility can pose a serious threat to the surrounding civilian population, the issue of proportionality may also become a source of controversy. Although

---

78. Colum Lynch, "Allied Doubts Grow About the US Strike on Sudanese Plant"; David L. Marcus, "Frank Criticizes Bombing of Plant in Sudan," *Boston Globe* (Sep. 25, 1998), p. A9.
79. Ibid.
80. Ibid.
81. Ibid.

a direct hit on a conventional ammunition depot will create a massive explosion, the resulting collateral damage will be limited to the immediate vicinity. In contrast, an attack on a BCW facility could result in the release of a deadly cloud.[82] The extent of the contamination of the surrounding area will depend on prevailing environmental conditions and the physical characteristics of the chemical or biological agent.[83] The actual effects of collateral damage of this type were demonstrated by an allied attack on an Italian ship, laden with 100 tons of mustard gas, during World War II. The attack resulted in the release of a poisonous cloud that drifted over the port town of Bari, Italy, killing more than 1,000 civilians.[84] During the Persian Gulf conflict, the US Department of Defense estimated that up to six million Iraqis could have been killed from the dispersion of anthrax and botulism viruses in a single attack of a BW facility.[85] Thus, all but the most carefully executed attacks on BCW facilities will likely fail the proportionality requirement of self-defense.

Consider a situation in which a particular state determines that another state plans to launch a chemical or biological surprise attack upon its population centers. Intelligence assessments reveal that the assassination of selected key figures would prevent this attack altogether. Intelligence further reveals that conventional forms of preemption would generate far greater harm, especially if the attack resulted in releasing the targeted chemical or biological agents. Under this scenario, would a preemptive assassination be lawful?

If international law is not a suicide pact, neither is it a license to kill. Assassination has traditionally been viewed as unlawful both in war and nonwar contexts. Where a condition of war exists between

---

82. Andrew D. McClintock, "The Law of War: Coalition Attacks on Iraqi Chemical and Biological Weapon Storage and Production Facilities," pp. 637–38.
83. Ibid.
84. Ibid., p. 637, n.10.
85. Ibid.

states, international assassination constitutes a war crime. Article 23 of the Hague Convention IV of 1907 provides that "it is especially forbidden . . . to kill or wound *treacherously*, individuals belonging to the hostile nation or army."[86] The US Army's field manual on the law of land warfare has incorporated this prohibition in the following terms: "This article . . . prohibits *assassination*, proscription or outlawry of an enemy, or putting a price upon an enemy's head, as well as offering a reward for an enemy 'dead or alive.'"[87]

Yet, the 1907 Hague Convention's prohibition on assassination is not as broad as it might appear at first blush. Focusing on the "treacherous" requirement of the Hague Convention, a recent military legal analysis of wartime assassination concluded that none of the following acts contravened the prohibition:

1. The November 18, 1941, raid by Scottish commandos at Bedda Littoria, Libya, whose goal was to kill German Field Marshal Erwin Rommel.

2. The April 18, 1943, downing of a Japanese airplane known to be carrying Admiral Isoroku Yamamoto by US aircraft.

3. The October 30, 1951, airstrike by the US Navy that killed 500 senior Chinese and North Korean military officers and security forces at a military planning conference at Kapsan, North Korea.[88]

When agents of one state assassinate an official of another state in a nonwar context, the action may constitute an act of terrorism. Article 2(a) of the Convention on Internationally Protected Persons,

---

86. Convention (No. IV) Respecting the Laws and Customs of War on Land, with Annex of Regulations, Oct. 18, 1907, art. 23 (b), 36 Stat. 2277, T.S. No. 539.

87. Department of the Army, *The Law of Land Warfare*, art. 31 (1956) (Army Field Manual No. 27-10, Washington, DC).

88. W. Hays Parks, "Memorandum of Law: Executive Order 12333 and Assassination," *Army Lawyer* (Dec. 1989) (Dept. of the Army Pamphlet 27-50-204), p. 5.

to which the US and most other countries are parties, criminalizes "the intentional commission of . . . murder, kidnapping or other attack upon the person or liberty of an internationally protected person," defined to include heads of state and other high-level officials.[89] It is important to note, however, that the Internationally Protected Persons Convention accords a head of state or state official protected status only when the official is outside his/her own country.[90]

Notwithstanding these international law prohibitions, according to the results of a 1975 Senate investigation, US presidents have instigated plots to assassinate foreign leaders in Cuba, Congo, Dominican Republic, Chile, and South Vietnam.[91] In response to these revelations, President Gerald R. Ford promulgated Executive Order 12,333, which provides that "No person employed by or acting on behalf of the United States Government shall engage in, or conspire to engage in, assassination."[92]

Although Executive Order 12,333 has been reissued by Presidents Carter, Reagan, Bush, and Clinton,[93] its value is more symbolic than real. A president can circumvent the ban posed by the Executive Order and legally carry out an assassination in four ways:

89. Convention on the Prevention and Punishment of Crimes Against Internationally Protected Persons, Including Diplomatic Agents, adopted Dec. 14, 1973, 28 U.S.T. 1975, 1037 U.N.T.S. 167.

90. The Convention defines "Internationally Protected Person" as: a "Head of State, including any member of a collegial body performing the functions of a Head of State under the constitution of the State concerned, a Head of Government or a Minister for Foreign Affairs, whenever any such person is in a foreign State, as well as members of his family who accompany him." Ibid., art. 1(1)(a).

91. Select Committee to Study Governmental Operations, with Respect to Intelligence Activities, Alleged Assassination Plots Involving Foreign Leaders, Sen. Rep. No. 465, 94th Cong., 1st Sess. (1975).

92. 46 Federal Register 59,941 (1985).

93. Boyd M. Johnson III, "Executive Order 12,333: The Permissibility of an American Assassination of a Foreign Leader," 25 *Cornell International Law Journal* 401 (1992), p. 403.

1. He can declare the existence of hostilities and target persons in command positions as combatants.

2. He can broadly construe Article 51 of the UN Charter and interpret certain criminal acts as legitimating assassination as a use of force in self-defense.

3. He can narrowly construe Executive Order 12,333, for instance, to prohibit only "treacherous" attacks on foreign leaders.

4. He can simply repeal or amend the order, or even approve a one-time exception to it.[94]

The contours of the Executive Order were tested by the 1986 bombing of Libyan leader Colonel Muammar Qaddafi's personal quarters in Tripoli in response to Libyan involvement in the bombing of the La Belle Disco in West Berlin. According to investigative reporter Seymour M. Hersh, who spent three months interviewing more than seventy current and former officials in the White House, the State Department, the CIA, the National Security Agency, and the Pentagon, Qaddafi's assassination was the primary goal of the Libyan bombing.[95] Hersh reported that nine of the eighteen US fighter jets that flew to Tripoli on April 14, 1986, had a specific mission to target Qaddafi and his family.[96] He quoted one well-informed Air Force intelligence officer as stating: "There's no question they were looking for Qaddafi. It was briefed that way. They were going to kill him."[97] The Reagan Administration characterized the attack as a legitimate self-defense operation under Article 51 of the UN Charter in light of evidence that Libya was planning future

94. Ibid., p. 417.
95. Seymour M. Hersh, "Target Qaddafi," *New York Times Magazine* (Feb. 22, 1987), pp. 17–19.
96. Ibid.
97. Ibid., p. 20.

terrorist attacks against the US[98]—an assertion that was rejected by an overwhelming majority of the members of the UN.[99] Shortly thereafter, senior US Army lawyers made public a memorandum that concluded that Executive Order 12,333 was not intended to prevent the US from acting in self-defense against "legitimate threats to national security."[100]

Then, during the Persian Gulf War in 1990, US Air Force Chief of Staff Michael J. Dugan publicly stated that the US might seek to "decapitate" Iraqi leadership by targeting Saddam Hussein, his family, and even his mistress.[101] This statement resulted in a great deal of outrage in the US and abroad, and refocused attention on the permissibility of assassination as an instrument of US policy.[102] Yet, in the aftermath of the Persian Gulf conflict, an increasing number of scholars have suggested that assassination has become a legitimate preemptive strategy in light of the growing destructiveness of cur-

98. President Ronald Reagan, Address to the Nation (Apr. 14, 1986), in *Department of State Bulletin* (Jun. 1986), pp. 1–2.

99. Of traditional US allies, only Britain, Israel, and South Africa supported the raid. Almost every other state, including many US allies, resoundingly rejected the legitimacy of the US reliance on Article 51 as legal authority for the Libya raid. The UN General Assembly adopted a resolution condemning "the armed attack by the United States of America in violation of the Charter of the United Nations and the norms of international law," and the US had to exercise its veto to prevent a similar resolution from being adopted by the Security Council. Stuart G. Baker, "Comparing the 1993 U.S. Airstrike on Iraq to the 1986 Bombing of Libya: The New Interpretation of Article 51," pp. 101, 104.

100. W. Hays Parks, "Memorandum of Law: Executive Order 12,333 and Assassination," p. 8. The Clinton Administration has recently reconfirmed this position. "Deadly Force against Terrorists Is Legal, White House Officials Assert," *Boston Globe* (Oct. 29, 1998), p. A29.

101. Robert F. Turner, "Killing Saddam: Would It Be a Crime?" *Washington Post* (Oct. 7, 1990), p. D1.

102. When Secretary of Defense Richard Cheney learned of Dugan's remarks, he immediately fired him, explaining to reporters that Dugan's comments constituted a potential violation of the US ban on assassination. Boyd M. Johnson, III, "Executive Order 12,333: The Permissibility of an American Assassination of a Foreign Leader," p. 403.

rent weapon technologies.[103] By analogy to the domestic criminal law concept of "necessity,"[104] these commentators argue that assassination can be justified under a balance of harms analysis, provided certain conditions are met, namely:

> First, a state must make a good faith effort to circumscribe potential targets to include only those authoritative persons in the prospective attacking state. Second, the assassination must comply with the settled rules of warfare as they concern discrimination, proportionality, and military necessity. Third, state-gathered intelligence must evidence, beyond a reasonable doubt, preparations for unconventional or other forms of highly destructive warfare projected against the acting state. Finally, the state must have decided after careful deliberation that an assassination would in fact prevent the intended aggression, and that it would cause substantially less harm to civilian populations than alternative forms of self-help.[105]

If self-defense can be subject to abuse, the risk of unleashing the assassination genie from the bottle is even greater. The prohibition on assassination provides protection to the country's own leaders who would be vulnerable to assassination plots by other states. A reversal of this customary restraint "could unleash a chain reaction of transnational assassinations and a substantial breakdown of dip-

---

103. Louis R. Beres, "The Permissibility of State-Sponsored Assassination During Peace and War," p. 240; Michael N. Schmitt, "State-Sponsored Assassination in International and Domestic Law," 17 *Yale Journal International Law* 609 (1992), p. 646; Robert F. Turner, "Killing Saddam: Would It Be a Crime?"

104. See Model Penal Code, Section 3.02 (1985) (providing that conduct believed necessary to avoid some harm is justifiable if "the harm or evil sought to be avoided by such conduct is greater than that sought to be prevented by the law defining the offense charged."); Arnolds and Garland, "The Defense of Necessity in Criminal Law: The Right to Choose the Lesser Evil," 65 *Journal Criminal Law and Criminology* 289 (1974).

105. Louis R. Beres, "The Permissibility of State-Sponsored Assassination During Peace and War," p. 240.

lomatic relations."[106] In addition to the risk of retaliation, targeting specific individuals may unintentionally strengthen enemy morale and resolve. Finally, the targeted individuals are likely to be replaced by others who will continue their threatening policies or even less acceptable alternatives. According to Professor Michael Reisman of Yale Law School, "While tyranicide might present a compelling justification for assassination, assassination in any form presents a cascading threat to world order."[107] For this reason, large numbers of other states are likely to oppose an assassination even if it can be legally justified as a legitimate act of self-defense.

It is noteworthy, however, that there was almost no international opposition to the August 20, 1998, US cruise missile attack against terrorist bases in Khost, Afghanistan, in an attempt to eliminate Osama bin Laden and his lieutenants.[108] International outrage has focused entirely on the attack on the Shifa plant in Sudan, which was launched on the same day.

The prohibitions embodied in the 1908 Hague Convention, the Geneva Protocol, the BWC, and the CWC are directed to the actions of states, not individuals. Although the BCW conventions contain provisions obliging each state-party to prohibit persons under their jurisdiction from undertaking activities that are forbidden by the treaties, these provisions fail to deal with the situation in which an offender is present in a state that has not established or otherwise lacks jurisdiction to prosecute, or is complicit with the offender.[109]

106. Ibid., p. 241.
107. W. Michael Reisman, "Covert Action," 20 *Yale Journal International Law* 419, 424 (1995).
108. CNN Interactive, U.S. Missiles Pound Targets in Afghanistan, Sudan (visited Sept. 16, 1998), at http://cnn.com.US/9808/20/us.strikes.02/index.html.
109. Unlike the "Grave Breaches" provision of the Geneva Convention, there is no universal jurisdiction or a duty to prosecute persons who violate the 1908 Hague Convention, the 1925 Geneva Protocol, the 1972 Biological Weapons Convention, or the 1993 CWC. See Michael P. Scharf, "The Letter of the Law: The Scope of the International Legal Obligation to Prosecute Human Rights Crimes," 59 *Law and Contemporary Problems* 41 (1996).

An approach with great potential which has not yet been pursued is to apply international criminal law to hold the offending leaders responsible and punishable before an international tribunal or domestic courts.

On May 25, 1993, the UN Security Council, acting under Chapter VII of the UN Charter, established the International Criminal Tribunal for the Former Yugoslavia to prosecute persons responsible for war crimes, genocide, and crimes against humanity during the Balkan conflict.[110] This was the first international war crimes tribunal established since the Nuremberg and Tokyo Tribunals following World War II.

During the next two years, the Yugoslavia Tribunal's judges were elected, Rules of Procedure and Evidence were promulgated, a Headquarters Agreement was entered into, the Tribunal's Prosecutor and Registrar were appointed, courtrooms, offices, and a jail were constructed at The Hague, a staff of over 500 persons was hired, seventy persons were indicted, and trials were commenced.[111] The expenses of the Yugoslavia Tribunal ($60 million in 1998) are covered by a combination of the assessed contributions of the member states of the UN and the voluntary contributions of states, international organizations, and private entities.[112]

110. S.C. Res. 827, U.N. SCOR, 48th Sess., p. 29, U.N. Doc. S/INF/49 (1994), reprinted in 2 Morris and Scharf, p. 177. See also the record of the debate leading to the adoption of Resolution 827, U.N. SCOR, 48th Sess., 3217th mtg., p. 16, U.N. Doc. S/PV.3217 (1993), reprinted in 2 Morris and Scharf, pp. 179, 188. Statute of the International Tribunal for the Prosecution of Persons Responsible for Serious Violations of International Humanitarian Law Committed in the Territory of the Former Yugoslavia since 1991, annexed to *United Nations, Report of the Secretary-General Pursuant to Paragraph 2 of Security Council Resolution 808* (1993), U.N. Doc. S/25704 (1993), reprinted in 2 Morris and Scharf, p. 1.

111. See generally 1 Morris and Scharf, *An Insider's Guide to the International Criminal Tribunal for the Former Yugoslavia* (1995).

112. *Third Annual Report of the International Tribunal for the Prosecution of Persons Responsible for Serious Violations of International Humanitarian Law Committed in the Territory of the Former Yugoslavia since 1991,* pp. 43–44, U.N. Doc. A/51/292-S/ 1996/665 (1996).

A year after the Security Council decided to establish an ad hoc tribunal for the former Yugoslavia, it created a second ad hoc tribunal to prosecute those responsible for the genocidal murder of 800,000 members of the Tutsi tribe in the small central African country of Rwanda.[113] The creation of the Rwanda Tribunal demonstrated that the international judicial machinery designed for the Yugoslavia Tribunal could be employed for other specific circumstances and offenses, thereby avoiding the need to "reinvent the wheel" in response to each humanitarian crisis of similar magnitude.

The two ad hoc Tribunals have jurisdiction over, inter alia, violations of the 1908 Hague Convention, which, as stated above, prohibits the use of poisonous weapons, as well as the deployment of weapons "calculated to cause unnecessary suffering." In addition to "use" of BCW, the Tribunals' jurisdiction covers "planning" and "preparation," which would include production and stockpiling.[114] The Security Council could go even further and expressly endow a new ad hoc tribunal with additional subject-matter jurisdiction covering breaches of the BWC and the CWC, in addition to the 1908 Hague Convention.[115]

On March 13, 1998, the US Senate passed Concurrent Resolution 78 by a vote of 93 to 0, "call[ing] for the United Nations to form an international criminal tribunal for the purpose of indicting, prosecuting, and imprisoning Saddam Hussein and any other Iraqi

---

113. Statute of the International Tribunal for Rwanda, annexed to S.C. Res. 955, U.N. SCOR, 49th Sess., p. 20, U.N. Doc. S/INF/50 (1996), reprinted in 2 Morris and Scharf, p. 3.

114. Yugoslavia Tribunal Statute, art. 7(1); Rwanda Tribunal Statute, art. 6(1).

115. Given the large number of parties, these conventions could be said to reflect customary international law. But even if they do not, it is perfectly fair to use them as the basis of an international court's subject-matter jurisdiction if the country where the acts were committed is a party to them.

officials who may be found responsible for . . . violations of international humanitarian law."[116] The Iraqi situation (including the production, stockpiling, and use of BCW) would seem to be an ideal candidate for a third tribunal to be created by the Security Council. After all, the Security Council has repeatedly condemned Iraq's violations of international humanitarian law and in particular violations of the conventions prohibiting BCW. It has warned Iraq that individuals, as well as the government of Iraq, would be held liable for such violations. It has called on member states to submit information of Iraqi violations of international humanitarian law committed during the Gulf War,[117] and it has established a commission to document subsequent Iraqi violations of the BCW conventions.[118]

It is important to bear in mind that the effectiveness of such a tribunal does not require that the violating state be vanquished and that the victor state(s) have custody of those accused of violating the BCW conventions. There is utility, for example, in obtaining an international indictment of Saddam Hussein, even if (as would undoubtedly be the case) Iraq refused to surrender him to an international tribunal for trial. The indictment would render Hussein a virtual prisoner in his own country, given the prospect of arrest if he stepped outside its borders.[119] Thus, the procedures for indictment and the issuance of arrest warrants set forth in the Statute and Rules of the ad hoc International Criminal Tribunals may be used to stig-

116. See 144 *Cong. Rec.* S1907-05.

117. S.C. Res. 674 (1990).

118. S.C. Res. 687, U.N. SCOR, 46th Sess., 2981st metg., U.N. Doc. S/RES/ 687 (1991), para. 8.

119. Michael Scharf and Valerie Epps, "The International Trial of the Century? A 'Cross Fire' Exchange on the First Case Before the Yugoslavia War Crimes Tribunal," 29 *Cornell International Law Journal* 635 (1996), p. 661; Remarks of Dr. Roy S. Lee, Principal Legal Officer at the United Nations, Office of the Legal Counsel, "Symposium on War Crimes Tribunal," 6 *Pace International Law Review* 93 (1994), p. 101.

matize and constrain accused persons, even if the accused cannot be arrested and tried immediately. Moreover, the Tribunal's process for confirmation of indictments, which has been described as akin to a "televised grand jury proceeding,"[120] would go a long way in documenting the international violations.

Yet, the other members of the Security Council have resisted US proposals for the establishment of additional ad hoc tribunals. There are several reasons why the Security Council has been unwilling or unable to continue with the ad hoc approach to international criminal justice that was employed for Yugoslavia and Rwanda. The first reason, which is sometimes referred to as "tribunal fatigue," is that the process of reaching a consensus on a tribunal's statute, electing judges, selecting a prosecutor, and appropriating funds has turned out to be extremely time-consuming and politically exhausting for the members of the Security Council.[121] At least one Permanent Member of the Security Council—China—has openly expressed concern about using the Yugoslavia Tribunal as precedent for the creation of other ad hoc criminal tribunals.[122] Second, the creation of ad hoc tribunals by the Council is viewed as inherently unfair by many countries because the Permanent Members of the Security Council can veto any substantive action by the Council and thereby shield themselves and their allies from the jurisdiction of such tribunals, notwithstanding any atrocities that

120. Michael P. Scharf, *Balkan Justice: The Story Behind the First International War Crimes Trial Since Nuremberg* (Durham, NC: Carolina Academic Press, 1997), p. 151.

121. See 1 Morris and Scharf, pp. 33–34 (explaining compromises necessary to gain support for the statute), 144–45 (describing difficulties in electing judges), 161–63 (discussing controversy in appointing the prosecutor).

122. See ibid., p. 344, n. 901, quoting statement of Mr. Li Zhaoxing of China at the time of voting on Security Council Resolution 827 (1993), which established the Yugoslavia Tribunal. U.N. Doc. S/PV.3217, 25 May 1993, pp. 33–34. China later abstained on Security Council Resolution 955 (1994), which established the Rwanda Tribunal.

might be committed within their borders. The final reason for the reluctance to create additional ad hoc tribunals is economic; that is, the expense of establishing ad hoc tribunals is simply seen as too much for an organization whose budget is already stretched too thin.

With the overwhelming approval of the Rome Statute for a Permanent International Criminal Court in July 1998,[123] it is unlikely that the members of the Security Council would be willing to support the establishment of an ad hoc tribunal to prosecute persons responsible for producing, transferring, stockpiling, or using BCW in Iraq or elsewhere. Instead, they would insist that such persons be prosecuted before the new Permanent International Criminal Court. However, with US opposition to the Permanent International Criminal Court,[124] the new tribunal's fate remains in doubt. At a minimum, it will be several years, perhaps as long as a decade, before the Statute for a Permanent International Criminal Court receives the required sixty ratifications to enter into force. Even when the Permanent Court is established, its jurisdiction over use of BCW will be largely restricted to cases of an international armed conflict.[125] Further, the jurisdiction of the Permanent Court would

123. Rome Statute of the International Criminal Court, U.N. Doc. A/CONF.183/9, 17 July 1998. The Statute was approved by a vote of 120 to 7, with 20 abstentions. Of the Permanent Members of the Security Council, the US and China voted against; France, Russia, and the UK voted in favor.

124. Michael P. Scharf, "Results of the Rome Conference for an International Criminal Court," *American Society International Law Insight* (Aug. 1998); Prepared Statement of Professor Michael P. Scharf Before the Senate Foreign Relations Committee," *Federal News Service* (Jul. 23, 1998) (available in Lexis, CURNWS File); Thomas W. Lippman, "Why the U.S. Objects to a World Criminal Court," *Washington Post* (Jul. 26, 1998), p. C1.

125. The Permanent International Criminal Court would have jurisdiction over "serious violations of the laws and customs applicable in international armed conflict" including:

(xvii) Employing poison or poisoned weapons;(xviii) Employing asphyxiating, poisonous or other gases, and all analogous liquids, materials or devices;(xx) Employing weapons, projectiles and material and methods of warfare which are of a nature to cause superfluous injury or unnecessary suffering or which are inherently indiscriminate in

not apply to the production, transfer, or stockpiling of such weapons unless they are ultimately used in combat.[126]

In the absence of a new ad hoc tribunal or a Permanent International Criminal Court, individual states can accomplish many of the same goals through the exercise of extraterritorial criminal jurisdiction over persons who violate the BCW conventions. The US recently enacted legislation that takes a step in this direction.[127] Section 2332a of title 18 the United States Code provides that any person "without lawful authority" shall be punished if that person uses, threatens, or attempts or conspires to use a weapon of mass destruction, including any biological agent, toxin, or vector, against a national of the US while such national is outside or within the US.[128] Section 2332c of the same title provides that any person "without lawful authority" shall be punished if that person uses, or attempts or conspires to use a CW against a US national while such

---

violation of the international law of armed conflict, provided that such weapons, projectiles and material and methods of warfare are subject of a comprehensive prohibition. Rome Statute of the International Criminal Court, art. 8(2)(b)(xvii), (xviii), and (xx). art. 8(2)(e)(i), U.N. Doc. A/CONF.183/9, 17 July 1998. In the case of an internal armed conflict, the Court has jurisdiction over, inter alia, persons responsible for "intentionally directing attacks against the civilian population as such or against individual civilians not taking direct part in hostilities." Ibid., art. 8(2)(e)(i).

126. Ibid., art. 25.

127. The provisions creating US jurisdiction over biological and chemical weapons attacks against US nationals were part of a package of antiterrorism provisions enacted in the aftermath of the bombing of the Alfred P. Murrah Federal Building on April 19, 1995, in Oklahoma City. See Roberta Smith, "America Tries to Come to Terms with Terrorism: The United States Anti-Terrorism and Effective Death Penalty Act of 1996 v. British Anti-Terrorism Law and International Response," 5 *Cardozo Journal International and Comparative Law* 249 (1997), pp. 260–62; Thomas C. Martin, "The Comprehensive Terrorism Prevention Act of 1995," 20 *Seton Hall Legislative Journal* 201 (1995), pp. 205–6. There is scant legislative history for the provisions on BCW, which at the time were not viewed as among the more important aspects of the legislation. See 1996 *U.S. Code Cong. and Admin. News* 924, 952–53, 955, 961–62.

128. 18 U.S.C. § 2332a.

national is outside or within the US.[129] These criminal provisions are based on the "passive personality" theory of jurisdiction; they provide jurisdiction to the US based on the nationality of the victim.[130]

A person such as Saddam Hussein would have several potential defenses to criminal proceedings under 18 U.S.C. §§ 2332a and 2332c. First, the law does not cover production or stockpiling; it covers only the *use* of BCW—and then only when such use is against a US citizen. On the other hand, production and stockpiling could be deemed overt acts that are part of a conspiracy to use such weapons, which is covered. Second, as leader of Iraq, Hussein's decision to order the production, stockpiling, or use of BCW would be within the scope of his presidential authority, thereby falling outside the statute's prohibition. However, since such acts are in violation of international law, a court might conclude that true "lawful authority" is absent. Finally, Saddam Hussein could rely on the doctrine of head-of-state immunity to quash an indictment brought under this statute while he continues to serve as President of Iraq.[131] However, recent cases involving Ferdinand Marcos of the Philippines, Manuel Noriega of Panama, and Radovan Karadzic of Bosnia[132] suggest that US courts might find the doctrine inapplica-

---

129. 18 U.S.C. § 2332c.

130. See generally, Geoffrey R. Watson, "The Passive Personality Principle," 28 *Texas International Law Journal* 1 (1993).

131. See Shobha Varughese George, "Head-of-State Immunity in the United States Courts: Still Confused After All These Years," 64 *Fordham Law Review* 1051 (1995).

132. See Doe v. United States, 860 F.2d 40, 45 (2nd Cir. 1988)("[T]here is respectable authority for denying head-of-state immunity to a former head-of-state for private or criminal acts in violation of American law."); U.S. v. Noriega, 746 F.Supp. 1506, 1519, n.11 (S.D. Fla. 1990) ("[T]here is ample doubt whether head of state immunity extends to private or criminal acts in violation of U.S. law."). Cf. Doe v. Karadzic, 866 F. Supp. 734 (S.D.N.Y. 1994) ("[W]e doubt that the acts of even a state official, taken in violation of a nation's fundamental law and wholly unratified by that nation's government, could properly be characterized as an act of

ble in a criminal case involving flagrant violations of international and US law.[133]

The Harvard-Sussex Program on Chemical and Biological Warfare Armament and Arms Limitation has proposed a "Convention on the Prevention and Punishment of the Crime of Developing, Producing, Acquiring, Stockpiling, Retaining, Transferring or Using Biological or Chemical Weapons" (Harvard Draft Convention; see *CBW Conventions Bulletin*, December 1998). The Harvard Draft Convention is modeled on the several antiterrorism conventions that provide for universal jurisdiction and require states to either prosecute or extradite (*aut dedere aut judicare*) offenders found within their territory.[134]

---

state."). But see Lafontant v. Aristide, 844 F. Supp. 128, 138 (E.D.N.Y. 1994) (rejecting the dicta of Doe v. United States and finding that such a "theory for circumventing head-of-state immunity is unacceptable").

133. Head-of-state immunity is based on the doctrine of comity. Thus, US courts traditionally defer to the State Department's view as to whether head-of-state immunity should apply in a particular case. Shobha Varughese George, "Head-of-State Immunity in the United States Courts: Still Confused After All These Years," pp. 1061, 1067. In contrast to a civil suit brought by a private party, in a criminal matter brought by the US a court should assume, even without specific State Department guidance, that the US government has weighed the foreign policy implications and determined that head-of-state immunity would be inappropriate under the circumstances.

134. See Convention for the Suppression of Unlawful Acts Against the Safety of Marine Navigation (1988), 27 *International Legal Materials* 672; Convention Against Torture and Other Cruel, Inhuman or Degrading Treatment or Punishment (1984), 23 *International Legal Materials* 1027, 24 *International Legal Materials* 535; Convention on the Physical Protection of Nuclear Material (1980), 18 *International Legal Materials* 1422, T.I.A.S. 11080; International Convention Against the Taking of Hostages (1979), T.I.A.S. 11080; Convention on the Prevention of Crimes Against Internationally Protected Persons, Including Diplomatic Agents (1973), 28 U.S.T. 1975, T.I.A.S. 8532, 1035 U.N.T.S. 167; Convention for the Suppression of Unlawful Acts Against the Safety of Civil Aviation (1971), 25 U.S.T. 564, T.I.A.S. 7570; Convention for the Suppression of Unlawful Seizure of Aircraft (1970), 22 U.S.T. 1641, T.I.A.S. 7192, 860 U.N.T.S. 105. The latest antiterrorism convention with the prosecute or extradite formula is the International Convention for the Suppression of Terrorist Bombings, which was opened for signature in January 1998. A/Res/52/164.

The Harvard Draft Convention avoids the deficiencies inherent in the current US legislation in three ways. First, the Harvard Draft Convention is based on the notion of "universal jurisdiction" rather than "passive personality jurisdiction," that is, it would provide state-parties jurisdiction over individual offenders present in their territory irrespective of any nexus to the offense. Like pirates, those who violate the international prohibitions related to BCW would thereby become "hostis humani generis" (an enemy of all humankind). Any state-party in which such persons are found would have a duty "without exception whatsoever" to either prosecute or extradite the alleged offender to another state or international tribunal for prosecution. Second, the Harvard Draft Convention would explicitly cover development, production, stockpiling, and transfer, as well as actual use of biological or chemical weapons. Third, it expressly provides that head-of-state or diplomatic immunity is inapplicable to these crimes,[135] and denies the defense of superior orders.[136]

---

135. Other international conventions that exempt offenders from claiming diplomatic or head-of-state immunity include: Convention on the Prevention and Punishment of the Crime of Genocide (1948), art. 4, 78 U.N.T.S. 277 ("Persons committing genocide or any of the other acts enumerated . . . shall be punished, whether they are constitutionally responsible rulers, public officials or private individuals."); and International Convention on the Suppression and Punishment of the International Crime of Apartheid (1973), 28 U.N. GAOR, Supp. No. 30, U.N. Doc. A/9030 ("International criminal responsibility shall apply, irrespective of the motive involved, to individuals, members of organizations and institutions and representatives of the State"). The Statutes of the International Criminal Tribunals for the former Yugoslavia and Rwanda similarly provide "The official position of any accused person, whether as head of State or Government or as a responsible Government official, shall not relieve such person of criminal responsibility nor mitigate punishment." *Statute of the International Tribunal for the Prosecution of Persons Responsible for Serious Violations of International Humanitarian Law Committed in the Territory of the Former Yugoslavia since 1991*, art. 7(2), annexed to *United Nations, Report of the Secretary-General Pursuant to Paragraph 2 of Security Council Resolution 808* (1993), U.N. Doc. S/25704 (1993), reprinted in 2 Morris and Scharf, p. 31; Statute of the International Tribunal for Rwanda, art. 6(2), annexed to S.C. Res. 955, U.N. SCOR,

Although it would certainly help close the gap between the international law prohibiting BCW and the enforcement of that law, the Harvard Draft Convention should not be viewed as a panacea. In light of past politically motivated false accusations of violations of the BCW conventions,[137] proceedings before domestic courts exercising universal jurisdiction may not possess the same credibility or carry with them the same international reprobation as proceedings before a neutral international tribunal. A second weakness inherent in a regime requiring domestic prosecutions concerns protection of sensitive intelligence sources and methods. It is one thing to share satellite surveillance photos, telephone intercepts, and information gathered by undercover operatives with other governments in a closed session of the Security Council (as may be necessary to justify use of force or imposition of sanctions); it is quite

---

49th Sess., p. 20, U.N. Doc. S/INF/50 (1996), reprinted in 2 Morris and Scharf, p. 5.

136. The illegitimacy of the defense of superior orders for international crimes was recognized in the Charter of the Nuremberg Tribunal and has been reaffirmed in the Statutes of the International Criminal Tribunals for the Former Yugoslavia and Rwanda. See 1 Morris and Scharf, pp. 262–68. Current U.S. law, in contrast, recognizes the defense of superior orders unless manifestly illegal, that is "a man of ordinary sense and understanding" would know the order was illegal. See United States v. Calley, 1973 W.L. 14894 (CMA), 48 C.M.R. 19, 22 USCMA 534 (U.S. Court of Military Appeals, 1973); see also Jordan J. Paust, et al., *International Criminal Law: Cases and Materials* (Durham, NC: Carolina Academic Press, 1996), 1373–76.

137. For years, the US government maintained that it had evidence of Soviet responsibility for the use of biological weapons known as "yellow rain" in Indochina from 1982 to 86. See Raymond A. Zilinskas, "Review of the Diplomacy of Biological Disarmament: Vicissitudes of a Treaty in Force, 1975–85, by Nicholas A. Sims." While many commentators continue to cite the yellow rain episode as a breach of the BWC, there is reason to believe that the story was fabricated by the US as part of its Cold-War disinformation campaign and as a way to justify further US biowar research and handsome congressional appropriations. Julian Robinson, Jeanne Guillemin, and Matthew Meselson, "Yellow Rain in Southeast Asia: The Story Collapses," in Susan Wright, ed., *Preventing a Biological Arms Race* (Cambridge, MA: MIT Press, 1990).

another to have to divulge such information in open court as would be required in a criminal prosecution.[138] Finally, international adoption of the Harvard Draft Convention would have a significant deterrent effect, but it could no more guarantee an end to all BCW use than the Genocide Convention[139] has prevented outbreaks of genocide in the years since its adoption in 1948.[140]

Conclusion

There have so far been three main stages in the evolution of international law governing BCW. First, there was the establishment of the prohibition of these weapons—a prohibition that is now recognized as customary international law. Second, there was the expansion and fortification of the prohibition through the filling of gaps. Third, there was the creation of verification regimes, enabling the international community to detect and publicize noncompliance. To retain vitality, the prohibition on BCW requires that there be an expectation of consequences to its violation. Thus, the next stage in the evolution will focus on strengthening the means of enforcement.

The traditional means of enforcement relies on the UN Security Council, which has the ability to impose a range of sanctions and even authorize the use of force to enforce the international prohi-

138. This prospect may deter governments from making extradition requests or indicting persons for violations of the BCW conventions.

139. Convention on the Prevention and Punishment of the Crime of Genocide, 9 Dec 1948, 78 U.N.T.S. 277.

140. The existence of the widely ratified Genocide Convention, with its similar universal jurisdiction regime and extradite or prosecute requirement, did not prevent the extermination of 750,000 Ugandans (1971–87), the annihilation of 2 million Cambodians (1975–79), the massacre of 200,000 East Timorans (1971–1987), the gassing of 100,000 Kurds in Iraq (1987–88), the slaughter of 250,000 Muslims in Bosnia (1992–95), or the mass murder of 800,000 Tutsis in Rwanda (1994). See Michael P. Scharf, *Balkan Justice: The Story Behind the First International War Crimes Trial since Nuremberg*, pp. xiii–xiv.

bition on BCW, as it has done against Iraq. However, the Security Council's robust response to Iraq's possession of BCW in the aftermath of its invasion of Kuwait has been the exception. More often, the Security Council has been paralyzed by the threat or use of the veto by the permanent members, and has taken no action in response to repeated violations of the BCW conventions.

In light of the Security Council's repeated failure to take effective action to eliminate the threat posed by a state's possession of BCW, states may increasingly be tempted to act unilaterally, following the example of the US attack on the Sudanese chemical plant in August 1998. However weak the evidence concerning the Shifa plant turns out to be, the attack sets an important precedent on which states may choose to rely in dealing with terrorist or state-sponsored BCW threats. There are very real risks to expanding the interpretation of Article 51 of the UN Charter to permit attacks on suspected BCW facilities, and even more so with respect to assassination of leaders who are responsible for using such weapons and pose a continuing threat. But at some point, the danger to international stability created by radical leaders such as Saddam Hussein, who are permitted to use BCW with impunity, exceeds the danger posed by the potential for nations to abuse an expanded interpretation of Article 51 for their own illegitimate ends.[141]

Thus, deterrence and enforcement of the BCW conventions presently rely on the threat or imposition of sanctions or military force, both of which are blunt instruments that tend to harm innocent populations and infrequently succeed in altering the policies of the responsible rulers. A third means of enforcement, which would supplement (rather than replace) the traditional approaches, is to apply international criminal law to hold the offending leaders re-

141. Stuart G. Baker, "Comparing the 1993 U.S. Airstrike on Iraq to the 1986 Bombing of Libya: The New Interpretation of Article 51," p. 116.

sponsible and punishable in domestic courts or international tribunals.

The international criminalization of BCW violations through the establishment of ad hoc international tribunals and/or a regime of universal jurisdiction (using the Harvard Draft Convention as a model) would have many benefits. It would potentially strengthen the norm against BCW, enhance deterrence of potential offenders, and facilitate international cooperation in suppressing the prohibited activities. Unlike sanctions and use of force, criminalization avoids collective punishment by directly targeting those responsible for the international violations. In addition, criminalization can strengthen international political will to maintain sanctions and take more aggressive actions if necessary. A criminal indictment can also serve to isolate offending leaders diplomatically and strengthen the hand of domestic political rivals.[142] Just imagine if every time Saddam Hussein's name appeared in the international press, it was followed by the moniker "indicted international criminal."

Ultimately, the success of the anti-BCW regimes requires the reestablishment of what, to paraphrase author Richard Price, can be called the "BCW taboo."[143] The addition of criminalization to the existing means of enforcement will go a long way toward that end.

142. This has proven effective with respect to Radovan Karadzic, the once powerful leader of the Bosnian Serbs who has been forced into hiding and politically marginalized by the international indictment and warrant for his arrest. See Interview with General William Nash, former Commander of the US forces in Bosnia (Sep. 29, 1998), Cambridge, MA (transcript on file with the author).
143. See Richard M. Price, *The Chemical Weapons Taboo*.

Commentary

The ultimate goal of national policy concerning BCW is prevention. To *prevent* attacks, the US and other target nations need effectively to *deter*, through a combination of threats, sanctions, and self defense. The conference panel on deterrence brought together some of the leading thinkers on this subject. The chapters by Richard N. Haass and Scott D. Sagan provide some key insights into the potential utility and dangers of ambiguity with regard to the possible use of nuclear weapons (NW). Most comments favored continuing a policy of ambiguity in this regard, but the grave risks of actually resorting to NW were forcefully advanced. Based on other discussions at the conference, the empirical case for credible non-NW threats in order to deter BCW use was strongly demonstrated.

In commentary on the Haass-Sagan exchange, Ariel Levite

noted that the threat of NW related to state action, and that when it comes to terrorists, we cannot seem to do much in the way of deterrence. With respect to rogue state actors, such as Iraq, he noted that the threats made between 1991 and February 1998 by all the relevant leaders—Israelis, Americans, British, and so on—shifted from more general statements to explicit attempts to try to deter BW and CW attacks. In all cases, moreover, while the target of such threats became more explicit, the type of response threatened was kept deliberately ambiguous. The terms of the threats use almost the same terminology: that responses to BCW use are to be swift, devastating, or even "overwhelming." Levite observed that: "Basically, nothing is ruled out. No one said anything about 'nukes,' but no one ruled out anything. The statements implied that we could use whatever was at our disposal. The threats have, moreover, been very much *public* threats." Finally, he noted, the threats against Iraq all suggest an element of automaticity and an element of disproportionality:

> That is, the threatened responses to BCW attack were automatically to be immediate and very stiff punishments. My assessment is that these kinds of statements worked and will continue to work. They worked because they convinced Saddam that there was a lot to be lost from actually engaging in BW and CW use against Israel, against the coalition forces, and against other countries in the region.

Levite addressed the suggestion that the threats against BCW use led to Saddam's predelegation of BCW decision-making authority to his trusted commanders. This issue, he argued, is much more complicated than has been assumed, because we now know that in some cases Saddam did not realize he was making decisions he would not be able to reverse given allied disruption of his communications command. The overwhelming success of the strategy of the US in managing the campaign made many of Saddam's decisions irreversible once he chose, for instance, not to deploy his chemical capability in the battlefield. "At the end of the day," Levite said:

> there are some qualities you cannot take away from even the ambiguous references to NW that have been discussed, or to the idea that they are not ruled out. NW communicate the gravity of a situation in a manner that nothing else does—basically saying: 'This is unacceptable.' It does not mean that the US would use NW, but it means that the US views BCW sufficiently gravely, to the point that it does not rule out anything. That is the message that one wants to communicate to Saddam and his ilk.

Levite also asserted the importance of holding leaders personally accountable, especially for crimes against humanity. This may be the one positive thing to learn from the tragic experience in the former Yugoslavia. "We must emphasize personal accountability—that eventually, wherever, we will catch up to, try, and punish the bad actors. I think that is an important message." With respect to defensive measures, he agreed with Haass' suggestions, and added that we need to give more attention to missile intercepts:

> Whoever wants to launch something against you should calculate that it is going to blow over his head as distinguished from over your territory. That is a quality that nobody can disregard, no matter how irrational, how crazy. It also makes legitimate using something that one would otherwise not use. Perhaps it is the most potent deterrence means available. And it does not actually have to work every time. The other side should know that there is a potential that it will blow over its own territory and that the resulting destruction is thus of its own doing. That is the only thing that is required.

Levite agreed that the utility of conventional attacks was limited "because one is torn between a situation where decapitation strategy becomes so difficult because of lack of intelligence, on the one hand, and massive retaliation or collateral damage on the other. That is why we are left with some very esoteric options—deep, buried penetration capability and things of that nature." He suggested continued cooperation with other states to reduce proliferation of BCW, and global pools, or at least pools among like-minded nations, of antibiotics, vaccines, experts, information, and so on, because the costs associated with, and limitations on possible deployment, make it unrealistic to expect that any county—even the US—can do it alone.

Michael Scharf's comprehensive review of defensive options in his chapter on sanctions and self-defense provided the legal backdrop against which strategists and political leaders function. One clear message that emerges from Scharf's discussion is that the international-law right of self-defense permits states to take unilateral action against suspected BCW facilities such as the US did against the Shifa plant in Sudan in August 1998. Where sufficient evidence of BCW exists, Scharf strongly advocates the full-bodied resort to such action in order to provide credibility to the desirable norms against the development, possession, and use of BCW.

Gidon Gottlieb's comments on Scharf's paper strongly endorsed his views of the permissible range of self-defense options, particularly the need to prevent the BCW threat even to materialize. He addressed specifically how the US should act with regard to the BCW threat, contending that it will act unilaterally (and not only multilaterally) when it is serious about getting something accomplished, as in the enforcement of securities, tax, narcotics, and piracy and slave-trade prohibitions. He cited President Truman's declaration of jurisdictional authority over the sea bed as an example of precedent creation through unilateral conduct, which led to other states following suit. Similarly, in dealing with BCW, the US "can issue influential, unilateral declarations, schedules of suspected materials, lists of suspected sites and facilities, making an effort at the same time to have other, like-minded countries do the same to-gether with us. It need not be universal." In addition, "we can certainly take action against foreign corporations and their officers that are training or assisting or developing the trade in BCW materials, and we can do the same for foreign professionals, scientists whom we suspect of being engaged in BCW-related activities." These people, he argued, should be seized in the same way the US presently seizes major narcotics violators. Retaliation is always a possibility when such actions are taken, but Gottlieb could not see "how we can delegate criminal law enforcement to international agencies and tribunals, which are essentially symbolic enterprises that can take action against only a limited number of individuals, and then only well after the event." These measures can in fact mitigate the need for the use of force in self-defense. Insofar as defensive actions are concerned, Gottlieb argued that the US could not be expected to meet an evidentiary standard like "beyond a reasonable doubt." Countries that "permit the development of BCW plants should bear the burden of proof that those facilities and installations are indeed harmless." In short, he advocated that we "think of our legal order as a way of liberating us to take the actions that are necessary for our survival, rather than limiting or restraining necessary actions in the face of the horrendous challenge of BCW."

Appendix

Conference Agenda
and Participants

HOOVER INSTITUTION CONFERENCE
Biological and Chemical Weapons (BCW)

Stauffer Auditorium
Hoover Institution
Stanford University
Stanford, California
November 16–18, 1998

Agenda

Monday, November 16, 1998

1:30 PM *Welcome and Introduction*
      John Raisian and George P. Shultz,
      Hoover Institution

1:45 PM *Session 1—Dimensions of the Problem*
     CHAIR: Sidney D. Drell,
      Stanford Linear Accelerator Center

    A. Chemical Weapons
      Michael L. Moodie, Chemical and Biological Arms
        Control Institute
    B. Biological Weapons
      Steven M. Block, Princeton University
    C. Intelligence: Warning and Detection
      Gordon C. Oehler, Science Applications
        International Corporation (SAIC)
    D. Attack Scenarios, Past and Future
      Dean A. Wilkening, Center for International Security
        and Cooperation, Stanford

3:30 PM BREAK

3:45 PM *Session 2—Dimensions of the Problem* (continued)
      Special Presentation: Rolf Ekéus, Embassy of Sweden
        (former Executive Chairman of UNSCOM)
      DISCUSSION: Session 1 participants and
        John A. Lauder, Nonproliferation Center, US CIA
        Lucy Shapiro, Stanford Medical Center

5:00 PM BREAK

6:30 PM RECEPTION AND DINNER, Stanford Faculty Club
      INTRODUCTION: George P. Shultz, Hoover Institution
      "The Role of Intelligence in Protecting
        Against BCW"
      SPEAKER: John C. Gannon, Chairman, US National
        Intelligence Council

Tuesday, November 17, 1998

9:00 AM *Session 3—Regulation of BCW*
        CHAIR: Abraham D. Sofaer, Hoover Institution and
        Stanford Law School

A. Current Status of BCW Treaties and Related Regimes
Jonathan B. Tucker, Monterey Institute of
International Studies
DISCUSSION:
John C. Yoo, University of California, Boalt Hall
Michael P. Scharf, New England School of Law
Robin Jo Frank, Legal Adviser's Office,
US Department of State

10:30 AM BREAK

10:45 AM *Session 4—Regulation of BCW* (continued)
CHAIR: Paul A. Brest, Stanford Law School
B. Legal Authority Concerning Intelligence, Inspection, and
Prevention
Lewis Libby, Dechert, Price and Rhoads,
Washington, DC (Department of Defense Role)
John C. Yoo, University of California, Boalt Hall
(Constitutional Issues)
DISCUSSION:
Pamela S. Karlan, Stanford Law School
Ronald D. Lee, US Department of Justice
Amy E. Smithson, Henry L. Stimson Center

12:30 PM LUNCH

1:45 PM *Session 5—Preparing for BCW Attacks*
CHAIR: Thomas P. Monath, OraVax, Inc.
C. Protection, Medical Response, and Cleanup
Robert F. Knouss, US Office of Emergency
Preparedness
Ariel E. Levite, Ministry of Defense of Israel

DISCUSSION:

Donald Prosnitz, Lawrence Livermore National Laboratory

Lucy S. Tompkins, Stanford Medical Center

Frances E. Winslow, Director, Emergency Services, San Jose, CA

3:30 PM BREAK

3:45 PM *Session 6—Preventing the Use of BCW*
CHAIR: Condoleezza Rice, Provost, Stanford University
A. *Strategies for Enhanced Deterrence and Defense*
Richard N. Haass, Brookings Institution
Scott D. Sagan, Center for International Security and Cooperation, Stanford
DISCUSSION:
Ariel E. Levite, Ministry of Defense of Israel

5:15 PM BREAK

6:30 PM RECEPTION AND DINNER, Stanford Barn
INTRODUCTION: John Raisian, Hoover Institution
"Two Incidents and the New Containment"
SPEAKER: Richard J. Danzig, Secretary of the Navy, US Department of Defense

Wednesday November 18, 1998

9:00 AM *Session 7—Preventing the Use of BCW* (continued)
CHAIR: Charles Hill, Hoover Institution and Yale University
B. *International Inspections and Remedies*
Tibor Tóth, Ad Hoc Group, Biological Weapons Convention Protocol

DISCUSSION:
Jonathan B. Tucker, Monterey Institute of
International Studies
Alan P. Zelicoff, Sandia National Laboratories

10:15 AM BREAK

10:30 AM *Session 8—Preventing the Use of BCW* (continued)
CHAIR: Abraham D. Sofaer, Hoover Institution and
Stanford Law School
C. *Sanctions and Self-Defense*
Michael P. Scharf, New England School of Law
DISCUSSION:
Sidney D. Drell, Stanford Linear Accelerator Center
Gidon Gottlieb, Hoover Institution and University of
Chicago School of Law

12:00 PM CONFERENCE CLOSES

Conference Participants

Steven M. Block—Professor, Molecular Biology Department, Princeton University

Paul A. Brest—Dean and Lange Professor, Stanford Law School

Richard J. Danzig—Secretary of the Navy, US Department of Defense

Sidney D. Drell—Senior Fellow, Hoover Institution, and Professor, Stanford Linear Accelerator Center (*BCW Conference Co-Chair*)

Rolf Ekéus—Ambassador of the Kingdom of Sweden to the United

States of America, and formerly Executive Chairman, United Nations Special Commission (UNSCOM)

Robin Jo Frank—Attorney Adviser, Office of Political-Military Affairs, Office of the Legal Adviser, US Department of State

John C. Gannon—Chairman, US National Intelligence Council

Gidon Gottlieb—Distinguished Visiting Fellow, Hoover Institution, and Professor, University of Chicago School of Law

Richard N. Haass—Director, Foreign Policy Studies, Brookings Institution

Charles Hill—Senior Research Fellow, Hoover Institution, and Diplomat in Residence, International Security Studies, Center for International and Area Studies, Yale University

Pamela S. Karlan—Professor, Stanford Law School

Robert F. Knouss—Director, Office of Emergency Preparedness, US Public Health Service, US Department of Health and Human Services

John A. Lauder—Director, DCI Nonproliferation Center, and Special Assistant to the Director of Central Intelligence, US Central Intelligence Agency

Ronald D. Lee—Associate Deputy Attorney General, Office of the Deputy Attorney General, US Department of Justice

Ariel E. Levite—Principal Deputy Director, Directorate for Foreign Affairs, Arms Control and Regional Security, Ministry of Defense of Israel

Lewis Libby—Member, Law Firm of Dechert, Price, and Rhoads, Washington, DC

Thomas P. Monath—Vice President, Research and Medical Affairs, OraVax, Inc.

Michael L. Moodie—President, Chemical and Biological Arms Control Institute

Gordon C. Oehler—Corporate Vice President for Corporate Development, Science Applications International Corporation

Donald Prosnitz—Senior Scientist, Nonproliferation, Arms Control, and International Security Division, Lawrence Livermore National Laboratory

John Raisian—Director and Senior Fellow, Hoover Institution

Condoleezza Rice—Provost and Professor, Department of Political Science, Stanford University

Scott D. Sagan—Co-Director, Center for International Security and Cooperation, and Associate Professor, Department of Political Science, Stanford University

Michael P. Scharf—Professor and Director, Center for International Law and Policy, New England School of Law

Lucy Shapiro—Ludwig Professor of Developmental Biology, Stanford University Medical Center

George P. Shultz—Distinguished Fellow, Hoover Institution

Amy E. Smithson—Senior Associate and Director, Chemical and Biological Weapons Nonproliferation Project, Henry L. Stimson Center

Abraham D. Sofaer—George P. Shultz Senior Fellow, Hoover Institution (*BCW Conference Co-Chair*)

Lucy S. Tompkins—Professor, Microbiology and Immunology Department and Infectious Diseases Department, Stanford University Medical Center

Tibor Tóth—Permanent Representative and Ambassador of the Republic of Hungary to the United Nations, Vienna, and Chairman, Ad Hoc Group of Governmental Experts

Jonathan B. Tucker— Director, Chemical and Biological Weapons Nonproliferation Project, Center for Nonproliferation Studies, Monterey Institute of International Studies

Dean A. Wilkening—Director, Science Program, Center for International Security and Cooperation, Stanford University

George D. Wilson—Research Fellow, Hoover Institution (*Assistant to BCW Conference Co-Chairs*)

Frances E. Winslow—Director, Office of Emergency Services, City of San Jose, California

John C. Yoo—Acting Professor, Boalt Hall School of Law, University of California at Berkeley

Alan P. Zelicoff—Senior Scientist, National Security and Policy Planning Department, Sandia National Laboratories

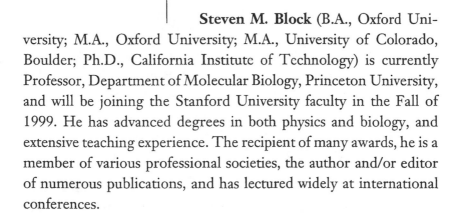

Contributors

Steven M. Block (B.A., Oxford University; M.A., Oxford University; M.A., University of Colorado, Boulder; Ph.D., California Institute of Technology) is currently Professor, Department of Molecular Biology, Princeton University, and will be joining the Stanford University faculty in the Fall of 1999. He has advanced degrees in both physics and biology, and extensive teaching experience. The recipient of many awards, he is a member of various professional societies, the author and/or editor of numerous publications, and has lectured widely at international conferences.

Paul A. Brest (A.B., Swarthmore College; J.D., Harvard Law School; Honorary Doctor of Laws, Northeastern University; Honorary Doctor of Laws, Swarthmore College) is Richard E. Lange

Professor of Law and Dean, Stanford Law School. He will step down as dean in the 1999–2000 academic year to return to teaching law full time at Stanford, where he has been on the faculty since 1969. A member of the American Academy of Arts and Sciences, he is the distinguished author of numerous publications.

Richard J. Danzig (B.A., Reed College; B.Phil. D.Phil., Magdalen College, Oxford University; J.D., Yale University) is Secretary of the Navy, US Department of Defense. The author of several books and numerous articles, his wide-ranging career has included positions at the RAND Corporation, Stanford Law School, and the law firm of Latham and Watkins. He served in the Defense Department from 1977 to 1981 and later as the 26th Under Secretary of the Navy, from 1993 to 1997.

Sidney D. Drell (A.B., Princeton University; Ph.D. and Sc.D. *honoris causa*, University of Illinois) is Emeritus Professor of Theoretical Physics, Stanford Linear Accelerator Center, and Senior Fellow, Hoover Institution, Stanford University. He has published extensively in theoretical physics and received many honors and awards for his work, including election to the National Academy of Sciences. An advisor to the US government on technical national security and arms controls issues since 1960, he is currently a member of the President's Foreign Intelligence Advisory Board, the Non-Proliferation Advisory Panel, and chairs the UC President's Council that oversees the Los Alamos, Lawrence Berkeley, and Lawrence Livermore National Laboratories.

Rolf Ekéus (graduate in law, Stockholm University) is Ambassador of Sweden to the United States, a post he has held since September 1997. A career officer of the Swedish Foreign Service, he has served in numerous high-level posts, including as Ambassador and Permanent Representative of Sweden to the Conference on Disarmament in Geneva (1983–88). He was Executive Chairman of the United

Nations Special Commission (UNSCOM) for Iraq from 1991 to 1997.

John C. Gannon (B.A., Holy Cross College; M.A., Ph.D., Washington University, St. Louis) is Chairman, National Intelligence Council, US Central Intelligence Agency. A US Navy veteran who has been active in local government politics in northern Virginia, he has had a long and distinguished career in the US Intelligence Community. Previously he served as Deputy Director for Intelligence at the CIA, and prior to that position he was Director of the CIA's Office of European Analysis.

Richard N. Haass (B.A., Oberlin College; M.Phil., Ph.D., Oxford University) is Director of Foreign Policy Studies at the Brookings Institution. He has served in the past in various academic and government posts, including: Special Assistant to the Under Secretary of Defense, US Department of Defense (1979–80); Director, Office of Regional Security Affairs, US Department of State (1981–82); Deputy Secretary for Policy, European and Canadian Affairs, US Department of State (1982–85); Lecturer in Public Policy and Senior Research Associate, John F. Kennedy School of Government, Harvard University (1985–89); and Special Assistant to the President on National Security Affairs and Senior Director, Near Eastern and South Asian Analysis, National Security Council (1989–93).

Robert F. Knouss (M.D., University of Pennsylvania School of Medicine) is Director, Office of Emergency Preparedness, US Public Health Service, US Department of Health and Human Services. Among the many US government posts in which he has served are Chief, Physician Education Branch, National Institutes of Health; and Director, Division of Medicine, Health Resources Administration. He was also for ten years the Deputy Director of the Pan American Health Organization.

Ariel E. Levite (B.A., Tel Aviv University; M.A., Cornell University; Ph.D., Cornell University) is Principal Deputy Director, Directorate for Foreign Affairs, Arms Control and Regional Security, Ministry of Defense of Israel; Adjunct Professor, Program for Security Studies, Tel Aviv University; and Member, Israeli Inter-Ministerial Steering Committee on Arms Control and Regional Security. He has held a variety of academic and government positions. The recipient of a number of awards, fellowships, and honors, he has published extensively on international and regional security and world politics.

Lewis Libby (B.A., Yale University; J.D., Columbia University) is a member of the Washington, DC, office of the law firm Dechert, Price, and Rhoads. The recipient of a number of awards and honors, he served as Deputy Under Secretary of Defense, US Department of Defense, from 1981 to 1993. He has also been Director of Special Projects, Bureau of East Asian and Public Affairs, US Department of State (1982–85).

Thomas P. Monath (B.A., M.D., Harvard University) is Vice President, Research and Medical Affairs of the biotechnology company OraVax, Inc., and Adjunct Professor, Department of Tropical Medicine and Public Health, Harvard School of Public Health. A member of numerous WHO, PAHO, and US Government committees, he has published over 285 scientific papers, reviews, and articles, and has edited five books. He has served in a number of posts, including as Director, Division of Vector-Borne Viral Diseases, Centers for Disease Control, Fort Collins, Colorado (1973–89); and, from 1989 to 1992, as Chief, Virology Division, US Army Medical Research Institute of Infectious Diseases, Fort Detrick, Maryland (with the rank of Colonel, US Army Medical Corps).

Michael L. Moodie (a graduate of Lawrence University and the Fletcher School of Law and Diplomacy) is President of the Chemical and Biological Arms Control Institute. The author of numerous publications, he has served as Assistant Director for Multilateral Affairs at the US Arms Control and Disarmament Agency (1990–93); and as Special Assistant to the Ambassador and Assistant for Special Projects, US Mission to NATO (1983–87). He has also held senior positions at the Institute for Foreign Policy Analysis, the Center for Strategic and International Studies, and Georgetown University's School of Foreign Service.

Gordon C. Oehler (B.S., Ph.D., Rensselaer Polytechnic Institute) is Corporate Vice President for Corporate Development at Science Applications International Corporation. From 1972 to 1997 he served in a variety of analytical and managerial positions at the CIA, including as Chief, Technology Transfer Assessment Center; Director, Office of Scientific and Weapons Research; National Intelligence Officer for Science, Technology, and Proliferation; and Director, Nonproliferation Center. He is a 1981 graduate of the National War College.

John Raisian (B.A., Ohio University; Ph.D., University of California at Los Angeles) is Director and Senior Fellow, Hoover Institution, Stanford University. An economist with numerous publications to his credit, he has had a distinguished career as a teacher, manager, and policymaker in academe, government, and business. He has been at the Hoover Institution since 1986.

Condoleezza Rice (B.A., University of Denver; M.A., University of Notre Dame; Ph.D., University of Denver) is a Senior Fellow at the Hoover Institution and a Professor, Department of Political Science, and Provost, Stanford University; she stepped down from the latter post in June 1999. An award-wining educator and prolific author who has been at Stanford since 1981, she is a member of the Council on Foreign Relations and of the boards of numerous organizations. From 1989 to 1991, she was on leave from Stanford, serving in Washington, DC, as Director of Soviet and East European Affairs in the National Security Council and as Special Assistant to the President on National Security Affairs.

Scott D. Sagan (B.A., Oberlin College; Ph.D., Harvard University) is Associate Professor of Political Science; Co-Director, Center for International Security and Cooperation; and Senior Fellow, Institute for International Studies, Stanford University. He has been an active consultant to numerous government agencies, serving as a special advisor to the Secretary of Defense and the Joint Chiefs of Staff, among others. He has published extensively and won numerous awards as an outstanding teacher and writer.

Michael P. Scharf (A.B., Duke University; J.D. from Duke University School of Law) is Professor of Law and Director of the Center for International Law and Policy at New England School of Law. From 1989 to 1993, he served in the Office of the Legal Adviser, US Department of State. An award-winning author, he has written numerous articles and several books.

George P. Shultz (B.A., Princeton University; Ph.D., Massachusetts Institute of Technology) is Distinguished Fellow at the Hoover Institution, Stanford University. In a long and outstanding career in public service, academe, and business, he has held four cabinet level posts as US Secretary of Labor (1969–70), Director of the Office of Management and Budget (1970–72), Secretary of the Treasury (1972–84), and Secretary of State (1982–89), and has taught at the Massachusetts Institute of Technology, the University of Chicago, and Stanford University. Among his many awards and honors is the US Medal of Freedom, the nation's highest civilian honor, which he received in 1989.

Abraham D. Sofaer (B.A., Yeshiva College; LL.B., New York University School of Law; Doctor of Laws, *honoris causa*, Yeshiva University) is the George P. Shultz Distinguished Scholar and Senior

Fellow at the Hoover Institution, Stanford University, where he directs Hoover's National Security Forum; and Professor of Law, by courtesy, at Stanford Law School. His professional positions have included: Assistant US Attorney, Southern District of New York (1967–69); Professor, Columbia University School of Law (1969–79); US District Judge, SDNY (1979–85); and Legal Adviser, US Department of State (1985–90). He has published extensively on transnational legal and US constitutional and national security issues.

Tibor Tóth (a graduate of the University for International Relations, Moscow) is Hungary's Ambassador and Permanent Representative to the United Nations office, Vienna. He has been active in diplomacy related to both the Biological and Chemical Weapons Conventions, and is currently Chairman of the Ad Hoc Group of Governmental Experts. A career officer of the Ministry of Foreign Affairs of Hungary, he has served in various posts at the Hungarian Ministry of Foreign Affairs.

Jonathan B. Tucker (B.S., Yale University; M.A., University of Pennsylvania; Ph.D., Massachusetts Institute of Technology) is Research Professor and Director of the Chemical and Biological Weapons Nonproliferation Project at the Center for Nonproliferation Studies of the Monterey Institute of International Studies. He has worked for the US Government in various capacities, including as an analyst at the Congressional Office of Technology Assessment (1990–93), and a foreign affairs specialist in the Chemical and Biological Policy Division of the US Arms Control and Disarmament Agency (1993–95). In February 1995, he was a member of a biological weapons inspection team in Baghdad, Iraq, under the auspices of the United Nations Special Commission (UNSCOM). He will be the 1999–2000 Robert Wesson Fellow in Scientific Philosophy and Public Policy at the Hoover Institution.

Dean A. Wilkening (A.B., University of Chicago; Ph.D. Harvard University) is Director of the Science Program, Center for International Security and Arms Control, Stanford University. A prolific author, he has held a number of positions at the RAND Corporation, including as Associate Director, Strategy and Doctrine Program, Project Air Force, and Senior Physical Scientist, International Policy Department (1990–94). From 1981 to 1982, he was a Ford Foundation postdoctoral research fellow at the Center for Science and International Affairs, Harvard University.

George D. Wilson (B.A., University of California, Berkeley; J.D., Georgetown University Law Center) is Research Fellow at the Hoover Institution, Stanford University. He practiced law in Washington, DC, and San Francisco from 1987 to 1993. In 1994 he joined the Hoover Institution as a research assistant, and in 1998 he was appointed a research fellow.

Frances E. Winslow (B.A., M.A., Drew University; Master of Urban Planning, Ph.D., New York University) is Director, Office of Emergency Services, City of San Jose, California; Consultant, Association of Bay Area Governments; and Member, Emergency Planning and Response/Recovery Committee, Seismic Safety Commission. She has previously held administrative and management positions in local government in southern California and New Jersey. She holds numerous professional affiliations and has received a number of awards and honors.

John C. Yoo (A.B., Harvard University, J.D., Yale University) is Acting Professor of Law, Boalt Hall School of Law, University of California, Berkeley. The author of numerous scholarly and journalistic publications, he served as General Counsel, US Senate Committee on the Judiciary, from 1995 to 1996. He has also been a federal judicial clerk, and has experience working for a number of law firms, at the White House, and for the *Wall Street Journal* and the *Boston Globe*.

Index